PRAISE FOR *Hacks, Sycophants, Adventurers, and Heroes*

"A thoroughly researched and comprehensive account of the character and events of the War of 1812."

> —**Lieutenant Commander John Pressagh**, Royal Navy Reserve, London Flotilla

"Colonel Fitz-Enz has again brought the War of 1812 to life with its varied cast of characters. The human side of the forgotten war is experienced in a smooth narrative, which will delight novice and professional historians alike."

> —**Joseph J. Ryan**, president of the Living History Education Foundation and fellow of the Company of Military Historians

"Another superb book on the War of 1812 authored by Colonel David Fitz-Enz. In this grouping of stories covering the key players in the war, he not only describes how they influenced the war, but his style of writing makes you feel that you are actually marching with Andrew Jackson to Talladega or manning the guns on the Saratoga under Commodore Macdonough. I thoroughly enjoyed the total view of the war presented by these twelve varied chapters.

> —**Colonel Robert Zoglman**, USA ret., U.S. Field Artillery, U.S. Army War College graduate

"Colonel David Fitz-Enz has brought a fresh approach to examining the War of 1812 and the leadership involved. The war ranged widely from Canada to the burning of Washington, to the Battle of New Orleans and the sea operations of the U.S. Navy against the British Navy. In that war leaders were selected for many reasons and sent off to do battle with the British. Communications were slow at best. The outcome of those battles was the result of the quality of the leaders and how well they accomplished their mission. Fitz-Enz paints the picture of these leaders and how they affected the outcomes."

> —**General John W. Foss**, USA ret.

D1271886

HACKS, SYCOPHANTS,

MADISON'S COMMANDERS IN THE WAR OF 1812

ADVENTURERS, & HEROES

OTHER BOOKS BY

COLONEL DAVID FITZ-ENZ, USA RET.

WHY A SOLDIER?
A Signal Corpsman's Tour from Vietnam to the Moscow Hot Line

THE FINAL INVASION
Plattsburgh, The War of 1812's Most Decisive Battle

OLD IRONSIDES: EAGLE OF THE SEA
The Story of the USS Constitution

REDCOATS' REVENGE
An Alternative History of the War of 1812

HACKS, SYCOPHANTS,

MADISON'S COMMANDERS IN THE WAR OF 1812

ADVENTURERS, & HEROES

TAYLOR TRADE PUBLISHING
LANHAM • NEW YORK • BOULDER • TORONTO • PLYMOUTH, UK

Published by Taylor Trade Publishing
An imprint of The Rowman & Littlefield Publishing Group, Inc.
4501 Forbes Boulevard, Suite 200, Lanham, Maryland 20706
www.rowman.com

10 Thornbury Road, Plymouth PL6 7PP, United Kingdom

Distributed by National Book Network

British Library Cataloguing in Publication Information Available

Library of Congress Cataloging-in-Publication Data

Fitz-Enz, David G., 1940–
    Hacks, sycophants, adventurers, and heroes : Madison's commanders in the
War of 1812 / Colonel David Fitz-Enz, USA Ret.
        pages cm
    Includes bibliographical references.
    ISBN 978-1-58979-700-0 (cloth : alk. paper) —
    ISBN 978-1-58979-701-7 (electronic)
    1. United States—History—War of 1812—Campaigns. 2. Command of troops—
History—19th century. 3. United States. Army—History—War of 1812. 4. United
States. Navy—History—War of 1812. I. Title.
    E355.F58 2012
    973.5'2—dc23   2012008141

∞™ The paper used in this publication meets the minimum requirements of American
National Standard for Information Sciences—Permanence of Paper for Printed Library
Materials, ANSI/NISO Z39.48-1992.

Printed in the United States of America

Maps on front and back pages are courtesy of the Department of History, United States
Military Academy, West Point.

To Carol

Happy Fiftieth Wedding Anniversary

Impressment—in my most fervent imagination,
I cannot conceive of a more barbaric practice.

—JONATHAN SWIFT, *Gulliver's Travels*

CONTENTS

PREFACE

WITHIN THE pages of the Oxford dictionary you will find the definitions for the following:

Hacks: *A producer of dull unoriginal work.*
Sycophants: *An informer, tale-bearer, malicious accuser; a calumniator, traducer, slanderer.*
Adventurers: *One who plays at games of chance, or adventures his money in such games; a gamester or engages in hazardous enterprises.*
Heroes: *Those renown supposed to be deified on account of great and noble deeds, for which they were also venerated generally or locally.*

Fifteen years ago, when I began to write books, I would never have written this book. Meeting book lovers last year, I noticed my readers had changed. Today's readers are bombarded from all directions with longer working hours, expanded television networks, high-demand handheld phones, and extended family obligations. Folks don't have the time to absorb detailed sagas of character motivation, even though they would like to know the whole story. Since history is not taught as it once was, the public knowledge is often summed up by a few notable events, such as that only three incidents occurred during the War of 1812: Dolly Madison saved George Washington's portrait when the British burned the White House, Frances Scott Key wrote the poem that became the *Star Spangled Banner*, and Andy Jackson won the battle of New Orleans after the war was over. Oh yes, nothing changed after the war was over. It seems there is no time to sit down and read a 300-page study about the life of a historic person, even though the reader would like to. So I have done that for you in *Hacks, Sycophants, Adventurers, and Heroes*. In this book, after researching through nearly all of the solid personal studies, I have condensed twenty-five of the fighting commanders under President Madison into one volume in hopes that once you have a complete grasp of this very complex tale of both sea and land, you will be driven to read more in depth about those who tweaked your interest.

This may be the only book one needs on the War of 1812.

This is the story of the good, the bad, and the outrageous men who served the commander in chief during the War of 1812. Only a few could boast Revolutionary War military experience from thirty-five years before. They ranged in age from twenty to sixty. The naval officers had sailed to the Mediterranean in pursuit of the Barbary pirates, stared down the French navy during the XYZ affair, and protected American merchant interests in the western Atlantic from British impressment. After a brilliant start, the American navy was overwhelmed, shattered, captured, or blockaded. On the North American continent, the land and lake campaigns were in fits and starts led by men of independent attitudes. This book is intended to provide the essential portrait of the officers who were given the burden to take on the most effective and efficient war machine of the day with the meager resources of a nation totally unprepared for war.

The time period, the Revolutionary War through the end of the War of 1812, some forty years, will find the commanders in youth and old age crisscrossing many times lending aid or sabotaging what seemed to be a good thing at the time.

This is not a chronology of the War of 1812 but rather tales of fighting men, on land and sea, who will tell you the story of the war they fought. As in every story, there are the good, the not so good, the bad, and the awful. Hanging around the fringe are the politicians who will speak for themselves. Featured are two presidents who took gambles with the lives of their citizens in an effort to chop off a tentacle of Great Britain but were nearly strangled in the end.

Spelling differs according to whom and where a quote is taken. The rules varied so widely across national borders and within communities that there were no standards. As a result, I have used the spelling as I found it. I have been criticized for using long quotes rather than putting the account in my own words. I think the reader gains from reading the words as they were written firsthand when available.

After 200 years, some are bound to differ with me over small points resulting from alternate research, but unfortunately none of us can boast the certainty that comes from speaking to a veteran of the War of 1812.

Acknowledgments

History is an unending argument.

I HAVE BEEN at the study of the Napoleonic Wars, of which the War of 1812 is but one of the campaigns, since my student days at Command and General Staff College. At the Army War College, I quickly opted to submit a paper on the same subject to the delight of my professor who couldn't read one more monograph on Patton. It is because Napoleon had swallowed up Europe that the British were decisively engaged, allowing Jefferson to slip Canada from England's grasp. The naval and land tactics, weaponry, uniforms, and equipage were echoed in North America for the two and a half years it took to decide the affair.

For that reason, a large portion of my research was done in England, Canada, and Portugal as well as the United States. I like to contrast the enemy's point of view of the same action with that of Americans who fought the war. So let me start overseas. My wife Carol, researcher and editor, and I began by writing numerous letters of introduction to military museums, libraries, and individuals. Most important, we made contact with Sir Christopher Prevost, 6th Baronet and direct descendant of Lieutenant General Sir George Prevost, the governor-general of Canada, who invited us to spend a weekend at his villa in southern Portugal. Lady Prevost's kind hospitality and access to the family papers, which had never been mined by historians, was invaluable. Major R. D. Cassidy, Royal Green Jackets museum and curator of the Light Infantry Museum at Winchester, gave me an appreciation for the rifleman. At Canterbury, housed in the town library on the high street, was a gold mine of information hidden in the archives of the East Kent *Buffs* infantry regiment. The demonstration of the Congreve Rocket system by Brigadier

K. A. Timbers, curator at the Royal Artillery Museum, was an unexpected bonus to learning the detail of both land and naval artillery, as was the tour of Chatham Royal Dockyard by Peter Dawson, who invited us into their library and introduced me to *Marinie Mirror, Society of Nautical Research.* Commodore Eric Fraser, RN, Court of St. James Naval Attaché, opened the doors of the private Admiralty Library in Whitehall, London, which was crammed with very rare periodicals from the time. They sent me to the British Museum's Newspaper Collection at Collingwood, where I found what Englishmen were saying about the war with America while in the grip of the Napoleonic campaigns. My eyes will never recover from reading every issue of the *Times* from 1812 to 1815 on half-sheet microfiche. A day spent at the Kew Gardens Records office saw us seated at a table filled with original naval and army accounts of courts-martial with most reveling consequences. On the army side, Andrew Robertshaw at both the National Army Museum and later the Royal Logistics Museum has stuck with me through countless questions. Tristan Longlois and Amy Cameron of the education department as well as Julian Farrance of marketing opened up the library and the hall of portraits to my endless probing. At the Twickenham Royal School of Music, Major Roger Swift opened my eyes to the role of the musicians. Dr. Paddy Griffith, former instructor at The Royal Military Academy and noted author, proofed my work, while Lionel Leventhal, publisher of many Napoleonic works, made significant contacts possible. Naval antiquities architect Allen Graham, one wet afternoon in February at the Naval & Military Club, introduced me to the wonder of HMS *Triconmallee*, restored at Hartleypool, England. The trip was long but highly memorable.

In Canada, there were two views to be considered. Mr. Donald Graves, a magical writer from the Ensign Heritage Group, strides the pages of the Englishman's history with master's insight. Rene Chartrand wants you to look more carefully at the complex picture, which is dominated by the courage of his French Canadians, who look back to the colony's beginning and remain a strong presence today. Ottawa's National Collection, close to the ground that was the host for this conflict, contained both insular history and image. It reminded us that the distrust between the English and French cultures was put aside during the War of 1812, as Canadians, for the first time in their history, banded together as a nation. It will be the Canadians who win the war. From that day forward, Great Britain took much of her greatness from the alliance with Canada.

In the United States, I will start with the most surprising tidbit. While having dinner at the Sovereign Military Order of the Temple of Jerusalem at West Point with Elbertus J. Prol and his wife Ann, curator of the Forge and

Manor of Ringwood, New Jersey, a bombshell was dropped. Prol's museum had a 12-pound gun from the USS *Constitution*, and the bill of lading establishing its authenticity was in the collection at the Academy Antiquities Collection. It was not in navy records. Sam Anthony and Becky Livingston of the National Archives opened the files on naval contests of the War of 1812. Jim Cheevers, curator of the United States Naval Academy museum, came through with a naval scrapbook filled with newspaper accounts from the period. Sigrid, the gracious hostess of the Beverly Robinson Collection, the best and most complete repository of naval prints, allowed a time-consuming day spent pawing through the images. Chief Marine Gunner Edward C. Sere provided access to the paintings of American Marines by Colonel Charles Waterhouse. Finally, I must thank Professor Donald Hickey, PhD, the national authority on the War of 1812 for assistance, knowledge, and support for more than fifteen years.

CHRONOLOGY OF THE WAR OF 1812

1796	Napoleon comes to power in France
1797	Quasi War with France, U.S. Navy established
1801, May 1	Tripoli declares war on the United States
1802, October	Capture of the USS *Philadelphia* in Tripoli
1803	Great Britain impressing U.S. seamen
1803, December	Louisiana Purchase
1804, February 16	Naval raid on Tripoli Harbor, Decatur
1805	Great Britain searches American ships to prevent France from getting contraband and impress seamen into Royal Navy
1805, October	Battle of Trafalgar
1807, June 22	USS *Chesapeake* attacked and boarded; President Jefferson imposes embargo
1811, May	USS *President* attacks HMS *Little Belt*
1811, November 7	Battle of Tippecanoe
1812, June 18	Congress declares war on Great Britain
1812, July	Major General Hull invades Canada
1812, August 19	HMS *Guerriere* captured by Captain Hull on USS *Constitution*
1812, October	Captain Zachary Taylor saves Fort Harrison
1812, October	Major General VanRensselaer invades Queenston, Canada
1812, October	HMS *Macedonia* captured by Decatur
1812, November	Brigadier General Alexander Smyth defeated in Canada across from Buffalo
1812, November	HMS *Java* captured by Commodore Bainbridge

1812, November	Major General Dearborn invades south of Montreal, Canada
1813, January	Battle of French Town won by British
1813, January 20	Battle of Raison River, Canada, won by the Americans
1813, February	USS *Hornet* captures HMS *Peacock*
1813, April	Americans attack and burn York, Canada
1813, May	British attack Sackets Harbor, New York
1813, May 1	Battle for Fort Miegs
1813, June 1	HMS *Shannon* captures USS *Chesapeake*
1813, August 30	Fort Mims massacre, Creek War
1813, September 10	Battle of Lake Erie; Commodore Oliver Hazard Perry destroys the Royal Navy fleet
1813, October 5	Chief Tecumseh killed at the Battle of the Thames
1813, October 25	Battle of Chateauguay
1813, November 11	Battle of Crysler's Farm, Canada
1813, January 20	Battle of the Raison River and Frenchtown
1814	Major General Jackson attacks Florida
1814, March	USS *Essex* captured off Valparaiso
1814, July 5	Battle of Chippewa, Canada
1814, July 25	Battle of Lundy's Lane, Canada
1814, August 18	Battle of Bladensburg; Washington burned
1814, September 1	British Army crosses the Canadian border to attack Plattsburgh/Lake Champlain
1814, September 11	Battle of Plattsburgh/Lake Champlain
1814, September 13	Battle of Baltimore; Key composes the poem "Star Spangled Banner"
1814, December 13	Royal Navy Admiral Cochrane's fleet arrives off New Orleans
1814, December	Major General Jackson attacks British army south of New Orleans
1814, December 24	Treaty of Ghent signed
1815, January 8	Battle of New Orleans, with Major General Andrew Jackson
1815, January 14	USS *President* captured by the Royal Navy
1815, February 16	Senate ratifies the Treaty of Ghent
1815, February 20	USS *Constitution* attacked by HMS *Cyane* and *Levant* off West Africa

1

A TALE OF IMPRESSMENT, ISSAC HULL, AND WILLIAM HULL

SAILING SCHOONER SEIZED

ON MAY 11, 1811, young John Leeds, a peaceful passenger on an American coaster out of New York City, was pressed, taken against his will, and imprisoned on a Royal Navy frigate—forced to fight another man's war. Leeds had clung breathlessly to the rail watching—fearing capture—as the American merchant captain tried to flee from the clutches of the British frigate HMS *Guerriere*. The menacing man-of-war lurked on station just off Sandy Hook, New Jersey, plying the turbulent waters along the Atlantic coast. The mission of the blockading frigate mandated her to "stop and search all commercial vessels for able seamen." England, a vulnerable island kingdom whose survival depended on her maintaining mastery of the sea lanes, was desperate for sailors to crew the expanding Royal Navy fleet in the face of Napoleon's global ambitions. A maritime nation in those early years, the new United States boasted over 100,000 able seamen on board her lucrative and enlarging merchant fleet. Trading as a neutral nation, the American vessels claimed immunity from the European conflict, but Great Britain could not allow the New World to support her enemies and restricted passage of cargo to continental ports.

As a warning to stop or else, the frigate fired a brace of guns aimed across the schooner's bow. The blast ripped apart the quiet sea, hurling a pair of sizzling 18-pound cannonballs that skipped across the wave tops before running out of energy and sinking harmlessly to the bottom. The unarmed American merchant captain had no choice: the slackened staysails fluttered, and the schooner lost way, radically slowing forward progress. Earlier that day, Leeds had witnessed *Guerriere*'s harassment and boarding of *Spitfire*, only minutes ahead of his own packet. He hoped that delay would allow an

1

escape down the Jersey coast, where ship traffic was thick and the threat of uncharted shoals kept the frigate seaward. But only an hour later, the speedy man-of-war easily overtook Leeds's hapless vessel.

A Royal Navy lieutenant, in a neatly tailored dark blue tailcoat splashed with gold decoration and high white collar, led a boarding party of rough-looking tars clad in rumpled slops. The passengers and captive crewmen were lined up along the exposed main deck for inspection. The officer was searching for able seamen or landsman in good health that could be pressed into service. The selection process allowed a wide margin of discretion. The lieutenant could take any British male he deemed useful to the conduct of his majesty's man-of-war. The judgment of the officer, as to citizenship, was based on his expert opinion alone. The ability to speak English was sufficient proof for seizure in most cases. Additionally, it was a license to kidnap since anyone born within the confines of the Crown was a citizen for life regardless of naturalization proceeding. *Once British, always British* was England's rule of law, and she possessed the might to make it right.

By applying the broadest interpretation to his instructions, the lieutenant held all males at risk. John Leeds, a young, strong landsman, declared that he was a native-born American and therefore immune from impressment under English law. The captain supported Leeds' appeal. However, the officer whose mission it was to increase the complement of the frigate snatched Leeds from the line-up against his will for servitude at his majesty's pleasure.

Written Off

In one of the surprisingly few personal accounts of impressment, James Durand describes his plight. "I was confined below decks in 'detestable bondage' by the Royal Navy."[1] Like many thousands forced to labor and fight, Durand, taken in 1809, was to disappear for the duration of the war into the sodden innards of the frigate HMS *Narcissus*. On board later in the notorious Dartmoor prison, he languished for the duration of the conflict.

Prior to his capture, Durand, age eleven, left his home at Milford, Connecticut, near New Haven, in 1797, apprenticed for five years to a farmer. Seeking adventure at sixteen, he signed on as a deckhand aboard a packet boat that plied the Long Island Sound. Competing for a deck job on a leaky ship bound for Charleston filled to the gunwales with produce, he raced a boy to the top of the mainmast garnering the job and to his surprise a pay hike as a *topman*. The ship then began routine porting between the Caribbean and the Eastern Seaboards' primary ports.

In 1804, while moored in the harbor of Dominico, an unwelcome gang of rough Royal Navy sailors boarded. Under the pretense of seeking deserters, they began interviewing crewmen. American members of the crew produced their "protections" issued by county clerks back home as proof of citizenship. Aware that many were copies belonging to others, purchased in any Eastern harbor, the Royal Navy contingent ignored the pleas and took several hardy members of the crew and pressed them into Royal Navy service for the duration of the war with France. Fortunately, Durand was confined to his bunk with fever at the time.

Soon after, an epidemic erupted on board that required the ship to be smoked. An infestation of rats called for extreme measures. Metallic tubs containing straw and tar were set alight and sealed below decks for twenty-four hours. The smoldering pots deprived the vermin of oxygen, killing hundreds of vectors of all kinds.

At seventeen, concerned after several bad experiences on poorly maintained and managed commercial ships, Durand signed on as an able seaman for a voyage on the USS *John Adams* (28 guns), a small frigate bound for the Mediterranean, there to engage the Barbary pirates. (During the early days of the U.S. Navy, there were no regular billets, and men served only for the duration of the voyage.) Enlisted as a foremast topman, second captain (leading man), he willingly took on leadership responsibilities. The American fleet, commanded by Commodore Edward Preble, had just concluded a naval campaign that squashed the Tripolian pirates and left little for the *Adams* to do but police the North African coast. With the treaty signing, a surprisingly healthy Durand witnessed the suffering of fellow crewmen with ophthalmia, dysentery, dropsy, and contagious fevers that ripped through the confined spaces of the crowded ship. Transferred to the USS *Constitution*, Durand chafed at the harsh treatment of the crew, taking a flogging from the first mate, renowned for his cruelty. Made boatswain of the young boys, he was required to flog them for minor transgressions. He reported that the duty sickened him.

Lying at Cadiz, Spain, the night before the battle of Trafalgar, Durand counted the ships of both the French and the Spanish fleets. In the morning, *Constitution* maneuvered out to sea past Lord Nelson's ships of the line, unaware of the historic battle that took place that very day. Later during a storm, he was washed overboard, but a desperate grab for a trailing rope saved his life.

In 1807, after two years of service, Durand was disgusted with the treatment he had received for his good and faithful service and jumped ship in Boston. He signed on a commercial brig bound for Goree, France, where he had the good fortune to witness Napoleon's christening of two men-of-war. Leaving port, the British frigate HMS *Shannon* came up like the wind and hailed Durand's ship to heave too. His ship was captured and the entire crew imprisoned at Plymouth, England, for six weeks. There, confined in the dungeon, they lingered in the dark on a starvation diet. Released when the brig

was auctioned off, Durand sought a mates job on a Swedish ship contracted
to take French prisoners to Spain. Upon return, the crew sought the Captain's permission to go ashore for a night of food and drink before the next
voyage. The captain warned, "I have no objections, but there is a very hot
press on shore and you'll all do better to stay on board." Taking the warning
to heart, Durand remained on board.[2]

> About eleven that evening there came along side a boat belonging to the
> Royal Navy frigate HMS *Narcissus*. The Royal Navy sailors boarded our
> brig and came below where I was asleep. With much abuse, they hauled
> me out of my bed, not suffering me to even put on or take anything ex-
> cept my trousers. In this miserable condition, I was taken on board their
> ship but did not think to be detained there for a term of seven years. Had
> I known my destiny that night, I would have instantly committed the
> horrid crime of self-murder. In this sorrowful condition I spent the night.
> At daylight, I found my way on deck and soon after heard the word given
> to un-moor the ship and get her ready for sea. At this I was overcome
> by grief. I ran below and tried to procure some paper, pen and ink from
> members of the crew, offering any price. I was able to offer money, as I
> had concealed some of my savings by tying the coins in a handkerchief
> about my neck. However, no member of the crew durst sell me pen, ink
> nor paper, as they guessed my intention of writing for aid to escape from
> a hateful service.
>
> There came along side a boat with stuff to sell. For a shilling, I pro-
> cured a sheet of paper on which I wrote a letter to the Captain of the (my)
> brig. I desired him to break open my chest and take out my protection
> and indenture and send them on board as quick as possible. I hired the
> boat to take this message to him immediately. The message boat made
> all possible speed; she had a mile and one-half to go, yet she went with
> such rapidity that in one hour and one-half after, the Captain was on
> board with my indenture and protection.
>
> The lieutenant of the Narcissus said he could do nothing about
> clearing me, but told the Captain of the brig that if he [the Captain]
> would go ashore and see the Captain of the frigate, he would direct him
> where to find him.
>
> There is an island to pass, between the spot where we lay on the
> frigate and the town. It is called Drake's Island. It was my bad fortune
> that the Captain of the brig carrying my protection and indenture passed
> on one side of the isle in the message boat, while the Captain of the Nar-
> cissus passed it on the other side. Therefore they missed each other and
> my last chance of regaining my liberty was gone. As soon as the Captain
> arrived on the *Narcissus*, he weighed anchor and put out to sea. I never
> saw the Captain of the brig again.
>
> In this unfortunate manner, I was dragged on board a British man-
> of-war, August 21st 1809. Despair so complete seized my mind, that

I lost all relish for the world. For the first twelve days thereafter, my entire victualing would not have amounted to the one ration as it was allowed us.

I lost, as I left behind me on the brig, more than 50 pounds sterling, a chest full of excellent and well-chosen clothes. Only lately I had quitted the service of the U. States' after enduring everything. The thought of serving with the British fleet deprived me of reason. I had been eight years from home and I began to despair of ever seeing that place again.

After I had been on board a few days, the Captain called me to the quarterdeck and asked me if I would enter. He said that if I would, he would give me 5 pounds. I utterly refused, telling him I was an American. I also said I would not do duty if I could help it.

"If you will not work I'll flog you until you're glad to set about it," said the Captain. "Go below for I won't hear another word out of you."

Below decks, I found twelve more Americans who had been previously impressed. One of them told me that, when he refused to obey an order, the Captain had given him four dozen lashes. "Therefore," said he to me, "I advise you to do as you are bid."

I thought this excellent advice and I went to work and made myself as contented as possible. I concluded I would write to the American consul when we came to port again.[3]

Able Seaman Durand began his long servitude aboard a foreign ship of war destined to attack America, his homeland. There was never a thought given to him being an Englishmen who took up American citizenship to avoid wartime service, as the British claimed. He was merely a target of opportunity snatched up from below decks of his ship like a stolen sack of wheat to be consumed or left to rot. And if he failed to please, what could he expect?

A Witness to Cruelty

Within the year, Royal Navy sailor Durand became engaged against French ships, ports, and colonies in the Caribbean, where his leg was broken during the siege of Guadeloupe. Returning to England in the summer of 1810, the ship was laid up for repair. Durand was transferred to a hulk (a dismasted ship permanently moored outside the port in a backwater at Plymouth harbor) for four months. Swinging around the anchor chair, lingering in the most wretched condition, he was restricted from going to town with the English sailors for fear he would slip away. So it would be for most of the impressed Americans for the duration of the war with France. They were restricted from ever landing, transferred at sea from one incoming ship to another outgoing. Voyages often lasted years rather than months.

As a result of his injury, Durand became a sail mender on his next ship. Off L'Orient, France, at battle stations, he was wounded in the leg. While an invalid, he joined the ship's band and learned the flute and clarinet. Back at Plymouth, his request to go ashore was denied: "you'll escape, be caught and flogged round the fleet," according to the captain.[4]

State-Sponsored Murder

Once again imprisoned at the Plymouth harbor, Durand chronicles the fate of an impressed American who did not heed the good advice given to him by his English captain.

> On the 9th of May 1812 two Englishmen and an American were tried for desertion. After what passed for a trial, the sentences were pronounced. Each Englishman was to receive two-hundred and fifty lashes and the American was to receive three-hundred. They were to be whipped through the fleet. Three days later, the sentence was carried out. A large boat came alongside, with the gallows erected on her. The poor prisoners were fastened to this naked from the waist up. All the time the music played the Rogues' March.
>
> After the sentence had been read out by the Captain, the boatswain' mate was ordered to proceed with the flogging. The American, whose name was Armstrong, first received 25 lashes and then each of the Englishmen received 18. This was repeated beside each ship, with the music playing (crews were forced to witness).
>
> As John Armstrong was alongside the last ship, he expired due the brutality of the punishment. So they gave his body ten lashes after he had died. His corpse was carried to the hospital and the doctors gave it as their opinion that some blood vessel broke inwardly and caused his death.[5]

To add insult to the treatment, Durand quoted British officers when lashing Americans, venting their fury, "You damned Yankees, we'll soon have all your ships in our ports and all your damned countrymen as our prisoners."[6] It is no wonder that in just over a month, President Madison, who had heard many a similar tale, had no difficulty in securing Congress's approval for a declaration of war.

THE ORIGIN OF THE WAR OF 1812

The march to the War of 1812 began earlier when Great Britain became decisively engaged in war with revolutionary France. French soldiers, participants in the defeat of the British at Yorktown, Virginia, returned home with an appreciation of an American adventure in government of, by, and for the people. More than wine began to ferment and age within the cantons across the most populated country in Europe. The Kings of France had bankrupted the country through foreign adventure and imprudent investments. Unable to provide a viable economy at home, the unmet needs of the people bubbled up from the cellar taverns in the capital city and spread unaided throughout the nation. The demand for liberty, equality, and fraternity turned ugly and spawned the great terror, which lopped off the heads of French nobility, decapitating the government. By 1795, six years of chaos was stabilized by the grip of Napoleon Bonaparte, who by 1804 had embroiled England in a global war of attrition.

Great Britain feared first for her possessions, which were secured by the ubiquitous Royal Navy. The rapid expansion of the army was eclipsed by a need for naval crews as the admiralty built scores of fighting ships for the defense of George III's realm. By 1806, more than 110,000 seamen of all classes were required. Traditionally, wartime crews were commandeered wherever they could be found. English merchant ships about to dock in London, Liverpool, Plymouth, and Portsmouth were raided for able seamen. No consideration was offered to masters for crippling their complement. Impressment gangs sent ashore from moored naval vessels kidnapped men from pubs and eating houses in coastal villages. When a son or father failed to come home in the evening, it was assumed that he had taken the king's shilling to serve at His Majesty's pleasure.

Service was hard and punishment vicious for those made to climb the 200-foot masts and stretch the heavy wet canvas sails in hammering winds and rolling seas. At least the food was superior to merchant fleet fare and better than army chow. Station and watch schedules allowed a sailor to rest and may have contributed to low desertion rates. It was a hardworking life made worse by confinement at sea for long, boring voyages. An English fleet sailed from the Bay of Biscay to the Caribbean and back in pursuit of the French, a six-month chase, but failed to make contact. By 1805, over 20,000 claiming American citizenship were impressed. Fully 10 percent of Admiral Lord Nelson's crew aboard his flagship *Victory* claimed American citizenship. Knowing that the war with Napoleon's France was a death struggle, the British turned the full force of the highly organized Naval Board shipbuilding and civil shipyard system to winning the war at sea. They would settle for nothing less than the destruction of the French navy and the restriction of neutral nations from trading with war-torn France. While the small British army struggled on the Iberian Peninsula, the massive combined Royal Navy and commercial fleet proudly dominated the seven seas.

WAR DECLARED

There was no military establishment in the United States equipped to conduct even a rudimentary swipe at war. Congress had feared the "Man on a White Horse." They believed that large standing military forces were as much a danger to the survival of the republic as a foreign invader. Besides, an army and navy cost a great deal of money which could not be sustained when federal funds were dependent solely on revenue collected by customs stations at ports of entry along the Eastern Seaboard. Procuring contributions from the states for federal projects was on a voluntary basis and up for negotiations. The results were disappointing.

Fair Warning

Earlier in 1807, an incident at Norfolk, Virginia, should have highlighted the need for large regular forces. The two countries collided on June 22 in full view of civilians along the shoreline. The captain of HMS *Leopard* (fifty guns), informed that some royal navy deserters had shipped over to the USS *Chesapeake* (thirty-six guns), hailed Captain James Barron and demanded to board and search for the miscreant crewmen. When Barron refused, the *Leopard* opened fire with a broadside from 18-pound cannons at 100 yards with predictably devastating results. The *Chesapeake*, less than an hour into her voyage, was unprepared for a major engagement. Three Americans were killed where they stood, and eighteen were wounded—Barron struck his colors to save his ship. Four men were taken. One, the leader, would be executed in Halifax, while the others were flogged for deserting His Majesty's colors. The British government admitted that the captain had been rash and made a halfhearted attempt to make things right.

Not satisfied, President Jefferson, rather than mobilizing, signed the Embargo Act on December 22, 1807, as a punitive measure that denied the importation of English goods and export of American products to England. Jefferson, a Francophile who hated all things English, believed it would bring London to its senses. The result was a huge loss of income to the federal government and the establishment of the smuggling industry in New England and along the Canadian frontier. The British depended on the New England merchants and the southern planters to support the Iberian Peninsula war with France. However, the trade was so lucrative that the New England merchants ignored Jefferson's ban, and the English no longer needed to pay the tariff while buying the goods and service, directly bypassing the American customs craft. The Royal Navy blockaded the American coast, but allowed merchant ships bound for English interests to pass unmolested. In the 1808 election, the Republicans lost seats in New England, and the unpopular act was heavily modified in 1809. Hostilities limped along while the new president, James Madison, and the American merchant marine fumed over increased impressment.

The *Guerriere* versus *Spitfire* incident of 1811 put the cork in the American bottle. Americans finally recognized the need for large regular forces to defend themselves against her old enemy, Great Britain.

The Growing Pains

The first line of defense would fall to the fledgling American navy. With the sale in 1784 of the *Alliance*, the last of the lingering colonial warships, the courageous Continental Navy was disbanded. Congress could not afford the bill to build or even maintain the largest, most expensive dynamic object on earth—a warship. Soon, because of the dual threat from the French (which turned out to be a so-called phony war) and the persistence of the Barbary pirates in spite of tribute paid to North African potentates, Congress reluctantly agreed with George Washington in 1797 to float out the U.S. Navy. Among the earliest captains during the War of 1812 was Isaac Hull, who had served as a junior officer on board one of the first large American men-of-war, the Boston-built frigate USS *Constitution*. Captain Hull would be in on the opening battle of the naval conflict.

ISAAC HULL

At age thirty-five, Captain Hull took command of a tired-out *Constitution*. She lingered for two years at the Washington Navy Yard undergoing extensive refurbishment. Hull sat and watched until the spring of 1812, when his time came. He was well regarded for the incident in April 1800 in the Caribbean where he led a contingent of marines and sailors on the innocent-appearing captured sloop *Sally*. Lieutenant Hull's vessel slid into the harbor of Puerto Plata and took a French privateer during the Quasi War.[7] Later, in 1804, while captain of the American sloop of war *Argus* (eighteen guns), Hull assisted Mr. William Eaton, an American naval agent to the Barbary States who hatched a plot to depose the Bey, the leader who had been capturing American merchant ships and enslaving their crews and passengers. Hull loaned Eaton the assistance of Marine Lieutenant Presely N. O'Bannon and a contingent of eight marines to augment his cobbled together force of itinerant Europeans and Arabs in the overthrow of the local ruler. Eventually, they attacked the fortress at Derna. Hull supported the land attack with naval gun support, while O'Bannon's marines assaulted the ramparts. After the victory, the Egyptian Mamelukes presented the marine lieutenant with a curve-bladed scimitar. The pattern is still carried today by Marine Corps officers while the exploit is found in the Marine hymn "from the halls of Montezuma to the shores of Tripoli."

On the eve of war, Hull was preparing his ship for action to meet Commodore John Rodgers, captain of the USS *President* off the coast of New York. He received the following message from the secretary of the navy.

> June 18th, 1812
> Sir:
> War has been declared between the "United Empire of Great Britain & Ireland" and their dependencies and the United States of America and their territories and you are with the force under your command entitled to every belligerent right to attack and capture and to defend —You will use the utmost dispatch to reach New York after you have made up your complement of men & cargo at Annapolis. In your way from thence, you will not fail to notice the british flag, should it present itself —I am informed that the Belvidera is on our coast, but you are not to understand me as impelling you to battle, previously to your having confidence in your crew unless attacked, or with a reasonable prospect of success, of which you are to be at your discretion to Judge. You are to reply to this and inform me of your progress.
>   Respectfully yrs.
>   Paul Hamilton[8]

The next day, one day following the beginning of the hostilities, Commodore Rodgers sent the Secretary his assessment of the enemy situation (not yet aware that war had been declared).

> U.S. Frigate President
> New York 19th June 1812
> British naval force at present on this side the Atlantic consists of one sixty four—seven frigates—seven sloops of war—seven Brigs, & two or three schooners—Halifax & Bermuda are their ports of rendezvous; & permit me to observe, Sir, that should war be declared, & our vessels get to sea, in squadron, before the British are apprised of it, I think it not impossible that we may be able to cripple & reduce their force in detail; to such an extent as to place our own upon a footing until their loss could be supplied by a reinforcement from England. The President & Hornet are ready for sea & the Essex will I hope be ready in ten days from this date.
>   It is this moment reported that the frigates UStates & Congress are off the Bar. The British frigate Belvidera & sloop of war Tartarus were

seen off Sandy Hook yesterday morning—The schooner Macherel with Mr. Ruff (English messenger) sailed last evening for Halifax,

With the greatest respect.

Jn Rodgers.[9]

Unaware of Rodgers's assessment, Hull maneuvered the big frigate, 204 feet long by 44 feet wide, out of the Navy Yard with the assistance of rowed boats and then sailed down the narrow confines of the Potomac River to the Chesapeake Bay. His plan was to rendezvous with Rodgers's squadron off New York Harbor. But Rodgers was over 100 miles off the coast chasing HMS *Belvidera*, which slipped through his fingers and escaped north. While searching in the waters off Massachusetts for the American squadron, Hull fell in with the enemy fleet from Halifax station. The Royal Navy formation contained a 64-gun ship of the line, HMS *Africa*, against which *Constitution* had no chance. Not alone, she was in company with *Belvidera* 36 (thirty-six guns), *Shannon* 38 (thirty-eight guns), *Guerriere* 38 (thirty-eight guns), *Acolus* 32 (thirty-two guns), and a schooner.

Alone, Hull had no option but to run, for it was suicide to stand and fight against the overwhelming odds. Off the coast of Cape Cod, at first the winds were fresh from the south, but soon they dropped off. The air seemed to hang on a hook, and steering could not be maintained. Through the night, nothing changed; by sunrise conditions were stark still and the bow of *Constitution* swung lazily around to face the enemy squadron, becalmed at sea five miles apart.

Captain Hull's after action report to the secretary of the navy was penned on July 21 chronicling the previous days' extraordinary slow motion chase.

[T]he Boats were instantly hoisted out and sent ahead to tow the Ship's head round and to endeavor to get her farther from the Enemy. . . . The boats of the Enemy were got out and sent ahead to tow which with the light air that remained with them, they came up very fast. Finding the Enemy coming fast up and but little chance of escaping from them, I ordered two of the Guns on the Gun Deck, run out at the Cabbin windows for Stern Guns on the gun deck and hoisted one of the 24 pounders off the Gun Deck, and run that with the Fore Castle Gun, an Eighteen pounder, out at the Ports on the Quarter deck, and cleared the ship for Action, being determined they should not get her, without resistance on our part. Notwithstanding their force, and the situation we were placed in. At about 7 in the Morning the ship nearest us approaching with Gun Shot, and directing astern, I ordered one of the Stern Guns fired to see if we could reach her, to endeavor to disable her masts, found the shot fell a little Short, would not fire any more.

At 8, four of the Enemy's ships nearly within Gun Shot, some of them having six or eight boats ahead towing, with all their oars, and sweep out to row them up with us, which they were fast doing. It soon appeared that we must be taken, and that our Escape was impossible four heavy ships nearly within Gunshot, and coming up fast, and not the least hope of a breeze, to give us a chance of getting off by out sailing them.

Hull said to his first lieutenant, Morris, "Let's lay broadsides to them Mr. Morris, and fight the whole. If they sink us, we'll go down like men"[10]— words, I am sure, in the heat of the moment. Isaac Hull's character was under siege; he wanted to fight, not run.

In this Situation finding ourselves in only twenty four fathoms of water [suggestion of that valuable officer Lieutenant Charles Morris] I determined to try and warp the ship ahead, by carrying out anchors and warp her up to them, Three or four hundred fathoms [1,800 to 2,400] of rope was instantly got up, and two anchors got ready and sent ahead, by which means we began to gain ahead of the Enemy. They however soon saw our Boats carrying out the anchors, and adopted the same plan, under very advantageous circumstances, as all the Boats, from the Ship furthermost off were sent to Tow and Wrap up those nearest to us, by which means they again came up. So that at 9 the Ship nearest us began firing her bow guns. Which were instantly returned by our Stern guns in the cabbin, and on the Quarter Deck. All the shots from the Enemy fell short, but we have reason to believe that some of ours went on board her, as we could not see them strike the water.

Soon after 9 a Second Frigate passed under our lee, and opened her broadside but finding her shot fall short, discontinued her fire, but continued as did all the rest of them, to make every possible exertion to get up with us. From 9 to 12 all hands were employed in warping the ship ahead, and in starting some of the water in the main hold to lighten her, which with the help of a light air, we rather gained of the Enemy or at least hold our own. About 2 in the afternoon, all the Boats from the line of Battle Ship (Africa) and some of the Frigates, were sent to the Frigate nearest to us to endeavor to tow her up, but a light breeze sprung up, which enabled us to hold way with her notwithstanding they had Eight or Ten Boats ahead, and all her sails furled to tow her to windward. The wind continued light until 11 at night, and the Boats were kept ahead towing, and warping to keep out of the reach of the Enemy. Three of their Frigates being very near us. At 11 we got a light breeze from the Southward, the boats came along side, and we hoisted up, the ship having too much way to keep them ahead. The Enemy still in chase, and very near.

19th [of July]. At day light passed within gunshot of one of the Frigates but she did not fire on us, perhaps for fear of becalming her as the wind was light. Soon after passing us, she tacked, and stood after us, at this time Six Sail were in Sight under all sail after us.

At 9 in the morning saw a Strange sail on our Weather Beam, supposed to be an American merchant ship the instant the Frigate nearest us saw her she hoisted American colours, as did all the Squadron in hopes to decoy her down. I immediately hoisted English colours that she might not be deceived, she soon halted her wind, and it is to be hoped made her escape. All this day the Wind increased gradually and we gained on the Enemy, in the course of the day Six or Eight miles, they however continued chasing us all night under a press of Sail.

20th [of July 1812] At day light in the Morning only three of them could be seen from the Mast head, the nearest of which, was about 12 miles off directly astern. All hands were set at work wetting the Sails, from the Royals down, with the Engine, and fire buckets and we soon found that we left the Enemy very fast. At ¼ past 8 the Enemy finding that they were dropped astern gave up the chase.

Signed
    Isaac Hull
    At sea,
USS Constitution

The site of a cluster of warships knotted together with wet towlines in a slow dance across a calm, motionless blue sea is difficult to believe if not seen. It was an incredible feat of tenacious endurance on both sides and as well as an exceptional feat of leadership. How the officers sustained the crew's energy is a wonder. The men must have been exhausted after the first day of rowing. To continue to wrap and haul all the next day and into the third must have been grueling work. While the two bower and single sheet anchors weighed nearly 5,000 pounds, the two kedge anchors rowed out in the boats came in at 700 and 400 pounds. The double capstans, one on each deck on the same axle, were normally used to raise the main anchors. But rather than pulling up an anchor, the capstan could be employed as a winch. Often in port, to move the ship a short distance or to turn it around at the dock, the light kedge anchor would be rowed out and dropped. Once it took a bite on the bottom, the line could be wound around the capstan, which was rotated by a party of men pushing around long wooden spokes until the ship was brought directly over the anchor. The action taken by *Constitution*, while extremely rare in combat, was also used to get a ship out of the "doldrums" in shallow water.

Captain Richard Byron of HMS *Belvidera* recorded the account of the chase in a letter to Herbert Sawyer, esq., Vice Admiral of the Blue at Halifax Station.

> At 3 pm on the 16th a strange sail was seen in the winds eye, which afterward proved to be the Constitution of 56 guns, on her way from Chesapeake Bay to NY. A general chase insued, and was continued during the night. At day light on the 17th it being then calm, the enemy's ship and her persuers hoisted out their boats to tow, and at 7:30 the former began warping herself ahead in 24 fathoms of water. She then bore from the Belvidera S.W. By S. distant four miles at 9 o'clock. A light air sprang up from the S.S.E., and the Belvidera trimed sail on the larbored tack. At 10:30 the breeze freshened, but in a few minutes died away to calm; when Capt. Byron, observing the benefit that the Constitution had dirived from warping, immediately commenced the same operation, bending all his hawsers to on another, and working two kedge anchors at the sametime, by paying the warp through on house-hole as it was run in through another opposite. The effect of this was soon visible, and at noon the American, whose *boomes* had just before been throuwn overboard, was with gunshot of Belvideria. At 2pm the enemy opened fire from his stern-chasers, which was returned occasionally by Captain Byron's bow guns. At 3, a light breeze enabled the Constitution to gain ground, and firing ceased; but the chase continued till day-light on the 18th, by which time she was four miles ahead, and being a clean ship she ultimately effected her escape.[11]

Better Days Were Coming

Having outsailed or, to put it bluntly, outrowed the enemy, Captain Hull and his crew were looking for a fight. It was humiliating to have had to run, even though the odds were so against them that it would have been foolhardy to risk the valuable ship at the start of the war to certain defeat and internment. The commander chafed for the hunt as the days crept by in Boston during a week of replenishment. Captain Hull wasn't looking for Rodgers's squadron when he returned to patrolling off Nantucket Island. The USS *Constitution* was going to go it alone. The noted author Henry Adams believed that Captain Hull anticipated relief of command by Captain Bainbridge, the yard commander, who had been busy refitting *Constellation*. Hull put to sea without orders before losing his command. The citizens of Boston watched her proud stern pass by Castle Island and turn north toward Halifax. She was going hunting!

However, historian William S. Dudley points to two letters of July 28 and August 2, just before departure, that Captain Hull wrote to his boss,

Secretary Hamilton. In them, he regrets that no orders were waiting for him and provides an analysis of what he believes the secretary would expect of him under the circumstances. He explains the need to get out of the harbor before a blockade can be thrown up.

As they sailed north, the weather was clear and the wind solid. Chains were put around the mast to secure the spars at the parrels, allowing the yards to be braced. It prevented the heavy yards from plunging to the deck from enemy cannon fire. Tons of loglike spars, strung with yards of smothering canvas, were not going to clutter and entangle the fighting men below when they met the British. Led farther north by an American privateer of fourteen guns from Salem, the brig *Decatur* reported a British frigate the day before.[12] Hull hastened on. At 2 p.m. on August 19, a month after his encounter with Broke's Royal Navy squadron, his lookout sighted a lone enemy ship on the horizon coming his way. She was a frigate not of American design.

Constitution *versus* Guerriere

The Englishman was the infamous frigate *Guerriere* who, in the spring of 1811, had mauled the American merchant brig *Spitfire* outside New York Harbor and later impressed John Leeds and several other men. Days later, Captain Rodgers, on *President*, had attacked HMS *Little Belt* (same as *lilli belt*) by mistake while searching for *Guerriere*. HMS *Guerriere* had also been one of the frigates chasing *Constitution* along with *Africa*. The crew of the *Constitution* wanted to settle the score with *Guerriere*.

Captain Dacres, the Royal Navy commander, would have said "that goes double for us as well." James Richard Dacres, Esq., was the son of Vice Admiral J. R. Dacres of Cambridge, England. Only three days before, Captain Dacres had entered on the log of a merchantman a challenge to any American frigate to meet him off Sandy Hook. Not only had the *Guerriere* for a long time been extremely offensive to every seafaring American, but the mistake that caused the *Little Belt* to suffer so seriously for the misfortune of being taken for the *Guerriere* had bred a corresponding feeling of anger in the officers of the British frigate. The meeting of August 19 had the air of a preordained duel.[13] Painted on her mainsail was the name of the ship, "*Guerriere*," while on her foresail the words "Not the Little Belt" was a challenge to fight it out. She had hoped to introduce herself as the avenger to Commodore Rodgers, captain of the *President*.[14]

There was no running before the wind in this engagement; they were going to go at it. Like two giant winged animals, they circled, backed, and warped, feeling each other out. Both wanted the weather gauge, and neither was looking to the lee for escape. *Constitution*'s first lieutenant sent men aloft to reef up the fore and main courses to be tied off by anxious hands. The men afloat kept an eye over their shoulder expecting the enemy to send a broadside of cannonballs at any moment to test the range and heat up the barrels. Topmen took to the ratlines for the pinnacle of the foremast and mainmast to secure the royals. They were counting on getting back down from 200 feet before the first shot. They tangled with the marines climbing into the tops; as they struggled through the soldiers' hole, some with their five-foot-long muskets, slung over their shoulder, got caught on the underside. Sailors avoided the tangle by seizing running rigging and coming down hand over hand, landing with a thud in their bare feet on the planked deck. The gallants and topgallants, along with the jib and mizzen sails, were quite enough to maintain way and provide maneuver speed. They didn't need to be piped to their stations. All were at hand by mid-afternoon. The guns were double shotted and run out. The black iron chunks stuck out through the white side stripe just above the water line. The officers, in dark blue coats piped in gold, drew their swords, the blades shining from the light coating of coal oil. The men waited in silence; if they did speak words, it was in whispered tones. Leaders alone were allowed voice on the gun deck. They guarded their prerogative jealously. With nearly 400 men crammed into a space of 170 feet long, 20 feet wide, and 5 feet high, communications was prescribed to only a minimum of voices. The marine drummer stood behind the captain on the quarterdeck, beating out the calls. At each of the twenty-five cannon/carronades, the crews were overstrength. They hoped it would remain so. The cabin boys scrambled down ladders below to the magazines, one forward and one aft. Running barefoot, they put the grey flannel bags in wooden boxes and closed the lid to keep the powder dry.

The blue-coated American marines in the swaying tops secured themselves to the mast with lines, more to steady themselves for better aim than to preserve their perch. The musket was hoisted up on a hip, the pan opened, and a sprinkle of black powder shaken into the primer slot. The remainder was poured down the musket barrel, the gun resting on its butt. The ball was spit into the open end of the metal barrel, a bit of paper stuck to the tongue. The taste of sulphur and charcoal remained in the mouth, while the lips were coated with the black lipstick. The last bit of paper was shoved down the barrel with the 4-foot slim steel ramrod and replaced in its holder under the musket. The ship lurched one way and then the other as the sailing master spun the wheel to gain position on the enemy frigate.

Now, before the battle, both crews stood by their guns straining to maintain balance—riding out the violent action of the careening men-of-war. Crew drill, a daily activity, prepared the men to service the guns with precise movements regardless of the horrors that combat was about to bring. Crisp orders had been passed and echoed from the quarterdeck to the lieutenants in charge of a section and on to midshipmen gun captains, each identified by their tailored dark blue coats. The officer's costumes were in sharp contrast to the slops worn by the crowd of crewmen that stood to the rail. Standing 20 inches above the rail were nets stuffed with rolled hammocks and bedding taken from the crew deck. There for the airing, this day they would provide a little extra protection from flying lead bullets and debris when the enemy closed within musket range. The massive fat black barrels rested calmly on squat wooden carriages that dwarfed the crewmen. The chunky wooden wheels appeared too flimsy to support the weight of the 2,000-pound iron guns. On firing, the recoil cradle carried the gun violently to the rear across the rough deck planks before the restraining hawsers snapped taut. The danger of being run down by careening cannons was paramount.

Idlers No Longer Idle

While the decks were cleared for action, the idlers were committed to specialty tasks. The surgeon and his mate were confined below in the cockpit at a trestle table to set out the frightful tools, probes, saws, and knives. Their devices appeared to be on loan from the carpenter—just a little shinier. The doctor was advised that the primary tactic of the day was surely not to sink the ship. The enemy guns and attendant Royal Marines would attempt to disable the ship's running gear and kill the crew. Then they would make *Constitution* their prize. No matter the outcome, the surgeon knew for certain that there would be hundreds of bloody casualties. Damaged limbs would be sawn off close to the trunk and the wound cauterized, seared to stop the bleeding. Alternately, hot tar could be smeared on the stump; if successful the man would live, forever an invalid. If the wound was to the trunk, there was little that could be done, for he would bleed to death, or later infection would surely kill him. Head wounds, a graze, could be overcome by trepan (crown-shaped skull saw and insertion of a metal plate). A pelt full of wood splinter, though painful, could be treated. Anesthetic took the form of alcohol, which, if spilled into the open wound, might also cleanse it. Leather buckets of seawater and fresh drinking water stood by, slopping over as the ship lurched violently. The chaplain moved through the ranks offering hope to those who fought for God and country.

The carpenter and his assistant were down on the orlop crawling around the catwalk attached to the inside of the double hull at the water line.[15] They were responsible for the integrity of the wooden walls against the sea. Scans of caulking hung from their belts while dragging several wooden shot plugs. The round flat plates were just the size of the enemy's cannonballs. At close range, a cannonball would make a neat hole that could be plugged like a stopper in a bottle and caulked shut. The sailmaker stood by on the orlop as well, dragging out spare sails that could be called up at any moment to replace ones torn to bits by chain and bar shot. The cook put out his precious fire in case the caboose was upset and spilled its hot coals on the wooden deck. He went below and broke out dried food that would be distributed as the day wore on. Hard ship biscuits and salt dried meat were not appetizing but would suffice along with plenty of drinking water.

The order was given to light the slow matches, an alternative to the flintlocks on the guns. The officers checked their pistols to ensure that the priming powder had not leaked out. Cutlasses were brought out of the arms locker in the wardroom by the marines and distributed at each gun position. A marine contingent was set on the forecastle and quarterdeck in a tight formation ready to respond once the enemy was within musket range. All the time, the ship answered the rough handling of the helmsman as the deck crew braced the yards in response to command. The wasters were up and down the ladders bringing up cannonballs and stacking them on brass monkeys (flat brass plate with holes to cradle the heavy balls to keep them from rolling around the deck) within reach of the gun crews. The distraction of a loose cannonball caromed around the deck like lethal bowling balls, crushing feet and banging shins, was a worry to all.

It was reported to Captain Hull that the ship was ready to make history.

The Royal Navy's Prospective

If naval history were to be made in 1812, the Royal Navy would surely make it. Later, a major British historian wrote in retrospect,

> It is a remarkable fact, that no one act of the little navy of the United States had been at all calculated to gain the respect of the British. First, was seen the Chesapeake allowing herself to be beaten, with impunity, by a British ship only nominally superior to her. Then the huge frigate President attacks, and fights for upwards of half an hour, the British sloop Little-Belt. And, even since the war, the same President, at the head of a squadron, makes a bungling business of chasing the Belvidera. While, therefore, a feeling towards America, bordering on contempt, had unhappily possessed the mind of the British naval officer, rendering him more than usually careless and opinionated, the American naval officer, having been taught to regard his new foe with a portion of dread, sailed forth to meet him, with the whole of his energies roused. A moment's reflection, taught him that the honour of his country was now in his hands; and what, in the breast of man, could be a stronger incitement to extraordinary exertions?[16]

Guerriere's Captain Dacres had seen *Constitution* weeks before and was not impressed with anything other than the ability of her crew to row. "Yes, she was a little bigger," C. S. Forester, the American author and historian observed,

> Dacres did not expect defeat; even the recent encounter had not convinced him of the quality of the American Navy. Nor could he have run away in any case without facing the gravest risk, the positive certainty, of a court martial. At that moment the captain of any British 38-gun frigate who refused battle with the Constitution would have been promptly condemned, not merely by legal process, but by the whole of the professional opinion of the Royal Navy.

England Expects

As at Trafalgar in 1805, Captain Dacres was expecting that each man *would* do his duty. Until then, the *Guerriere* had not fought another frigate. The Royal Navy had a long history and was expected to write one more glorious chapter that day. His crew consisted of long-serving professionals. His Royal Marines were smart, dressed all in red with dark blue collars and cuffs, crossed with wide white belts. They took to the tops just as the American marines had done and clung to the driving masts as the British man-of-war maneuvered in slow arcs. The two vessels, alone on the blue sea, churned up the water, leaving white bubbling corkscrew wakes in the foaming water. Each ship prepared alike; they looked like twins not adversaries. The overwhelming size of *Constitution* became abundantly clear now that both parties were drawn close together. The American's masts were taller, her beam was wider, and her hull was longer. The British had painted their ships black to make them look small and vulnerable. It was intended to invite attack. *Gueirrere* was about to get her wish.

Close With and Kill

William James, *the* recognized authority, gives us the English account of the start of the engagement.

> Guerriere . . . opened her starboard broadside at the Constitution. The Guerriere then filled, wore and, on coming round on the larboard tack, fired her larboard guns, "her shot," says Captain Hull, "falling short," a proof, either that the Guerriere's people knew not the range of their guns, or that the powder they were using was of an inferior quality: both causes, indeed, might have co-operated in producing the discreditable result.

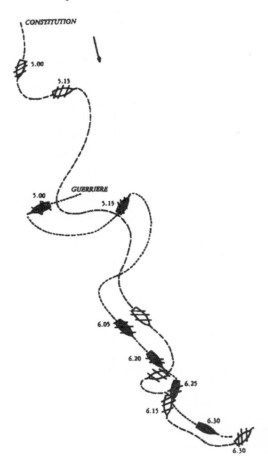

CONSTITUTION

5.00

5.15

GUERRIERE

5.00

5.15

6.05

6.20

6.25

6.15

6.30

6.30

HMS *Guerriere* attacks the USS *Constitution* in August 1812 off the coast of New England.

Black powder is a mixture of charcoal, saltpeter, and sulphur, which, when ignited in a closed space, creates gas pressure that propels the shot out of the open end of the barrel as the gas tries to escape, taking the path of least resistance.

The effectiveness of the powder depends on the following:

1. The quality of the ingredients
2. The proportions within the mixture
3. The size of the powder particles
4. The efficiency of firing, which is the rate of combustion within the chamber
5. The gun quality: bore accuracy and the tightness of the charge ego, that is, the degree of "windage" and the seal provided by the wadding
6. The weight of charge in proportion to shot weight and barrel length[17]

It was known that powder, after prolonged storage could be contaminated and lose its punch. Therefore, it was tested on a regular basis.

Forester's account says that

> The Constitution came rushing down on him, he did his best to cut her up during the important minutes of the approach. But he was opposed to a man whose judgement of time and distance was superior to his. Dacres awaited his coming with his ship hove-to fired a broadside when he judged the ships were within range, and then put his ship before the wind on roughly the same course as the Constitution's, in order to prolong as far as possible the period of the approach, and he yawed first to port and then to starboard so as to present his broadside to the advancing enemy and rake him as he came down. Dacres' eye was not keen enough, or excitement may have clouded his judgment, or his gunners were not well enough trained, or the gunnery control there was an elementary system practiced at the time in all ships was ineffective.[18]

The Words of the American Commander

The after-action letter to the secretary of the navy tells the tale of the victor:

> Sir,
> . . . after all was clear the Ship was ordered to be kept away from the Enemy, on hearing of which the Gallant crew gave three cheers, and requested to be laid close alongside the chace. As we bore up she hoisted an English Ensign at the Mizen Gaff, another in the Mien Shrouds, and a Jack at the Fore, and Mizentop Gallant mast heads. At 5 minutes past 5PM as we were running down on her weather quarter She fired a Broadside, but without effect the Shot all falling short, she then wore and gave us a broadside from Larboard Guns, two of which Shot Struck us but without doing any injury. At this time finding we were within gunshot, I ordered the Ensign hoisted at the Mizen Peak, and a Jack at the Fore and Mixentop Ballant mast head, and a Jack bent ready for hoisting at the Main, the Enemy continued wearing, and maneuvering for about 3/4 of an hour, to get the wind of us. At length finding that she could not, she bore up to bring the wind, on the quarter, and run under her Topsails, and Gib, finding that we came up very slow, and were receiving her shot without being able to return them with effect, I ordered the Maintop Gallant sail set, to run up alongside of her.
> At 5 minutes past 6 PM being alongside and within less than Pistol Shot [fifty yards] we commenced a very heavy fire from all of our Guns, loaded with round and grape, which some great Execution, so much so that in less than fifteen minutes from the time, we got alongside, his Mizen Mast went by the board, and his Main Yard in the Slings, and the Hull, and Sails very much injured, which made it very difficult for them to

manage her. At his time the Constitution had received but little damage, and having more sail set than the Enemy she shot ahead, on seeing this I determined to put the Helm to Port, and oblige him to do the same, or suffer himself to be raked, by our getting across his bows, on our Helm being put to Port the ship came too, and gave us an opportunity of pouring in upon his Larboard Bow several Broadsides, which made great havock amongst his men on the forecastle and did great injury to his fore rigging, and sails. The Enemy put his helm to Port, at the time we did, but his Mizen Mast being over the Quarter, prevented her coming too, which brought us across his Bows, with his Bowsprit over our Stern, (they collided). At this moment I determined to board him.

American Marines Forward

At that moment, Lieutenant of American Marines William Bush, at the head of his boarding party, yelled to Captain Hull near him on the quarterdeck,

"Shall I board her, Sir?" and is shot dead.[19]

Constitutions surgeon, Amos A. Evans's, words are chilling,

During the engagement she came against our stern with her bows twice, and carried away her Jib boom and injured our Taffrail. It was when in that situation that Lt. Morris and Lt. Bush were shot. Mr. Morris first jumped on the Taffrail with an intention of boarding her and was instantly wounded in the parietes of the abdomen. Mr. Bush jumped into his place the instant he fell and immediately one musket shot entered his face and passed into his brain.

Second Lieutenant of Marines John Contee wrote to Lewis Bush, brother of the slain marine,

In the heat of the action the Marines were called aft, led by the illustrious Bush who mounted the taffrail sword in hand, and as he exclaimed "Shall I board her," received the fatal ball on his left cheek bone which passed thro' to the back of his head. Thus fell that great and good officer, who, when living was beloved, & now gone is lamented by all. His loss is deeply regretted by His country & friends, but he died as he lived, with honor to both.[20]

The *Constitution* captain's account continues,

But the instant the Boarders were called, for that purpose, his Foremast, and Mainmast went by the board, and took with them the Gib-boom, and every other spar except the Bowsprit. On seeing the Enemy totally disabled and the Constitution received but little injury I again to renew the action, not knowing whither the Enemy had struck or not, we stood off for about half an hour, to repair our Braces, and such other rigging, as had been shot away, and wore around to return to the Enemy, it being now dark, we could not see whether she had any colours, flying or not, but could discover that she had raised a small flag Staff or Jurymast forward. I ordered a Boat hoisted out and sent Lieutenant Reed on board as a flag to see whether she had surrendered or not, and if she had to see what assistance she wanted, as I believed she was sinking. Lieutenant Reed returned in about twenty minutes, and brought with him, James Richard Dacres Esqr. Commander of his britanic Majesty's Frigate the Guerriere, which ship had surrendered, to the United States Frigate Constitution, our Boats were immediately hoisted out and sent for the Prisoner, and were kept at work bringing them and their Baggage on board, all night.

At daylight we found the Enemy's Ship a perfect Wreck, having many shot holes between wind, and water, and above Six feet of the Plank below the Bends taken out by our round Shot, and her upper works so shattered on pieces, that I determined to take out the sick and wounded as fast as possible, and set her on fire, as it would be impossible to get her into Port.[21]

The remainder of the report tells of the heroic conduct of his officers and men and provides a list of casualties. There is little bravado in the victory report that will come later when the press elevates Isaac Hull to national hero. I believe that a professional naval officer of the day had little hatred for defeated men and did not relish the destruction of a beautiful man-of-war like *Guerriere*. I don't doubt that looking into the eyes of the surrendered Captain Dacres, he saw the despair that was to follow the Englishman all his life and knew that the positions could have been reversed.

The captive Royal Navy captain watched as his men were evacuated from his shattered command.

An examination of H.M.S. Guerriere and an attempt at towing demonstrated the impossibility of getting her into port, so Captain Hull of U.S.S. Constitution gave orders to burn her. Just before setting fire to the disabled warship, Captain Hull asked Captain Dacres if there was anything he would like to save from his ship. Dacres replied. "Yes, my mother's Bible which I have carried with me for years." An officer was sent to get it and from this moment a friendship sprang up between these two captains that lasted until Hull's death in 1843.[22]

In a sinking condition, she was set on fire by the American sailors and sunk. Captain Darces wrote his lamentable report to his commander from the deck of the enemy's ship.

Captain James R. Dacres R.N. to
Vice Admiral Herbert Sawyer, R.N.

Sir,

I am sorry to inform you of the Capture of His Majesty's late ship
Guerriere by the American Frigate Constitution after a severe action on the 19th of August. . . . At 2 PM being by the Wind on the
starboard Tack, we saw a Sail on our Weather Beam, bearing down
on us. At 3 made her out to be a Man of War, beat to Quarters and
prepar'd for Action. At 4. She closing fast wore to prevent her taking
us. At 4:10 hoisted our Colours and fir'd several shot at her. At 4:20
She hoisted her Colours and return'd our fire, Wore several times,
to avoid being raked, Exchanging broadsides. At 5 She clos'd on our
Starboard Beam, both keeping up a heavy fire and steering free, his
intention being evidently to cross our bow. At 5:20, our Mizen Mast
went over the starboard quarter and brought the Ship up in the Wind.
The enemy then plac'd himself on our larboard Bow raking us, a few
only of our bow Guns bearing and his Grape and Riflemen sweeping our Deck. At 5:40 the Ship not answering the helm, he attempted
to lay up on board at this time. [they collide] Mr. Grant who commanded the Forecastle was carried below badly wounded. I immediately order'd the Marines and Boarders from the Main Deck: Master
was at this time shot thro the knee, and I receiv'd a severe wound
in the back. Lieutenant Kent was leading on the Boarders, when the
Ship coming too, we brought some of our bow guns to bear on her
an had got clear of our opponent when at 6:20 our Fore and Main
Masts went over the side, leaving the Ship a perfect unmanageable
Wreck. The Enemy shooting ahead, It was hoped to clear the Wreck
and get the Ship under Command to renew the Action but just as we
had clear'd the Wreck our Spritsail yard went and the Enemy having
rove new Braces &c, wore round within Pistol Shot to rake Us. The
Ship laying in the trough of the Sea and rolling her main Deck Guns
under Water and all attempts to get her before the Wind being fruit-
less, when calling my few remaining officers together, they were all of
opinion that any further resistance would be a needless waste of lives, I
order'd though reluctantly, the Colours to be struck.

Later, in the letter, he alludes to the early misses from his broadside:
"on coming into action, the Enemy had such an advantage from his Marines
and Riflemen, when close and his superior sailing enabled him to choose his
distance."[23] It is true that once within "pistol range," the accurate musket fire
was devastating. The captain could swear to that since an American Marine

shot him from the tops. Captain Hull had achieved the first frigate-to-frigate victory in the history of the Royal Navy. In London, the newspapers bemoaned the loss, and citizens petitioned the Naval Board over the loss, which in their eyes was totally inexplicable. But there was more to come.

THE AMERICAN OFFICER CORPS

The good, the bad, and the outrageous made up the senior officer corps of the American military community during the War of 1812. Each service had its own homegrown hero or goat torn from civilian endeavors and thrust into battle against the most professional military machine the world had ever known. Some were courageous and savvy, while others, often caught up by their own ambition, were wholly inadequate. There was one who would become a national scandal. The minor conflicts with the French and the Barbary pirates over the past seventeen years culled out the majority of poor performers in the navy. But since there was no regular structure to the U.S. Navy, that is, no government yards, depots, procurement, or personnel, each captain scratched the port for officers and crew prior to sailing. However, once signed on, the captain could be sure that endless sea voyages honed his young officers' skills at ship handling, gunnery, and leadership. The result was a naval officer corps of exceptional men who stepped up at just the right moment and proved the equal of the Royal Navy captains.

The Sad Story of the Army

The first land action shared a distinction with the first naval action. Captain Isaac Hull's uncle, Governor William Hull of the Michigan Territory, was selected by the president to command the western arm of the invasion force sent to Canada. A newly appointed brigadier general, Governor Hull, a loyal Republican, met the criteria used to select officers from lieutenant to general. General Hull had been a junior officer during the Revolutionary War but had no further contact with things military over the next forty years and was reluctant to assume the position in view of the tense relations with the British across the Canadian border. Captain Hull took the *Constitution* to sea at precisely the same time his uncle was ordered to invade Upper Canada. While the ship gained immortality as *Old Ironsides*, when the British cannonballs failed to dent her hull, his uncle was not so fortunate. Thrust into command of a far less lethal alliance of untested regulars and uninspired militiamen, the general was not provided with officers or troops who had ever fought more than bands of rampaging Indians along the burgeoning frontier.

William Hull

At age twenty-three, Hull, a native son of Connecticut, joined the fight for independence in 1775. In 1805, his service to the Jefferson administration paid off
with the governorship of a very promising territory. The overly ambitious invasion plan of sixty-two year-old Major General Henry Dearborn, commander of
the army, would send Hull across the Detroit River into what would become
Windsor, Canada. Formerly the Secretary of War under Jefferson, Dearborn
supported Jefferson's avaricious desire to add Canada to the stars and stripes as
a punitive measure for the impressments of American sailors and a land grab of
unprecedented arrogance. The former president was infamous for declaring that
"the taking of Canada this year is a mere matter of marching." Jefferson ardently
believed that French Canadians, who outnumbered the English in Ontario five
to one, reflected the rebellious spirit of '76 in view of their own French Revolution of 1789. The mere sight of an American soldier on Canadian soil would
spark revolution and kick the British out of Upper Canada. Henry Clay of Kentucky boasted that his state militia could take all of Canada. Jefferson had witnessed revolutionary France as the Ambassador earlier and had become a Francophile as a result. Additionally, his experience as a young man in the colonies
during the American Revolution had fostered a deep hatred of everything English. Dearborn's plan, written prior to the declaration of war, called for a four-
pronged attack. The first was Detroit, followed by Niagara and Kingston, with
the final blow delivered by the main force under Dearborn at Montreal. He had
saved the best for last and for himself. Knowing that regular British forces were
positioned to the west along the northern shore of the Great Lakes, he planned
to prevent them from going east and spoil his attack on the capital city. The absence of an experienced staff, seasoned officer corps, and trained and equipped
regular troops was not a concern. Dearborn and his political leaders in the executive and legislative branch of the new republic chose to misread the lessons of
the war they had learned when fighting the British as young men. Disregarding
the pivotal intervention of the French as a mere footnote, they were convinced
that the militia had won the war and would rise to do the same once again. It
was not only an opinion held by the government; most citizens would have
agreed that England would never attempt to put a land army in the United States
after their humiliating defeat forty years before. Besides, Great Britain could not
afford to fight the United States and Napoleon at the same time. Jefferson and
Madison, having monitored Napoleon's glorious string of victories since 1795,
convinced them to ride the emperor's coattails with their own military adventure. How could they foresee the emperor's disastrous winter campaign that
froze his army in Moscow and began the meteoric decline of Bonaparte?

In his zeal to take Canada and please his benefactors, Dearborn chose to
overlook the absence of a functioning and funded department of supply and

services normally identified with the conduct of land warfare. Over the past year, the roster of 6,000 regular army troops had added only 3,800 recruits in spite of increased benefits. In great haste, the two infantry regiments, one artillery regiment with a handful of horse guns and a dragoon regiment with no horses were increased by doubling the number of formations. The regular and militia regimental cadre of officers and sergeants was recruited from the local community's membership of the reigning political party. Winfield Scott, a lawyer who volunteered for service in 1808 remarked that "swaggerers, dependants, decayed gentlemen and others fit for nothing else, made up the officer corps."[24] The blue-coated regulars marked with red collars and cuffs, while splendid, lacked every aspect of an effective fighting force. The new regiments formed that year were a shadow fighting force not fit for a parade. In the west, small garrisons of a few hundred old soldiers huddled inside crumbling fortifications at the mercy of Indian raiding parties who roamed freely, killing settlers and burning their crude attempts to tame the wilderness east of the Mississippi.

Although Congress had authorized a substantial increase in the size of the army, the populace seemed uninterested. They didn't swarm to the colors as in 1775 because business was booming and young men found a future outside soldiering. There was little support for the annexation of Canada except in the heart of Jefferson and the westerners. Henry Clay and others feared the Indians, who were being increasingly armed and trained by the border crossing British in Canada. While Congress appropriated the billets for a regular army of 36,000, the reality put the figure well under 10,000, and nearly half of those were recruits in training.

When called, the states were expected to release over 100,000 militiamen to federal control. Few believed that the governors would give up their private army's to fight outside their borders unless the country was being invaded. Hull was the exception since Michigan was under constant threat along its long, watery border. He petitioned Congress for regular forces to bolster Fort Detroit earlier in 1812, which resulted in his appointment to the regular army and command of the just minted 4th Infantry Regiment. Hull was expected to combine them with his own militia and that of Ohio and strike Canada. Homesteaders around the edge of Lake Erie felt the pressure of Indian marauders led by British officers who supplied victuals, blankets, hatchets, muskets, and gunpowder, and could be counted on, that is, once crops were planted, to supplement the 4th Regiment.

Hull Leads the Invaders

General Hull began to muster his force south of the Michigan border on June 10, nine days before the declaration of war. The 4th Regiment and the gathering militia were compelled to build a military road 200 miles long through the wilderness and swamps before reaching Detroit and crossing into Canada. Early on June 18, Secretary of War Eustis sent Hull a warning that Congress was expected to declare war that day. Hull acknowledged it on June 24 while leading a combined force of 2,000 still 40 miles south of Detroit. Surprisingly, Hull wrote back, "I feel confident the force under my command will be superior to any which can be opposed to it."[25]

On the same day, a messenger from the north notified him that the British were aware of the declaration of war and had promptly captured Hull's only lake vessel, cutting off his communications by water to the east. He quickened his march toward Fort Detroit, where a small garrison of 120 regulars protected the 500 citizens employed in the fur trade. On July 12, the American command crossed the Detroit River with great difficulty, established a beachhead, but could not find the British army. Augmented by Tecumseh's Indian war parties, 1,000 redcoats under Major General Isaac Brock opposed Hull. The formidable Brock was an experienced professional officer who had fought in India and numerous engagements throughout the empire. First blood went to Brock, who sent a small, seasoned force north to capture Mackinac Island in the straits between Lakes Michigan and Superior. With first-rate intelligence provided by Indian scouts, Brook's main force moved south to confront Hull. American scouting parties were sent north to find Brook. On hearing their disturbing reports of redcoats and Indians, Hull, fearing the worst, managed to cross back to Michigan before Brook could catch him. At Fort Detroit, Hull lost his nerve once again, believing that the British were south of him, cutting his line of communication and about to release the Indian war parties to ravage the surrounding communities. Hull split his force by 400, sending them south to form a defensive line, while the remaining 1,400 manned the fort. He was hemorrhaging troops to disease and desertion at a high rate and feared that the command would dissolve while the British pressed forward. On Hull's heels, Brock crossed his entire command under the cover of a bombardment from ships and gunboats just to the south of the American fort. By the time the British assembled an infantry attack on Fort Detroit, 600 of the Michigan militiamen had fled. Brook didn't want to risk losing seasoned soldiers who were very difficult to replace in the northwestern wilderness. Hull was offered surrender terms, readily accepting them on August 16, knowing that without the protection offered in the agreement, the women and children would be slaughtered by the Indians. The immediate effect after the surrender and evacuation was the rampaging of the Indians throughout the nearby western territory. As a result, Major General William Henry Harrison, the victor over Tecumseh at Tippecanoe and future president of the United States, fought the Indian nations anew. With captains like

Zachary Taylor, another future president, they tried to stabilize the frontier once again. General William Hull was court-martialed for treason and cowardice and found guilty of only cowardice and neglect of duty. It is said that the court was stacked with political enemies. The court recommended that he be shot, but President Madison commuted the sentence. Hull was released because of his age and prior service to the nation.

CHRONOLOGIES

Isaac Hull

1773, March 9	Born at Derby, Connecticut, nephew of William Hull
1790s	Captain of merchant ships
1798, March	U.S. naval lieutenant on USS *Constitution*
1802	First lieutenant on USS *Adams*
1803, fall	Isaac Hull took command of *Argus* from Decatur
1804	Master and commander of the USS *Enterprise*
1806	Promoted to captain
1809–1810	Constructed gunboats and commanded *Chesapeake* and *President*
1812, August 19	Captain of USS *Constitution* and captured HMS *Guerriere*
1812, September	Commandant of the Portsmouth Navy Yard, Maine

William Hull

1753, June 24	Born at Derby, Connecticut
1772, June	Law graduate from Yale
1775	Captain of the Litchfield, Connecticut, militia
1781	Judge in Newton, Massachusetts, and state senator
1805, March 22	First governor of the Michigan Territory
1812, February	Appointed brigadier general for the Army of the Northwest
1812, July 12	Hull's command crossed the Detroit River and invaded Canada
1812, August 16	Hull surrendered Fort Detroit to British

NOTES

1. James R. Durand, *The Life and Adventures of James R. Durand*, ed. George S. Brooks (1820; reprint, New Haven, CT: Yale University Press, 1926), 1.

2. Durand, *The Life and Adventures of James R. Durand*, 47.

3. Durand, *The Life and Adventures of James R. Durand*, 50.

4. Durand, *The Life and Adventures of James R. Durand*, 59.

5. Durand, *The Life and Adventures of James R. Durand*, 65.

6. Durand, *The Life and Adventures of James R. Durand*, 65.

7. Extract from journal of Lieutenant Isaac Hull, U.S. Navy, of U.S. frigate *Constitution*, Captain Silas Talbot, U.S. Navy, commanding, Wednesday, March 5, 1800, courtesy of the National Archives.

8. William S. Dudley, ed., *The Naval War of 1812: A Documentary History,* vol. 1, 1812 (Washington, DC: Navy Historical Center, Naval Historical Center, Department of the Navy, 1985), 136.

9. Dudley, *The Naval War of 1812*, 138.

10. Leland P. Lovette, ed., *Naval Customs, Traditions and Usage* (Annapolis, MD: U.S. Naval Institute Press, 1939), 196.

11. John Marshal, *Royal Naval Biography: or Memoirs of the Services of the Flag-Officers, Rear Admiral, Captains & Commanders*, vol. 2, pt. 2 (London, 1825), 625.

12. Dudley, *The Naval War of 1812*, 232.

13. Henry Adams, *The War of 1812* (New York: Scribner, 1889; reprint, New York: Cooper Square Press, 1999), 41.

14. Donald Hickey, *The War of 1812: A Forgotten Conflict* (Champaign: University of Illinois Press, 1989), 94.

15. The orlop is the lowest deck in a ship just above the bilge.

16. William M. James, *The Naval History of Great Britain, during the French Revolution and the Napoleonic Wars*, vol. 6, 1811–1827 (1857; reprint, London: Conway Maritime Press, 2002), 98.

17. *Mariner's Mirror* 59 (November 1973): 453 (Society of Nautical Research Paper No. 4, Chatham Royal Dockyard Historical Society).

18. C. S. Forester, *The Naval War of 1812* (London: Michael Joseph, 1957), 54.

19. Edward Howard Simmons, *The United States Marines: A History* (Annapolis, MD: Naval Institute Press, 1974), 24.

20. Michael L. Bosworth, Lieutenant John Contee of the United States Marines, USS *Constitution*, and the Nautical Showdens of Montpelier, essay written for Montpelier Mansion of Laurel, Maryland, *Journal of the War of 1812,* 6, no. 2 (Spring 2001).

21. Dudley, *The War of 1812*, 238.

22. Edgar K. Thompson, The Outfit of a Naval Cadet in the Reign of George II. *Mariner's Mirror* 61 (1974): 191.

23. Dudley, *The Naval War of 1812*, 243.

24. John Elting, *Amateurs to Arms: A Military History of the War of 1812* (New York: DaCapo Press, 1995), 2.

25. Henry Adams, *The War of 1812* (New York: Cooper Square Press, 1999), 5.

2

ANDREW JACKSON

A wounded British officer at New Orleans was approached by a volunteer woodsman, "Are there no regular officers in your army? I would like to be attended by a gentleman."

"Lets leave the conceited bastard to wallow in his own blood," said a scruffy American militiaman.

"No," said the Kentucky Lieutenant. "Don't mind his imprudent tongue, His wound makes a gentleman of him, nothing else could."

—Military anecdote

A WOUND THAT WOULDN'T HEAL

EARNED DURING his many personal disputes, Jackson carried a bullet within his body to old age. But that is not the wound that never healed. When just fourteen, a messenger during the American Revolution, the boy was captured and confined. A British officer took him on as a personal servant, but Andrew Jackson refused to polish his captor's black riding boots. Outraged by Jackson's behavior, the officer slashed at him with his sabre. The swirling blade brushed across the boy's forehead, breaking the skin. The minor wound soon disappeared. However, the injury to his soul would last a lifetime. He also hated the British allies, the American Indian, who killed one of his brothers. His other brother died as a result of British military prison conditions. His mother's life was stolen when she contracted cholera while nursing American prisoners of war in Camden, New Jersey. Jackson carefully nurtured those festering wounds to the grave.

Like his ancestors in the Highlands of Scotland, Andrew Jackson was born fighting. "There was a willingness to take the law into his own hands rather than waiting for the solution to come down from above."[1] The 1707 Act of Union, joining Scotland and England, was bitterly opposed by the clans. Many a battle was fought over the prospect of London rule and the dissolution of the Highland feudal culture. Bonny Prince Charlie's failed rebellion brought the same contempt in the English. The Disarmament Act denied Scots their arms, clan tartans, and playing of the bagpipes. The total defeat brought immediate cruel and degrading consequences to the clans of the north. Six months in jail was pronounced on anyone wearing any portion of the Highland dress.

Soon, an English government clearance program to weaken the clans began to drive the small families off the land. The Jacksons, weavers like most crofters, were moved to villages where they could be watched—and controlled. Coastal towns became overcrowded with poor, vagrant clan families. The solution to the overcrowding was to transport Highlanders to the northern counties of Ireland. The assimilation of the churchgoing Scots and Roman Catholic majority was explosive. There, Hugh Jackson, Andrew's grandfather, set up a weaving business, while his four sons farmed the nearby hills. The uneducated and unweary peasant farmers wandered into the new towns in large numbers seeking employment. Factories brought steady wages, but the overcrowding in slums haunted by disease made the people yearn once more for the freedom and open spaces of the farms. Andrew Jackson's father, a farmer, felt unwelcome in Catholic Ulster. In these dire circumstances, many clansmen took matters into their own hands. They would go to the crown colony of America, with its free land and the lure of a frontier so remote that surely the king's greedy reach could not disturb them. Elizabeth, Andrew's mother, had four sisters living in the Carolinas. Letters encouraged the family to give up on Ulster as they had. Kin meant a great deal to the Highlanders, and the invitation was all it took to risk the voyage for the promise of a new land and the opportunity to build a homestead. In the spring of 1765, the Jackson family, mother, father, and two young sons, Hugh and Robert, ages three and one, landed in America with few possessions. They walked the long roads to the Catawba Valley set on the western frontier of North Carolina.[2] It was Indian country, and Elizabeth was surprised to find that her sister's home was fortified against an occasional attack by marauding braves. Squatting on poor land miles away from the family was the best the Jacksons could do. That fall, Elizabeth was pregnant once again. Knowing that a third child was expected in the spring of 1767, Andrew senior labored alone to clear the land of white oak in time for planting that spring. Misfortune struck that fall, rendering him incapable of work. His condition worsened that winter in the drafty little cabin he had managed to provide. He died before the birth of his third and most impressive offspring. Andrew Jackson, the younger, was born on the fifteenth of March fatherless, consoled only in that he would bear his fathers' name. His aunt took the young family in, out of necessity, where Elizabeth would combine her family with the Crawfords. Andrew's mother thought of her Andrew as someone special and did all she could to have him educated by a local minister in hopes that her son would go to the cloth. But the nature of that youngster was tyrannical, hot-blooded, and difficult to hold in her hand.

As he grew, he "terrorized the neighborhood." Local folks said not only that he was uncontrolled but that he nurtured a wall of ignorance about himself. Of his mother, of whom he often spoke, Jackson said she was as gentle as a dove and as brave as a lioness. She taught him to stand up for himself and fight to preserve his honor as a man and a Christian. She saw the Indians as a threat to the land and the family and turned her son into an Indian fighter. Today, it is suspected that Indian war parties had killed members of the clan, including at least one of his older brothers.

Young Andrew learned to shoot a bow and could read the Indians' bird and animal calls as they crept up on settlers' farms. He is known for one incident in which he saved a family with a prompt warning. Throughout his life, he always called Indians savages and never trusted their promises or agreements. He believed it to be war between the white and the Native American communities that would end with the extinction of one. Jackson, determined that it was to be the Indian, was stubborn, impetuous, quick to anger, and extremely contentious when he believed he was right. He was always right. However, he was unwaveringly loyal to friends even when he thought them in the wrong.

Described as tall, thin, and wiry, with large bright blue eyes and thick unruly hair that he sported all his life (even when the color prematurely turned white), he tended toward violent behavior that was most fitting on the frontier of the Carolinas and Tennessee. There was little sophistication in the backwoods, where life was not only hard but dangerous. Survival of the fittest was no idle phrase. He was nine when the Revolutionary War began. Again, the Indians were on the other side, supported this time by the British army.

At age thirteen, Jackson had his first contact with the British army when Lieutenant Colonel Banester Tarleton, leading his infamous dragoons, attacked a force of several hundred militia near Jackson's home. Nearly all were killed or wounded, and he and his mother nursed the wounded. His hatred spread to the redcoats at that early age. Allied with the Indians, the British burned the homesteads, and the people fled time and again to the mountains along with Jackson and his mother. Jackson saw the Indians as pawns for any invader to use to disrupt and destroy the valley he called home. "They must go" is a phrase he used throughout his life.

He became a messenger in the militia in 1780, attending drills and learning the political importance of the formation as well as its duty. The young irregular was captured in 1781.

His mother arranged a prisoner exchange and took her son, suffering from smallpox, home. Once her boy was safe, she traveled 160 miles on foot to the prison ships in Charleston to nurse American militia, some her kin. She soon contracted cholera and died. Orphaned at fifteen, he finished his local schooling at age seventeen and went to the big city to become a lawyer.

A two-year law student in Salisbury, North Carolina, he was described by a companion as "the most roaring, rollicking, game-cocking, horse-racing card-playing mischievous fellow that ever lived in the town."[3] However, he possessed a charismatic presence that drew people to him. At 6 feet 1 inch with bushy hair that stood as erect as a butter bush, his thin body disguised its great strength. He had a strong jaw pushed far forward, making his eyes look sunken. A long, straight nose had a sharp end, but his shabby and often patched dress caught the eye.

In September 1787, at age twenty Jackson qualified to practice law in North Carolina. In Salisbury, his studies and attendance at the law offices of Spruce McCay entitled him to go out on his own, roaming the state's courtrooms, picking up fees for service. Jackson's education in the law didn't temper his explosive personality. Remarks passed between Waightstill Avery, a prominent lawyer on the circuit, concerning Jackson's skill at the bar that were taken as a personal insult, and Avery was called out to duel. Pistols were fired, but neither man was hit. Dueling, though illegal, was tolerated and regarded as a fair fight if the two men were known to be gentlemen.

A year later, the western district of North Carolina, through the Cumberland Gap on the far side of the mountains, beckoned the young lawyer to the Tennessee Territory. The danger of western Indian attacks that dominated the newspapers had no effect on the young lawyer. Partnered with several young buck members of the bar, Jackson joined the McNairy party, some sixty families, and took the new road that led through known raiding party country. The young men were headed for Nashville and recognized the safety in numbers offered by the wagon train. The 183-mile trail that had been opened up through the gap by Daniel Boone was described as narrow and treacherous. Breaking out of the pass brought a real hazard to life when signs of Indians were picked up by the wary Jackson. His misspent youth, marking trails and learning the sounds of war parties and sniffing the wind, was about to come into play. Jackson advised the party to keep moving, stopping for only a few short hours day and night. Deep in Indian country, game paths, known to the natives like highways, crisscrossed the wagon trail and allowed hunting parties to move quickly and quietly ahead to ambush the settlers. On one occasion, the wagon train moved for over thirty hours, not risking to camp until they found a clearing they could defend. Just after dark, while others slept, Jackson propped up against a tree, smoking a pipe to fend off the bugs, to listen in the dark. Soon, he heard the unmistakable hoot of owls. He reckoned that they were wingless owls since it was too early for owls to be hunting. Within minutes, he roused the camp and got them on the move to safety. Nashville learned later that a small party of white trappers took up residence and warmed themselves around the smoldering campfires. Little remained of the men and equipment found by the next passersby. The incident established Jackson as an Indian fighter, the highest calling in that fragile outcropping of the new United States. Jackson was true to the calling, which he valued, and would drop everything to lead the militia in the defense of farm or family.

Spain's influence crept north. The Spanish weren't going to give up the hold they had on the southern Gulf Coast because the settlers paid a 15 percent fee to ship from Spanish ports. Yet Spain played both sides, maintaining friendly ties with the United States. Small Spanish garrisons let the Indians fight their battles for them by stocking Chickasaw Bluffs, now Memphis, which was on U.S. soil. It was a message to the Indians that they could defy the American government. The Indian support costs were picked up by the Spanish shipping tariff paid by the settlers, thereby funding their own destruction. The federal government attempted to mediate claims to Indian lands with grant money for land taken by squatters. Overtures were made to the Spanish officials, and while good words passed, settlers continued a relentless creep deep into Creek Indian strongholds with every passing season. In 1793, the federal government threw up its hands and left the matter to resolve itself by bloodshed, ambush, and war parities. Jackson took a prominent role in the new territory of Tennessee administered by the provisional governor, William Blunt. Tired of fighting Indians and prosecuting settlers for squatting on Indian land, Judge Jackson threatened the federal government, "If you don't settle this matter we'll look elsewhere for protection." By this, it was plain to the federal government that Jackson meant Spain or even England.

Jackson led a bid for statehood that succeeded in June 1796. He became its first and only member of the House of Representatives at age twenty-nine. Secretary of the Treasury Albert Gallatin, on seeing him on the street of Philadelphia, described Jackson "as tall, lank, uncouth-looking personage, long locks of hair hanging over his face, and a queue hanging down his back tied in an eel skin, his dress singular, his manners and deportment of that of a back woodsman."[4] The short time spent as a representative and shorter time as a senator, resigning in April 1798 during his first term, brought him home to his beloved wife Rachel and his home beyond the Allegheny Mountains. The ever growing number of Tennesseans topped 77,000 in its early years. The regular army, which numbered just over 1,000, was scattered among coastal forts, leaving the new state to raise a militia for its own survival. The federal government would contribute arms and power but little else other than a manual written on the experience of the Revolutionary War army and sprinkles of wisdom from the land forces of Europe fighting Napoleon. Members of the militia elected their leaders by popular vote. A major general as commander with three brigadier generals was to provision, train, and lead the widely scattered force. Jackson was highly disturbed when he lost the election to command. He thought that his reputation as an Indian fighter would suffice, but an older man, a hero of the Revolutionary War, was selected. It would be 1802 before his friends and neighbors presented him with the pair of silver starred epaulets on a dark blue frock coat. It meant more money than a state judge. The state constitution allowed him to serve in both capacities and draw two pays. His election was contested since the other candidate, John Sevier, split the district vote, resulting in a tie. Sevier proposed another ballot, but Jackson refused and threw the decision to the sitting governor, Archibald Roane. It seems that history turns on such moments. Roane and Jackson had been friends in North Carolina when both received licenses to practice law in the same county.[5]

Sevier's criticism of Jackson was well known. Sevier, the hero of the Battle of Kings Mountain during the Revolutionary War, called Jackson "a poor, pitiful petty-fogging lawyer." Sevier challenged Jackson to a duel outside the state boundaries to prevent Jackson's blood from defiling the Tennessee soil. It all came to nothing when Sevier's horse was frightened by the bravado of the meeting and ran off with the dueling pistols.

Jackson had a reputation of protecting his honor in the face of a loaded pistol. Once a man who was involved in a horse race dispute challenged that honor. A fellow member of the bar, Mr. Joseph Erwin, esq., pulled out of a scheduled private race match between Jackson's stallion Truxton and his horse Ploughman. To save face, Erwin's son-in-law, Charles Dickenson, published remarks in local rags concerning the conduct of Jackson over the cancellation. The accusation went back and forth for more than a month. Jackson saw it as an attempt to advance the reputation of Erwin by airing the affair in public, a common tactic of the day.

The rules were read out, "It is agreed that the distance shall be 24 feet, the parties are to stand facing each other with their pistols perpendicular. When ready, the word fire will be given, at which they are to fire as soon as they please. Should either fire before the word fire is given, we, the seconds, pledge ourselves to shoot him down instantly."[6]

The pistols fire a light ball half that of a musket, usually wounding the victim and allowing the wounded man to take his time in returning a shot. Some say that it was wise to absorb the first shot and then take one's time to aim for a kill. Dickenson was a renowned marksman, often goading an opponent into the duel so that he could kill him with honor. Dickenson raised his pistol while Jackson stood ramrod straight and still, waiting to absorb the impact. Dickenson's gun barked, sending the ball directly to Jackson's midsection. His loose coat concealed the tall frame so that Dickenson's shot missed the heart by an inch and lodged between the sternum and a rib. Jackson raised his weapon and fired, but the half-cocked position of the hammer prevented the strike, and Jackson fully cocked the hammer and fired, sending the ball deep into Dickenson's stomach. The wounded man doubled over and sunk to the ground. Jackson and his second left the field. It was only then that it became apparent that Jackson was wounded. He carried the ball within his body for most of his life along with other bits and pieces.

Jackson's popularity with the militia was based on his experience in the field along with a previous performance when a member of Congress. Tennessee's governor submitted a claim for militia soldiers' pay after an extended campaign to protect settlers from an onslaught of Indian raiding parties. The Congress tabled the matter for four years and finally refused to pay, believing that the militia attacks were purely offensive, an effort to take Indian land in support of unlawful claims. Jackson rose for the first time on the floor of the House and declared that some 1,200 attacks had taken place, causing the militia to defend the communities and farms "by taking the fight to the Indians." He said that "the troops were called out by their superior officers and should not be expected to get clarification from Washington before honoring the order to mobilize. A contrary doctrine would strike at the very root of subordination. Before you obey the command of our superior officer, you have the right to inquire into the legality of the service upon which you are about to be employed, and, not until you are satisfied, you may refuse to take the field? Admit to this," he shouted, "and you destroy the very basis on which military authority rests. When a force is called to service the men expect that they will be paid for their service and not negotiated out of it by uninterested parties at the federal level years later."[7] The militia was paid in full.

JUDGE JACKSON GAVE NO QUARTER

His reputation as a judge was as fiery as his time in Congress. A defendant, Mr. Bean, who in a drunken rage had cut off the ear of his child, cursed the court and stomped out of the courthouse. The sheriff and posse were cowed when Bean threatened to kill anyone who got in his way. Jackson, infuriated at the behavior, told the sheriff to deputize him. Jackson then left the courthouse and confronted Bean in the street. The armed man threatened the crowd with a pistol. Jackson stormed into the accumulation of onlookers with two cocked and loaded pistols. At the top of his lungs, the tall, resolute judge, who had taken on the mantle of justice like a suit of armor, screamed, "Now surrender you infernal villain, this very instant; or I'll blow you through." Bean dropped the gun and declared later, "I saw shoot in those eyes."[8] When it came to land disputes, Jackson believed himself to be evenhanded. He told Captain Sam Houston to arrest and prosecute those white settlers who violated the treaty agreements and squatted on Indian land. Their stock was sold at auction. The judge believed that such white behavior only destabilized the law-abiding settlers and put them in jeopardy from retaliating Indians. But he did not burn them out, kill them, and send their woman and children into captivity, as he was known to do to offending Indians.

Jackson grouped Indians and slaves into the same category. He called them "lower grade." He defended them as long as they acted within the law, a position that he felt was his sacred honor to uphold. "The land would never be civilized and safe for women and children if the rule of law was subverted," remarked the judge. Indian land was acquired by demanding payment for the goods purchased from frontier merchants. So it is true that they were paid in kind for their land. However, the price was absurdly low, and the Indians did not fully grasp the concept of landownership. The merchants did not want them to fully comprehend the gravity of the transactions. Additionally, the chiefs were often bribed by land-grabbing factions that encouraged them to sign numerous treaties granting large tracts of land.

EXPANSION

In 1800, Napoleon made good on his insistence that Spain return Louisiana with the signing of the Treaty of San Ildefonso. However, providence smiled on the United States with the British victories in the Caribbean in 1801, compelling Napoleon to give up his dream of a North American empire. France settled with Jefferson, who had been ambassador to France prior to his presidency. In 1803, a price of $15 million was finalized. By 1809, Jackson had grown in power on the frontier and in Washington. He proposed to the new governor, Willie Blount, brother of the former governor, that an exchange of territory was the only solution to the ubiquitous Indian raiding parties that kept Tennessee out of the mainstream progress. Jackson proposed to move the tribes to the southernmost portions of the Louisiana

Territory, thereby displacing Indian communities and forcing them onto the shoulders of the federal government. It was said that it was the perfect solution, "as clear as two and two make four."

He reckoned that the vacant land had fish and game and a culture of resident tribes close to that of their own. The idea had support in Washington since the original suggestion came from Jefferson. It fit in with the president's agronomy. Opposed to factories and commercial manufacturing, Jefferson saw the new world as the breadbasket and supplier of fibers for Europe. He pointed out that the eastern tribes of Delaware and Yamasees had been wiped out over land disputes and that the removal of the Cherokee would save them from the inevitable takeover by the white man in ever-evolving Tennessee. He found it a good thing for the Indians to leave in order to save themselves.

When dealing with chiefs, Jackson always spoke to them like naughty children. In a letter from Judge Jackson to a half-breed chief who he believed knew the whereabouts of a raiding party that had killed children and taken their mother as a slave, he wrote,

> Could you not also have taken the woman? The creeks have killed our women and children, we have sent to demand the murderers, if they are not given up, the whole creek nation shall be covered with blood, fire shall consume their Towns and villages; and their lands shall be divided among the whites. I am your friend, and the friend of your nation, but if you persist in allowing Creeks to have access through your Nation, my friendship and the friendship of the United States will stop. Remember how the entire Creek Nation came to destroy your towns and how a few hundred Chickasaws aided by a few whites chased them back to their nation, killing the best of their warriors, and covering the rest with Shame, Remember brother, we will do the same if the creeks dare to touch you for your friendship to us. So be warned. Mark what I say. If you suffer any more scalps or stolen horses to be carried through your nation by the Creeks your Father the President will know that you have violated your treaty with us and have taken our enemy by the hand. Give me the names of the murderers, the identity of their towns, and the place where they have carried the woman prisoner. You say you are the friend of whites, now prove it to me.

THE WAR OF 1812 IN THE SOUTH

Jackson had commanded the militia of Tennessee for ten years, confining his field actions to protecting the settlers. With the declaration of war on Great Britain in June 1812, Jackson offered his force of 1,500 trained and experienced fighters to President Madison. But Jackson's reputation in Washington politics was not stellar. Being a tyrant in the House of Representatives, combined with his abandonment of his seat in the Senate, left him friendless at the capital. He was looked on as a meddler and a spoiler. Former President Jefferson had pushed for the invasion of Canada, which was not going well. An adventurer and scoundrel, Major General James Wilkinson was in New Orleans lobbying Washington to allow him to attack Florida, thus adding a large southern tier to the map of the United States. Madison and Jefferson championed Wilkinson's aggression. Jackson was pleased to receive a commission as a Major General of volunteers and called for his Tennessee militia to take up the nation's colors. Jackson hated Wilkinson, whom he referred to as that "publick villain," but would accept command under the Major General. The volunteers were called to assemble in mid-December, but it took until January 7 for the expedition's equipage, along with the two infantry divisions, to prepare for the winter/spring campaign. The trek to New Orleans, nearly 600 miles south, began with embarkation on board flat bottom boats that were poled out onto the freezing Cumberland River. At the intersection of the great Ohio, which was thick with ice floes, frozen hands paddled with the current to the welcome the fast flowing Mississippi. Five weeks later, in spite of the ice-clogged Ohio, they met General John Coffee's cavalry command on the banks of Natchez. The 2,000 men were told that they were going to take Mobile, Pensacola, and St. Augustine, destroying Spanish control and making history.

Politics took over. Wilkinson and others in Washington attempted to maneuver Jackson out of the picture. Additionally, the international climate changed at the peace talks that the Russian Czar sponsored in St. Petersburg between delegations from Great Britain and the United States. The unthinkable had happened: Napoleon was defeated by the Russian winter and was in full retreat back to France.

Jackson was unaware of developments huddled on the banks of the Mississippi waiting for orders to proceed. Wilkinson left him there while the government dithered. Finally, on the fifteenth of March a curt order arrived from the secretary of war, John Armstrong, a political animal of the first order:

Office of the Secretary of War   February, 5, 1813
Sir, The causes embodying and marching to New Orleans the Corps under your command having ceased to exist, you will on receipt of this letter, consider it as dismissed from public service and take measures to have it delivered over to Major General Wilkinson all orders of public property, which may have been put into your possession.

You will accept for yourself and the Corps the thanks of the President of the United States I have the honor to be Sir, With great respect.

Your Most Obedient Servant

Jackson, ever wary of his enemies in Washington, sensed that there was a plot to purloin the army he had built, send him home alone, and then re-enforce Wilkinson with Jackson's troops. Jackson believed that the "croakers" in Washington were out to get him and that Armstrong expected his corps to join the regular army under Wilkinson since they were unpaid, short on rations, and vulnerable to Indian massacre if they tried to walk home on their own. Jackson would never abandon his boys. Before leaving, Jackson sent a reply telling the secretary that he had no intentions of complying but would keep his command together and return it intact to Nashville. He shamed the secretary for the treatment of his volunteers, who in good faith took on this dangerous and foolhardy adventure. The corps began the 500-mile march through the wilderness. Jackson knew that if the command dissolved and the men meandered home, foraging in small bands as they went, the Indians would decimate their ranks. At his own expense, he supported the endeavor on his own authority.

Little did Jackson realize that the president had presented the general with his finest hour; his reputation would be formed not in conflict but in adversity. The terms "tenacious," "unyielding," "dauntless," "bullheaded," and "uncompromising" fit Jackson, but so did "compassionate," "loyal," "supportive," and "kind." The strong current of the rivers that brought them south were against them now. It would be a foot march in the wet and mud of spring while clouds of Indian braves snapped at the edges for a white man's scalp. With only a dozen wagons, space was made for the sick. No one was left behind. Those who could stand but not walk were given the officer's horse, including Jackson's own. Jackson hardened as the march threatened to exhaust the resolve of the soldiers. He cheered them with the thought of going home each time the column faltered. It wasn't for cause or country now, it was for home. He cajoled, cussed, wheedled, and demanded, moving up and down the long, thin column, plodding on ever deteriorating tracks. He was tough, the toughest man on the march. Some who had been admonished for falling behind said that he was as tough as *old hickory*. Within a month, he brought them through safe and sound to a man. The *Nashville Whig* newspaper gushed, "Long will the General live in the memory of his volunteers of West Tennessee—for his benevolence, humane, and fatherly treatment of his soldiers; if gratitude and love can reward him, General Jackson has them. It affords us pleasure to say, that there is not a man belonging to the detachment, but what loves him." All his past bad behavior and temper-strewn incidents were excused. Noted detractors reneged and admitted that there was no finer fellow in Tennessee than Old Hickory.

THE CREEK WAR

The Creek War began in August 1813, a little over a year after America declared war on Great Britain. It was brought on by a serious incident that sparked a larger conflict. A faction of young braves, stimulated by Tecumseh's plan of devastation, split from the Creek tribal council. Known as the *Red Sticks*, the warrior faction butchered over 200 men, women, and children at Fort Mims, forty miles north of Mobile, Alabama. Their chief, the half-white William Weatherford—known as Chief Red Eagle—led the large raiding party. Newspapers wrote of children being swung by the legs and having their heads battered against trees. Pregnant women were scalped and, while still alive, had their stomachs sliced open, spilling infants out onto the ground.

Militia Major General Andy Jackson called out the Tennessee, Georgia, and Mississippi militia, a force that would number 5,000, for a period of three months. Georgia and Mississippi did not respond, balking at command under Jackson. The general persisted and put out a clarion call through the newspapers of Tennessee: "Your frontier is threatened with invasion by a savage foe! Already do they advance towards your frontier, with their scalping knives unsheathed to butcher your wives, your children, and your helpless babes? Time is not to be lost! We must hasten to the frontier, or we will find it drenched in the blood of our fellow-citizens."[9] He got less than half the number, all of which came from within Tennessee.

Fall of 1813

President Madison supported Jackson's resolve and directed that the Creek renegades under Red Eagle be defeated. General Jackson, a man of action, assembled 1,200 infantry and 800 light cavalry/mounted infantry within days of the order and struck south to Alabama. The movement of the frontiersman is recorded to be the unbelievable pace of thirty miles a day. The pickup army was intent on destroying the renegade Indian warriors who had terrorized not only the white communities but the peaceful Native American villages as well. Red Eagle let it be known that all tribesmen must support his campaign, or they would be killed along with the white settlers. The Tennessee militia transited along the western spine of the Lookout Mountains, where they established two supply forts: Deposit and Strothers. As soon as Fort Strothers was cut from the wilderness, his friendly Creek scouts sent him on a forced march thirteen miles to the hostile village of Tallushatchee. The cavalry and mounted infantry under Brigadier General John Coffee surprised a band of Red Stick, slaughtering them where they stood. The young fighter Davy Crockett reported that they shot them down like dogs. Trapped inside cabins, they were unable to fight in the open. The entire town was set alight and razed to the ground as an example to all of the Red Stick followers.

Examining the battlefield, Jackson came across a dead mother holding a living infant in her arms. Since the entire family had perished and there was no one to care for the baby, Jackson's Indian scouts told the general that the baby should be killed. But Jackson remembered his own experience as an orphan and took the child to his own tent and fed it brown sugar dissolved in water. Then he dispatched an officer, who was returning to Tennessee with the wounded and to get supplies for his exhausted army, to take the child to his wife at the Hermitage. He sent along a letter to Rachael asking her to raise the child as their own, even though the baby was as savage.

Jackson was a very complex man. The child, Lyncoya, was bright, and his adopted father intended to send him to West Point for a military education, but the child wanted to be a saddler, one of the trades that Jackson himself was trained for as a boy.

The Battle of Talladega

Within the month, the renegade chief prepared to reap vengeance on the town of Talladega, which sheltered Creeks friendly to Jackson. Red Eagle pledged in letters to Big Warrior and other chiefs that they could depend on his support. While waiting for badly needed supplies to feed his little army at Fort Strothers, Jackson received word from his scouts that Talladega was soon to be under Red Stick attack. The village could not hope to hold out from a combined attack of 1,000 braves. Leaving immediately that night on a thirty-four-mile trek through the wilderness, Jackson hoped to catch the Red Sticks from behind as he concentrated the combined Indian force around the beleaguered village.

The general moved in his fighting square formation with the mounted troops on the sides and the reserve behind them. There was no time to lose according to a messenger who informed the general that Red Sticks were within a quarter mile of Talladega. At dawn, not pausing to organize further, Jackson went into the attack from the march. Even though the men had not eaten or rested, Jackson could not pass up this opportunity to catch the enemy with their backs to him. He thrust the lead elements of the infantry forward and told them to engage the Indians and to withdraw quickly back up the center of the box. He sent the mounted formations on either flank forward like the horns of the bull and kept the reserve in place across the back of the box. The general expected to draw the Indians into the killing ground formed at the middle of the U-shaped defensive position.

It went according to plan, and 1,000 screaming savages turned about and charged the withdrawing militia. Unfortunately, the militia's center gave way with the shock of the Indians response, risking Jackson's entire command. However, seeing the center weaken, Jackson led the reserve into the hole, putting a stopper in a bottle. He stabilized the center, and the fleeing infantry returned in time to see the mounted horns of the bull close in behind the trapped enemy. It was like shooting fish in a barrel, according to the eloquent Davy Crockett. The Indians swirled in ever-smaller numbers until they broke through a weak spot in the left flank, where an infantry unit had failed to close with the mounted infantry. The panicked Indians spurted through, leaving nearly half their force dead or dying on the killing ground.

Jackson led the triumphant entry into Talladega, where he used his personal funds to purchase food for the militia. In the two battles, the militia had suffered 20 killed and 121 wounded. Although there was no count of Indian wounded, the Red Stick had lost nearly 700 dead and captured. Jackson believed that, if nothing else, the renegade chief would have difficulty recruiting additional braves to his cause now that Tecumseh had gone back north and the news of the defeats spread.

The general had hoped to finish the Red Stick menace there at Talladega, but it was not to be. One tangible result was the surrender of the Hillabees and Fish Pond tribes without a shot being fired. Indians believed in war if it was entertaining and profitable, but they would not go anywhere near a line of battle where artillery was present. Jackson knew how they feared cannons and always dotted his formations with small, highly mobile horse drawn guns. The general put out the word, "Long shall they remember Fort Mims with bitterness and tears." However, Jackson was aware that as long as Red Eagle could recruit a fighting force, there would never be peace. The uprising, though severely wounded, was not dead.

The Twin Specters

With success in battle, Jackson now faced the greatest challenge of his military career. Competent leadership in combat is a much-coveted talent of which too few could boast. Jackson provided that calm, cool control in the face of danger, which the men expected and deserved. However, he soon learned that when a battle was over, the war was not. Shortly after the acceleration of combat, boredom sets in, bringing thoughts of home and dreams of comfort. When hardship and poor living conditions combine with skimpy rations, leadership at every level is pressed hard. And so with enlistments running out as fast as the food at Fort Strothers, those twin specters of desertion and mutiny loomed as the temperatures dropped and mountain nights became bone chilling. Those long-ago promises to serve were nearly up for a large portion of his men as December approached. Armed forage parties left in swarms each morning to return at night with little to show for their efforts.

In the cold of December, the troops were on the move and in no mood to return to the fighting. A company got up and started for Tennessee. Jackson rode ahead and, with a small band of cavalry, he blocked their way. Sitting on his horse, he demanded that they return to the others, or he would shoot them down as deserters. Tense moments passed as they surveyed the stern face of the general and the cocked carbines of the horseman behind him. There was no doubt in their faces that he would end their lives, so they returned. Once back in camp, an entire brigade swelled up and started to prepare to leave to the north and home. As they took to the road, Jackson, alone, rode in front, turned, and stopped. Even though his injured left arm would not respond because of the recent wound and the bullet that was embedded in his shoulder, he laid a musket on the pommel of his saddle and pointed it at the head of the column. The general declared that he would shoot the first man who stepped toward him. A long pause intervened. The men believed him. Perhaps, like Mr. Bean, they saw shot in his eyes. They turned and reluctantly followed him back to Fort Strothers with Jackson in the lead. During the slow ride back to camp, his aide remarked that the musket was not loaded. "I know he said, do you think I would shoot an American soldier."[10]

Two weeks later, the brigade of volunteers packed up and formed ranks to leave. Jackson, exasperated, put the artillery in battery on the Tennessee road and sat his horse in front of the loaded cannons. He pleaded with the formation to remain until the replacements arrived. Jackson was bluffing once again; no word had come to his inquiries concerning the availability of fresh troops. Finally, when the men remained in ranks failing to fall out, he ordered the gunners to light their matches—in preparation to fire. The men melted back to their encampment. He wrote to his wife that he "was forced by circumstances to turn cannons on my own men. This is the worst moment of my life."

By January, he had allowed the brigade to go home while the remaining 500 men wintered over. In deep despair, Jackson's morale was as low as the hangers-on who tended the fires and consumed provisions. Suddenly, General Cocke appeared with 850 recruits in mid-January. Jackson wasted no time and mounted an expedition south to catch Red Sticks at their winter camp.

Three miles north of the Indians' encampment, Red Eagle, who had been alerted to the presence of the white man's column, suddenly struck from ambush. Jackson reeled back and retreated to the water line at Emuckfew Creek. There he established a line of battle. The Indians pursued but remained just out of reach of his rearguard. As the artillery were crossing over the creek, a band of Red Sticks struck once again. This time, Jackson's rearguard stood the assault, and the general deployed his cavalry and mounted infantry as before on both sides while the artillery formed in battery. But the untrained recruits could not sustain their courage and began to break up into small groups. The braves isolated the bands of huddled youngsters and were about to destroy Jackson's center. But Old Hickory rode in among the troops of his wavering line and seized the moment in his good right arm. Leading from the front (his style), the unschooled military commander showed that he was a born combat commander. He appeared to be oblivious to the chaos and danger that surrounded him. Rather than killing Indians, he focused on re-forming the line. Yelling commands, encouraging the slackers, and directing the reserve into the gaps, Jackson was at his very best. Once the artillery began the rolling fire and the grapeshot played about the warbonnets, Red Sticks had no choice but to withdraw.

Jackson retreated to Fort Strothers; the Indians did not pursue. The loss had been his fault, and he knew it. Raw recruits should not be expected to fight like veterans. Training dominated camp life spent on two subjects: fighting drills and rank discipline. Jackson offered no quarter, and he punished every infraction. They would not run again.

The Last Big Battle of the Creek War

In Washington, the news that the peace talks sponsored by the Czar of Russia were busted spurred the Secretary of War, John Armstrong, into action. As the army expanded in early March 1814, most of the regular army units were given to Major General James Wilkinson, who was transferred from New Orleans to conduct an attack on Montreal. Former President Jefferson had made headlines once again in London when he invited the Marquis de Lafayette to have tea with him in Montreal that spring. However, the danger of a victory by the Indians, like the near-run at Emuckfew Creek, could open up a southern front that Armstrong was sure would include the British army. Therefore, the militia of Tennessee was strengthened by the arrival of the 39th Regular Infantry Regiment. Jackson was overjoyed with their arrival now that he had trained his soldiers for the next and final round. With nearly 5,000 troops at his disposal and well provisioned, he struck out for the Horse Bend Indian cantonment. There, 1,000 braves from the scattered Creek nation were meeting with their prophets, gaining courage to strike the white communities. They felt that they had routed Jackson at the last encounter and now were high, ready to wipe him out at Fort Strothers. But Jackson was full of himself this time and determined, with the weapon that he had the honor to command, to send the last vestige of the Creek portion of Tecumseh's insurrection to their "happy hunting ground."

Leaving a force behind at Fort Strothers to guard the provisions, he moved straight south with a force of 2,000 infantry, 700 cavalry and mounted infantry, 500 Cherokees, and 100 friendly Creeks. When he arrived two days later, he was astonished at the preparations the Red Sticks had made. A thousand braves, along with 300 women and children, were settled on a piece of land that was nearly surrounded by the river in a colossal loop of land. Across the open end, they had constructed a breastwork of logs over six feet high, cut through with loops for rifles. The barricade was saw-toothed, providing covering fire on anyone attempting to assault the wall. The Indians had learned the tricks of building a safe defensive position from their enemy. It was true that a good fort could provide as much as a four to one advantage to the defender. The more he thought about it, the more he realized that the Indians had built their own cage. Sending the cavalry and Indians around to the opposite side, Jackson easily surrounded the fortification. While he was moving his artillery into position opposite the log wall, Jackson's Cherokee Indians set fire to the log houses with flaming arrows.[11] This premature diversion gave Jackson just what he needed. While the gunners bombarded the breastwork, Jackson sent in the 39th Infantry to carry the outer defenses. Jackson was in his glory, as happy as a man could be. He knew that the Creeks would crumble and that their war whoops would not be heard again in Tennessee or anywhere else. At the wall, the infantry used the loopholes for firing positions and were protected by the same work the Indians had counted on to separate them from the white man. They routed the Red Sticks, who ran in a swirling mass of mayhem and war paint. Clearly outnumbered inside the cantonment, they frantically looked for an escape route, but their years of defiance and promises to Tecumseh were coming to a calamitous end within a box they had built themselves. Used to fighting in the open where they could melt away into the dark, dense forest, only to regroup, on this bloody day they had run out of options. The fighting was now at close range, hand to hand, and the vengeance of the white man was ferocious. For years, they and their families had lived in fear of night-raiding parties that had burned them out, killing their women and children or carrying them off to a fate that no one could countenance. Now, there in the dust bowl, dead center within the stronghold, the Red Sticks gave up the ghost to the Great Spirit.

Of the 1,000 Creek warriors presumed to have been present in the camp, twenty survived the attack to escape into the woods and carry the tale to the surviving elements of the Creek nation. Jackson had lost a total of seventy-two from his various elements and double that in wounded. Unfortunately, many wounded would not survive long without medical treatment.

Epitaph

An epitaph to the story is that Red Eagle walked into Jackson's tent unannounced days later and declared that he wanted peace since his army was dead and he had no other choice but to lead his people into captivity. The general knew that no one else could fill his moccasins without more bloodshed so he agreed to release the chief to save his people from starvation. At Fort Mims, Jackson found the remains of 130 whites who had been scalped. Many were women. Several slaves taken from other Indian tribes were released back to the community along with Polly Jones and her three children. As Napoleon fell that March, so did the Red Sticks, freeing Jackson and his combat hardened Tennessee militia.

JACKSON IS RECOGNIZED BY THE PRESIDENT

In May 1814, Jackson's position in the regular army became permanent as Brigadier General (brevet promoted to Major General)[12] in command of the 7th Military District, which included virtually the whole southern portion of the United States. Jackson realized that the deposition of the French emperor ensured the transfer of excess British navy and army formations to the Gulf of Mexico.

Jackson had the bit in his teeth as commander of all the troops in the southern states and territories set to take on the Spanish and British wherever he found them. Under orders, on November 7, Jackson invaded Pensacola and took it from the Spanish, allies of the British, who were arming and training 4,000 Seminole and Creek Indians to invade the United States as part of their plan to take Mobile and New Orleans.

In late August 1814, Jackson received a letter from a close friend, George Grigg, in Washington, informing the newly appointed regular army major general that the Senate and House of Representatives, the arsenal, the dockyard, the Treasury, the War Office, the Presidential Palace, the ropewalk, and the great bridge across the Potomac were burned. He described it as a dark red glow across the sky that was both striking and sublime. Jackson was humiliated that America could not defend its capital.

Because decisive victory was rare during the War of 1812, Jackson's triumph at Horseshoe Bend was the lead in every newspaper in the country. A national hero, the etchings in the newspapers made him recognizable on the streets wherever he went. His brevet general's commission did not last a month when William Henry Harrison resigned and Andrew Jackson put on his second star. At home in Nashville, the 7th District was responsible for Tennessee and the territories of Alabama, Mississippi, and Louisiana.

He hated the Indians. In his view, the tribes should not have resisted the western expansion, and he imposed harsh terms on the defeated people under his control. The general made no distinction between those Indians who had supported the white communities and those who had fought against him. His was a punitive peace treaty imposed by the stronger over the weaker. Jackson regarded the Creek War as a part of the War of 1812 against the British since the enemy encouraged, organized, and equipped the Indians and gave them sanctuary within Spanish Florida. He told those elements that refused to sign the treaty that they would not receive food and would be hunted down and killed.

THE BATTLE OF NEW ORLEANS

Highly defensible, New Orleans lies 100 miles above the muddy mouth of the Mississippi River. Freshwater lakes, streams, swamps, and bayous surround the center of the sleepy city, which is barely above sea level. If Royal Navy Vice Admiral Sir Alexander Cochrane was looking for a vulnerable target, he should have taken Mobile instead or at least landed his army there and marched to New Orleans as Jackson did. The admiral had talked the London government into the adventure, which might result in an English claim of the Louisiana Territory. Great Britain had been opposed to the sale of the Spanish territory to America by Napoleon, believing that the emperor had cheated the Spanish throne out of the land. "Personally, Cochrane was hungry for prize money, which made that city irresistible. Her warehouses were packed with two year's accumulation of sugar, cotton, hemp, and lead, which, its ships tied up in harbor for the last two years, would have a contemporary value of $10 million."[13] Cochrane got the go-ahead in the last week of November and began his planning. The western approach was blocked by Jean Lafitte, prince of pirates at Barataria Bay, who held sway for forty miles of bad ground and defensible beaches approaching New Orleans. As early as September, a British emissary had tempted Lafitte with an offer of amnesty for his past high-seas piracy. The cunning fellow stalled the British while he bargained with the authorities in New Orleans for a pact of mutual defense, one that he secured. The southern approach up the Mississippi could accommodate the big ships of the Royal Navy fleet, and therefore a host of naval guns that could destroy the city in minutes was blocked by Fort St. Philip and farther along by Fort St. Leon at the English Turn. The river switchback was so severe that sailing ships lost the wind and would have to wait under the fort's guns for a change of direction before moving upriver. The only water approach lay to the east through shallow Lake Borgne, which lapped against Bayou Boemvemie at Fisherman's Village. While unoccupied by Jackson's army, the approach could be secured by a line of five American naval gunboats.

In Mobile, Jackson was tipped off in early December concerning Cochrane's plans by a message from Secretary of War James Monroe. Informants in Cuba sent word of the movement of the large British fleet with embarked troops. Sixty ships, frigates, sloops of war, transports, horse carriers, and supply vessels joined the expedition with more troop carriers filled at the Cape of Good Hope. It contained many of the troops and officers who had raided both Washington and Baltimore and was expected to be commanded by Major General Ross, but he perished at Baltimore. His deputy, Major General John Keane, and Colonel William Thornton would be the field commanders until Ross's replacement, Major General Sir Edward M. Packenham, the Duke of Wellington's brother-in-law, could make his way from England. A former adjutant and division commander during the lengthy and successful Peninsula Campaign against the French in Spain, Packenham was well suited for the job.

Jackson's Order of Battle

Monroe took the threat seriously, ensuring that Jackson had the tools to do the job. He assigned regular infantry regiments to the 7th Military District for the defense of New Orleans. The 2nd, 3rd, 7th, 39th, 44th, and 350th Artillery Gunners were alerted and put on the road to the southwest. A regiment should contain 1,000 fit troops, but these were at half strength or less. As they trickled in at just over 2,000, some were short of serviceable muskets. Monroe called on the governors of Kentucky, Tennessee, Mississippi, Indiana, and Georgia for their militias. Many volunteered, but they were short of muskets, prompting the secretary to send 4,000 pieces by slow boat down the Ohio. Jackson would have to wait to see who showed up and with what before he could construct a workable defense. With the Spanish and the remainder of the Red Sticks dispersed, Old Hickory left Mobile on November 22 for New Orleans. Those who met him on the trail noted his sallow countenance and were told that he was under the weather. Hearing the scuttlebutt about his frail health, Jackson carried himself with vigor and ferocious vitality to hide his inner conflicts. The general moved about the byways and bayous for the next two weeks accompanied by his chief of engineers, Major Howell Tatum, while his command congealed in the city. They discovered that the complex terrain was their most dependable ally. Yet Jackson was concerned with the direction of the main attack and the probable diversions and ruses that the British might employ. He could not afford to cover all bets with the pickup force he was allocated. The general sent out numerous local scouts to watch the approaches, depending on early warning and interior lines to meet the enemy with his full strength, such as it was. Never before had a commander on the eve of battle had such a hodgepodge of disparate combatants under his orders. In addition to the understrength of the regular regiments and a pair of 6-pounder field cannons, he counted on U.S. Navy Commodore Patterson's company of Marines, a battalion of local citizens from New Orleans, a battalion of "freemen of color," a local unit (Beale's rifles), Jean Lafitte's roving pirates, Hind's Mississippi dragoons, John Coffee's battalion of mounted rifles, and eighteen Choctaw Indian scouts.[14]

First Contact

Royal Navy Admiral Cochrane lay off the coast waiting for news from his probes on the Mississippi River. By water, Lake Borgne and Bayou Bienvenue were the only way to New Orleans. A singular advantage lay in the short distance his troops would have to transit across the Villeré Plantation once they landed. The only obstacles were half a dozen American gunboats and sixty miles of shallow waters dotted with sandbars. American Naval Lieutenant Catesby Jones, leader of the gunboat flotilla on Lake Borgne, strung out his vessels to make them appear formidable and slowly retired in the face of forty-five boats and barges that were rowed directly at his formation. Through the night of December 13, the dance continued with the Americans staying just out of range, as Jones gathered vital information that he sent back to Jackson. Early the next morning, Jones had been pushed between two islands and decided to make a stand. He knew that the might of the pressing enemy was beyond his ability to destroy or even disrupt, but he could make a stab at resisting the onslaught. Drawing his five boats, 185 sailors who manned twenty-three guns, into line, he fired on myriad black dots that had pursued him for the last day and a half. Initially, Jones sunk two English boats while sustaining considerable damage in the fray. Soon his boat and all the others were overwhelmed by British tars who closed in, boarded, and swarmed onto the decks of the American defenders. Jones was seriously wounded. It was all over in minutes. Captured American sailors, together with the truce party that Jackson sent to look after his men, gave false accounts of Jackson's command. Interrogated, they rendered inflated facts and figures, identifying 20,000 infantry, cavalry, and artillery waiting in the city for the Redcoats' attack. The information tempered the enemy's planning process.

Jackson, grateful for the sacrifice of the sailors, knew that he must disrupt the British timetable with a swift strike to the nose of the advancing force. Declaring martial law on December 16, he hurried dependable General Coffee to secure his left flank while the other unit commanders were sent to the southern side of the city. Consolidated under Jackson, they prepared to move along the eastern side of the river, depending on Patterson's ships for gun support from the American flotilla and the fort on the western side of the Mississippi.

The wet, tangled terrain significantly slowed the progress of the British troops. Landing on tiny Pea Island, the troops were unnerved by hundreds of torpid alligators slowed by the winter chill. It rained during the day and frosted all exposed surfaces by morning. The tiny island gave pause to the weary soldiers and sailors, while flat-bottomed boats were provided to transship the formations to the edge of the Villeré Plantation set on solid ground. It had been sixty miles of sodden boats, endless rowing, and cooling temperatures, quite unlike the delightful Caribbean rest home they had enjoyed since the attack on Baltimore.

The British Army Makes Its Move

Major General Keane directed Colonel Thornton, who had gained his reputation leading the vanguard of British forces at the battle of Bladensburg, to embark his command on boats and make contact with the American army. On the morning of December 22, Thornton's command had to be ferried in waves since there were only enough boats to transport 2,000 troops per lift. That long day, Thornton's advance guard of the 95th Rifles, the 85th and 4th Foot Infantry, a rocket element, and a detachment of sappers and miners, accompanied by Admiral Cochrane and General Keane, left Pea Island for Bayou Bienvenuee. The 21st, 44th, and 93rd Foot Infantry along with Royal Artillery detachments, would follow as soon as the boats could complete the round-trip. On the morning of December 23, the advance guard picked their way through the tangled bayou to Fishman's Village at the western corner of the Villeré Plantation, just twelve miles from the city of New Orleans. The American outpost was captured, but one man ran free and three days later staggered into the city with the belated news. At the edge of the Villeré, they disembarked onto solid ground and began to trek west toward the Mississippi. They broke out of the cypress trees to the cut sugarcane fields and spread out. Once more in company formation, the Redcoats of the 85th and 4th contrasted with the forest green of the 95th Rifles, which found its origins fighting Indians in the eastern forests during the Revolutionary War. Soon they were in sight of the plantation house, where the son of the family was sitting on the veranda watching for enemy activity. Leading British skirmishers were on him a moment later, but he broke free and scampered into the swamp with the Redcoats hot on his heels. Once again, prisoners told the British inflated tales of American formations in and around the city, which confirmed earlier accounts taken from Jones's sailors. Two of Thornton's regiments were light infantry and could be at the gates of New Orleans within a couple of hours, but the consistent testimony taken from prisoners warned the colonel off. His lack of field guns made him overly cautious.

Admiral Cochrane survived the situation. He sat safely in the middle of 2,000 top-notch troops, backed by rockets, waiting for 2,500 more, which should close in by midnight. His highly efficient artillery staff was in the process of bringing up field artillery and heavy naval guns. To his left was the levee containing the 1,000-yard-wide Mississippi. To the front was a mile of flat, open ground cut by plantation fences, deep drainage ditches, dirt roads, and scattered plantation complexes. Beyond lie the city of New Orleans and the booty he so deeply desired. He contemplated the risk. His opponent, Jackson, not a professional soldier but an Indian fighter, used duck-and-cover woodman's tactics and was known for his fiery temper and unorthodox leadership. Jackson's command lacked cohesion, having been thrown together from hither and yon. He doubted that there was any depth to his defenses, and a quick breakthrough would allow the British to pour through the lines like the water of the mighty Mississippi. Cochrane felt confident that once everything was in place, the victory was a matter of time since no one was coming to Jackson's rescue. The admiral thought that he could afford to wait until his new ground commander, Lieutenant General Packenham, was on the field.

Jackson Gets Word of the Redcoats

By the morning of December 23, reports had trickled in that the Redcoats had landed to the south in some large number and were headed for New Orleans. The first reliable account came from Jackson's chief of engineers, Major A. Lacarriere Latour, a former member of Napoleon's army who saw nearly 2,000 British infantry near the Villeré Plantation. With expected ire, Jackson issued curt orders to, "Send Hinds' dragoons to scout and blunt their lead element, put the 7th on the road south of the city and get everyone else on the road behind the 7th."[15] Not only were Major Thomas Hinds's Mississippi dragoons scouts, but their presence showed the British the mobility of mounted horsemen that Cochrane did not enjoy. The 44th Regiment, a pair of 6-pounders, two battalions of local volunteers, and a company of American marines—a complement of nearly 2,000 odd—were gathered up off the streets within the hour. Not forgetting the navy, Patterson's *Carolina* slipped south from her moorings in the city and rested within range of the British encampment that hugged the east bank of the river. The guns of the *Carolina* disturbed Cochrane's musings at 7:30 that evening, blasting the tents and cooking fires of the complacent enemy. The gallant British regiments sheltered behind the levee while the rocketeers dithered to find a suitable site for their rockets. Thirty minutes later, Jackson prematurely attacked before his command was closed. The broken ground, wet ditches, and high fences slowed a cohesive attack. The city militia, unaccustomed to running, fell well behind. Excited, the militia paused, then fired to the south in the general direction of the enemy and the U.S. 7th Infantry. The naval bombardment slackened when the American infantry closed to within fifty yards of a thin line of redcoats that Thornton had managed to form. The wet ground steamed with fog when combined with a heavy volume of white smoke given off by the naval guns and chattering muskets, which restricted visibility. Soon the veteran British regiments righted themselves and counterattacked. The tightly bunched company of American marines gave way, leaving the pair of field guns exposed, while the 7th Infantry brought Thornton's assault to a standstill. Old Hickory, on horseback, rallied the marines while his trailing staff officers gathered up the militia and brought them to contact in good order. There the two sides stood, hammering each other for nearly an hour. No quarter was given, but the white smoke from the black powder blotted everyone's senses. It was a stalemate. Jackson knew that he could not afford the losses. When General Coffee's mounted horsemen appeared on the British right flank, pouring accurate volleys into the redcoats, Jackson took the opportunity to pull the plug. The time had come for his command to follow him to the rear. The *Carolina* covered the retreat as Coffee's dismounted troopers became entangled with the Redcoats. Woodsmen and Tommy, tooth and claw, fought each other man to man.[16] The American tally could have been worse. Of the 884 regulars and 560 militiamen who made the assault, 215 were casualties, while the British figures were slightly more at 275.[17] The Americans were fortunate that General Keane didn't commit the 44th Foot, which was held in reserve fearing an attack from American units that were falsely reported south of the English Turn. More than any other factor, the lack of good information handicapped Cochrane on this mixed and unfamiliar ground. Jackson, repeating his mistake that occurred toward the final days of the Creek War, overestimated the ability of the untrained, inexperienced, and recently minted militia. Rash and assuming that everyone in his command had the same innate abilities, the general failed to train and integrate novices with regulars. Reconstituted a mile north Jackson discovered that in addition to the casualties, sixty-four militia had either deserted or been taken prisoner. He could not allow panic to set in. Five miles south of New Orleans, Jackson put the men to hard work digging a line of defense. They had fallen back two miles from the engagement to the Rodrequez Canal. The old millrace, 1,000 yards long, emptied into the Mississippi. A man-made gift, straight as a die, it was dug deeper now, the dirt thrown up to form a six-foot-high berm reinforced with wooden posts and set with loopholes for musket and cannon. Slaves and free men labored side by side day and night to build a line that must hold. Patterson's navy secured the American river flank by moving a second ship, the *Louisiana*, into position while dismounting fortress guns to an emplacement on the west side of the river that was able to lob shells into the British left flank should they choose to hug the edge of the river. Jackson anchored the west end of the breastwork with a log redoubt, while Coffee turned the east end into a hook to prevent the American flank from being turned. The old shallow millrace was now eight feet deep and fifteen feet wide. Work begun on Christmas was completed two weeks later. Not content, Latour convinced Jackson to begin work on a second and then third defensive line each a mile distant. Cautious, Jackson divided his force. Major General William Carroll's Tennessee militia, Jackson's former comrade at arms, along with three elements of Governor Claiborne's Louisiana militia, were charged with securing the western edge of Lake Pontchartrain. It was a second but less likely route for Cochrane's advance, but it bore watching. Jackson kept those 2,500 troops in his back pocket as a reserve in case the barricade was breached and the American main line was forced back to the second or even the third line of defense.

The British weren't idle when General Packenham arrived on Christmas Day. While the infantry regiments accumulated on the field, Colonel Alexander Dickson, Royal Artillery, Department of Ordinance, who was assigned to support Cochrane's expedition, put his gunners to work. The artillery set a contrast to the redcoated infantry. The gunners were clad in dark blue coats with red collars, cuffs, and turn-backs piped in bright yellow lace. Their black shakos, stuck with red and white chicken feather plumes, white cross belts, and brown leather packs, were piled in heaps nearby while they toiled in the sticky gumbo mud of the riverbank. Atop the levee, two 9-pounders, four 6-pounders, and two 5½-inch howitzers, along with embrasures for heating cannonballs, were dug in. On December 27, from 800 yards, the limit of the field pieces, the Royal Artillery's white-hot cannonballs not only struck *Carolina* but set her on fire as well. She exploded when the flames spread to the powder magazine below. *Louisiana* took the hint and wrapped her way upstream, against the current and out of range. Jackson could plainly see that he was up against a professional army and not a bunch of redskins. The British 14th Light Dragoons (Duchess of York Own), in short blue jackets, white chest cording with scarlet collars, and gray overalls with two red stripes down the leg, were on foot.[18] Native horses, found while foraging, were harnessed to Dickson's cannons and ammunition wagons. In the age of sail, it was not uncommon for more than half the horses to perish during a long sea voyage, often forcing armies to procure animals locally. However, an infantry foray attempted on December 28 to probe Jackson's defenses was strongly rebuffed. Packenham came forward to have a look and decided that the fortified millrace was too strong for anything other than an artillery preparation followed by a deliberate frontal attack. Cochrane agreed and sent for heavy naval cannons to be dismounted from the fleet and brought the long torturous water, swamp, and bayou route to the front. The iron cannons and carronades, which weighed in the realm of a ton, were propelled on wide, stout wheels the size of large dinner plates. Transported the seventy-five miles by crews taken from the West Indies regiments, the soldiers suffered mightily on those cold nights and morning frosts. Many died of exhaustion. At 800 yards, well within the range of Jackson's gunners, gun positions had to be prepared in the dark. British redoubts were constructed next to the river and toward the center of the battlefield and crammed with cannons, carronades, field guns, mortars, and rockets. Prepared without the benefit of torches, the gun platforms were not level, a major hindrance to effective on-target projectiles. As a rule, the Royal Artillery installed large stockpiles of cannonballs and bags of powder since many early salvos would have to be adjusted from the strike of the previous shot. Dickson was concerned that the scarcity of both limited the impact of his guns. On the morning of January 1, 1815, the infantry regiments lined up behind the guns in sight of the American line, ready to step off into history.

Dotted along his barricade, Jackson had a considerable amount of artillery in place. While the Royal Artillery had managed to set twenty guns in battery to support the imminent infantry attack, the American artillery riveted only twelve. At the top of the list were a 32-pound cannon, three 24-pound long guns, one 18-pounder, three 12-pounders, three 6-pounders, and a 6-pound mortar. The *Louisiana* mounted one 24- and two 12-pound long guns. A barrier made of stacked cotton bales protected the barricade's guns. Jackson's gun crews were regular artillerymen augmented by sailors from the sunken *Carolina* and experienced pirate gunners, a contribution from Jean Lafitte.

January 1, 1815

Packenham's plan called for Keane's 3rd Brigade to conduct a feint north, up the eastern side of the levee, to draw interest and fire. A small portion of the 21st would attack on the right through the woods to occupy Coffee. The Royal Artillery intended to concentrate their fire on the center of the American line. Once breached, a hundred skirmishers would rush the line, firing to keep the Americans down, while 300 soldiers carrying fascines— bundles of branches—to fill the defensive ditch to provide footing. Colonel Gibbs's 2nd Brigade, consisting of the 4th, 21st, and 44th Regiments and the West Indian Battalion, advancing quickly in column under the cover of the skirmishers, would exploit the breach—a forlorn hope—followed by the remainder of the army.[19]

Fog shrouded the battlefield at 9 a.m. on New Year's Day, when the guns on both sides banged into action with a crescendo easily heard by the nervous citizens of New Orleans. Panic screamed through the streets, and horses bolted, running down pedestrians, smashing through fences, and trampling men and gardens. Rampaging chickens, ducks, and geese scattered feathers, while clouds of rolling white smoke began to billow above the rooftops. The infantry commanders, pressed against cold brass eyepieces of their collapsible field telescopes, twisted the barrels to focus through the debris on the center of the American line. Straining at the leash, the troops wanted to end the suspense and get going. The leaders, together in a wad of colorful gilt-edged uniforms, stood up in their stirrups, seeking vindication for their careful plans. For three hours, the cacophony raged uninterrupted, deafening the gunners and bystanders. There was no joy for the invaders. Sustaining only light damage, the American guns raked the Royal Artillery's first line of forward light guns, putting them out of action. A dozen British gunners were dead, and twice that number were wounded. As suspected, the ammunition supply was not sufficient to complete the mission. The heavy carronades and cannons were too unstable on their makeshift platforms to be effective. Dickson reluctantly called a cease-fire, and the plan had failed before it began.

Darkness gave the British an opportunity to withdraw the heavy guns to safety within the original line beyond the reach of the American artillery. An unwelcome cold, persistent rain hindered the operation. The sugarcane fields, already saturated, pooled under the feet of the gunners who became bogged down. The Redcoats left their cooking fires and sunk up to their knees as teams of soldiers dragged the unyielding iron guns to a safe haven. Patterson's naval guns continued to harass the Englishmen's struggle to withdraw the artillery in good order.

The Americans filled in shell holes with shovels full of liquid mud. Several limbers had been splintered by rocket blasts. Horse-drawn high-wheeled rigs, specially made for the heavy work, replaced the huge cotton bails, some of which had caught fire during the action. On January 2 Jackson happily welcomed the addition of 700 Kentucky militiamen. Monroe had called up 2,300. It was a boost to morale and the combat strength of the American defenses. Jackson's assortment of desperate amateur elements should have been of concern when the British withdrew to safer ground and prepared for a renewed assault. Old Hickory never doubted their ability to follow orders and make the British pay for past sins. Scouts reported fevered activity along the rear of the enemy cantonment. Yet the general displayed a calm demeanor going about the preparations for the coming attack with an air of victory about his person.

The British commander agreed that Jackson had used the ground well and lodged himself behind a strong defensive line, giving Jackson a three-to-one advantage over their offensive actions. It would take a great deal more of everything to drive the Americans off the line and into the city, where the disciplined Redcoats would take Yankees apart one by one. Expected on January 4, Packenham waited for the arrival of Major General John Lambert's 1st Brigade, which consisted of the 7th Fusiliers and the 43rd Foot, to form a reserve for the main attack, freeing Thornton to swing around to the west. There was added work for people who had signed up to dig, not to fight. The Villeré Canal, which had ferried troops from Lake Borgne, would have to be widened and lengthened through the levee to allow the forty-five boats, filled with the 2nd Brigade, to cross the wide Mississippi, land, and then pierce Patterson's interfering naval and fortress cannons. Continued scouting through the woods on the right of the British line, seeking a viable path around Coffee's lodgment, failed once again. The tropical forest, swollen swamp, and tangled bayou defeated the probe as surely as if the land had enlisted in Jackson's army. Thornton's shortened brigade, consisting of a partial 85th Foot, the 5th West India Regiment, 200 Royal Marines, 200 tars, a pair of 9-pounder field artillery pieces, and a brace of howitzers, embarked after dark on January 7. They were expected to clear away all opposition on the west side of the big river.

The Final Dawn

At dawn on January 8 the main attack came from the 2,200 soldiers of the 2nd Brigade, reinforced by the famous 95th Rifles, who skirted the woods along the western edge of the battlefield, remaining beyond the range of Patterson's naval guns. Along the east bank of the river the lead element of the

3rd Brigade's 1,200 soldiers, formed from the light companies of the 7th, 43rd, and 93rd and a company from the West India Regiment, waited until Thornton made contact with Patterson. Advancing unhindered along the riverbank, they would attack Jackson's redoubt set atop the west end of his defensive line, preventing it from interfering with the main Redcoat attack. General Gibbs's brigade, the 4th, 21st, and 44th, would march up the center and, with support from Dickson's field guns, assault the middle of Jackson's line. Patterson, unaware that the British intended to land on his side of the Mississippi to kill and capture his guns and 450 militia, mounted three more guns and pointed them east to interdict the main British attack.

Thornton, on which everything rested, found that the cut through to the Mississippi was too shallow, and the boats, full of men and grounded, had to be drawn through to the river, costing valuable time. The guns proved too heavy and were left behind along with the West India troops, who were exhausted from the effort. The Mississippi, running fast from continuous winter rain, raged into the Gulf at four and a half miles per hour. The big river, like the swamp on the east side of Jackson's defense, refused to ally with Redcoats. Thornton's reduced command was swept south, landing some distance from their original target. Packenham knew that his plan was not surviving intact from the very start and thought of amending it before dawn.

Under the cover of the thick morning fog and wet ground, Dickson's artillery stepped off at first light, but couldn't find their original positions. Within the 3rd Brigade, the 44th retuned to get the ladders and fascines that had been forgotten in the excitement of the general advance, throwing the timetable off even further. Suddenly, the fog lifted, allowing the American artillery to rake the field slowing the entire British front. When the Redcoats came within a hundred yards, Jackson shouted, "Fire at will." The British line faltered. General Gibbs, mounted at the head of the 3rd, rallied his men but fell dead before his infantry could reach the ditch and drop their bundles or erect ladders. Major Wilkinson, leading the 21st, scrambled up the muddy slope of the barricade and died in his tracks. The rifle regiment out in the open on the British right was swept away by well-aimed rolling musket fire. Thornton, struggling to catch-up, was unable to subdue Patterson's guns, which devastated the 93rd as it attained the American redoubt next to the river. None of the elements of the Redcoats had achieved their goals, and they began to slide backward amid the smoke, noise, and confusion.[20]

In an effort to save the day, General Keane lead the 93rd Light Highland Infantry diagonally across the open battlefield under cover of Dickson's supporting cannon fire. They reached the barricade at the deepest part of the ditch and flung themselves at the American defenders. Jackson appeared in the midst of his men as they repelled the assault. His words could not be discerned, but his appearance was electric. Keane was struck in the throat, and his field commander, colonel of the Scots, died in the trench. Packenham rode to fetch Colonel Lambert's reserve regiments. Wounded in the leg, he was trapped under his dying mount. Helped to the saddle of his aide's horse, the Major General sustained a mortal wound. The British commander had died while rallying his troops. Packenham's body was shipped to England for burial. "Our lamented General's remains were put in a cast of spirits and taken home by the Military Secretary."[21] The open battlefield was a killing zone.

By 8:30, the general retreat began. Thornton finally made contact with Patterson and completed his mission. In silencing the guns, he was badly wounded. Patterson and his militia withdrew in good order.

Aftermath

The British lost nearly 300, with 1,260 wounded and nearly 500 missing and taken prisoner. Jackson's genius was proved when the tally of thirteen killed and thirty-nine wounded was published in the *New Orleans Picayune*. To cover their withdrawal, the British relied on a large mortar that could throw a projectile 4,000 yards. The bombardment of the barricade continued until January 17. A thousand bombs were launched in nine days, killing two Americans and wounding seven. Jackson's line could do little else other than hunker down and wait them out, knowing all along that the British had been defeated once again by a rag-tag military force made up of free citizens of a republic.

Great Britain would learn their lesson, and from that day to this, we have been trading partners, allies in numerous wars, and, some would say, members of the same family. I certainly would.

CHRONOLOGY: ANDREW JACKSON

1767, March 15	Born in Waxhaws, Carolina
1780	Joined the Carolina militia as a courier
1787, September	Carolina Country lawyer
1791	Tennessee lawyer
1796	U.S. Representative from Tennessee
1797	U.S. Senator from Tennessee
1798	Judge, Tennessee Supreme Court
1801	Colonel, Tennessee militia
1802	Major general Tennessee militia

1813, January	Major general of volunteers, march toward New Orleans
1813, Spring	Jackson on return march becomes known as "Old Hickory"
1813, August	Creek War begins
1813, Fall	Battle of Talladega
1814, March	Battle of Horseshoe Bend
1815, January 8	Battle of New Orleans

NOTES

1. James Webb, *Born Fighting: How the Scott-Irish Shaped America* (New York: Broadway Books, 2004), 78.

2. H. W. Brands, *Andrew Jackson, His Life and Times* (New York: Anchor Books, Random House, 2005), 12.

3. Robert V. Remini, *Andrew Jackson and the Course of American Empire—1767/1821* (New York: Harper & Row, 1977), 30.

4. Remini, *Andrew Jackson and the Course of American Empire*, 91.

5. Brands, *Andrew Jackson*, 105.

6. Brands, *Andrew Jackson*, 136.

7. Remini, *Andrew Jackson and the Course of American Empire*, 97.

8. Remini, *Andrew Jackson and the Course of American Empire*, 47.

9. Remini, *Andrew Jackson and the Course of American Empire*, 190.

10. Remini, *Andrew Jackson and the Course of American Empire*, 199.

11. American Indians of the South lived not in the tepees of animal skins but rather in dwellings of wood and logs, much the same as white settlers did.

12. Brevet allows the rank to be worn but the pay to be withheld.

13. John R. Elting, *Amateurs to Arms: A Military History of the War of 1812* (New York: Da Capo Press, 1995), 282.

14. Elting, *Amateurs to Arms*, 297.

15. Elting, *Amateurs to Arms*, 298.

16. "Tommy" is slang for a regular British soldier in 1796 and comes from the brown bread ration provided to soldiers. The term may have been used earlier from the Scottish soldiers who eat "tammie," or bread roll.

17. Donald R. Hickey, *The War of 1812: A Forgotten Conflict* (Champaign: University of Illinois Press, 1990), 209.

18. John Pimlott, *British Light Cavalry, Nations at Arms 1800–1815* (London: Almark Publishing, 1977), 39.

19. A "forlorn hope" was a term given during the Peninsula War in Spain for the first commander and his unit to rush through a breach in the defenses. If carried out, the man and the unit were honored. However, much of the time, they perished.

20. Vincent J. Esposito and John R. Elting, *The West Point Atlas of American Wars* (New York: Frederick A. Praeger Publishers, 1959), map 12.

21. Hickey, *The War of 1812*, 212.

3

OLIVER HAZARD PERRY

Commodore Oliver Hazard Perry was the American Navy's brightest ornament.

—Commodore Stephen Decatur

BORN TO the sea, Oliver Hazard Perry of Bristol, Rhode Island, clung to the water's edge, salty or fresh. His puritan grandfather's family fled England in 1639 and took root on Cape Cod. His father, Christopher Raymond Perry, unlike his Quaker roots, was not a pacifist. Raymond, at the start of the American Revolution, was drawn into the militia. The teenager soon found his home aboard a privateer tweaking the nose of the British merchant fleet until captured by the Royal Navy and surviving incarceration on a prison hulk in New York Harbor. A crewman on board the Continental Navy's *Trumbull*, he was captured once again, suffering a second term at His Majesty's pleasure at Newry, Ireland. Held this time in a more relaxed atmosphere, he became acquainted with an Irish lass while serving his sentence. Escaping, he found a billet on a merchantman, sailing free until the end of the Revolutionary War. As a crewman aboard a ship from Dublin to New York, he renewed his friendship with the girl he had met while a prisoner, who by chance was a passenger. Back home, he married her, the pretty Sara Alexander, a direct descendant of Scotland's Sir William Wallace. Their first of five sons and three daughters was given the distinctive name of Oliver Hazard Perry, honoring his great grandfather, Colonel George Hazard. Growing up on a farm, like so many of the age, he learned the ways of the land and to care for animals. By the age of eight, his family had moved to larger quarters in Newport, adjacent to the sea.

A town devoted to ships, shipbuilding, and the countless details that go into the complex task of moving with the wind, his hometown was a one-industry mecca. From a schoolmaster, he learned navigation by the stars, the science at the heart of every voyage of every craft. His dominating mother imposed the Church of England's Book of Common Prayer on the family, leaving the Puritan ancestors on his father's side of the family estranged. His father, Raymond Perry, turned toward the sea to become an officer on small merchant coasters at first and then transitioned to bigger ships and longer voyages. He left his wife behind to cope with the growing family. A natural-born sailor, Raymond not only captained but also owned a series of vessels, making a name for himself in Newport.

The Quasi War of 1798, a result of the confused XYZ affair, forced the government to raise a navy. Not capable of maintaining an expensive navy, the last Continental Navy warship was sold in 1786. Political patronage, the best method of the day for success, brought a commission as post Captain to Raymond Perry, who would serve alongside Stephen Decatur Sr. His ship, *General Greene*, was built in the Newport shipyard. The twenty-four gunner was similar in design to the Royal Navy's frigate class that carried two dozen 12-pounder long guns and half a dozen 6-pounders. Launched in January 1799, it remained unfinished until spring. Named for the Rhode Island hero of the Revolutionary War, the *General Greene* was left to the Captain to establish the complement of officers and crew since the U.S. Navy had no regular rooster from which to draw. Oliver needed little coaxing and wrote the obligatory letter requesting service as a midshipman on board his father's vessel. Appointments were at the discretion of the master and were submitted to the secretary of the navy, who asked that men of good character be submitted for his approval. Sea captains during the time in all Western nautical nations often took their kin and that of their friends' children to sea as midshipmen. The position educated future officers in the absence of organized schools. Set between able seamen and lieutenants, the midshipmen led small gangs organized around functional tasks, such as gun crews, wasters, and topmen.

MIDSHIPMAN, U.S. NAVY, 1799

On active service, under his father, Oliver was assured of a career. Not completely pleased that Raymond Perry had scrupulously followed the Secretary's guidelines in the selection of the ship's complement, the captain's organizational skills were found wanting in politically charged Washington. It was a bad start for Perry's father. The *General Greene* entered service in June 1799 with a strongly worded yet simple mission. The ship was to proceed to the Caribbean and capture all French vessels (privateer, merchant, and naval) and protect American interests to include the capture from the French of any vessel that was once American. In particular, pirates were to be dealt with in the usual fashion. The midshipmen mess, belowdeck, was set far forward, where the youths slept and ate in close quarters, resting between watches, practicing their knots, reading up on navigation, and quizzing each other over questions bound to be asked by the lieutenants. Promotion depended on demonstrated accomplishments and navigation skills. It would be a matter of long voyages and longer years before a midshipman could wear the splendid uniform of a naval lieutenant. It was vital that a midshipman get on with his fellows. Teamwork was the hallmark of a good crew, and friendship in the mess meant everything to Perry.

Captain Perry was burdened with officers and crew that he had picked himself from friends and acquaintances, accepting recommendations and trusting in his own rather limited judgment. The *General Greene* was not a merchantman transporting cargo with as short a crew as possible to maximize profit. She was a man-of-war representing an entire nation under orders from the president not only to defend American interest but also to act on the nation's behalf. Once at sea, the limited orders left a great deal of latitude in the hands of the captain. The summer sea voyage to the south, into the teeth of hurricane season, caught him fighting the weather and coping with an inexperienced crew and a newly minted ship that leaked. Drawn through the ringer in a severe squall, the *General Greene* put into Haiti for repairs to her masts, rigging, and sails. The seepage was rather severe, keeping the new ship in port for extensive work. The yellow fever season was in full swing, while progress to make her seaworthy was dreadfully slow. The crew suffered badly, forcing Captain Perry to head home rather than, as his orders dictated, take his station. Illness spreads quickly in the confines below deck. The fever ran wild through the complement, forcing the captain to turn north for home. Once again, the power in Washington reprimanded the captain but did not relieve him. Midshipman Perry learned that valuable military lesson at his father's knee.

Returning to service late in the year, the *General Greene* was called to assist in the reduction of the harbor fortifications at Jacmel, a Haitian port. The *General Greene* swept in on the tide, and within the hour, her 12-pounders shattered the walls, reducing the fortress to a pile of unrecognizable rubble. Young gun captain Perry stuck to his cannon and crew while pounding away with a sizzling cannonball shot out once every two minutes. Deafened by his gun and the cannons about him, his head was ringing by the time the action was finished. It was his first action, and he was exhilarated by the energy expended, as the ship seemed to come alive for the purpose for which she was built. His father was somewhat redeemed by the action.

The Quasi War in the Caribbean was a tangle of diplomatic intrigue involving colonial Frenchmen who changed direction as often as the tropical winds. One day they were staunch Francophiles and the next freebooters with no particular allegiance. Sea captains, operating under broad orders, needed more than just nautical skills if they were to survive in those shark-infested waters. Both the captain and his superior, Commodore Silas Talbot of the USS *Constitution*, leader of the Haitian squadron, were strong willed and unbending. Talbot directed Perry to return to Newport with the *Constitution*'s diseased sailors and to exchange healthy crewmen from the *General Greene*. Perry chaffed at the order when told to abandon his orders to participate in the work at hand. It was asking too much for Captain Perry to obey orders that he believed were ill-conceived. After long delays, unauthorized side trips, and the refusal to conduct operations in accordance with naval regulations, Talbot reported the miscreant behavior. Back in Newport, the end result was a three-month suspension that beached Raymond Perry. Throughout the inquiry, Oliver Hazard Perry supported his father's actions, as did others, to no avail. Young Perry learned firsthand the importance of political and military connections that he would contend with during his own naval career.

BY THE SKIN OF HIS TEETH

After the election of a new president in 1801, Thomas Jefferson appointed a new secretary of the navy. The former Congressman Robert Smith, by direction of the new austerity program, cut the number of ships, captains, lieutenants, and midshipmen to the bone. He wiped out the *General Greene*'s quarterdeck and retained only one man on active service: Midshipman Oliver Hazard Perry.

The young United States was a maritime nation with a long coastline, numerous natural harbors, a mild climate, and sweeping trade winds. The virgin forests between the seaside and Appalachian Mountains provided the best live oak in the Western world. Shipyards, apprenticed joiners, carpenters, blacksmiths, and all manner of trades would fill the demand for sailing craft of all sizes and tasks. Staysail coasters, square-riggers, fishing boats, horse carriers, and timber transports were launched from the Carolinas to the territory of Maine. Farming and fishing were the prime wage providers, but merchant seaman and whalers were close behind. The American merchant fleet plowed a path in the Atlantic to the British Isles, Europe, and the Mediterranean. No longer protected by the Royal Navy, the Barbary pirates who rimmed the southern edge of Mediterranean targeted American trading ships, commandeering cargo and enslaving passenger and crew on their vessels. The demand to protect American commercial interests forced Jefferson to reactivate the American navy.

The *John Adams*, a light frigate of twenty-eight 12-pounder long guns, plus a couple of pair of smaller guns fore and aft, needed a crew. The captain, Hugh G. Campbell, selected his officers from the secretary of the navy's list, picking Oliver Hazard Perry from the ranks of the midshipmen. Perry, a thin, dark-haired, handsome lad, bid good-bye to his father and joined the *Adams* in New York Harbor in early June 1801. Sailing with an American squadron in the Mediterranean, the *John Adams* was detached to bottle up a corsair, the command ship of the Tripoli fleet, taking on supplies in the harbor of Gibraltar. While the duty excused the *John Adams* from all the action against other pirates, Perry distinguished himself through diligence at whatever duties he was given. As a result, the captain assigned the seventeen-year-old to be an acting lieutenant. It was recognition of his knowledge and leadership.

Pressed into courier duty, Perry's ship transported diplomats and their families between posts. Rejoining the American fleet off the shore of Tripoli, the *John Adams* sent a party ashore to burn three beached grain-carrying barges. While Perry remained on board, Lieutenant James Lawrence led a shore party to destroy the craft. During the raid, the party sustained injuries before completing the mission.

In late November 1803, Perry was back home in Newport. The now taller and strikingly handsome acting lieutenant, in a well-fitted dark blue uniform, shiny row of brass buttons, and single gold epaulette on his left shoulder, was a catch for the young ladies of Newport. Events in the Mediterranean were not going according to plan under Commodore Preble, captain of the USS *Constitution*. The harbor at Tripoli was a tough nut to crack. The American fleet, while active, was not successful in curtailing pirate operations. The secretary of the navy added the USS *Constellation* to the fray. Captain Campbell, the ship's new commander, sent for Perry to join the departure from the Washington Navy Yard in the early spring of 1804.

BACK TO THE MEDITERRANEAN

Constellation joined an impressive fleet off Norfolk, Virginia. In the lead was the USS *President* under Commodore Samuel Barron, the USS *Congress* under Captain John Rodgers, and the schooner USS *Essex*. Sailing northwest with the trade winds, the formidable fleet reached Gibraltar by August. Even though this was his second tour with Campbell, who had assigned Perry to the *Constellation*, during the voyage Perry had a difference of opinion over improper orders and requested transfer to another ship in the fleet. Captain Rodgers, commander of the fleet by 1805, sent Perry to the USS *Nautilus* for the remainder of that tour of duty. Although his new ship was much smaller, Perry assumed duties of first lieutenant, though a downgrade was nonetheless key to his development. His position demanded that he oversee all departments on an hourly basis. The other officers and crew depended on him to intercede with the captain since he had access to the commander that none other possessed. Oliver Perry, like so many of his time, was beginning to take on the mantle of a self-righteous man of honor who, like so many men of his time, believed totally in his own judgment and damn the outcome. In other words, he became a naval officer.

For the past year, the war against Tripoli, Morocco, and the pirates had swirled around *Nautilus*, yet only once had the ship seen real action, and Perry was not aboard at the time. He had a talent for always finding himself on the sidelines, a witness to the affair. Once again, he asked Rodgers for a transfer back to a major vessel. He requested the billet on the *Constellation*, which was under a new captain. A few months later, when the fighting had subsided and diplomacy took its place, Rodgers brought Perry to the *Constitution*, where he remained for the rest of the tour.

HOME WITH NEW DUTIES

By the fall of 1806, with no enemy abroad, Perry was beached. Sent to the Newport boatyard, he was to supervise the construction of seventeen gunboats for harbor duty. Proud of their boy, his mother and father showcased his return to society. He was a knockout to the young females and a number set their cap at him. Newport society was highly class conscious, restricting Perry's reach for a young miss from a prominent family. Finding his first love, she was more than willing. His parents approved, but the opposition was overwhelming. Perry moved on now that the gunboats were to be commissioned and sailed brokenhearted with his flotilla for New York Harbor.

GREAT BRITAIN IGNORES AMERICAN SOVEREIGNTY

President Jefferson was becoming frustrated with a new crisis. Great Britain had become decisively engaged on the Continent with the postrevolution expansion of France. Napoleon, since 1796, had been tumbling one throne after another. England was being isolated, losing her markets under the Emperor's Continental economic trade system. Great Britain stepped in when Portugal fell to the French with a new army at the expense of her colonial holdings. In 1805, the Royal Navy defeated the combined fleets of France and Spain. That morning, October 5, off the coast of Spain, the USS *Constitution* sailed by the fleet only hours before the great naval battle Trafalgar. On board HMS *Victory*, Lord Nelson's flagship, 10 percent of the crew were captured American seamen, kidnapped off American merchant ships, and impressed into Royal Navy service. By 1807, the count of missing sailors had reached nearly 10,000. In June, the USS *Chesapeake*, leaving the Norfolk, Virginia, harbor, was fired on and seized by the British man-of-war *Leopard* within sight of the shore. Several Americans were killed and wounded, while four suspected British deserters were taken. Jefferson reacted by imposing a moratorium on all trade with Great Britain. The embargo was meant to punish the British, but the loss of trade reverberated through the entire American mercantile and agrarian sectors. Britain retaliated, blockading American ports and seizing American ships and cargos before they could dock in Europe. At first, the country supported retaliation against its old enemy, but soon reality set in when businesses began to fail and imports dried up. Extremely unpopular, the embargo spawned an entirely new enterprise—smuggling. Along the St. Lawrence and the southern shore of the Great Lakes, struggling frontier Americans sold foodstuffs, timber, and potash to neighboring Canadians. The lack of roads to the south, combined with the harsh climate, prevented a quest for new markets.

Returning to Rhode Island, Perry spent the next year building more harbor-bound gunboats while the navy was crying for seagoing men-of-war to break the British blockade. In days of sailing, it took a ship-of-the-line—sixty guns and more—to influence an action. The biggest American ships were four large frigates, mounting only fifty-five total guns. Ships fought at close quarters, side by side, often less than hundred yards apart. As a rule, the cumulative amount of cannonball weight a ship could throw at the enemy determined the victor. This put all twenty-one American fighting ships at a disadvantage. American captains could not punch above their class, limiting their challenge to frigates and smaller ships. Of the 600 ships sailing under the white flag with the red-crossed ensign of St. George, 300 were ships of the line.

PERRY SERVES WITH LAWRENCE

Placed in command of a gunboat section, Perry served along side Lieutenant James Lawrence, whom he had met as a midshipman in the Mediterranean.

They patrolled the busy entrance to the harbor where the masts of tall ships ringed both sides of Manhattan Island like a forest in winter. In 1809, after serving once again under Commodore Rodgers, who had hemmed him in in New York Harbor, Perry was placed in command of the small schooner USS *Revenge*. A member of the small naval officer corps of those days relied on patronage for assignments and promotion. It may have been not *what* one knows but *who* one knows. Serving next to the flagpole, where the commodore could get to know an officer, was always a wise career move. Rated at ten 6-pounder guns, *Revenge* patrolled outside New York Harbor.

A CHANCE TO SAIL FREE

In June 1810, the *Revenge* was shifted to serve under Captain Campbell's (Perry's nemesis) command, patrolling the Gulf Coast seeking privateers who ignored the American tax laws. *Revenge* was an ideal ship for the duty since she carried staysails that enabled her to maneuver across the wind and, with her shallow draft, chase smugglers inshore. A warrant put out by the owners of a merchant ship, *Diana*, came to Perry's attention off the coast of Georgia. Sailing under false colors, she was recognized and captured. The British had been providing her protection, but Perry chased her down, boarded the privateer, and dared the Royal Navy to attempt to take her back. Done under the guns of stronger vessels, the action was honored by Secretary Hamilton. It read,

> The firmness and decision, properly tempered with moderation evinced by Perry, when it seemed probable, from the reports in circulation, that a hostile course might have been adopted against the Diana, and of the complete state of preparation in which you constantly held yourself to repel any attack upon the sovereignty of the United States.[1]

Returning the *Diana* safely to her owners, the commendation was waiting for him when he next met Captain Campbell.

Returning to Commodore Rodgers, Perry was ordered to conduct a nautical survey of the coastal waters along the Connecticut coast to Newport, Rhode Island. It was tricky water, particularly in fog and winter storms. Who better for the job than Perry, who had sailed the waters much of his life, aboard *Revenge*, a light coaster, ideal under the circumstances. In January 1811, he began the task, which took considerable time because the area was shrouded in thick fog and pelted with rainy squalls. Having pleaded for more time, concerned that the request would reflect badly on his ability to act alone in the matter, he began to cut corners, testing the skill of his pilot and crew. Unwittingly disoriented even though in familiar surroundings, he misidentified his position and left the quarterdeck temporarily in the hands of his brother, midshipman Raymond Perry. The *Revenge* grounded within a short distance of Perry's childhood home. He sprang into action, throwing everything overboard (including the cannons), chopping off the masts, and discarding all canvas. Nothing freed the stricken vessel. A sailor was sent for help, and rescue boats appeared as a storm replaced the fog, driving *Revenge* farther into the sandbar. They fought into the darkness, but Perry was forced to abandon his command. Once confronted with the appalling incident, Perry acted in compliance of the finest code of the sea. Ensuring that not a man was lost, but efforts to pull the wreck back to sea the next day failed. The Naval Court of Inquiry gave faint praise for his actions, but everyone in the naval community knew that Perry had failed to preserve his vessel. It was a good and timely lesson, but remained an open sore all his life. Running the nation's vessel up on the shore was always frowned on regardless of the conciliatory language in the after-action report. The incident would follow him when war came.

DISGRACED

By August, Perry was back to harbor duty and gunboat herding, just as before. Gunboats were as ugly as the name implies. Competing for way in the close confines of Newport and New York harbors, they plodded deep in the water, with little freeboard showing. Their true value came from their ability to scout the enemy fleet a mile offshore and report its strength. Within the harbor they acted as messengers for the harbormaster in positioning merchantmen or as traffic cops. The duty was soul destroying for a young officer who watched his contemporaries pass by on the quarterdeck of seagoing fighting ships. Even though there was no state of war between England and America, tensions were high. After the attack on the *Chesapeake*, the two navies circled each other waiting, indeed wanting an incident so that they could go at it once again. The Royal Navy officer corps, who plied the waves of the world as if it were a private lake enjoying imperial status aboard massive men-of-war, held nothing but contempt for the Yankee sailors and their captains.

Oliver Perry picked that moment in 1812 to end his long engagement and he was married to the twenty-year-old Miss Elizabeth Mason.

As that turbulent year dragged on, Perry could feel tension rise daily; war was inevitable and perhaps imminent. He feared that his loss of the

Revenge would penalize him when war came and men were assigned to ships. Secretary of War Paul Hamilton's list would be the fountainhead of all assignments. He made himself known in a letter, as did all those seeking a billet at sea. Once war was declared by Congress on June 18, 1812, Commodore Rodgers is believed to have interceded with the Secretary and secured a wartime billet that no one else wanted. Rodgers assured the young lieutenant that he had his interests at heart.

The Navy Department employed only a couple of clerks, reducing the production of personnel orders from the Secretariat to be ground out slowly in those turbulent times. High on the seniority list, Perry was told of Rodgers's overture. Not a patient man, Perry wrote the Navy Department for relief from the gunboats and assignment to noteworthy duties. In the meantime, further confusion and delay were caused by the appointment of William Jones as the wartime secretary. Navy talk confirmed rumors, whispers carried his name, assurances were conveyed, and confirmation was all but received, and still no orders arrived in Newport. That summer and on into the fall and Christmas, the horrendous events of the first six months of the naval war with Great Britain made daily headlines. The young nation rejoiced while Perry sat and stewed. Ships he had known and ships he had sailed became famous for their stunning victories against all odds. Shipmates with whom he had shared bleak hours under sodden decks were men of note. Locals, relations, and the men on those awful gunboats all knew why their lieutenant was still paddling around the estuary. It was the blot on his record, the loss of *Revenge*, just one absentminded moment stuffed in between years of good service that would prevent him from fulfilling his destiny.

INDEPENDENT COMMAND AT LAST

It was not until the clear, cold days of January 1813 that Perry received orders to take command of the Lake Erie squadron as master and commander, a grade between lieutenant and captain. Commodore Isaac Chauncey, the overall naval commander of Lake Ontario and Lake Erie, headquartered at Sackets Harbor, New York, near the mouth of the St. Lawrence River, pushed for Perry. There was no flotilla on Lake Erie. There, Perry's unique experience of boatbuilding and years of sailing skill made him the only choice for command on that faraway yet strategic backwater.

Former President Jefferson's statement that "the taking of Canada this year is a mere matter of marching" was taken seriously in London and Montreal. While he prepared to leave, Perry understood the magnitude of his orders and the burden he had willingly assumed. While his contemporaries sailed the saltwater theater garnering the headlines, his command would be mired in a ground-pounding war of attrition, laboring under the most primitive conditions, scrounging for materials, suffering in a severe climate, and being harassed by Indian war parties. The days of lace tablecloths, silver service, and polite neighbors would be replaced by rustic quarters, scarce vittles, and frontier ruffians. While dominating the lake, the craft he was expected to construct would be called upon to transport troops and their equipage since a road network did not exist. Indeed, the first land action of the war occurred on the very far western end of Lake Erie when Governor Hull attacked across the Detroit River within a month of the declaration of war. Many Americans had to go to a map to locate the first battle and subsequent defeat of the army. Perry vividly remembered General William Hull's disgrace since it coincided with his nephew's, Captain Isaac Hull's, complete and unexpected victory over HMS *Guerriere*.

THE NAVAL CAREERS OF PERRY AND CHAUNCEY BECOME INTERTWINED

Major General Henry Dearborn, former Secretary of War under Jefferson and commander of the army, planned the taking of Canada a month before the declaration of war. He kicked off the campaign in July 1812 with an attack on Amherstburg (Windsor), Canada, across the river from Detroit. When the unfortunate General Hull requested naval craft to move his troops, he was told to capture the boats from the enemy. Taken as an illustration of the state of American naval presence on both Lake Ontario and Lake Erie, it is understandable why the secretary of the navy, in all haste, sent Captain Isaac Chauncey to Sackets Harbor on Lake Ontario with orders to do what was necessary to secure both lakes during the conflict. At forty years of age, Chauncey carried a dual background. He had been involved with operations against the French and Barbary pirates in the Mediterranean but most recently had commanded the New York Navy Yard, which built and repaired naval crafts of all sizes. He was well acquainted with Perry and had championed his appointment to the Great Lakes. Sackets Harbor had been a tiny jewel of a natural harbor perfectly situated for boatbuilding. Before he could assume command, an attack by the Canadian Provincial Marine,[2] which realized the value of the harbor, had been driven off. Chauncey's journey northwest was slow and cumbersome against the Hudson River current and on up the Mohawk to Oswego, New York, and along the intermittent coastal track to Sackets Harbor's boatbuilding yard, some 600 miles through hostile Indian country. Amazingly, 170 sailors and marines and 140 shipwrights and joiners, along with tools, 100 cannons in varied sizes, and all manner of supplies, were waiting when he arrived in October.[3] Three years before, the USS *Oneida*, an 18-gun brig, was constructed at the yard and remained the only warship at Chauncey's disposal.[4] Over the past two months, sporadic skirmishes occurred among the shoreline communities on the St. Lawrence River. The New York state militia, commanded by Brigadier General Jacob Brown and assisted by an element of the regular rifle regiment under Captain Benjamin Forsyth, used Sackets Harbor as a supply base as well. It was a neat, small isolated pocket that lived on the very edge of the conflict. Under construction was the corvette USS *Madison*, which would be completed just before the sailing season ended in November.[5] In October, the conflict on the Niagara River swelled up, and an attempt to capture two enemy vessels and sail them past the British defenses down the Niagara River into Lake Erie failed. The new secretary of the navy put Chauncey under the gun. "The success of the ensuing campaign will depend absolutely upon our superiority on all the lakes & every effort & resource must be directed to that object . . . and would be important to the success of Major General Harrison's campaign."[6] That poignant ending, which swung the attention away from Lake Ontario to Lake Erie, was most significant to Perry, who would by circumstance alone be in direct contact with the western attack on Canada. Harrison had the ball as far as Madison was concerned. The newly appointed brigadier general was expected to raise a force not only to recoup the loss of Detroit but also to complete Hull's mission to invade Canada. For that, Harrison would need naval support from Perry. Chauncey would be in a support role to his own subordinate. If the emphasis was laid on Lake Erie, Chauncey should place Perry at Sackets Harbor, but that was not an option. The lines of command were blurred. Perry was to direct the action and thus get the money, supplies, and interest. Suddenly, Lake Ontario was the backwater, something the commodore found perplexing. It appeared to Chauncey that Washington thought of Lake Erie as a separate and distinct command, and he was concerned that Perry, a very headstrong officer, would get the same impression. Additionally, the vital naval construction supplies for the Lake Erie fleet came by way of Pennsylvania to Erie, a more direct route with better roads. Chauncey concocted a cunning plan to secure his place in history.

In the early days of 1813, Perry sent his complement ahead by a separate route to the base at Erie, Pennsylvania, pealing off to conference with his boss at Sackets Harbor. Chauncey briefed his subordinate on the content of the secretary's instructions, directing the new master and commander to build ships that winter and prepare to campaign by June. Chauncey would shift his headquarters and join Perry as leader of the new Lake Erie squadron, and together they would take control of water and cooperate with General

Harrison's plans to regain the lost territory. This may not have been what the secretary had in mind, but out on the frontier, that is the way Chauncey intended to proceed. Because of the traveling conditions, Perry did not close on his headquarters until the last week of March. He had a little over two months to build a battle fleet capable of defeating a strong Canadian Provincial Marine. Preparing the boatyard were 140 craftsmen and sailors who laid the foundation for the slips and prepared for the cordage and hardware that had been purchased in Pittsburgh. That winter at Buffalo, New York, Chauncey had stored the guns and all the paraphernalia that went with them. The Erie's naval agent contracted for a blacksmith to make iron components and a facility to assemble a large quantity of wood blocks. Perry was at home in command and more than qualified to mass-produce the small ships that could navigate the sandbars and shoals that made Lake Erie such a treacherous body of water. Now the winter was his ally. The enemy, marooned on the north side of the lake, could not raid his yard, and work progressed as if it were peacetime. Like the lake navy, the army went into winter quarters, and the militia went home.

While winter bound in Amherstburg, Canada, in ice, the Provincial Marine worked efficiently to construct a fleet capable of ruling the lake and preventing Harrison from crossing the river as Hull had done the previous year. By April, the enemy's craft were on the prowl, sailing off the Presque Isle shipyard, evaluating Perry's progress, and watching the militia ganged on the bluffs with their field guns pointed north. Perry was sure that the British were preparing a raid. A strong force put ashore could surely fire the yard and turn all his work to ashes in a couple of hours. He asked the militia and regular army commander, Brigadier William Winder, cousin of the governor of Maryland and political appointee of the Madison regime, to maintain a presence sufficient to deter the British from landing.

Chauncey: A New Nemesis

Chauncey's spring plan called for the destruction of the Provincial Marine boatyard at York (Toronto) and Kingston, Canada, securing Lake Ontario and thus preventing the British from supporting their troops fighting on the *Niagara* against American infantry units. While Kingston was never attacked, York was destroyed. With that in hand, he planned to move with the American army to the eastern mouth of Lake Erie and, together with Perry and the army, attack Fort Erie, which blocked the southern end of the Niagara River. At that point, Perry would get a portion of his seamen to man the new Erie fleet. Of course, that was contrary to Secretary Jones's instruction, but Chauncey felt that the view of the commander on the ground had a better grasp of the military situation. Jones was more interested in Harrison's progress,which had picked up the gauntlet dropped by Hull when he failed in Canada at Detroit and allowed the Redcoats and their Indian allies to run free in Michigan and northern Ohio. Jones's interest in Harrison led him to communicate directly with Perry, bypassing the chain of command. Chauncey bristled at the news and suspected Perry of disloyalty. Chauncey stopped communicating with Perry, slowing progress unnecessarily. Chauncey, a combat veteran who had commanded the frigate *John Adams* in the saltwater navy and had extended service in significant posts, was not to be snubbed while a serving as a commodore.

In late May, Perry left his base to join Chauncey's element in support of the American army's attack on Fort Erie at the eastern mouth of the lake. He intended to confront Chauncey concerning the absence of qualified crewmen. Jones's efforts to recruit in the east had fallen short. Sailors feared the lake fever, which was rumored to abound on the northern freshwater lakes. The Secretary had to turn to the idle crews in blockaded ports for relief. Perry informed a frosty Chauncey of the completion of his mission to construct a naval force on Lake Erie that was able to campaign as soon as several hundred crewmen arrived. Perry's command would require over 700 to crew the new squadron on Erie, but he had less than half that on hand. With added commitments on Lake Ontario, the Commodore was more than likely to husband the limited assets for himself.

Perry joined Chauncey to support the army's attack on the British Fort Erie. Placed in command of the small squadron of American craft providing transport and cannon support, Perry saw his first action under his own flag. In addition to the praise from General Dearborn, Chauncey thawed out, transferring the ships that Perry had directed to the Lake Erie fleet.

Commander Robert Barclay

Things were not rosy for newly arrived Commander Robert Barclay, Royal Navy, who was forced to travel cross-country now that the Niagara was under American control. Son of the Reverend Peter Barclay of Fife, Scotland, Barclay, at twenty-seven, was the same age as Perry. A lieutenant at Trafalgar, in 1809 he lost an arm while leading a boarding party against the French. Arriving on June 5, he waited impatiently for *Detroit* to be completed at the Amherstburg boatyard. Sir James Yeo was expected to provide seamen taken from the ships at Montreal that were discharging troops and supplies for the coming campaigns. Barclay, on board a fast schooner, probed and then blockaded the Erie boatyard. The British were well aware of the added threat posed by Perry's extra complement of vessels newly acquired after the Battle of Fort

Erie. The addition of five American craft from Black Brook—no longer held at the mouth of the Niagara River after the fall of Fort Erie—was a considerable boon. Barclay's squadron crisscrossed beyond the sandbar that protected the harbor at Presque Isle well within sight but out of range of the American defenses. Perry found it maddening to watch them prowl through his glass, but he knew his day would come. His big brigs would have to be lifted up over the sandbar, which was impassable under Barclay's guns. On July 28 the severe weather forced the Provincial Marine to leave for safer water. Before the enemy returned three days later, Perry was able to stand out on the lake. Without the *Detroit*, Barclay retreated and waited until September, when the men and supplies arrived. The American domination on the Niagara peninsula forced the use of the slow overland route. The summer rains had turned bad roads into quagmires. British Major General Procter, whose army threatened Fort Malden near Sandusky, Ohio, was consuming supplies at a high rate and could not survive on foraged vittles. A resupply run across the western tip of the lake opened Barclay up to attack from Perry sweeping in from the east. On the water loomed Perry's burgeoning squadron, while Harrison was beginning to roll up the southwestern bank. As crewmen trickled in, Barclay prepared his fleet for one decisive battle.

While Perry exercised his new understaffed ships, he pleaded with his commodore for more men. Perry was unaware that while Chauncey was assisting the army on the Niagara, British General Prevost and Commodore Sir James Yeo were attacking his headquarters at Sackets Harbor. The resulting failed attack nonetheless tempered Chauncey's thinking about the defense of Lake Ontario and made him conserve those crews that were intended to be sent west. Navy Secretary Jones did not validate the threat to Lake Ontario. Chauncey's estimation was ignored. Jones ordered the Commodore to send Perry a considerable number of men from the draft that Jones had recently provided from the fleet. Chauncey discovered that Jones had been sending bits and pieces since July directly to Perry without informing him. Jones told Perry that he believed that the Provincial Marine was shorthanded and that he should attack immediately. The Secretary upgraded Perry, giving him combat command of the lake without telling Chauncey. It was amateur to intervene between serving officers at that critical point and could have led to resignation and disaster.

An angry Chauncey complied, sending just over 100 men. Like so many commanders in history, when compelled to support, they complied by number but not by skill. Perry complained about the quality of his draft. "Boys, blacks, and soldiers, I need sailors." Neither Jones nor Chauncey understood that Perry was about to fight a major battle that would determine the fate of the invasion of Canada. Chauncey answered, "I have yet to learn that the Colour of the skin, or the cut and trimming of the coat, can affect a mans qualification or usefulness."[7] Perry gave up on the commodore and turned to Marine Lieutenant John Brooks, who, together with his officers, beat the bushes for men with ship knowledge. They raided the Pennsylvania militia, promising prize money for a four-month enlistment. Over 100 volunteered, some with maritime skill. Soldiers before and after the battle served in large numbers on board lake navy vessels, although there was a navy and army regulation that strictly prohibited officers of either service from doing so. Perry ignored the rule and welcomed anyone who was willing to serve. In the first week of August, under pressure from Washington, Chauncey reluctantly sent the final installment with Lieutenant Jess Elliot and 100 men from his command to flush out the roster of the Erie fleet. Chauncey could not believe that he had been bypassed after all the service he had given, and now the secretary was looting his command at a very critical moment.

ARMY AND NAVY

Perry was more than ready, having been harassed by Barclay for the past month. Ordered to cooperate with Harrison ever since the first day of his assignment, he felt that the time had come for the alliance to be formed. Perry was supremely confident that the force he had at his disposal was a punitive force equipped to punish the enemy. He was also aware that if he failed, there was no one who would defend the loss of a weapon he had built with his own hands, certainly not the commodore. He presented his complements to Major General Harrison, who received him warmly. Harrison depended utterly on the lift and guns that the navy did not provide earlier to the unfortunate General Hull. In mid-August, Perry sailed to the water off the mouth of Sandusky Bay to meet with the army's planning staff. Procter's Indian scouts reported the meeting where the field guns of the army met the guns of the navy. The Indians did not stand and fight when cannons were present. They believed that war should be amusing and profitable.

The army officers were given the capabilities of the ships and, most important, the restrictions posed by the wind to aid their planning. In the coming days, the two staffs and unit commanders acquainted themselves with the land and naval artillery. The range and weight of projectiles were compared. Guns were fired at targets, cavalry integration was planned, troops carrying row boats were inspected, and a good time was had by all. Perry established his order of battle for the fleet to practice in the calm waters of the southern summer lake. He performed a formal reconnaissance of the Fort Malden area and tested the waters for depth and current. Local fishermen were consulted about the winds, the most important variable. His schooner, staysail rigged, was much more forgiving in the face of the wind. As in modern-day maneuvers, ships came into line, signals were hoisted, and craft responded. Most importantly the amateur crews learned cannon drills while the boatswain's mates ran the men and rigging up and down with impunity. Observed by Barclay's scouts from afar, few secrets survived on either side. It was going to be a pounding. Barclay's preponderance of long guns provided an advantage, however, if the Americans could fight in close, the advantage would go to Perry's carronades. According to Theodore Roosevelt's *The Naval War of 1812*, "The Americans were certainly very greatly in force . . . naval battle was a slugfest."[8]

UP ANCHOR

By 7 a.m. on the clear morning of September 10, 1813, sixteen months since war was declared, Master and Commander Oliver Hazard Perry moved his squadron from the safety of Put-in-Bay and into the history books of every schoolchild in America.

At the call *Sail Ho*, shouted and echoed from ship to ship and deck to deck, the two fleets were committed to battle. Many would certainly die, some would be maimed for life, and others would remember that morning every waking day for the remainder of their lives. Well within sight of Rattlesnake Island, the sails filled with a stiff breeze, and the two commanders applied their skill to position their men-of-war for the kill. "After more than three hours of exhausting and frustrating labor, Perry finally yielded to nature's force and ordered Master William V. Taylor to wear ship—to turn with the wind as opposed to tack—and bear down to the northeast. Perry's intention was to fight the battle either among or to the east of the islands. Taylor objected to his commander's bidding, aware that such a maneuver would defer the wind advantage to the British. "I don't care, to windward or to leeward they shall fight today."[9]

BATTLE OF LAKE ERIE

Eyewitness Account

On the morning of the 10th of September, at sunrise, the enemy were discovered bearing down from Malden, for the evident purpose of attacking our squadron, then at anchor in Put-in-Bay. Not a moment was to be lost. Perry's squadron immediately got under way, and stood out to meet the British fleet, which at this time had the weather gage. At 10 am the wind shifted from S.W. to S.E., which brought to windward. The wind was light—the day beautiful. Not a cloud obscured the horizon. The line was formed at 11, and Commodore Perry caused an elegant flag, which he had privately prepared, to be hoisted at the mast head of the Lawrence. On this flag was painted, in characters legible to the whole fleet, the dying words of the immortal Lawrence:—"Don't Give Up The Ship." Its effect is not to be described—every heart was electrified. The crew cheered—the exhilarating can was passed. Both fleets appeared eager for the conflict, on the result of which so much depended. At 15 minutes before 12, the Detroit, the headmost ship of the enemy, open upon the Lawrence, which for 10 minutes, was obliged to sustain a well directed and heavy fire from the enemy's two large ships, without being able to return it with carronades, at 5 minutes before 12, the Lawrence open upon the enemy. The other vessels were ordered to support her, but the wind at this time was too light to enable them to come up. Every brace and bowline of the Lawrence being soon shot away, she became unmanageable, and in this situation, sustained the action upwards of two hours, within canister distance, until every gun was rendered useless, and but a small part of her crew left unhurt upon the deck.

At half past two the wind increased and enabled the Niagara to come into close action—the gun-boats took a nearer position. Commodore Perry left his ship in charge of Lieutenant Yarmer, and went on board the Niagara. Just as he reached that vessel, the flag of the Lawrence came down. The crisis had arrived. Captain Elliot at this moment anticipated the wishes of the Commodore, by volunteering his services to bring the schooners into close action.

At forty-five minutes past two the signal was made for close action. The Niagara being very little injured, and her crew fresh, the Commodore determined to pass through the enemy's line. He accordingly bore up and passed the head of the Detroit, Queen Charlotte and Lady Prevost, pour a terrible raking fire into them from the starboard guns, and on the Chippewa and Little Belt, from larboard side, at half pistol shot distance. The small vessels at this time having got within grape and canister distance kept up a well directed and destructive fire. The action now raged with the greatest fury. The Queen Charlotte, having lost her commander, and several of her principal officers, in a moment of confusion, got foul of the Detroit. In this situation, the enemy in their turn had to sustain a tremendous fire, with the power of returning it with much effect. The carnage was horrible. The flags of the Detroit, Queen Charlotte, and Lady Prevost, were struck in rapid succession. The Brig Hunter, and the Schooner Chippewa, were soon compelled to follow the example. The Little Belt attempted to escape to Malden but she was pursued by two of the gun-boats and surrendered, about three miles distance from the scene of action.

The writer of this account, in company with five others, arrived at the head of Put-in-Bay island, on the evening of the 9th, and had a view of the action at the distance of only ten miles. The spectacle was truly grand and awful. The firing was incessant, for the space of three hours and continued at short intervals, forty-five minutes longer. In less than one hour after the battle began, most of the vessels of both fleets were enveloped in a cloud of smoke, which rendered the issue of the action uncertain, till the next morning, when we visited the fleet in the harbor, on the opposite side of the island. The reader will easily judge of our solicitude to learn the results. There is no sentiment more painful than suspense, when it is existed by the uncertain issue of an event like this.

If the wind had continued at S.W. it was the intention of Admiral Barclay to have boarded our squadron. For this purpose he had taken on board of his fleet about two hundred of the famous 41st regiment. They acted as marines, and fought bravely; but nearly two thirds of them were either killed or wounded.

The carnage on board the prizes was prodigious. They must have lost 200 in killed, besides wounded. The sides of the Detroit and Queen Charlotte, were shattered bow to stern. There was scarcely to place ones hand on their larboard sides without touching the impression of a shot. A great many balls, canister and grape, were found lodge in their bulwarks, which too thick to be penetrated by our carronades, unless within pistol shot distance. The masts were so much shattered that they fell overboard soon after they got into the bay.

The loss of the Americans was severe, particularly onboard the Lawrence. When her flag was struck, she had but nine men fit for duty, remaining on deck. Her sides were completely riddled by the shot from the long guns of the ships. Her decks, the morning after the conflict, when I first went on board, exhibited a scene that defies description—for literally covered with blood, which stilled adhered to the plank in clots—brains, hair, and fragments of bone were still sticking to the rigging and sides. The surgeons were still busy with the wounded. Enough! Horror appalled my senses.

Among the wounded were several brave fellows each of whom had lost a leg or an arm. They appeared cheerful, and expressed a hope that they had done their duty. Rome and Sparta would have been proud of these heroes.

It would be invidious to particularize instances of individual merit, where every one so nobly performed his part. Of the nine seamen remaining unhurt at the time the Lawrence her flag, five were immediately promoted, for their unshaken firmness, in such a trying situation. The most of these had been in the action with the Guerriere and Java.

Every officer of the Lawrence, except the Commodore and his little brother, a promising youth, 13 year-old, were either killed or wounded.

The efficacy of the gun-boats was fully proved in this action, and the sterns of all the prizes bear ample testimony of the fact. They took raking positions and galled the enemy severely. The Lady Prevost lost twelve men before either of the Brigs fire on her. Their fire was quick and precise. Let us here the enemy. The general order of Adjutant General Baynes, contains the following words: "His [Perry's] numerous gun-boats, [four] which had proved the greatest annoyance during the action, were all uninjured."

The undaunted bravery of Admiral [Captain] Barclay, entitled him to a better fate to the loss of the day, was superadded grievous and dangerous wounds. He had before lost an arm; it is now his hard fortune to loos the other, buy a shot which carried away the blade of the right shoulder; a canister shot made violent contusion in his hip. His wounds were for some days considered mortal. Every possible attention was paid to his situation. When Commodore Perry sail for Buffalo, he was so far recovered, that he took passage on board our fleet. The fleet touched at Erie. The citizens saw the affecting spectacle of Harrison and Perry, leading the wounded British hero, still unable to walk without help, from the beach to their lodgings.

On board the Detroit, twenty-four hours after her surrender, were found, snugly stowed away in the hold, two Indians Chiefs, who had the courage to go on board at Malden for the purpose of acting as sharp shooters, to kill our officers. One had the courage to ascend into the round top and discharge his piece, but the whizzing of shot splinters, and bits of rigging, soon made the place too warm for him—He descended faster than he went up. At the moment he reached the deck, the fragments of a seaman's head struck his comrades face, and covered with blood and brains. He vociferated the savage interjection, "quoh" and both sought safety below.[10]

U.S. Brig Niagara off the western Lister,
Head off Lake Erie,
Sept. 10th 1814, 4 o'clock p.m.
Sir—It has pleased the almighty to give to the arms of the United States a signal victory over their enemies on this lake,

The British squadron, consisting of two ships, two brigs, one schooner and one sloop, have this moment surrendered to the force to my command, after a sharp conflict.

I have the honor to be sir,
Your obedient servant
O. H. Perry

To General Harrison, his message was short and very informal: "Dear General—We have met the enemy and they are ours."

Analysis

Perry let it be known at the inception of the battle his personal feelings, "don't give up the ship," which must have been on the lips of every man on both sides. The Americans saw it as a call to duty, while the British saw it as a fight to the death. Perry's transfer under fire, in view of both fleets, inspired his men to ever-greater heights. The most remarkable item in the battle that took place within "range of half a pistol shot" was the sailors, soldiers, and marines who held their duty stations, surrounded by shot, shell, musket balls, smoke, noise, confusion, blood, and dismemberment.

CHRONOLOGY OF OLIVER HAZARD PERRY

1797, April	Midshipman; served one year under father, Raymond Perry, on the USS *General Greene* in the Caribbean
1802	Served in the Mediterranean on board the USS *Adams* frigate
1804–1806	Acting lieutenant of the USS *Constellation, Nautilus*, and *Constitution*
1806–1809	Built gunboats for harbor use
1807, January 15	Promoted to lieutenant
1809–1811	Captain of the schooner USS *Revenge*
1811–1813	Master and commander of the Newport Squadron
1813	Master and commander of the Lake Erie Squadron
1813, September 10	Promoted to captain with victory, Battle of Lake Erie
1814–1817	Commander of the frigate USS *Java* in the Mediterranean
1817–1819	Commander of the Newport gunboat flotilla
1819	Commodore of the U.S. Naval Squadron Caribbean; diplomatic duty in Venezuela, dies of yellow fever; buried at sea near Trinidad

NOTES

1. David Curtis Skaggs, *Oliver Hazard Perry* (Annapolis, MD: Naval Institute Press, 2006), 40.

2. The Canadian "Provincial Marine" was a naval force of craft of all kinds led by Commodore Sir James Yeo, Royal Navy, which operated on the Great Lakes, Lake Champlain, and the St. Lawrence, now at war and determined to dominate every aspect of the watery frontier.

3. J. Mackay Hitsman, *The Incredible War of 1812*, updated by Donald E. Graves (Toronto: Robin Bass Studio, 1965), 104.

4. "Brig," originally a brigantine, a two-masted ship square-rigged on both foremast and aft mast.

5. A corvette is a flush-decked warship with a single tier of guns, smaller than a frigate but shipped rigged on three masts.

6. Hitsman, *The Incredible War of 1812*, 128.

7. Skaggs, *Oliver Hazard Perry*, 73.

8. Theodore Roosevelt, *The Naval War of 1812* (New York: Putnam, 1882), 243.

9. Gerard T. Altoff, *Oliver Hazard Perry and the Battle of Lake Erie* (Put-in-Bay, OH: The Perry Group, 1999), 32.

10. John M. Niles, *The Life of Oliver Hazard Perry* (reprint of William S. Marsh [Hartford, CT, 1840], taken from a firsthand account transcribed in 1820).

4

WILLIAM HENRY HARRISON, CHIEF TECUMSEH, AND ZACHARY TAYLOR

A standing army is one of the greatest mischiefs that can possibly happen.

—President James Madison

WILLIAM HENRY HARRISON

"TIPPECANOE & Tyler Too," a political election cry in 1840, brought the 67-year-old William Henry Harrison to the White House as the ninth president. It was a long, hard trek that began when his ancestors opted for the New World. There were no more prominent men of the colonial time than those who bore the name of Benjamin Harrison. The first, late of England, bought land in Virginia in 1632. Later, militia Colonel Benjamin Harrison of the House of Burgesses sat in the first Continental Congress. The Wakefield and Berkeley plantations spawned five additions to the name Benjamin Harrison, and each would contribute to the growing of America while increasing the family's wealth and influence. Benjamin Harrison V looked for a profession for his son, who was not the heir to the family land. William attended numerous medical schools, all of which became unsuitable because of religious affiliation. On arrival at the Pennsylvania University, he was told that his father had died. Soon after, his brother informed him that the money had run out and that he must leave school. Harrison, the son of wealth and privilege, turned to patronage and through an acquaintance petitioned President Washington for a commission in the army.

The following day, he took the oath and became Ensign William Henry Harrison of the 1st U.S. Regiment of Infantry. In 1791, the regular army was at its lowest strength. Other than Ensign Harrison's regiment, there was only one other, an artillery regiment that was short guns, limbers, and horses. Most of the government officials were veterans of the Revolution and believed that the war had been fought and won solely by volunteers and state militiamen. In these early days of the nation, Congress did not receive funds from the states but relied on tariffs collected at the ports for federal income. Yet Congress was charged with the protection of settlers whom they encouraged to "go west."

The ensign, in splendid uniform, assisted in the recruitment of young men off the streets of Philadelphia. There was no military education for officers except that they must be able to read and write. The same was true of sergeants because they conducted muster and read the rolls. With fewer than 100 raw recruits, the company marched west 300 miles, through mountain passes, to Fort Pitt at the confluence of two mighty rivers, the Allegheny and the Monongahela. The nineteen-year-old ensign was not conditioned and learned what it meant to be in the infantry. It was a great relief to board crude boats and float their way to Fort Washington at Cincinnati, Ohio. On their arrival in November 1791, a party of women and children, family supporters of the 600-man expedition of General Arthur St. Clair, staggered into the fort with a horrific tale of a massacre. Ambushed 100 miles west by a large horde of Indians, the command was slaughtered, women and children were killed, and the general was slain. The braves roamed the area after the battle and killed the wounded with tomahawks.

Confined for the winter in primitive conditions while fellow officers turned to drink and duels, Harrison had the good fortune to come across the military history books of an artillery officer who had lost a duel. Absenting himself in the evening from the merriment, he began to educate himself on the art of war. Comrades assured him that there would be no suicidal winter forays in the back country where the Indians could snuff out intruders with abandon. Major General James Wilkinson, now in command, proposed an expedition to Fort Jefferson to recover the equipment left at St. Clair's defeat and bury the bodies exposed on the freezing ground before attacking an Indian village twenty-five miles west. Harrison, at the head of his platoon, marched toward the fort, struggling for a week in deep snow and cold for eighty miles. With supplies running out, Wilkinson, true to form, lost heart. He sent the infantry home, splitting his command into two small vulnerable parts. The mounted militia pressed on to Fort Jefferson. The savages had mutilated the bodies, which were found dismembered and frozen. After burial, the same band of Indians attacked the column as it left. The militia, bent on revenge, beat off the attack before returning to Fort Washington with horrific tales of blood and gore.

The British Persist

The 1783 Treaty of Paris called for the British to vacate the Ohio and points west, withdrawing to Canada. However, they maintained a hold on the western Indians, supplying them with guns and ammunition. Stirring up the tribes, three British Indian agents remained to direct the marauding war parties. Supplied with blankets, food and high-quality tomahawks, bands of braves were sent to slow the spread of settlers in Ohio. Washington, a former Indian fighter in his youth, commissioned Major General (Mad) Anthony Wayne to rid Ohio of the Indians.[1] Once again, General Wilkinson had overplayed his hand and was superseded by Wayne. How Wilkinson got the command in the first place can only be put down to political pressure. In charge of the Northwest Indian War, Wayne created the Legion of the United States and built the settlement of Legionville devoted solely to basic training, a unique idea of the time. At the behest of their British agents, the Indians terrorized farms, burned barns, grabbed stock, slaughtered farmers, and kidnapped women and children. In the face of civil discontent over the lack of protection afforded settlers, Congress authorized an army force of over 5,000 regulars to subdue the territory. At Fort Fayette, north of Philadelphia, Harrison trained with other young officers, to include Solomon Van Rensselaer, Meriwether Lewis, and William Clark, future national heroes. With the loss of his captain to the charge of conduct unbecoming of an officer and a gentleman, Harrison was promoted to lieutenant and breveted to captain in order to take the officer's place.[2] While training, he learned of his mother's death. In his sorrow, he decided to make the army his career and never looked back. Back at Fort Washington that spring, his pay and prospects were given a boost when he was appointed aide to General Wayne. The winter of 1792 found 200 trained infantry settled near the site of St. Clair's defeat in a new fort they called Recovery—they picked up the bones of the soldiers, which had been disinterred by the Indians, and put them in a common grave. Fort Recovery was furiously attacked in the spring, much to the surprise of all who believed that the negotiations were leading to a treaty.

In July 1794, Wayne assembled an expedition comprised of 3,000 infantry and General Charles Scott's two regiments of mounted Kentuckians. They struck out 200 miles west into the wilderness deep into virgin forest devoid of farms or hamlets and surrounded by nothing but oppressive heat and bug-infested bogs. The Indians retreated before them to take refuge at the British fort at the Rapids. A few miles south of the Michigan border, Wayne stopped to build Fort Defiance, where he stockpiled the food he had taken from abandoned Indian villages. At an officers meeting, General Wilkinson suggested a radical formation, while Captain Harrison countered with a more conventional attack that took in the likely response of the Indians. The result was the following:

> General Order # 1
> The Army will March tomorrow Morning at five O clock agreeable to the constant order of March, with this difference; That the column will March two deep and in close Order as Circumstances will permit, of being totally Divested of Baggage, the Center will be left free for artillery and spare Ammunition.[3]

Harrison knew the value of artillery, a concept that Wilkinson had never noticed. The accepting of the captain's plan over that of the outspoken Wilkinson embarrassed the general, who was not a forgiving man. The following morning, the attack was delayed until noon because of wet ground, which gave the Indians time to spy on the preparations and set up a good defense. High winds accompanied the rain so violently that it knocked over the virgin forest, creating a natural abatis. The combination of grassy riverbed in the center, wooded ridges to either side, and thick forest caused the line to lose synchronization. Waiting at this convenient barrier were 1,000 Indians steadied by a company of British soldiers and Canadian militia. Under British command, the enemy force opened up with a wall of musket balls, sending the American dragoons and mounted Kentuckians into chaos and disrupting the attack. Harrison thought that his duty was clear, and he left Wayne's side and spurred his horse in the direction of the fault. Picking his way through the debris, he stopped the horsemen and turned them back toward the enemy line. Wayne witnessed the gallant aide as he traversed the line, putting units in place and leading them forward in spite of musket balls that filled the air. The Indians fell back in the face of the American charge. Retreating to the fort's gate they discovered that it had been closed as soon as the white-skinned allies were safely inside. Taking their wounded, the braves scattered into the surrounding woods.

Scouring the battlefield, Harrison found Captain Van Rensselaer—killed later at Queenston—suffering from wounds and took him to headquarters, where his life was saved by surgeons. Wayne surveyed the British fort at the Rapids and determined that it would cost too many lives for too little gain to take the ramparts, which bristled with cannons. A short distance away, the troops labored for two months building Fort Wayne and stocking it with troops and provisions before returning in October—thus the battle of Fallen Timbers entered the history books.

During the coming year, General Wayne dickered with a delegation of Indians over the terms of a treaty in which the chiefs finally agreed to exchange land rights for $20,000 in goods to be distributed among the tribes and an annual annuity of over $9,000 in kind. The administration of the Greenville Treaty was given to Harrison, who traveled the area for compliance.

The army was contracting once again, and promotions were a thing of the past. Harrison offered his resignation when he purchased land at North Bend with the intention of settling down. In the spring of 1798, after seven years of service, Harrison was promoted to captain. Friends were the valuable component in the career of an upward-bound young man of that long-ago period. Through a friend and a set of circumstances, he suddenly received an appointment as the Secretary of the Northwest Territory from President John Adams.

Politics

By 1799, the Territory qualified to be represented in the House of Representative. Harrison, a former Virginian and therefore opposed to the Federalists of New England, won the vote of the newly established Territory House seat. In Philadelphia, he became vocal on the questions of the day, which revolved around the rights to and cost of land in the West. He was quick to make a name for himself over the issue of partial payment of land. He championed the cause of the smallholder over that of rich speculators in the east who would purchase land outright and then lease it back to poor farmers, making them sharecroppers instead of landowners. The Harrison Land Law was his first national contribution.

In the election for Vice President Thomas Jefferson to take the office of president, Harrison expected to be looked upon with favor. Once Jefferson took the oath in January 1801, he turned to the popular Harrison and appointed him to the governorship of the new territory of Indiana. Harrison took it in stride. He found that he was at home out of uniform and wondered why he had not thought of it at the beginning of his adult life. Governor Harrison set up shop at Vincennes, Indiana, on the Wabash River, a 200-hundred mile trek due west from the Ohio River. The following spring, Harrison's travels acquainted him with the plight of the Indians who abounded throughout the territory. He wrote to Secretary of War Henry Dearborn, who had supervision over Indian affairs,

> All profess and I believe that most of them feel a friendship for the United States . . . but they make heavy complaints of ill-treatment on the part of our Citizens. They say that their people have been killed—their lands

settled on—their game wantonly destroyed & their young men made
drunk & cheated of the peltries which formerly procured the necessary
articles of Clothing, arms and ammunition to hunt with. Of the truth of
these charges I am well convinced.[4]

Harrison's eyes were opened by the daily Indian testimony of rough
men who took young squaws, spreading disease and disrupting their families.
White men took advantage of the Indians' penchant for liquor, offering it in
trade for pelts. Drunken braves were found in the morning passed out on the
humble streets of Vincennes. As the governor, he evoked his power to revoke
trading licenses and detain those who attacked or killed an Indian. Juries, as
a rule, acquitted a white man who was accused of killing an Indian. Settlers
looked on the Indians as unwanted guests in their country. Even good Christians saw all Indians as subhuman and a threat to their lives. With the addition
of white settlers in ever-growing numbers, game was diminishing, which the
Indians depended on for food. Harrison adopted Jefferson's program "Hoes
for Bows": "Your father, the President, wishes you to assemble your scattered warriors and to form towns and villages, in the situations best adapted
to cultivation; he will cause you to be furnished with horses, cattle, hogs, and
implements of husbandry, and will . . . instruct you in management."[5] In the
south, the Creeks and Cherokees had taken up the offer, which was succeeding in "civilizing the natives." The Council of Chiefs, after extensive negotiations with Harrison, agreed to deed a portion of their land across the southern
portion of Indiana, which extended west into Illinois country. By the fall of
1802, the governor was content in his role, as were the citizens who petitioned the president to extend Harrison in his position.

The Louisiana Purchase of 1803 added 900,000 square miles to the
United States for the sum of $15 million. The French influence in Indiana
had been strong; many Indians relished their return. French traders positioned
along the Mississippi and Ohio rivers paid out, in advance, gold coin to those
who agreed to future trading rights. The Louisiana Purchase was good for
the United States but another blow to the future enrichment of the tribes
in Illinois. Harrison found that his primary duty was the acquisition of tribal
land through negotiations with gangs of chiefs, many of whom wanted special
treatment on their behalf. Often the "good of the tribal members" came last.

In 1805, the population of Indiana reached the requisite 500,000, and
a second-grade government with a standing house and delegate to Congress
was granted. By popular acclamation, William Henry Harrison remained as
governor. His ardent negotiation with the Indians while keeping the approval of the white citizens was a balancing act at which he was most adept.

Harrison considered himself a frontier diplomat who learned the culture of the Indian tribes and understood their chiefs. He found that Indians were people and were motivated by the same good and bad traits found with the white settlers of the small settlements that were to spring up on former Indian land. While some Indians were true representatives of the tribe intent on getting the best deal for all, others were greedy and only concerned with feathering their own nest. He was becoming expert at separating them out during long, tedious negotiations.

TECUMSEH (SHOOTING STAR)

Tecumseh and his Shawnee brother, "the Prophet," were devoted to driving the white man back into the sea. With British backing, they began a campaign to unite all the tribes, north to south, along the leading edge of the American frontier to seal off their tribal land and exterminate those who tread on their land. It was not an arbitrary movement but rather a real and organized threat to the expansion west. A true warrior, he could not be bought, and he refused to sign the Greenville Treaty, which annexed the Ohio country. Those chiefs who settled with Harrison and sold their land were the enemy of Tecumseh, and he wasted no time in deposing them. After an encounter with Chief Tecumseh, Harrison wrote a worrying phrase, "Where ever he goes he makes an impression favorable to his purpose."[6]

The Prophet, Tenskwatawa, a holyman, claimed contact with the Great Spirit on long solo treks in the forest. He, like his brother, demanded that the native people return to ancient ways and rid themselves of all the white man's trappings. They must join him in the destruction of the invader and no longer negotiate away their heritage.

BACKFIRE

In 1806, the two troublemakers preached their poison in a most convincing manner. Incited, a war party attacked a small missionary station where several white families were converting the Indians to Christianity. Tecumseh's favorite trick was to burn someone until he told the truth. In this case, a disgraced chief who had signed a treaty confessed under distress that the Christians had poisoned his mind and made him sign. A war party raided the tiny church camp and took several men prisoner. The Prophet had them burned alive to cleanse the village of their sins. Tales of the Prophet's powers were strewn about the landscape and spread like a summer wild fire. Harrison knew without looking that the holy man was a fraud and told the Indians to have him perform a miracle. "Have him stop a river from flowing or make the moon change her habit and then you will unmask him as a fraud." The British Indian agent on the border told Tecumseh that on the sixteenth of the month, the earth would shadow the moon. The Prophet called a council of the tribes from far and wide and at exactly the correct moment commanded the moon to go dark. The throng beseeched him to return the light, which he did in due course. The story was told throughout the Indian nations, often precluding a visit by the two brothers. Their power grew.

By the summer of 1807, the brothers were making inroads to Indian village life. Young men gave up planting and prepared to wipe out all vestiges of the white man on their tribal land. Militia Colonel William Wells was sent with two companies of troops to calm the newest uprising. He reported that the British were supporting the movement, and this was alarming the settlers. All along the frontier, Tecumseh's railings were heard and accepted by the young hotbloods of the tribes who had experienced the decline in the prowess of their nation. It was hard to dispute the message of the Prophet, who would have dissenters dismembered or burned alive. Governor William Hull of the Michigan Territory became alarmed by the reports of hostilities along his border with Canada. Harrison agreed and together they asked the federal government for stands of muskets, cartridges, and equipment for their neglected militia. Jefferson wrote a note to Tecumseh to which the Chief replied, "This land is ours, the Great Spirit has appointed this place for us and here we will remain."[7] Jefferson had his hands full at the time with the British blockade of American ports and the incessant kidnapping of seamen. Reports from the west informed Jefferson that the British were inflaming and supplying the tribes. Talking down to Tecumseh like a child, the president told the Indians that they should stay out of the dispute between the two nations and mind their own business. Of course, it only aroused more anger.

1808: ANOTHER TERM

Harrison, his wife, and five children left the center of Vincennes for a place on the Wabash to build a mill and boatyard. Tecumseh moved west and established Prophetstown, where the Wabash and Tippecanoe met. It was situated at the center of Indian tribal villages in north-central Indiana, 200 miles from Vincennes. Harrison worried that it was a power base for a bloody campaign against white man rule. The Prophet was seen in Amherstburg, Canada, courting the British. Tecumseh arrived at the same time as the Canadian governor-general, Sir James Craig, an Anglophile. "The Shawnee war chief had in his hands a great belt of wampum—thousands of small coloured shells sewn together—given to his predecessors by the British after the defeat of the French, a talisman, sacred in Indian eyes, symbolizing a treaty of friendship between the British and the natives."[8] He gave assurances that the king would not abandon them but would protect their interest. He favored an exclusive Indian state, free of white men in the Michigan and Ohio valleys. Such provocation meant that no good could come from this frightening development. Afterward, the Prophet went directly to meet with Harrison and flaunt his newfound ally. Harrison, like many, believed that food, not politics, would calm the tribes.

As June 1810 warmed the peaceful farmland of the Midwest, old friends delivered warnings. Rumors of war plans crept out of Prophetstown. Tecumseh had marked Vincennes and other population centers for massacre. They would arrive as friends and then strike the towns dead. Then proof arrived by way of some French river men who had been assaulted by Tecumseh himself when they tried to deliver casks of salt. If they had been Americans, the boatmen were assured, they would have been killed. The cauldron simmered all that winter.

By the summer of 1811, Tecumseh seemed to have taken over from his brother and was calling the shots. He arrived at the governor's home and set his tent under a large walnut tree. He would not go into the house but insisted that they talk in the open. Several hundred braves who remained a distance away backed him. Perhaps they feared an arrest of the great chief who spoke of violations to the treaty. The governor feared an attack at close quarters. Tecumseh raved on for two days while Harrison listened. Harrison sent word to call up two companies of infantry and a troop of dragoons as a show of force. The next day, Tecumseh complained that a man from the east had come to him and told him that Harrison had lied and that the boundaries were not in place and the money would not be paid. Assured that it was not true and that surveying teams were on the job delineating the treaty, Tecumseh was told that he could depend on Harrison to see that his word was kept. In private, Harrison was aware that the Indians were often cheated, shortchanged, and hoodwinked, but there was little he could do about it. Cartels in the east were always meddling when so much land was up for grabs, and the Indians held no sway in the marbled halls of investment and finance. Tecumseh brought his large party of braves a little closer to the old walnut tree but was cowed by the extent of armed military elements lurking on the grounds of the governor's house. The mounted dragoons, menacing with swords drawn, their long shiny blades reflecting in the sun, moved slightly forward in line. Harrison felt that any moment, violence could erupt. Once again, it was a stalemate. Tecumseh threatened the lives of settlers who encroached on Indian land. Harrison countered, "The moon will fall to earth before the President will suffer his people to be murdered, and he would put his warriors in petticoats before he would give up the land fairly acquired from its rightful owners."[9] Suddenly, with a final flourish of complaints against other tribes and their chiefs, he turned and left.

Tecumseh had bigger plans than just the northwest. In an effort to unite tribes, his vision was wider than Harrison imagined. For the next six months, he and his brother moved south, inciting the tribes of the south as he went. His intent was to council with the chiefs of the Creek Nation in Tennessee, Mississippi, and Alabama. There, he intended to spread his magic and stir up trouble for Andrew Jackson.

Harrison was tired of threats, rumors, and raids. A man of action from his youth, it was time to drop the diplomacy and exert leadership.

THE BATTLE OF TIPPECANOE

The governor had been the referee for several years and had managed to satisfy no one. He knew that Tecumseh was out of the area inciting more mayhem and that his return would be marked with the massacre of some quiet village and the taking of hostages and would mandate an outpouring of grief. Forced to react, the outcome would cause more upheaval, hostilities, and loathing. Tension had been building for years and if Harrison didn't take action, the territory, which was about to bid Congress for statehood, would be looked on as unstable—not yet fit. He had the tools, the militia, and now was the time to strike. Harrison believed the Prophet to be unhinged and not capable of leading his braves in the absence of his brother. Washington was teetering on war with Great Britain and had cautioned the governor about hasty action unless provoked. Harrison had written to Dr. Eustis, Secretary of War, about his concern of being preempted by an attack, something that would devastate the territories' status quo. He told Washington that an attack on Prophetstown would be a demonstration of the determination to back up the "Great Father's" word that peace must be maintained and disputes were to be settled in council.

Harrison proposed a simple, straightforward movement of two regular infantry companies added to 150 more from the 4th U.S. Regiment, fourteen companies of militia, and two troops of mounted dragoons. He invited Colonel Joseph Davies, a comrade from the Northwest Indian War, to commit his Kentucky dragoons to the expedition. Counting on the territory militia, which was keen to eliminate the threat to their farms and families, the total force would be just over a thousand. It meant a flat-bottom-boat pulled up the Wabash River for the infantry while the mounted soldiers stuck to the north bank along the towpath. Above the halfway point north of Terre Haute, the column assembled and spent the next four days building a log fort named after the governor. Once all the troops had trickled in and forage parties scrounged for game, local farmers provided cattle and hogs that would make the march alongside the soldiers. With a two-story log blockhouse disappearing behind them, the little army, devoid of cannons, trudged up the road in good spirits. Harrison had no trouble filling out the ranks of the militia, who thought it was about time the Indians were taught a lesson as to just who was in charge. From time to time, Indians were seen and were shot at to show that the white men meant business. Prophetstown had considerable warning since there was little doubt where the little army was headed. Three days later on November 2 they paused again when they sighted a party of Indians. Once again, they put together a crude log structure and gathered the boats. There were 1,000 men, split between land and water, strung out for several miles. More signs of Indians on November 4 made Harrison cautious, and he carefully crossed the river at a low point. He was concerned that an ambush was set, and he put out experienced scouting parties to probe the countryside and pick the best approach route for the command.

Nearing the town, Chief White Horse came forward with a white flag. Harrison knew him as one of the Prophet's leaders. The chief said that they had been expected and that a delegation had gone down the other side of the river to greet them. Harrison had not seen the party. The governor had set up camp for the evening overlooking the fortified village surrounded by log barriers. It was set on a grassy plain above the marsh and next to a creek several hundred yards from the Indian village.

THE MORNING OF NOVEMBER 7, 1811

That evening, the Prophet sprinkled his fairy dust, shook his rattle, danced his primitive steps, mixed his potion, and proclaimed that the enemy's bullets could not harm the braves when they attacked the white men. Two British officers present convinced Tecumseh's mystic brother to attack before dawn while the soldiers were most vulnerable. Faces painted black, armed with shiny new English tomahawks, they crept and crawled in bands of a dozen or more until they were in position on all sides. While still dark at 4 a.m., a nervous picket felt something brush by in the wet gloom. Moving forward, the braves didn't make a sound until they tipped off a sentry at the sleeping camp. Shocked awake, the soldiers, who had slept next to their loaded and bayoneted muskets, struggling to stand, were bludgeoned to the ground by swing war clubs. Mounted troops were not able to get to their horses but fought hand to hand in the gloom, with campfires providing the only illumination. Dashing silhouetted figures yelled and whooped, swinging tomahawks with deadly fighting force. The camp area was small, with hardly enough room to accommodate the 450 additional bodies that raged from tent to tent killing in the shadows. Under British direction, a band gained the edge of the cantonment, fired in unison, and retreated to load and then repeated the exercise. Kentucky Colonel Davies was killed. Harrison, mounted on a borrowed horse, maintained remarkable composure even though a musket ball had grazed his forehead. A private in the ranks recalled, "The awful yell of the savages seeming rather the shriek of despair . . . the tremendous roar of musquetry—the agonizing screams of the wounded and dying, added to the shouts of the victors, mingling in the tumultuous uproar, formed a scene that can be better imagined than described."[10] Once the element of surprise was exhausted and a glimmer of dawn silhouetted the attacker, Harrison organized a defense that turned into an assault on the village.

The Indian attack stalled and slid off the edges of the American cantonment. Widely separated bands gathered there, wounded, and where they found cover behind the log barriers. The Kentucky dragoons pursued the retreating braves among the log houses, setting fire to a few to drive out the savages. The Indian squaws who had been promised a captured white slave by the Prophet to do their work wailed in despair over their dead braves. The Prophet, not a fighting man, was desecrated and left the village with the retreating war party.

General Harrison rested his troops, buried the dead, and tried valiantly to save the wounded. However, with little medical assistance, many more died from their injuries over the next few days on the road home. In all, the Yankees' loss was nearly fifty dead and three times that wounded. The Indians left thirty-six dead within American lines, and more must be added to the number found in the village and on the retreat. Between 15 and 20 percent of the Prophet's strength of 600 was lost.

It was said that the governor intended to punish the Indians; others said that he intended to curry favor with the citizens of Indiana by standing up to the Indians, whom they feared. Historians differ widely on the efficacy of the expedition. Harrison was both criticized and honored for his bold initiative. It is difficult to find fault when considering the years of aggravation, meddling, external government pressure, moral standards, and intransigence on both sides that were heaped on Harrison's shoulders. I put it down to utter frustration in an effort to balance the needs of the natives with the inevitability of western expansion.

The Shawnee chief Tecumseh, after failing to enlist the Creek Nation in his alliance, turned to the British and never looked back.

SPRING OF 1812

Many saw the advent of war as a chance to end British interference in the territories along the Mississippi. The governors agreed with the war in principle, but were concerned that the militias were poorly equipped and trained to take on a campaign in a wilderness teeming with Indians backed by regiments of Redcoats. They expected the federal government to deploy regular infantry and artillery on their behalf. Most knew that those formations needed in numbers did not exist and could not be ready for the field for many months.

In July, Harrison, watching from Vincennes, thirsted for every bit of war news now that Hull had been launched to invade Canada. Isolated in the remote western states and territories, the skirmish at Tippecanoe was the spark that began the War of 1812. Harrison's militia, along with Senator Henry Clay's noted Kentucky mounted rifles, met in Cincinnati, where militia Major General Harrison assumed command of the combined command intent on relieving Major General Hull at Detroit. Initially, 2,000 assembled, to be joined by an equal number of amateur soldiers toting their own firearms. Sportsmen and hunters flocked to join in the sport. In high spirits, they didn't consider the presence of Redcoats as a threat.

In the late days of August, Harrison received a request from the citizens of Fort Wayne who had been alerted of an attack by a combined Indian and British force. Like Hull during the defense of Detroit, the thought of prowling Indians pillaging around the edge of a disciplined British onslaught brought panic, as it should have. Harrison moved quickly and reached Fort Wayne with 3,000 infantry and dragoons before the enemy could rout the eighty defenders at nearby Maumee. Harrison's large, unorganized force ranged in an arc sixty miles north, burning Indian villages, farms, and crops to deny the approaching British the luxury of living off the land. This frontier war was brutal.

In the meantime regular Major General James Winchester, age sixty—a hero of the Revolutionary War in which he was promoted in the field for gallantry, captured twice, and wounded and participated in the final battle at Yorktown—was appointed to command in Harrison's place. Winchester didn't have the presence of Harrison, a vibrant inspirational man who talked to the troops in their language and led from the front. The troops were unfamiliar with the interloper and made fun of the old man who needed help mounting his horse. The undisciplined part-time soldiers played jokes on the aged general when he went to the latrine, resulting in the embarrassing sight of his uniform drying on the roof of his tent. Even the officers gave the old codger a hard time, which bordered on mutiny. Harrison petitioned Secretary Eustis to refrain from putting a political appointee in command, as this would destroy the discipline and morale he had established. Eustis reneged, subordinating Winchester to second in command of the Army of the Northwest.

At the start of October, Harrison received orders to subdue the Indians, relieve Fort Detroit, and invade Canada. Winchester was given command of the west wing of the army. The old man gallantly buried his pride and vowed to stay on until Amherstburg was taken. Following orders, the army fanned out to ravage the land north of Fort Wayne in two columns while securing food for the long winter and establishing quarters at the Maumee Rapids, where they were joined by a column from eastern Ohio. The supply chain, like the army, was an amateur affair, and the men began to starve as the winter settled upon them. Uniform items lag behind the temperature, and boots don't materialize. Everything was in short supply. Eustis had forgotten how fast an army can go through supplies. A quartermaster system designed to service the Eastern Seaboard failed miserably the farther west it was expected to function.

ZACHARY TAYLOR

Welcome news arrived that Captain Zachary Taylor's tiny company of militia and civilians had successfully defended Fort Harrison from a relentless three-day attack by the Miami and Wea Indians. Zachary Taylor's origin, as so many participants in the War of 1812, went back to Carlisle, England, the border country between Scotland and England. In the mid-1600s, borderers left the British Isles to seek freedom in colonial Virginia. His father, Colonel Richard Taylor, a Revolutionary War soldier, was one of the earliest settlers of Kentucky and played a prominent role in statehood. Growing up on an impressive estate near Louisville, Kentucky, young Zachary was a rough-and-tumble lad who romped in the forest with his brothers always on the lookout for Indians. The last duty before bed was to barricade the doors and check to see that the rifles were primed and ready. Contemporaries described him as "a thick set lad with short legs and a chest like a barrel. His skin was fair, his eyes sharp and gray, frequently twinkling with fun."[11]

Zachary was a good student, according to the family tutor, who later founded a school for the landed children of Louisville. The boy's favorite subject was military history. When Aaron Burr passed by on his way to take over Louisiana, Taylor, like many others, swelled the ranks of the Kentucky militia, fearing a threat to their hard-earned claim. In May 1808, Taylor applied for and was commissioned a first lieutenant in the 7th Regular Regiment. A year later, he was posted to New Orleans, but the assignment in fact was none too fortunate; the commanding officer, General James Wilkinson, was of dubious character. He had taken part in the Conway cabal against Wayne and as a reward he had superseded "Mad Anthony" (Major General Anthony) Wayne. Wilkinson had attempted to ally Kentucky with Spain; he had been implicated in Burr's conspiracy, but had been acquitted in a court-martial.[12] Shortly after arrival, Taylor contracted yellow fever and was sent home to Louisville. That June of 1810, age twenty-six, he married Peggy Mackall Smith, twenty-three, who was visiting from Maryland. Stationed at Fort Pickering near Memphis on the border between Tennessee and the Mississippi Territory, they made their first home. As an independent commander, he was promoted to captain. Patronage was most significant in an officer's life, and Taylor was in the right place at the right time. Two years later, his regiment joined the 4th, assigned to Harrison's Army of the Northwest, which was engaged with Tecumseh. Taylor trailed along behind Harrison when the general attacked Prophetstown. Left behind to maintain Fort Harrison, the intermediate supply point established during the march to Prophetstown, the oak and honey locust structure of the fort was barely 150 square feet. Fifty men, many sick with fever, as was Taylor once again, were marooned there all alone. The tiny fort's only hope of surviving an attack was its elevation above a sharp bend in the Wabash River. The second story protruded out, giving a view of the stockade walls. There was a log guardhouse over the gate that provided coverage of the four-foot ditch beyond the outer walls.

One evening, soldiers reported hearing shots, and the next morning Taylor was told that a war party had murdered several close-by farmers. A patrol found the bodies and brought them to the fort for burial. Taylor dispatched a report to Harrison on September 10 concerning the incident and said that he had been alerted to the Prophet's intention to attack the fort.

The operational report of Captain Taylor read,

> Late on the evening of the fourth instant old John Lenar and between thirty and forty Indians arrived from Prophet's town with a white flag, among them about ten women, and the men chiefs of the different tribes that compose the Prophet's party. A Shawanoe man who spoke good English informed me that Old Lenar intended to speak to me next morning and try to get something to eat. At retreat, beating, I examined the men's arms and found them all in good order, and completed their cartridges to sixteen rounds per man. . . . For some time past, as I had just recovered from a very severe attack of the fever, I was not able to be up much throughout the night. After tattoo I cautioned the guard to be

vigilant, and ordered one of the non-commissioned officers, as the sentinels could not see every part to prevent the Indians taking any advantage
of us, provided they had any intention of attacking us. About eleven
o'clock I was awakened by the firing of one of the sentinels. I sprang up,
ran out, and ordered the men to their posts. My orderly sergeant, who
had charged of the upper blockhouse, called out that the Indians had
fired the lower blockhouse. . . . The guns had begun to fire pretty smartly
from both side.

I directed the buckets to be got ready, and water brought from the
well, and the fire extinguished; but, from debility or some other cause,
the men were very slow in executing my orders. The word 'fire' appeared
to throw the whole of them into confusion; and by the time they had
got the water and broken open the door the fire had communicated
to a quantity of whisky (the stock having licked several stored there),
though the Indians had introduced the fire without being discovered,
as the night was very dark; and in spite of every exertion we could not
extinguish it.

As the blockhouse adjoined the barracks which made part of the
fortifications, most of the men immediately gave themselves up for
lost, and I had the greatest difficulty in getting my orders executed; and
sir, what from the raging of the fire, and yelling and howling of several
hundred Indians, the cries of nine women and children (a part of them
soldiers' and a part citizens' wives, who had taken shelter in the fort),
and the desponding of so many of the men, which was worse than all, I
can assure you that my feelings were very unpleasant; and, indeed, there
were not more than ten or fifteen men able to do a great deal, the others
being either sick or convalescent; and to add to our other misfortunes,
two of the stoutest men in the fort that I had every confidence in, jumped
the picket and left us.

But my presence of mind did not desert me, I saw that, by throwing
off part of the roof that joined the blockhouse which was on fire, and
keeping the end perfectly wet, the whole row of buildings might be save,
and leave only an entrance of eighteen or twenty feet for the Indians to
enter after the house was consumed; and that a temporary breastwork
might be erected to prevent their entering even there. I convinced them
that this could be accomplished, and it appeared to inspire them with
new life; never did me act with more firmness or desperation. Those that
were able mounted the roofs of the houses with Dr. Clark at their head
under a shower of bullets, and in less than a moment threw off as much
of the roof as was necessary.

This was done with only the loss of one man killed and two wounded,
and I am in hope neither of them dangerous; the man who was killed was
a little deranged, and did not get off the house as soon as directed, or he
would not have been hurt. Although the barracks were several times in a
blaze, and an immense quantity of fire against them, the men used such

exertion that they kept it under, and before day they raised a temporary breastwork as high as a man's head, although the Indians continued to pour in a heavy fire of ball and an innumerable quantity of arrow during the whole time the attack lasted, in every part of the parade.

I had but one other man killed, nor any other wounded inside the fort, and he lost his life by being too anxious; he got into one of the galleries in the bastions and fired over the pickets, and called out to his companions that he had killed an Indian, and neglecting to stoop down, in an instant he was shot dead.

One of the men that jumped the pickets returned an hour before day and, running toward the gate, begged for God's sake for it to be opened. I suspected it to be a stratagem of the Indians to get in, as I did not recognize the voice: I directed the men in the bastion where I happened to be to shoot him, let him be who he would; and one of them fired at him, but fortunately he ran up to the other bastion, were they knew his voice, and Dr. Clark directed him to lie down behind an empty barrel that happened to be there, and at daylight I had him let in. His arm was broken in a most shocking manner, which he says was down to the Indians; I suppose that was the cause of his returning; I think it probable that he will not recover. The other they caught about one hundred and thirty yards from the garrison and cut him all to pieces.

After keeping up a constant fire until about six o'clock the next morning, which we began to return with some effect, after daylight they moved out of reach of our guns. A party of them drove up horses that belonged to the citizens here, and as they could not catch them very readily, shot the whole of them in our sight, as well as a number of their hogs. They drove off the whole of the cattle, which amounted to sixty-five head, as well as the public oxen.

I had the vacancy (in the wall) filled up before night with a strong row of pickets, which I got by pulling down the guardhouse. We lost the whole of our provisions, and must make out to live on green corn until we can get a supply, which I am in hopes will not be long. I believe the whole of the Miamis or Weas were among the Prophet's party, as one chief gave his orders in that language. It resembled Stone Eater's voice, and I believe that Negro leg was there likewise. A Frenchman here understands their languages and several of the Miamis or Weas, that have been frequently here were recognized by the Frenchman and soldiers the next morning.

The Indians suffered smartly, but were so numerous as to take off nearly all that were shot. They continued with us until the next morning, but made no further attempt on the fort, nor have we seen anything of them since. I have delayed informing you of my situation as I did not like to weaken the garrison, and I looked for some person from Vincennes' none of my men were acquainted with the woods, and therefore would either have to take the road or the river, which I was fearful was guarded by small parties of Indians that would not dare to attack a company of rangers on scout; but, being disappointed, I have at length determined to send a couple of my men by water, and am in hopes they will arrive safe.[13]

The Indians lurked in the surrounding woods, preventing the men, women, and children in the fort from foraging for food. Their stock was nearly gone. The orderly sergeant was dispatched to Vincennes for help. Six long days passed, and the survivors were getting desperate. They knew for certain that their man had not gotten through and contemplated death at the hands of the savages. Women thought of how they would kill their children and themselves. Then a column of 1,200 militia arrived with a bang, scaring away the braves in short order. Zachary Taylor must have surely earned his nickname at Fort Harrison long before they called him "Rough and Ready" later during the Mexican War. The president promoted Taylor to brevet major—without an increase in pay.

HEADQUARTERS KNOWS BEST

Harrison's army was stuck in the mud for the winter, short of rations and low on morale. November found the sodden roads in northern Ohio impassable for artillery and supply wagons. The enemy faced the same conditions returning to Amherstburg to wait for spring. Harrison wanted to send the majority of the militia home for the winter to save supplies, but General Dearborn's plan had suffered another setback. Major General Stephen Van Rensselaer's attempt to take Queenston was a disaster. His regular force was captured, and the main body of the New York militia refused to fight. Eustis directed Harrison to keep his force intact even though his boats were frozen fast and he couldn't reach the Maumee Rapids with his whole army.

Winter Misery

The following is taken from the journal of Private Elias Darnell, Christmas Eve 1812:

> Obstacles had emerged in the path of victory, which must have speared insurmountable to every person endowed with common sense. The distance to Canada, the unpreparedness of the army, the scarcity of provisions, and the remaining part of our time. . . . Our suffering at this place have been greater than if we had been in accommodation! The sufferings of about three hundred sick at a time, who were exposed to the cold

ground, and deprived of every nourishment, are sufficient proofs of our wretched condition! The camp has become a loathsome place.¹⁴

General Winchester spent three months idle before he received two days' rations and clothing and orders to join the army near Maumee Rapids. On Christmas, the weather turned to cold and snow. His command stepped off, but the going was terrible. The column could be easily confused with Napoleon's retreat from Moscow the previous year. On the third miserable day, the general received counter orders to return to his station. Word came that Indians under Tecumseh were pursuing them. But the old campaigner had enough and pressed on in complete disregard of his orders. If his command was to survive, it must close with the main body and not be left to freeze. It was not until January 11, 1813, that Winchester arrived with his miserable frostbitten army wing, eighteen days on the trail without an Indian in sight. Harrison's intelligence machine was absolutely broken.

Harrison's and Hull's campaigning had not only inflamed the Indians but also provided every frontier citizen with a license to kill Indians wherever they found them. Indians were shot on sight, and raiding parties of young braves rampaged from farm to farm, killing and burning at random; no one was safe, not even children, on either side.

FRENCHTOWN AND THE RAISIN RIVER

Enjoying a well-deserved rest at Maumee Rapids, General Winchester's arm of the Army of the Northwest camped sixty miles north of the main body of Harrison's winter encampment. Surprisingly, he found that his officers were restless. They obsessed over reports that Frenchtown, a dot on the banks of the Raisin River, was occupied by a handful of Canadian militia and Indians. A proper village with warm houses and plentiful food was the main attraction to men who had slept on the ground and had been huddled around open campfires for the past two months. Goaded into action, Winchester sent two messages. The first was to militia General Perkins, near Sandusky, for reinforcements, and the second was to his boss, General Harrison, informing him of his intention to take independent action. Alarmed, Harrison denied the proposal, but the messenger found that Winchester's command had marched for Frenchtown. Informed days later that his order was not acknowledged, Harrison pursued through a winter storm followed by two regiments and artillery that struggled through the snow. On horseback, Harrison abandoned the march and went on ahead alone.

Meanwhile, Winchester sent an attack force forward under Lieutenant Colonel William Lewis with 450 infantry followed the next day, January 18, by 100 more infantry. Together, Lewis formed his line on the slippery river ice and led them across and up the bank into the village. The two sides clashed in the streets of the little town, scrapping for three hours. The Canadians slowly contracted as they were pushed out of town two miles into the forest. On January 20 Winchester arrived with the bulk of the command and partook in the good food and gracious hospitality. While Winchester sorted his units between the good quarters and improved living conditions inside the homes of the villagers, Harrison sent word that he was a few days behind with the army.

Only eighteen miles north, the British were preparing a counterattack. Winchester heard news of an approaching British force, but for the first time in several months, he and his men were comfortable and didn't put any stock in the reports. They believed that the British didn't fight in the winter. It was another case of amateurs playing soldiers, risking his force while recalling the comforts of plantation living. Besides, Harrison was on his way. A rampart of pointed logs that formed a breastwork protected three sides of the village. His regulars were not in position but were stuck out on the right flank. Their commander demanded his prerogative when formed with militia. (In formation, the regular army was always on the right of the formation as the premier unit.) It was an extremely cold night. Soldiers were reluctant to leave the barracks in the freezing night air. They didn't believe that the enemy that they had chased into the woods could mount a counterattack at night.

Hell in the Night

At 4 a.m., when all the Americans were safe and warm in quarters, the three British 3-pounders and three small howitzers that were mounted on skids opened up with a roar to announce the attack of 600 Redcoats and 500 Indians. "American militiaman, Private Frederic Rolette, was struck in the head by a musket ball. The tightly rolled silk bandanna saved his life. The ball was caught in the fold and flattened against his skull, increasing his headache and causing a goose egg but no further damage."[15] Chaos, shock, regret, and fear gripped the Americans as they tumbled out into the black lanes, running half-dressed, gripping unloaded muskets with cartridge boxes dangling over one shoulder. Neglectful officers searched for their men, who had been scattered haphazardly throughout the houses. Sergeants grabbed passersby enlisting them into small groups before running to the log barricade in the direction of the enemy attack. The British were in control, sending mounted Indians around the flanks while they dominated the center, breaching the nearly undefended log obstruction. The militia congregated in the center of town while the 17th Regiment of Regulars was pushed off the flank and dashed for the riverbank. Half-dressed, Winchester and his two battalion commanders, who shared his quarters, separated in the street. The general seized a horse and retreated to the river, where the press of the Indians denied him a moment to stop and make a stand. Many men, without weapons, ran across the ice only yards ahead of the screaming braves, playing the game they loved the most. They clubbed, chopped, and scalped, the soldiers turning the snow red. The savages stopped just long enough to scalp and tuck the blood-dripping hair into their belts before taking up the foot race once again. Fleet on horseback, small bands of braves got ahead of the fleeing troops and ambushed them from behind when they tried to stop and form a defense. When one squad was caught, they were ordered to ground their arms and surrender. Resigned, a soldier knew his fate: "Dam you—tomahawk me, it is all you can do."[16] The Indians moved in on the praying Christians and tomahawked the lot and scalped the dying soldiers. An Indian chief captured General Winchester, taking his uniform coat for himself, and led him to British Colonel Henry Procter outside the village. There, the general was informed that a small band of militia had managed to erect a stronghold in the town, and Procter felt that it was best for all concerned that the fighting stop and the remaining Americans surrender. Winchester, after some convincing, agreed, and a flag of truce was offered to Kentuckian Major George Madison. The terms were generous since capitulation to the British meant humane treatment. Madison knew that the Indians would be sent in to murder his men if he resisted. The battle for the Raisin River and Frenchtown was a complete victory brought about as a result of the irresponsible command of an old political hack. Only thirty-three of Winchester's men made it to Harrison. All the others were either killed or taken prisoner.

1813: WINTER QUARTERS

In 1813, one thing had gone Harrison's way. The secretary of the navy's interest in Lake Erie could secure his watery right flank and hinder the military support provided the British force at Amherstburg on the Thames River across from Detroit. Harrison's mission remained the same: "restore Detroit, invade Canada and secure the Michigan." In the west, the people were dumbfounded by the disaster at Frenchtown. Men wore black armbands, and women donned widow weeds to church on Sunday. Anger grew along with the grief and was accompanied by thoughts of revenge against the Indians. Horror stories of the monstrous deaths suffered by their defenseless soldiers abounded. Slogans were chanted under the breath: "The only good Indian is a dead Indian" and "Remember the Raisin."

The new Secretary of War, John Armstrong, was taking the recruiting, training, equipping, and fielding of the regular army seriously. Expecting to have nearly 17,000 regulars under arms by the summer of 1813, he increased Harrison's Army of the Northwest from three regiments to six. To the 17, 19, and 24, the 26, 27, and 28 were added, but because of the losses suffered on the last campaign, the first three numbered elements contained only a couple hundred soldiers. Those remaining were mere shells, sick and broken. There was few fit to construct the ramparts of Fort Meigs at Maumee Rapids. Harrison was unable to move forward and finish the mission. The militia from surrounding states and territories had melted away during the winter, leaving the regulars to secure Fort Meigs. Harrison traveled to Cincinnati since the wet spring prevented Procter from any offensive action. Additionally, Harrison had heard that Colonel Procter was not in much better shape, but he had a considerable number of healthy Indians to back him. Procter's Indians were barely under control and might or might not follow orders. He sought the assistance of Tecumseh, who had arrived just before the battle of Frenchtown.

BATTLE FOR FORT MEIGS

In early April 1813, Harrison got word that Procter was preparing to attack Fort Meigs on the Maumee River. He marched out of Cincinnati with 300 troops and a brigade of Kentucky militia close behind. Crossing the end of the lake with the assistance of the Provincial Marine, Procter led a considerable force consisting of 500 regulars, 450 Canadian militia, and 1,500 of Tecumseh's Indians. Embarked were two 24-pounders taken from Detroit, several small dismounted field guns, and a brace of gunboats each carrying a 9-pounder. Protected by the infantry, it took several days of backbreaking work to drag the 2,000 pound 24-pounders into position. On May 1, 1813, the American garrison of 1,100 was secure inside the log and dirt fort on high ground above the river, a position that dominated the surrounding terrain. Harrison got a messenger through the British lines directing Kentucky's Brigadier General Green Clay to split his 1,500 militia, sending one by boat to attack the heavy guns from the rear and the other to break through the Indian formation and enter the fort.[17] Tecumseh's Indians were fixed on the fort and failed to protect the river attack. When the Kentuckians appeared behind the Indians, they broke and were chased into the woods. With revenge in their hearts for the slaughter, Tecumseh's braves reaped what they had sewn—Indian scalps were taken by the white militia. Tecumseh's Indians reassembled at the rear of the British position where American prisoners were corralled. They stole away the Americans from the prison stockade and dragged them to the head of a gauntlet. The savages ran the American prisoners through the double line of murderous braves, who clubbed them to death before the Shawnee chief could stop them. The war in the west was the most brutal, foretelling the plight of settlers moving beyond the Mississippi in a few years to come. The fort held firm, and after two days of sniping, the Indians, who were weary of the fun, slipped away, taking as much food as they could carry back to their families. The Canadian militia pleaded to return home for the spring planting. Their growing season was short, and if they didn't get the crops in the ground, there would be no harvest.

THE END IS NEAR

General Harrison had breathing room now that Procter was back in Canada and moved to Cleveland, Ohio, close to Erie, Pennsylvania, where the U.S. Navy was constructing a boatyard. While Harrison was building back his regular army strength, he saw the value of the fleet that Commander Oliver Hazard Perry was constructing that spring. The general realized that General Hull was hampered by the lack of naval support. Procter was depending on a strong Provincial Marine to protect Canada from invasion. While he was away, a supply storage site was constructed near the Upper Sandusky called Fort Stephenson. There he stockpiled food, clothing, powder, and shot for his coming campaign to invade Canada.

In July, in the absence of Harrison, Tecumseh convinced Procter to attack Fort Meigs. The rather complicated plan called for the Canadian force to stage a mock battle in the woods a mile away. General Clay was supposed to be tricked into coming to the aid of some American column trapped a short distance away and weaken his defense by sending a relief force that would be ambushed and then, with the fort poorly defended and Clay off balance, attack the fort. This had been done successfully in the past by the Indians on a small scale, but Clay didn't bite, and the whole expensive operation returned to Amherstburg with egg on their faces. Procter would never listen to Tecumseh again.

Procter, if nothing else, was tenacious. In early August, he tried again to push Harrison back away from the Canadian border. Loaded once more on a Provincial Marine transport, he landed at the Upper Sandusky and attacked Fort Stephenson intent on destroying the American supplies stockpiled for the invasion at Fort Malden, the key to Canada at Amherstburg. For two days, Major George Croghan, in command of 160 regulars, held out even though he had been ordered to abandon and burn the fort and supplies in the face of the coming attack. Croghan refused to relinquish his command and remained to fight. The log-and-mud walls were too strong for the 6-pounder that was pulled by the gunners up to within range of the ramparts. It was another misstep for Procter and Tecumseh.

PREPARATION FOR THE FINAL BLOW

Harrison was worried when the 6,000 regulars turned out to be only half that promised by Armstrong. Turning to Kentucky once more, Governor Isaac Shelby provided 3,000 militia, which was a thousand more than Harrison requested. The citizens of Kentucky were the most militant of all the frontier states in the northwest. The Pennsylvanian militia, called on for Harrison's campaign, refused to fight outside their home state. Armstrong pulled Johnson's regiment off their regular patch to reinforce Harrison's strike. Everyone involved felt that Procter was weaker than ever after two failed forays that netted him nothing but exhaustion and diminished war supplies. It was known that the Indians were eating him out of house and home since he fed not only the braves but their extended families as well. Foodstuffs had been a constant problem for the Canadian defense across the entire nation's border. The majority of meat and grains were bought for gold coin from American smugglers. At the end of 1813, Governor General Prevost would publicly thank the Americans for feeding his entire army.

At first, Perry and Harrison had planned an amphibious assault at Fort Malden. That meant that Perry would have to fight for control of the lake while transporting the army. Wisely, after a conference with the two leaders and their staffs, it was decided that Perry should lure the Provincial Marine out into the lake with a ruse of an all-out attack and lie in wait for the enemy fleet in the conduct of a purely naval engagement. On September 10, 1813, a ferocious lake battle took place near Put-in-Bay near the western end of Lake Erie. At the conclusion, Perry sent Harrison the welcome message: "We have met the enemy and they are ours."

Harrison, more than ready, asked Perry to begin to ferry his army in stages toward the Canadian coast. On September 27, the first stage of 4,500 troops landed unopposed in Canada just three miles south of Fort Malden. The securing of Lake Erie proved the secretary of the navy right and Commodore Chauncey on Lake Ontario wrong. The British could not sustain operations west of Kingston at Detroit or the Niagara peninsula without control of Lake Erie. Supplies in the harsh northern climate needed on a

President James Madison, fourth President of the United States. A great mind but no commander-in-chief; he was prodded into war by Jefferson and the War Hawks. Print from engraving, courtesy of the Navy Art Collection, Naval History and Heritage Command.

Secretary of War John Armstrong was appointed because of his military background in the Revolutionary War and service in Europe as an observer in the wars of Napoleon. The trust was misplaced. He directed a campaign lead by a sycophant, which he abandoned before it began. His assessment of the British intensions at Plattsburgh and the Chesapeake Bay bordered on bad judgment and military incompetence. By John Wesley Jarvis, Oil on wood, © 1812, stretcher: 76.2 cm x 61cm (30 in. x 24 in.), National Portrait Gallery, Smithsonian Institution.

William Hull, politically appointed governor of the territory of Michigan and militia major general, was selected to be the first leader to invade Canada in July 1812. He had no military association since his service during the Revolutionary War, which he proved at the surrender of Fort Detroit. Engraved by P. T. Stuart after painting by Gilbert Stuart, one print from engraving, courtesy of the Library of Congress, LC-USZ62-70643.

Her first action in the War of 1812, USS *Constitution*, nearly becalmed with studding sails out, is rowed out of danger at sea, pursued by the Royal Navy flotilla, July 1812 off the coast of New England (US Navy Historical Center)—05.USS Const-Royal.tif. By J. Font Mahan, oil painting on copper, © 1841, courtesy of the Navy Art Collection, Naval History and Heritage Command.

Sailing captains of men-of-war chose to ram and board their opponent, subdue the crew, and take the vessel to be sold in prize ports. The victorious crew shared the spoils when the fighting was over. By Carlton T. Chapman, print from photograve, courtesy of the Navy Art Collection, Naval History and Heritage Command.

The first engagement of an American frigate, USS *Constitution*, with a Royal Navy frigate, HMS *Guerriere*. Until this engagement, the British believed that their war ships were superior to the Yankee navy. By John Trumbull, oil painting on canvas, courtesy of the Navy Art Collection, Naval History and Heritage Command.

HMS *Java* attacked the USS *Constitution* off the coast of Brazil, believing she was a smaller frigate. The *Java* was blasted to utter destruction and her battered crew rescued. By Anton Otto Fiscer, oil painting on canvas, © 1960, courtesy of the Navy Art Collection, Naval History and Heritage Command.

Andrew Jackson's close family members were killed by Indians. As a boy prisoner in the Revolutionary War, he received a malicious wound from a British officer. Jackson grew into a renowned Indian fighter and destroyer of everything British. Painted by Thomas Sully; engraved by James B. Longacre, © 1820, one print from engraving, courtesy of the Library of Congress, LC-USZ62-435.

A youthful Tennessean, Davy Crockett joined Andrew Jackson in his struggle to subdue the rebellious Red Sticks and bring calm to the territory. Courtesy of the Library of Congress, LC-USZ62-21489.

The Battle of New Orleans is famous for being fought after the Treaty of Ghent was signed on Christmas Eve 1814. Due to the sluggish dissemination of information, the participants were unaware of the settlement on the day of the battle, January 8, 1815. By Hyacinthe Laclotte, © 1840, print from lithograph, courtesy of the Navy Art Collection, Naval History and Heritage Command.

A widely disseminated print of the naval heroes of the War of 1812; it was seen as victory over the almighty kingdom of Britain and hung in many parlors across the young nation. As people moved west, they named many a town, village, county, and child for these men. Oliver Hazard Perry tops the list. By Nathan Currier, lithograph, © 1846, courtesy of the Navy Art Collection, Naval History and Heritage Command.

Commodore Isaac Chauncey, best known for his shipbuilding ability, commanded the Great Lakes fleet. While he remained overly concerned with Lake Ontario, Chauncey competed with his subordinate Oliver Hazard Perry on Lake Erie over supplies, crews, and command structure. Joseph Wood, artist; David Edwin, engraver, print from stipple engraving, © 1814, courtesy of the Navy Art Collection, Naval History and Heritage Command.

William Henry Harrison was a professional soldier who turned politician and was appointed to several positions by the serving administration culminating in the Governorship of Indiana. His thrust at the Indian population at the Battle of Tippecanoe elevated him higher in the party. He prided himself on his knowledge of Indian culture and dominance over Chief Tecumseh. By Rembrandt Peale, oil on canvas, © 1813, stretcher: 72.4 cm x 60.3 cm x 2.5 cm (28½" x 23¾" x 1"), National Portrait Gallery, Smithsonian Institution; gift of Mrs. Herbert Lee Pratt Jr.

The premature battle of the War of 1812, November 7, 1811, was designed by William Henry Harrison to preempt an Indian uprising, but only exacerbated the state of affairs. It is difficult to tell who was the winner. Courtesy of the Navy Art Collection, Naval History and Heritage Command.

Zachary Taylor shown here during the Mexican War. As a young regular army captain, he commanded a slapped-together log fort against a Tecumseh-inspired raiding party of well-armed Indians. The odds were horrific, but Taylor managed to save the fort and its inhabitants. Drawn by S. Wallin; engraved by Wm. and J. T. Howland, one print from engraving, image 50.8 cm x 36.2 cm, courtesy of the Library of Congress, LC-DIG-pga-03849.

daily basis by the troops were the determining factor for the defense of Upper Canada.

Procter, with his tail between his legs, under orders from Montreal, had pulled out and headed east on foot for a long march to Lake Ontario, where he expected to be picked up by the Northwest Company's Voyageurs' canoes. He took his troops, rations, wagons, artillery, families, and cattle herd with him, leaving the Indians an empty fort. Procter moved on a road along the Thames River that supported his supplies in a trail of flat-bottomed boats since the road was fit only for dismounted troops. Tecumseh was outraged by the British resolve and saw his nation once more abandoned by fickle British promises. He tried to talk Procter into stopping to fight and finally convinced him that if he didn't, Johnson's mounted infantry, which was snapping at his heels, would overwhelm his column, which was in extended order. Behind Johnson was Harrison, plodding along with 3,500 infantry, dragging their supplies up the ragged road.

On October 5, 1813, near Moraviantown, on the banks of the Thames River, battle was joined. Procter, who had been at the head of the retreat with his wife and children, returned to establish a defensive position between the river and a swamp. He put the 41st Redcoats between the river and the road with the support of one 6-pounder. On the right, Tecumseh's Indians, eager to fight since this was their native land, bunched up in the trees. It took all day for Harrison to come up and join Johnson's Kentucky mounted rifles. Harrison clearly outnumbered the British force two to one. He looked at the thin red line and assumed that there was a considerable number of Indians in the woods. His dragoons alerted him to the swamp, a trap for his exhausted troops. Johnson, who had been pressing the enemy for days on that solitary road, interrupted his plans. Johnson suggested that his mounted force could smash the line with a frontal charge. Harrison, unfamiliar with such open-field tactics, doubted that it could be done alone with horsemen but agreed. Johnson took one battalion straight at the gun and the other against the Indians to the left into the woods, where the troopers would dismount and fight from tree to tree. The action against the 41st had immediate success. The cannons never got off a single shot, the red line crumbled, and a large portion was captured. In the trees, the Indians fell back. James Johnson, son of the commander, believed that he shot and killed Tecumseh. In less than a half an hour, it was all over. Those British who were not wounded, dead, or captured ran east. Harrison did not pursue but was content that his force had accomplished his mission at last. Detroit was his and would remain his. There was no British, Canadian, or Indian force capable of threatening the western migration of the American settlers.

CHRONOLOGY: WILLIAM HENRY HARRISON

1773, April 4	Born at Berkeley Plantation, Virginia, to Benjamin Harrison V
1790, June	Entered the University of Pennsylvania
1791	Commissioned an ensign in the 11th Infantry, regular army
1792, July	Promoted to lieutenant
1793	Aide-de-camp to commanding general during the Northwest Indian War
1794	Fought at the Battle of Fallen Timbers
1795	Treaty of Greenville, opening up the Ohio
1797	Secretary of the Northwest Territory, acting governor
1799, March	Northwest Territory delegate to the U.S. Congress
1800	Governor of the Indiana Territory
1803	Negotiated treaties with the Indians
1804	Treaty of St. Louis
1805	Treaty of Grouseland
1809	Treaty of Fort Wayne
1810	Chief Tecumseh begins an Indian uprising
1811, November 6	Militia General Harrison fights the Battle of Tippecanoe
1812, September 17	Regular Major General Harrison takes command of the Army of the Northwest
1812–1813, winter	Establishes Fort Meigs
1813	Conducts a campaign through Indiana and Ohio before retaking Detroit and invading Canada
1813, October 5	Wins the Battle of the Thames and kills Chief Tecumseh

NOTES

1. His exuberance and fiery presence on the battlefield gave him the nickname "Mad," but he was a brilliant commander, legislator, negotiator, and long-serving patriot.

2. Brevet promotion allows the officer to wear the rank and assume the higher duties but not the pay.

3. Freeman Cleaves, *Old Tippecanoe: William Henry Harrison and His Time* (Newtown, CT: American Political Biography Press, 1939), 17.

4. Cleaves, *Old Tippecanoe*, 34.

5. Cleaves, *Old Tippecanoe*, 36.

6. Cleaves, *Old Tippecanoe*, 53.

7. Cleaves, *Old Tippecanoe*, 58.

8. Pierre Berton, *The Invasion of Canada 1812–1813* (Toronto: Anchor Canada, 1980), 63.

9. Berton, *The Invasion of Canada 1812–1813*, 68.

10. Cleaves, *Old Tippecanoe*, 102.

11. Silas B. McKinley and Silas Bent, *Old Rough and Ready: The Life and Times of Zachary Taylor* (New York: Vanguard Press, 1946), 32.

12. McKinley and Bent, *Old Rough and Ready*, 35.

13. McKinley and Bent, *Old Rough and Ready*, 38.

14. Berton, *The Invasion of Canada 1812–1813*, 280.

15. Berton, *The Invasion of Canada 1812–1813*, 294.

16. Cleaves, *Old Tippecanoe*.

17. John Elting, *Amateurs to Arms: A Military History of the War of 1812* (Chapel Hill, NC: Algonquin Books, 1991), 105.

5

HENRY DEARBORN, JACOB BROWN, AND WINFIELD SCOTT

You have all heard of Father Dearborn, what is your conception of him?
Chicago school children answered: *He was one of our early settlers named for Fort Dearborn*. Another answered: *He ran a big department store near Fort Dearborn in the first ward.*

—*Chicago Tribune*

HENRY DEARBORN

IT ISN'T surprising that Henry Dearborn never saw Chicago or ran a department store. Unlike most of the commanders in the War of 1812, he was nearly a professional soldier. Born in New Hampshire in 1751, he studied medicine and was the local doctor in Nottingham in 1776, when he and his fellow townsmen heard of the first shot fired at Concord Bridge. He formed a company and marched the fifty-five miles that very day. Returning the following day, there was nothing to do since the British had withdrawn to Boston; he was elected captain in New Hampshire's militia regiment. Soon, he marched at the head of his company to Boston, where he saw action for the first time at the Battle of Bunker Hill. On that hallowed ground, he served with Captain James Wilkinson, and a partnership began that would last into the War of 1812. Dearborn fought his way from the coast of Maine to Quebec on a horrendous wilderness trek up the Kennebec River in the early winter of 1775 only to fall ill with fever on the way. Rejoining his company in time to fight, Dearborn was captured and became an early prisoner of war and feared that he would be sent to England and hanged. Paroled in May 1776, he returned home, was promoted to major, and helped form the 3rd

New Hampshire Regiment, which marched to Ticonderoga and Saratoga in May 1777. On the day of the victory, he wrote in his diary, "On this Day has been fought one of the Greatest Battles that ever was fought in America, & I Trust we have convinced the British Butchers that the Cowardly yankee Can, and when there is a Call for it, will, fight."[1] It's easy to see the hatred that was spawned during the long Revolutionary War on the soul of the young doctor and that would spill over once again in old age. He endured the terrible starvation of the winter of 1778 at Valley Forge with Washington, and in the spring he was prominent at the Battle of Monmouth, New Jersey. Dearborn was present at Yorktown when Cornwallis surrendered in 1781. At the time of the signing of the Treaty of Paris in the spring of 1783, Colonel Dearborn returned home to his wife Dorcas, his beautiful daughter Julia, and his son Henry after eight years of honorable service in the front lines. A most human man who lived the same life as his beleaguered soldiers, he wrote, "I ate part of a fried rattle snake today, which would have tasted very well, if it hadn't been snake."[2]

The Dearborn settled in Pittston on the Kennebec River in the territory of Maine. When Washington became president, he designated Dearborn as U.S. marshal for the District of Maine. Massachusetts promoted him to militia major general, and in 1792 he was elected to Congress. In 1801, Jefferson appointed him to his cabinet as Secretary of War. General Reid said of him, "He is a noble fellow, there is no man I esteem and love more, and if Jefferson had always made as good appointments as Dearborn to the War Office, I should think much better of him than I now do."[3] In 1795, Major General "Mad" Anthony Wayne, after the victory at Fallen Timbers, signed a land acquisition treaty that gave the United States the major portion of the Ohio Valley and certain selected tracks in the west. One of those was a six-square-mile portion at the mouth of the Chicago River that emptied into Lake Michigan—an ideal location for a trading post and fort. The following instructions were given to the military officer resident on the Detroit River across the Michigan Territory from Chicago:

> The officer of the Secretary of War   March 9, 1803
> To: Colonel John Hamtramck,
> Commanding Officer, Fort Detroit
> Sir, Send a suitable officer, six men and one or two guides across the
> country to the mouth of St. Joseph's at the mouth of Lake Michi-
> gan and thence to Chikcago to examine the situation with the view
> of establishing a post. . . . If it should be found that a company with
> pack horses can march with light baggage and such provisions as may
> be necessary, a company under a judicious Captain to take post. Two

field pieces and a quantity of ammunition should be sent by water . . . barracks and strong stockade should be erected.

Signed

Thomas H. Cushing
Adjutant General[4]

So it was done. Cushing, as was the custom, named the fort after the Secretary of War: Fort Dearborn.

The Burr Affair

In 1805, former Vice President Aaron Burr, who had killed Alexander Hamilton in an "Affair of Honor," was on the move. On his way to usurp the land named in the Louisiana Purchase and split if off as a country under his despotic rule, he called on Andrew Jackson at Nashville, Tennessee. Using his close acquaintance with Secretary Dearborn, he intimated that his mission had the approval of Dearborn, his old comrade. Jackson gave tacit approval to Burr's plot, thinking that it was part of national policy. A year later, with the arrival of Captain Fort, a Burr agent, he learned the real purpose and notified Dearborn of the affair that Burr and Major General Wilkinson were cooking up with the Spanish. With the heat on, Wilkinson tried to distance himself and abandon Burr in a letter to Jefferson, who exposed the plot in the newspapers on November 16, 1806. Even though Jackson had notified Washington of the attempt to steal Louisiana, his name was blackened in the capital. Dearborn, playing dumb in an effort to distance himself, wrote to Jackson,

> You have been among the opposers of any such unlawful expedition, as appears to have been initiated, by a set of disappointed, unprincipled, ambitious or misguided individuals, and that you will continue to make every exertion in your power, as a General of the Militia, to counteract and render abhortive, and such expedition. At Pittsburgh it is industriously reported among the adventurers, that they are to be joined, at the mouth of the Cumberland, by two regiments under the command of General Jackson—such a story might afford you an opportunity of giving an effectual check to the enterprise if it is not too late.[5]

Jackson was livid, as he often was with any communication from Dearborn or Jefferson:

> The first duty of a soldier or citizen is to attend to the safety and interest of his country. The next is to attend to his own feeling where ever are

rudely or wantonly assailed. The Tenor of your letter is such and the in-
sinuations so grating—The ideas and tenor so unmilitary, stories alluded
to, and intimations, of conduct, to stoop, from the character of a general
to a smiling assassin.

Jackson's draft of the letter went on to discuss the character of Wilkinson
and concluded with the following, "Colo B (Burr) received at my home all
the hospitality that a banished patriot . . . was entitled to. . . . But sir when
proof shews him to be a traitor, I would cut his throat with as much pleasure
as I would cut yours on equal testimony."[6]

As a rule, if Jackson had been within traveling distance of Dearborn, he
would have put a ball between his eyes in a duel. Jackson stewed over the accusation that he was in cahoots with Burr in the plot. On March 17, 1807,
Jackson sent another letter to Dearborn, ending the matter:

> After I have given, the most deliberate consideration to your expres-
> sion, then, in a degree, ambiguously made I can not draw from them
> any other conclusion than this: that you believed me conserned in the
> conspiracy, that I was a fit subject to act the traitor of traitors, as others
> have done, and that it was only necessary for the Secretary at War of
> the United States, to buy me up without honour, money or price. . . . It
> is well known fact that you have been uniformly the intimate friend and
> supporter of genl. Wilkinson. . . . It has been not only storied in this part
> of the western country, but has been reported on the most respectable
> authority, that Colo. Burr and his adventurers held your order as Secre-
> tary at War, purporting a furtherance and governmental support of the
> enterprise. . . . The government must indeed be tottering with its own
> imbecility when principal supporters of it, shall be thus insulted, thus
> assailed by an officer of government, devoid of talents integrity and all
> together ignorant of the duties attached to his elevated station. The
> nominal dignity that the Secretary at war acquires at the first entrance
> upon the duties of his office, will always give to his assertions a degree
> of credit. I know what he has done is unworthy the character of a genl.
> Or a man of honor.[7]

Jackson was beyond anger.

A New Era

Tarred by the "Burr affair," in 1809 President Madison appointed Dearborn
to the position of Collector of the Port of Boston, one of the most highly
paid posts in the administration. Incidents at sea and increased meddling in
the maritime affairs of the United States made it clear to the Madison administration that the nation should think about mounting a land force to defend

its shore. In January 1812, Henry Dearborn was called to Washington to accept command of the regular army as the senior major general.

A sexagenarian, he enjoyed good health and believed himself just the man for the job. He had long courted the Virginians who dominated the White House, serving in one government post after another, and was considered one of their trusted cronies. In a letter to his son, he reveals his prime concern on his first day in office: "We are engaged in forming a list of nominations of officers for several states. I hope to complete these soon." Regular officers' commissions and state militia posts at the level of colonel and above were controlled along party lines. Loyal party service in elected or appointed positions along with social standing and wealth could overcome a lack of military experience.

From the very start, at the urging of Jefferson (now out of office, but still stirring the pot), Madison remembered Dearborn's service on that dreadful march to Quebec and the winter of 1775 spent in a prisoner-of-war camp. Jefferson was intent on taking Canada to punish the British. Dearborn, like Jefferson, thought only of offense, while the states were consumed by defense. The New England states balked at the thought of contributing sons in support of the regular army and dug in their heels. If they were to participate, it would be the "good old militia," supplied with equipment from the federal government but leaving command in the hands of the governors. The citizens of Massachusetts believed that their "minutemen," who saw the British off once before, could do it again thirty-five years later if invaded by the Redcoats. They didn't realize that the times and the structure of society had been altered. No longer did men who shot their own food and lived off the land populate a solely agrarian landscape. The current generation of military-age men had no intention of dropping everything to conquer Canada. Only in the west could Dearborn find the kind of enthusiastic support for a large land army. Manufacturers beat a path to his door once war was in the air. They were thick on the ground and occupied the lobby of the tiny War Department and office of the commanding general.

Winfield Scott, a young officer who would have the misfortune to serve under Dearborn's generals, despaired, "Swaggerers, dependents, decayed gentlemen and others fit for nothing else always turned out to be utterly unfit for military purpose what so ever."[8] Dearborn also left an impression on young Scott: "old, vain, respectable and incapable."

Dearborn Takes the Field

In the spring of 1812, the regular army authorization, which had been increased to 10,000, stood at an untrained and poorly equipped 6,750. Muskets, bayonets, powder, or ball ammunition were in very short supply. Weapons had been scattered between arsenals and untouched since 1781 so that those few issued were often unserviceable. While Dearborn had championed the integration of artillery into the force, the single artillery regiment at the start of the war was short of cannons. As money manager, he ruled that, "officers could not commit to more than $50 without his approval." In a far-off, isolated post, it meant that rations and medical care could be postponed until the correspondence went both ways, a matter of months.

War Plan

In April and May, Dearborn authored a plan to invade Canada with a four-pronged attack along an 800-mile front by a handpicked force of state and territorial militia backed by small elements of the regular soldiers. It called on Governor Hull in the Michigan Territory to attack across the Detroit River at Amherstburg, militia Major General Van Rensselaer to cross the raging Niagara River at Queenston, an attack on Kingston on the St. Lawrence River, and a main attack under his own personal command on Montreal. The first attack under Hull was set for July. When Hull failed due to poor planning on Dearborn's part, Hull was court-martialed. Dearborn was president of the court, and a young Martin Van Buren was the judge adjutant prosecuting the case. Hull had little chance since his defense rested on Dearborn's ineffectiveness, which contributed in a significant manner to bringing about the surrender of Fort Detroit. Hull proclaimed that "the president (Dearborn) of the court-martial which has condemned me, which his own misconduct had been a great cause in producing."[9] The court condemned Hull to death, but the president pardoned the old man for service to his country.

Ironically, the loss of Fort Detroit meant that Fort Dearborn in Chicago could no longer be supported and so was evacuated in August. "A little band of soldiers and their families left the stockade at Fort Dearborn and made their way along the sand dunes of Lake Michigan on route to Fort Wayne. The Indians swept down on them from ambush."[10] All were killed and scalped.

Temporary Truce

The London government and the Governor of the Canadas Sir George Prevost, hoping to avoid the war, proposed a truce in August 1812. Monroe agreed to talk so that Dearborn and Stephen Van Rensselaer could take advantage of the lull to prepare a force worthy of taking Queenston. A few miles south near Buffalo, a regiment of regular rifles, under the command of Brigadier General Alexander Smyth, was ordered by Dearborn to "cooperate" with the Van Rensselaer attack. Even though Smyth, a Washington lawyer and friend of Jefferson, had no military experience, he was commissioned a colonel in 1805. He ignored Dearborn's order and opted for a plan of his own for the invasion. His reluctance to support the October attack at Queenston with his regulars was decisive in the loss of the battle. He then deserted his post and returned to Washington to resume his law practice. He no longer engaged himself in the war—nor was he court-martialed.

Dearborn's Coup de Main

After the losses at Queenston, late in the year, Major General Dearborn managed to assemble his invasion force at Plattsburgh, New York. Winter came early in the north country twenty miles south of the border while the swirling winds turned calm Lake Champlain into dangerous waters. The village that clung to the icy waters of Cumberland Bay supported less than 1,000 citizens, many of whom were engaged in smuggling food, raw materials, and lumber for shipbuilding to Canada.

Dearborn had saved the best troops for himself. He led 6,000 soldiers, including seven regiments of regulars, artillery, and mounted light dragoons. A contingent of New York militia infantry from the four northern counties tagged along when they crossed the border between Champlain and Rouses Point along the shoreline of Lake Champlain. It was late November, and the cold had descended, burning their lungs and freezing their feet. The militia refused to cross the border, stating that they didn't join with the army to fight in foreign wars. Left behind, Dearborn pressed on and was met by a gallant collection of French Canadian troops and Indians led by Major Charles-Michael d'Irumberry de Salaberry, leading a force of only about one-fourth that of the Americans. A skirmish took place in fog blown off the warmer water of the lake, confusing and confounding the general. Dearborn lost heart and withdrew across the border late the next day with his army intact. He offered to resign his commission, but unfortunately it was not taken from him. Dearborn remained at his post in Albany that winter, directing new formations forward as they came on line. However, he had at long last exhausted his political appeal and was threatened with relief. His friends in Congress dumped him when he needed them the most. The impressive list of failures was too much for Secretary of War Armstrong, who had been at his side during the Revolutionary War, which, under the current circumstances, had faded from memory.

NEW YORK'S JACOB BROWN

The time had come for young men, fresh in wind and limb, to take up the sword. Jacob Brown's background, like nearly all the other leaders of his time, began when his family arrived in colonial America in the mid-1600s. Originally from Leicestershire, England, they settled in Bucks County, Pennsylvania, and fell in with the Quaker community, where Jacob was born to Samuel and Abbey Brown in May 1775. Young Jacob was taught in the local Quaker school, where he excelled. His father prospered in land speculation and other financial holdings, which turned out badly, forcing the family off the land. Jacob maintained a living as a teacher in a Quaker school in New Jersey while learning the surveying trade and seized the opportunity to go to the Ohio Valley, where the land was opening up to the settlers. By the late 1790s, he was teaching once again in New York City, grinding out days, months, and years teaching the same subjects while the new United States was expanding into the fertile river valleys that he had marked out years before. The newspapers were full of adventure along rivers and lakes where a man could create a future. Jacob agreed that the western frontier held prospects for any young man who was willing to gamble. Together with one of his six brothers, John, he struck out for the land they had purchased in New York state. His father had recovered enough of his holdings to join in the purchase of 2,000 acres of good bottomland near the mouth of the Black River, where it met the St. Lawrence on the very northern frontier with Canada. The report of the condition of the track was so favorable that in the spring of 1799, brothers, sisters, and cousins, some twenty in all, made the long, arduous journey by boat and packhorse and established Brownsville, New York. As head of the clan, Jacob grew in influence, accepting outside work as a land agent and a few minor state posts. Sixty miles south in Utica, Jacob met the sister of a local businessman, Miss Pamela Williamses. They married in 1802, and their first son was named for Jacob's patron, Governor Morris, who had befriended the teacher in New York City years before. In 1807, with the trouble over excesses by the British government, the state militia was revived, and Jacob was appointed a captain in an infantry regiment that was a military formation in name only. A supporter of the new governor, David Tompkins, his political affiliation brought him to promotion to colonel after only two years. However, from the start of his commission, he took his duties and the welfare of his citizen soldiers seriously. Constantly pressing the state to furnish weapons, powder, and equipage, he limited costly drills, accomplishing little before they turned into drinking bouts. Brown recognized that in the harsh northern land, men had little time to spend away from tending the land and preparing for the long winter.

His years of teaching gave him a commanding presence that was combined with fine, manly features. At six feet with broad shoulders and a fine head of thick brown curly hair, his face was both friendly and firm. He was the very image of a professional soldier in his fitted dark blue short coat with gold epaulets and a single row of gold buttons worn with well-fitted white deerskin pants tucked in calf-high black boots.

Embargo Devastates the North

President Jefferson's outburst to punish Great Britain by restricting trade with, among others, Canada brought the northern economy in Vermont and New York to its knees. The farmers depended mostly on the sale of potash to their northern neighbors, along with foodstuffs and cut timber. It was a matter of survival. There was no alternative market since the roads and waterways to the south were long, unimproved, hazardous, and highly seasonal. There was nothing for it; smuggling was forced upon the hapless population.

A commodity nearly unknown today, potash is obtained as the remnant of burning wood. The forests of the north encumbered the growing of crops. The first task was to clear the land of trees and stumps, a soul-destroying labor. However, the wood ash sold in Montreal for hundreds of dollars per ton, a considerable compensation that in turn sustained land clearing. The ash was used in making soap, bleach, and fertilizer and as an oxidizing agent. As potassium nitrate, it is a key ingredient in gunpowder. Federal customs agents were abundant along the northern frontier since tariffs were the sole source of federal funding. Interfering with the primary source of income for a frontier family became a hazardous occupation. Agents were harassed, shot at, and ostracized from the communities in which they lived:

> The state militia was added to the enforcement when states passed laws supporting the embargo. A British army officer, buying beef to feed his troops, reported that he questioned a militia brigadier general, in full uniform, while buying a herd of cattle that had been driven into Canada. "Don't you consider it treason to trade with the enemy?" asked the red-coated officer. The militiaman replied, "While trading with the enemy is forbidden, I could not regard anyone who offered me such a good price for my cattle as being my enemy."[11]

Jacob Brown could have been that officer since he was known as "Embargo Brown" by many. Brown was opposed to the punitive embargo because of the hurtful effect it had on every citizen who scratched a living from the harsh climate and unforgiving rocky ground.

Brown's War

With the declaration of war, Lieutenant General Sir George Prevost published his thanks to the American smugglers for feeding his army and encouraged them to continue. While Brown backed away from his family's enterprise, he was well aware that smuggling had become a cottage industry as more and more goods found their way by roads that had been cut to the border expressly for the purpose of selling to the British. They paid in gold coin, preferable to Yankee paper dollars.

Brown was statically placed at Brownsville between Kingston, Canada, and Sackets Harbor, New York. The militia, under his command in the northern counties, where the St. Lawrence met Lake Ontario, was a hot spot. Sackets Harbor was the only natural haven along the southeastern coast of Lake Ontario. The tiny enclosed harbor opened to westerly winds, making it hard for an avenging Canadian Marine fleet to maintain their station and bombard the boatbuilding yard that it protected. Brown was sent to fortify the outer limits, which he accomplished, by throwing up an earthen fort poked with holes for artillery. Although totally unschooled in military engineering, he was intuitive in his thinking. A man who could carve an estate of a couple of thousand archers, build homesteads, put up bridges, construct mills, and organize both a community and a defense was a formidable leader. He could count on only 600 militiamen at any one time because crops had to be planted, nurtured, and harvested by his part-time soldiers. The militia belonged not to Madison but to Governor Tompkins. Brown sent a constant plea for supplies of all kinds, but in particular muskets, powder, lead, rations, and blankets were always on his list. The governor put the case for federal support to Congress, which favored militia over regular troops but failed to provide the states with essentials. The procurement of artillery pieces was a constant problem. Just south of the New York border at Ringwood, the Cooper foundry had worked gunmetal since before the Revolution. The state convinced Congress to build an arsenal at Watervelliet next to Albany on the Hudson River. There, the gun tubs were married with the gun carriages and limbers before being matched with teams of horses for the new artillery regiments. Some were sent by barge up the Mohawk to the Oswego River and transshipped to Sackets Harbor on unimproved tracks and old Indian hunting trails. While guns were expensive, they were also costly to transport and thus lagged behind all other requests. Yet field cannons and naval guns were often the deciding factor in backwoods battles. The Indians never stood a chance in the face of artillery fire.

Secretary of the Navy Paul Hamilton had done little to support the Great Lakes, suggesting that ships should be captured from the enemy to save money. Within days of the start of the war, several Canadian Marine craft were taken and sailed to Sackets Harbor joining the sixteen-gun brig USS *Oneida*. The American facility was strategically significant to both sides in the conflict. Brown expected that it wouldn't be very long before the British retaliated in force. In addition to saving face, the destruction of the boatyard and the rescue of their vessels would allow the British to dominate lake transport, which was vital to movement along the frontier. Three naval 9-pounder cannons arrived just in time to expand the firepower of the defenders at the harbor. The master of the *Oneida*, Captain Melancton Woolsey, encountered an enemy fleet of five ships entering Black River Bay preparing to attack the harbor, which lay to the eastern edge. He could see that infantry were ganged aboard and feared that boots on the ground could tip the battle in England's favor. Woolsey sailed on ahead to alert the militia and then moored off the far end of the point where the earth fort housed the 9-pounders and added his starboard guns to the fight. A 32-pounder naval gun that had been destined for *Oneida* but that was too heavy for the brig's rails to support was added to the defenses.[12] The winds, the determining factor in all things naval, didn't allow the Canadian Marine fleet to take up a threatening position until the militia and sailors had unloaded the guns from *Oneida*'s port side, significantly increasing the throw weight of the battery. Laying off the harbor entrance, unable to get in close or send boatloads of infantry ashore, the enemy fleet suffered, locked down by the steady pounding from Captain Woolsey's accurate bombardment. Realizing that there was no chance to take the secure little harbor, the British fleet pulled off, but would return to fight another day.

Brown's Mission

A civilian in uniform, Jacob Brown accepted a mission impossible from the political planners who masqueraded as military masters. He was directed to secure the St. Lawrence shoreline, Cape St. Vincent across from Kingston, Canada, and Sackets Harbor, a distance of 200 miles, with 600 untrained and poorly supported militiamen who rotated home to tend crops and prepare the homestead for winter. No trained and experienced professional officer would have ever accepted the mission under similar conditions. Brown was a man of enormous capability driven by relentless ambition to please his political boss for personal gain. It is a harsh analysis but one that could be applied across the board to a host of noteworthy persons in the early days of national expansion with little to lose and a great deal to gain. Patronage ruled all fields of endeavor.

Ogdensburg

A particular sore spot and hotbed for smugglers was the town of Ogdensburg, which lay downstream midway to Montreal. Brown sent several gunboats full of troops and supplies northeast with the river's flow to garrison the town. That August and September, the temporary armistice arranged by Prevost aided in the deployment of troops and supply shortages. Not honored in good faith, the American unit commanders used it as a break in the action to prepare for the winter and to train with newly supplied weapons. By the end of August, the first regular soldiers arrived. Major John Forsyth of North Carolina marched in with a company taken from the rifle regiment. Sharpshooters, they were trained with a weapon superior to the smoothbore musket that could shoot a man in the head with an aimed shot at over 100 yards. Shorter than the musket, the single-shot rifle was easier to load but still required a ball to be rammed down the barrel. The rifleman was not expected to charge the enemy, so the weapon was not equipped with a bayonet as a rule. Riflemen carried a short sword that could be attached to the muzzle, but it unbalanced the weapon and was impractical. Clad in faded forest green deerskin head to toe, the rifleman blended into the woods where they acted independently in a skirmish role, picking off the officers and other key leaders. It was said that the British felt that skirmishers were unfair, but they had similar units in the days of the Revolutionary War. In fact, Sir George Prevost's father and uncle founded the 60th Light Infantry, which became known as the Royal Green Jackets. The reason all the troops in the British army were not skirmish riflemen was that it was too expensive and took too long to train and maintain the elite force.

The war was beginning to roll on that fall after all the fits and starts unnecessarily killed and maimed too many well-intentioned patriots who fought under incompetent officers appointed out of purely private ambition. Governor Tompkins raised funds from the wealthy citizens of New York City and surrounding counties who saw the threat to their well-being by way of a British invasion from the north. The governor spent the winter correcting the deficiencies attributed to the nearly unresponsive federal departments.

ISAAC CHAUNCEY

The new secretary of the navy, William Jones, recognized the importance of Lake Ontario and Lake Erie and appointed a commodore, Captain Isaac Chauncey, whose specialty was boatbuilding. Snatched from his comfortable billet at New York City, where he was commander of the navy's boatyard, the commodore would have preferred command of a ship, but the Royal Navy, at the close of 1812, was in the process of shutting down the American Navy after a summer and fall of heavy losses to both commercial shipping and men-of-war. The pressure on England from a ten-year string of Napoleon's victories was coming to an end with his foolhardy invasion of Russia. If forty-year-old

Chauncey, a native New Yorker, were to make a name, it would have to be on the Great Lakes. At Sackets Harbor, his base of operations, he was charged with both building warships and fighting them. Energetic, he dispatched a crew of builders from his old yard to the new before his own arrival. By October, timber was being milled, hardware was being pounded into shape, and masts were soaking in the pools when 500 newly minted militiamen arrived and took their share of wood planks to build barracks for shelter from the oppressive winter that would soon descend on them.

Brown, frustrated with the trickle down of everything basic to warfare, sent Governor Tompkins a note: "Are we always to rely upon ourselves or are we to rely upon government next month, next spring, or any future period."[13] Jacob Brown was beginning to make the transition from party sycophant to military commander. On arrival at Ogdensburg, he discovered that the local townsmen and militia were complicit. Their passive attitude to enforcement of the law was sinister. Far too much trading money was dominating every phase of life in the tiny village a few hundred yards across the frontier on the St. Lawrence River. Those brought before the local judge for violating the law were given the lightest of sentences, often commuted to nothing. While Embargo Brown himself had been active in smuggling, the declaration of war meant that servicing the enemy was killing his men. Brown ordered his artillery to fire on the boats carrying contraband to Prescott, Canada. Angered at their loss of smuggled goods, the British poured hundreds of cannonballs into the center of the American village. The citizens of Ogdensburg, siding with their customers in Canada, petitioned for Brown to leave the area. On the morning of October 4, British Colonel Robert Lethbridge, leading 500 militia and a pair of companies of Glengarry fencibles in rowboats, attacked as the mist was lifting off the St. Lawrence. It was a punitive exercise that was ill-advised. Brown's artillery threw the attack into confusion when soldiers abandoned their equipment and swam for the Canadian shore in an effort to avoid the cannon shot. The Governor General, Sir George Prevost, relieved Lethbridge for the offensive action, which he had discouraged. Prevost had no patience for a commander who would risk his scarce British troops on a hotheaded prank.

After the battle, Brown was retained in the area as fall rains began to restrict travel. Governor Tompkins believed that there was a threat from the British. He was totally unaware that Prevost had no intention or ability to invade the United States that winter or the next one to come. With autumn came the reinforcements. Brown placed nearly 3,000 militia along the St. Lawrence, reducing the free flow of contraband to a trickle. Nevertheless, enterprising smugglers managed to get their produce to the Canadian market when the British upped the going rate. As the snows of December arrived, the militia departed for home, leaving only local militia who were known to consort with the enemy who provided an income for everyone on the American side of the border. Governor Tompkins and General Brown were aware of this, but it was a way of life as both sides of the border huddled around hearth fires and waited for the spring thaw of April or perhaps May.

FORSYTH, A MAN OF ACTION

No one told Major Benjamin Forsyth, who was left in charge of defending Ogdensburg, to sit still that winter. Isolated by ice and snow from contact with higher command (all appeared to be hibernating), he became aggressive. In late February, he surprised everyone along the frozen St. Lawrence River when his company sallied forth with his 150 regulars and a handful of militia to Brockville, Canada, where he seized prisoners. A punitive raid to discourage smugglers and their potential buyers, it shocked Prevost, who gave in to his local commander, Colonel George Macdonnell, a Scotsman with a reputation as a fighter. The outraged colonel mounted a force of several hundred, including the Glengarry light infantry, which had been fired on in boats earlier and suffered the disgrace of having to swim back to Canada. Done in a fit of pique, Macdonnell's men routed Forsyth's rifles from their little fort and sent them packing back to Sackets Harbor for the winter. Even though Brown had been advised to take several hundred militiamen to assist Forsyth, he was unable to raise the troops at that time of year. The citizens of Ogdensburg and Prescott settled into a peaceful winter, happily trading without interference.

Tompkins and Brown expected the regular army to replace the militia as the prime land force that winter. The first to arrive was Colonel Alexander Macomb's 3rd Artillery Regiment, which he had raised himself. Under the worst of winter snow and blizzards, he moved the men and guns hundreds of miles to Sackets Harbor, closing in just before Christmas.

PIKE BEGINS THE 1813 CAMPAIGN IN THE NORTH

Secretary John Armstrong, a lieutenant during the Revolutionary War and publisher of a book on "advice to young army officers" (that James Monroe said wasn't worth the paper it was printed on), issued a campaign plan. In the north, Kingston, York, and the Niagara were to be attacked by 4,000 infantry and artillery transported by Commodore Chauncey from Sackets Harbor.

The field commander was to be newly promoted regular Brigadier General Zebulon Pike leading two regiments with gun support from the navy. Dearborn, still hanging around, jumped at the chance to redeem his reputation and traveled with the troops to Sackets Harbor and meddle in the affair. Believing false reports that Kingston was too strong to attack, Dearborn altered the plan and chose York instead for the first attack. Of course, Kingston, at the mouth of the St. Lawrence, was the strategic target, not York, which was a provincial capital, housing only a boatbuilding complex. In the last week of April, a force of 2,000 sailors and soldiers attacked York, which was poorly defended. Within the day, the town was taken and the boatyard destroyed along with a number of ships that were under construction. The tragedy was that General Pike was killed when an ammunition wagon nearby exploded. The unexpected death of the land commander left the troops leaderless, and they burned and looted much of the town. Dearborn, who had remained on board during the fracas, sailed with Chauncey to Fort Niagara on the American side of the Niagara River. The troops were landed to begin a campaign expected to cut western Canada from the east.

EVERY ACTION HAS AN EQUAL
AND OPPOSITE REACTION

At the end of May, Chauncey transported Macomb and most of his artillery regiment to beef up the efforts on the Niagara, leaving the harbor in the hands of 500 regulars. They were a mix of sick, lame, and lazy who were left behind. Sir James Yeo, who took the burning of York personally, was prowling around the entrance to Black River Bay when he saw Chauncey leave with his flotilla filled with troops for Niagara. Yeo called in Prevost, and they mounted an attack by 1,000 infantry on board seven ships to avenge York. The naval artillery alone, totaling 106 guns, was capable of smashing the little defenses thrown up by Brown earlier. But it was the days of sail, and positioning the ships in shoal water driven by trailing wind called for great skill and luck. The prevailing west wind could sweep Yeo's ships directly into the guns of the American fort. His captains would have to fight to maintain a firing position while the transports could be driven onto the sandbars on either end of the tiny peninsula just south of the harbor opening.

The British intended to attack on May 28, but the winds were fitful, and control of the fleet turned into a slow dance when they were sighted by an American schooner in the bay. The alert was given and word sent to Brown to gather the militia to defend the port. Meanwhile, the regular troops manned the earthworks along the west-facing shore that protected the harbor entrance. On a cleared plain 300 yards long, every available cannon was arrayed.

Yeo got cold feet and was about to call off the attack when a flotilla of boats carrying over 100 regular American infantry was spotted to the south headed for the bay. Prevost sent a number of canoes filled with warriors to capture the troops. Soon the winds picked up, and Yeo sent the fleet into the bay the next morning. By then, General Brown had assembled 500 militia and mixed them with the defenders along the open shoreline. The leading edge of Brown's defense looked like a porcupine bristling with shiny pointed bayonets, and the eager mouths of brass field guns stuck out in grand anticipation.

The enemy fleet sailed in a line and belched out a broadside. Whistling cannonballs fell short, splashing the water and sending up plumes of white spray. The ships' gunners were finding their range. Soon the balls were bouncing past the American lines and crashing into the homes behind the battlefield. The ships came even closer on their second run. Those filled with infantry turned in toward Horse Island on the extreme left flank of the Americans. It was obvious to Brown that any troops that landed would strive to disembark beyond the island and then attempt to roll up the defenders as they pushed the Americans back into the harbor itself. Brown anchored his men just below the point while the cannon fire prevented the British from getting south of Horse Island. Forced to land on the vacant island, they were canalized onto the narrow strip connecting the island with the mainland. Perfect targets, the British suffered heavy losses as they approached Brown's line of shooters. The British expected the militia to run in the face of their onslaught, but Brown had them withdraw to a prepared position that forced the enemy infantry to wheel to their left and face the regular American units as they pulled back toward the town along with their cannons. That day Brown found that he had the soul of a warrior, as he rallied his formation in the face of the enemy's volleys. Sometimes only yards in front of the redcoats, Brown remained in control and settled his line. The British formation fell victim to an L-shaped ambush. Enemy in front, enemy on the right, and the lake shore on the left, the only path open was to the rear, and they took it, withdrawing back to Horse Island and onto their transports. Unfortunately, Commodore Chauncey's brother, Lieutenant Wolcott, waiting nervously in the harbor, witnessing the noise, smoke, and confusion all around, assumed that they had lost and set fire to the ships in the yard and the naval stores to save them from being captured. In a way, Walcott Chauncey accomplished Yeo's mission for him, the destruction of the American boatbuilding capability, at least for the next few months. At the conclusion of the battle, the British, under a flag of truce, asked that they be allowed to retrieve their wounded, which Brown allowed. Hard to comprehend in the world of today, commanders were gentlemen who played by rules set down long before in the days of chivalry.

THE REGULAR ARMY'S SCHOOLROOM

In Washington, Brown's bid for a regular commission as a colonel, which had been ignored the previous winter, was honored with promotion to brigadier general—his was the single star given up by Zebulon Pike's death. At about the same time, March 1813, Major General James Wilkinson, commander of the Southeastern Military District, was made commander of the army on the relief of General Dearborn, who was in poor health and advanced age. Secretary of War John Armstrong made it plain: his objective was the destruction of Kingston and the capture of Montreal. Armstrong, a veteran of the Battle of Saratoga in 1777, was still fighting the war of his youth where he was a staff officer under Granny Gates.

As with everything Wilkinson, confusion reigned. He insisted that the attack on Kingston and subsequent maneuver toward Montreal start with an attack on the Niagara 180 degrees to the west, in the wrong direction. Wilkinson departed Sackets Harbor to tour Niagara, while Brown and the staff accumulated the equipage for the campaign in the other direction. Wilkinson thought it wise to avoid the arrival of Secretary Armstrong, who had decided to go along on the expedition, fearing the duplicity of Wilkinson once the old general was out of sight of Washington. It was truly the despicable leading the bewildered. On his return, Wilkinson held a war council with all the luminaries and Brown, who had been doing all the work as the new general on the block. Of five plans, the one selected was to send the entire force down the St. Lawrence, feint an attack at Kingston, and link up with Major General Wade Hampton marching from Plattsburgh toward St. Regis and then proceeded to Montreal. It required water transport for 7,000 troops and their equipment through 200 miles of hostile territory.

While Brown prepared the move, Wilkinson left to gather up 3,500 regular troops at Niagara, asking one more time of Armstrong if he shouldn't linger and attack the British on the Niagara front first. It is true that Wilkinson was very ill at the time and was using opium to control his pain, and this could be an explanation of his erratic behavior.

By mid-October 1813, Armstrong sent Hampton on the move toward St. Regis, and the boats were loaded at Sackets Harbor. Wilkinson changed his mind and called for a halt at Kingston and a reduction of their defenses by artillery bombardment. Armstrong vetoed the modification at that late date and ordered Wilkinson to execute the plan as written. At that critical point,

Armstrong said that he was not well and pulled out for Washington, leaving Wilkinson to coordinate with Hampton, whom he hated.

On Grenadier Island, in the middle of the St. Lawrence River just short of Kingston, the American force gathered in the middle of an October storm that dumped ten inches of wet snow on the unprotected troops. It was not until the second day of November, two weeks later, that the sick were evacuated to Sackets Harbor and the command moved downriver toward Montreal. Brown managed to pull his second brigade out three days before and spearhead the expedition down the St. Lawrence. On November 1, Brown landed on a point, moving inland, just below French Creek. Two British brigades and a pair of gunboats that got past Chauncey attacked Brown. Field artillery had been dismounted to protect Brown's infantry as they landed. The field guns drove off the British gunboats, and the enemy infantry backed off. Wilkinson moved the bulk of the army, landing south of Ogdensburg on November 6. It was getting cold, and they were only halfway to Montreal. Hampton was asking for direction, and since he had been told to go through Armstrong for orders because of bad blood between himself and Wilkinson, Hampton halted after several skirmishes with the Canadians. Wilkinson sent orders to Hampton to meet him at St. Regis with supplies. Hampton didn't have any supplies.

Following behind on the river, Brown caught up with the main body that was prepared for battle on the north (Canadian) side of the river. Colonel Macomb's artillery joined Brown's 2nd Brigade and moved ahead to Crysler's Farm. The British brigades that had crossed with Brown several days before were following the Americans. A rearguard was formed to block them. The next morning, November 11, after a bitter cold night, Brown encountered sporadic contact with one militia unit after another but swept them aside, securing the north bank of the river clear to Cornwall. Wilkinson was ill and after brief orders went to bed, leaving his field unit commanders to deal with the British. Wilkinson's main force attacked the British under freezing, wet, miserable conditions and was effortlessly thrown back across the St. Lawrence. The following day, Wilkinson continued the march down the river and joined with Brown and Macomb; a messenger brought word that Hampton was unable to comply with the request for supplies. By unanimous consent of his commanders, Wilkinson agreed to end the expedition not because of the weather or the loss at Crysler's Farm, but because of Hampton's failure to supply the army. The army took up winter quarters at French Mills.

To be expected, Wilkinson, through illness, left the army on November 18 for convalescence at a comfortable house in Malone, New York, placing Brigadier General Jacob Brown in charge of constructing the winter quarters. French Mills was a village in name only, containing six houses and adjacent barns lying helplessly in the snow on the bank of the frozen river. The soldiers, tired and lonely, devoid of the victory over Canada, who expected to spend the winter enjoying the admiration of their countrymen and the comfort of warm, dry quarters, built shelters and prepared to sit and watch a border that neither side wanted to cross. The tone of the camp was similar to the desperate Valley Forge winter of 1778. Now, at last, the smugglers had a resident market feeding the American army cantonment. This cut the cost of transportation, raised profits, and avoided the risk of border customs collectors.

Secretary Armstrong took action on January 20, 1814, and split up the cantonment. The army was divided into fragments with Brown taking 2,000 men to winter at Sackets Harbor and the others ending up at Plattsburgh and Burlington, Vermont. Wilkinson would remain in the east, while Brown and Scott would go west.

OUT WITH THE DEAD WOOD

In February 1814, Brown was rewarded with a promotion to major general. Wilkinson, to curry favor with Madison and Jefferson, attacked Montreal once again that March and was defeated by his own folly and court-martialed for his conduct of the campaign. Secretary Armstrong reached down into the ranks of colonels who had proven records and promoted a new crop of brigadier generals, which included Winfield Scott.

NEW DIRECTION

In April, Brown concurred with Tompkins and Armstrong and moved his regulars, along with the militia at hand, early that season to the New York side of the Niagara River. He was the commanding general of the department taking on the responsibilities of not only fighting battles but also administering the war along that critical frontier. It was quite a stretch for a man who had begun as a sycophant to the political bosses intent on gaining an enclave for himself in the new west to find himself a couple of turbulent years later as the point of the spear. Under his command were a collection of regular units, individual soldiers of which had little combat experience. General Winfield Scott, commander of the largest formation, the first brigade, recognized the flaw.

> *General Winfield Scott was a great commander and an overpowering conversationalist.*
>
> —Ulysses S. Grant

WINFIELD SCOTT

Winfield Scott's career in the army began back in the tidewater of Virginia. Born to William and Mary Mason Scott in 1786 at Petersburg, the second son of five children, he was an orphan by age seventeen. Issue of a wealthy landowning family, young Winfield studied law at William and Mary College, graduating in 1806. With Jefferson's embargo came an increase in the authorized strength of the army, and Scott, angry at the treatment of America by Great Britain, sought a commission as a captain of light artillery that was granted in 1808. A year later, his unit was sent to Louisiana under the command of Major General Wilkinson. Scott previously witnessed the general's evidence at the trial of Aaron Burr in a Richmond court and was troubled with the tone of Wilkinson's testimony. In 1809, Scott fell afoul of the commanding general, who had taken a dislike to the young officer. Wilkinson ordered a court-martial of the captain citing two charges: "withholding money from his men placed in his hands for their services and disrespectful language to a superior officer," namely, Wilkinson. The first charge was dismissed, and Scott pled guilty to the second, bringing a one-year suspension. He spent the year studying the profession of arms and reading books on the ancient wars and recent European conflicts. Available was a translation of Frederick the Great's campaigns. He continued his studies on his own for the next few years while serving in the tiny American army and becoming known for his discussions concerning the profession of arms among his colleagues. He was one of few in his time who understood all phases of planning, training, maneuver, and support. In 1812, he was promoted to lieutenant colonel of the artillery and posted to General George Izard's 2nd Regiment on the Niagara. He was stationed at Black Rock on the American side of the Niagara River near Buffalo. On October 9, 1812, Scott assisted in the capture of Fort Erie across the water from Buffalo, his first battle in which his field cannons were of great assistance. Later in October, Scott took his gunners to support General Van Rensselaer at Queenston and fired in support of the first wave of soldiers to cross the river and attack the city.

When Solomon Van Rensselaer, the nephew of Major General Stephen Van Rensselaer and who had been rescued on a battlefield years before by William Henry Harrison, was killed in the street fighting in Queenston, Scott agreed to lead the next wave to cross the treacherous river and take command. General Van Rensselaer promised to send wave after wave of militia across in the few boats that were fully engaged. When the returning boats filled with wounded and covered in blood were emptied, the troops refused to go and remained on the American side. It didn't take long for the remaining Americans to abandon Queenston for fear of being overwhelmed, wounded, killed, or taken prisoner. After the battle, Scott and his command were marched off to prison. The militia was paroled, but the regulars were taken to Quebec as prisoners of war.

Colonel Scott was exchanged during the winter of 1813 and assumed the duties of adjutant general to Dearborn. On the passage to Fort Niagara that mid-May, Dearborn was ill and deferred to Scott to take command of the assault on Fort George since none of the three brigadier generals, John Boyd, William Winder (defender of Washington to come), and John Chandler, were capable of the hazardous undertaking.

Scott the Professional Soldier, Summer of 1814

"Scott got his chance to affect all units under Brown's command by introducing a camp of instruction in which the American army—both officers and men—should be drilled and disciplined in the utmost perfection in the tactics of the French army."[14] Scott was in his glory, at last turning his brigade and others into a professional force equal to the veteran redcoat's regiments. For three uninterrupted months, "one copy of the French *Manual of Tactics* was in the camp—belonging to General Scott. All studied from it. Scott would drill his staff and general officers—these would drill the grades below, and they in turn the noncommissioned officers and privates."[15] The effect was dramatic.

Strategy

Now that Armstrong had purged the army, he came up with a plan to meet Madison's original objective: the invasion and the taking of Canada. Over the past two years, an army had been built that could stand against the British. He convinced Madison that the trust should be made in the Niagara to seal off the west, which would please the politicians known as the "western war hawks." Once the land around Lake Ontario and Lake Erie was occupied, Montreal could be rolled up without threat from enemy troops in the rear.

Sir George Prevost was no longer interested in the west. He possessed a different approach now: he was going to be capable of taking the offensive for the first time. Sir George had put his strength in the west because that is where he was sustaining attacks. The treaty talks in Ghent would soon resume. What was needed was a stunning demonstration not in the west but in the east, clearly visible, aimed at a negotiated settlement to the war that would benefit England without the necessity of a long, costly campaign. But it was clear that the Americans were interested in the west, so he would humor them by feigning an attack.

The Fighting Season of 1814

After two years of missteps, corruption, neglect, hacks, sycophants, and adventures, the heroes were about to take the field. At dawn on July 3, Brown sent his army across the Niagara River at the south end to attack British Fort Erie. With 4,000 soldiers, the tiny fort was soon overwhelmed and surrendered. The objective was to cause mayhem on the Canadian side of the river. Brown's campaign would track north with the mighty river roaring on their right flank. The new commanding general intended to fix the British and then fight them on their own terms, European style.

Brown and Scott appeared to be twins, a brace in identical dark blue uniforms and flat hats worn fore and aft over the eyes, as they rode side by side. Both were tall, thin, and athletic with Scott bigger at six feet six inches. They talked and rode slowly at the head of the column along the towpath and into history. The army moved slowly, plodding at first, knowing that they were to cover twenty miles to the Chippewa River, the site of their first camp. The aggressive British general Phineas Riall, who had burned and sacked Buffalo and Black Rock earlier, was comfortable commanding militia and was also known to have no respect for the courage of American soldiers. He sent Lieutenant Colonel Thomas Pearson south to obstruct the American advance while he gathered as many regular units to make a stand. Pearson, accompanied by sappers, withdrew in front of the American column, burning bridges over the numerous small tributaries that fed into the mighty Niagara. Scott, an artillery officer, had a couple pair of gallopers (light field guns pulled by two pair of horses designed to keep up with cavalry) brought up to disrupt Pearson and drive him off the bridges. The action was successful, preventing any interference in the flow of the American column. A mile prior to Chippewa River, at Street's Creek, just short of dense woods, Scott stopped the column for the night, waiting for the other brigades to catch up before the light faded. Brown, knowing that the Chippewa was wide and fast just before it entered the Niagara, broke off and rode west to find a crossing point. Colonel Peter Porter arrived at the head of his regiment and pushed into the woods to clear it of some pesky Indians and rode right into Major General Riall accompanied by the 100th Foot Regiment.

Riall expected to meet the New York militia from Buffalo, which he intended to blow through and scatter. At the run, Porter pulled out, while General Brown rode off for Scott. As the Redcoats emerged from the wood line, Scott immediately deployed his brigade in line as trained at the summer camp and prepared to send the British a volley. Riall responded with several field guns, but was surprised when the enemy didn't run as militia tended to do when confronted by artillery. As Scott's line advanced into the guns, Riall suddenly realized what he had done. "Those are regulars, by God!" "Regulars by God" is a motto found today in the halls of the American infantry school.

Riall pressed the attack with three regiments, not realizing that more American elements were closing in behind Scott. The light artillery fired rapidly, sending cannonballs in salvos that ripped through the ranks of rigid Redcoats. Riall lost his guns to counter battery fire. Scott extended the classic line of four regiments that turned in at the ends, allowing musket fire to pour in on the advancing enemy from three sides. The Redcoats couldn't absorb the fusillade and faltered. To Riall's amazement, Scott called for fixed bayonets and charged. Riall pulled up and then out, back toward the woods, and across the river in disorder and into prepared positions on the far side. Later Scott wrote, "The English mouldered away like a rope of sand."[16] The momentum of the land war changed at Chippewa that evening when 1,300 American regulars routed 1,500 Redcoats. For every six enemy killed or wounded, one American also suffered.

Brown wanted to pursue, but cooler heads convinced him to consolidate at Chippewa and consider his options. The American objectives were the occupation of Fort George in Canada and Fort Niagara on the opposite side of the river. British forces under Major General Gordon Drummond held the forts. Brown knew that naval gunfire support, which only Chauncey could provide, was essential if he was to succeed in dislodging the British. Chauncey was reluctant to vacate Sackets Harbor and leave his headquarters open once again to the avaricious Yeo. Not a natural supporting player, he sought to lead, not follow. Although directed to assist Brown by the naval secretary, Chauncey needed a bigger stage and rejected the support role. Needing an excuse, Chauncey pleaded lake fever, but wouldn't relinquish command to his subordinate. Even though he possessed new ships capable of doing the job, the commodore was unwilling to risk them or leave his home port under current conditions.

Lundy's Lane

The British and American composite armies, a collection of veteran, regulars, militia, artillery, cavalry, and Indians of all tribes, swirled around both sides of the mouth of the Niagara River north of the falls. There was little direction from either headquarters, allowing forage parties to clash over a squalling pig, barnyard chickens, or a shed stuffed with fodder. Brown became aware that Drummond did not intend to be trapped between the American army and the navy and intended to choose the offense inland away from the forts. Drummond's aggression relieved the American commander of concern with the obstinate Chauncey. It was to be a land battle. Pulling back elements from the east side of the river, Brown consolidated at Chippewa.

Riall marched south with the lead element of the British army and settled at Lundy's Lane, three miles north of Chippewa, to wait for the main body and further instructions. His 1,200 militia and Glengarries were soon swelled by an additional 800 regulars late in the afternoon. Drummond moved from the American side to the west bank of the river, leaving only a skeleton force to guard Fort Niagara. Somehow, he surmised that the American fleet was not coming.

Intelligence gathering was never a strong point in the American army, but under Brown, that changed. As his elements began to coalesce, they brought alarming reports of Redcoat movement on the American side of the river, threatening Brown's supply depot. Scattered contacts and brief sightings told the commander one thing: Drummond was consolidating north of Chippewa, but for what purpose? Why had they abandoned the forts and come out in the open? The American general concluded that it was the arrogance of the British officer corps. They were certain that the Americans could not stand against the thin red line that had dominated the war against Napoleon's hordes. Brown and Scott conferred while their strength increased above and below Chippewa. Confident, Brown sent Scott "to find the enemy and beat him!"[17]

Scott moved off cautiously at the head of his 1,200-man brigade accompanied by dragoons and a considerable amount of artillery. At just after 5:00 p.m., within the sight of Niagara Falls off to the right, bugle calls were heard coming from the north. It was July 25 in the northern latitude, where the sun would not set until after 9:00 p.m. The dragoons, in the advance took fire, perking up the infantrymen as they emerged from the confines of the woods a half a mile short of the long, low hill at Lundy's Lane, a road east and west leading to the river. Drummond had picked the high ground, a fundamental element in early nineteenth-century tactics. Looking up from the open plain, Scott's brigade advanced rapidly to contact before the Royal Artillery guns and rockets would mow his men down like ninepins. He sent a courier back to tell Brown before sending one regiment into the woods on the right and drawing his other three up in line of battle. He positioned the field guns in the center and moved off amid screaming rockets and bouncing cannonballs. The main British force of regulars arrived shortly before Scott stepped off and were still taking up positions. The battle was very much on the fly and not the set piece that Drummond had envisaged.

Scott was committed and was assured in his own mind that Brown couldn't be far behind. He took the colors forward with him and began the assault on the hill, which was long and low, only fifty yards high at the acme.

Major Thomas Jesup's 25th Infantry Regiment on the right discovered a road north that came back to the left at the point of the left flank of Riall's brigade, which was preparing to advance. Surprised by the sudden show of force, the Canadian militia, covering Riall, broke up and exposed Riall's brigade. General Riall was captured, but Drummond quickly stuffed the reserve in to bolster his flank.

By 9 p.m., with the July sun setting, Scott's line was suffering and had to be consolidated by Major Henry Leavenworth into a single formation. Still in the van, Scott was wounded but continued to police the line, driving his blue-coated infantry, who took on the shadows as they crept up the slope enveloped in their own smoke.

Brown arrived at last, leading three fresh brigades and the remainder of the artillery. The 21st Regiment was called on to take the Royal Artillery guns that were doing appalling damage. Their commander replied, "I'll try Sir"—today's motto of the regiment. That low mound of earth, hardly noticed before by travelers along Lundy's Lane, became a pinnacle brawled over by desperate men, nearly unseen in the gathering doom. The Americans slowly pushed their way to the top and then were shoved back off. Drummond, Brown, and Scott were wounded. As for Scott,

> Two horses were shot out from under him and he had to pass the last hour in the conflict on foot. One ball struck his side injuring his two ribs badly; but, tieing his scarf tightly over the wound he continued with his men. Late in the fighting he received a second ball in the left shoulder, which shattered the joint and compelled him to give up to the surgeon. Weak from the loss of blood from the first wound, the last shot, added sharp pain to the depletion, prostrating him utterly and the surgeon gave him little hope of early or easy recovery.[18]

Drummond was having unforeseen difficulties. His Indians had melted away when the American artillery found the range. He lost control of his local militia and had them removed from the field when they began to fire in all directions. A fresh regiment under British Major Hercules Scott marched and countermarched, never finding a place until late in the battle. Drummond had the high hand on the hill with more troops than the Americans, but late in the battle it didn't seem to matter. Drummond, recovered from his graze in the neck, organized a three-regiment counterattack and drove up the hill against the Americans silhouetted against the bright night sky. Scott reorganized a unit and charged into Drummond's flank in an attempt to dislodge the British assault. In the darkness, Scott was fired upon from both sides. Scott, shot through, collapsed and was taken from the field.

Leaders on both sides relinquished control, and the American formations lost heart with the wounding of Brown. Word passed to "pull back." It was over. The British remained on the hill.

CHRONOLOGIES

Henry Dearborn

1751, February 23	Born at North Hampton, New Hampshire
1775	A doctor, he was elected captain of the militia and fought at Bunker Hill and Quebec with Benedict Arnold
1777	Battle of Saratoga
1778	Valley Forge and Trenton
1781	Battle of Yorktown, Massachusetts; promoted to major general in the state militia after the war
1792	Elected to Congress
1801	Appointed Secretary of War under President Jefferson
1805	Involved with the Aaron Burr plot
1809	Collector of the Port of Boston
1812	Appointed commanding general of the U.S. Army under President Madison; authored a plan for the invasion of Canada
1812	Invades Canada intending to take Montreal, but fails and is relieved

Jacob Brown

1775	Born in Bucks County, Pennsylvania
1790s	Teacher in Quaker schools in New Jersey and New York City
1799	Buys land in northwestern New York state and founds Brownsville
1803	Land agent and minor New York state official
1807	Jefferson's embargo against Great Britain turns Brown and his neighbors into smugglers; appointed captain in the militia
1809	Appointed colonel in the militia
1811	Appointed brigadier general in the New York militia
1812	Builds the defenses at Sackets Harbor
1812	Defends Ogdensburg, New York

1813	Commissioned a brigadier general in the regular army
1813	Commands a brigade in an expedition to capture Montreal
1813	Missed the Battle at Crysler's Farm
1813	Establishes the French Mills Cantonment
1813	Commissioned a major general in the regular army
1814	Leads the army in the Niagara at the battles of Chippewa and Lundy's Lane

Winfield Scott

1786	Born in Petersburg, Virginia
1806	William and Mary College, lawyer
1808	Appointed captain, light artillery, regular army
1809	Court-martialed by Major General Wilkinson
1812, October	Fought at Queenston, Canada, and captured
1813, November 20	Fought at Battle of Crysler's Farm, Canada
1814, March	Promoted to regular brigadier general
1814, July 5	Battle of Chippewa, Canada
1814, July 25	Battle of Lundy's Lane, Canada

NOTES

1. Lloyd Brown and Howard H. Peckham, *The Revolutionary War Journal of Henry Dearborn, 1775–1785* (Chicago: The Claxton Club, 1939), 11.

2. Brown and Peckham, *The Revolutionary War Journal of Henry Dearborn.*

3. Brown and Peckham, *The Revolutionary War Journal of Henry Dearborn,* 16.

4. Brown and Peckham, *The Revolutionary War Journal of Henry Dearborn,* 17.

5. Brown and Peckham, *The Revolutionary War Journal of Henry Dearborn,* 20.

6. Brown and Peckham, *The Revolutionary War Journal of Henry Dearborn,* 20.

7. Brown and Peckham, *The Revolutionary War Journal of Henry Dearborn,* 22.

8. John R. Elting, *Amateurs to Arms: A Military History of the War of 1812* (Chapel Hill, NC: Algonquin Books, 1991), 2.

9. Brown and Peckham, *The Revolutionary War Journal of Henry Dearborn,* 16.

10. Brown and Peckham, *The Revolutionary War Journal of Henry Dearborn,* 14.

11. David G. Fitz-Enz, ed., *The Final Invasion: Plattsburgh, the War of 1812's Most Decisive Battle* (New York: Cooper Square Press, 2001), 7.

12. John D. Morris, *Sword of the Border: Major General Jacob Jennings Brown, 1775–1828* (Kent, OH: Kent State University Press, 2000), 23.

13. Morris, *Sword of the Border,* 28.

14. Orville James Victor, *The Life, and Military and Civic Services of Lieut-Gen. Winfield Scott: Complete Up to the Present Period* (New York: Beadle & Co., 1852), 83.

15. Victor, *The Life, and Military and Civic Services of Lieut-Gen. Winfield Scott*, 84.

16. Elting, *Amateurs to Arms*, 187.

17. Morris, *Sword of the Border*, 115.

18. Victor, *The Life, and Military and Civic Services of Lieut-Gen. Winfield Scott*, 47.

6

ALEXANDER MACOMB AND
THOMAS MACDONOUGH

Keeping an army in America has been nothing but a public nuisance.

—President John Adams

ALEXANDER MACOMB

IN THE spring of 1782, the last year of the Revolutionary War, an adventurer, Alexander Macomb, and wife, Marie Catherine, began a family at the tiny far western frontier log fort that clung to the banks of the Detroit River. The boy, named for his father, increased the outpost's population to one more than 200 white people. Tied to the British government as a land agent, fur trader, and surveyor, Macomb lost his position with the signing of the Treaty of Paris, ending the Revolutionary War. Like many British colonial civil servants, paid by the Crown, who supported the revolution and therefore remained behind when the British went home, Macomb was free of the king and unemployed.

The following year in New York City, he used his knowledge to speculate on large tracts of western wilderness, becoming an affluent commercial magnate in the financial capital of the new United States. At one point, he acquired the southern shore counties along the St. Lawrence River and Lake Ontario, which became known as the Macomb Purchase. From the beginning of his term as president of the United States of America, George Washington resided with the Macombs at their mansion, Number 7 Broadway. Buying and selling parcels of tractless land and risking large amounts on government securities in the volatile financial market eventually reduced the family to ruin and bankruptcy. Once the richest man in the state, Alexander Macomb senior spent time in debtor's prison.[1]

Alexander and his four brothers were educated in Episcopal schools, learning to fit into the society of the New England merchant class that was about to figure prominently in the coming conflict. As a teenager, Alexander took on the classics and military arts of fencing and marksmanship, knowing that a gentleman might have to defend his honor. His sister May married a son of an Earl who settled in New Jersey, where the youthful Alex was introduced to the finest of society. He grew to be strong and outgoing; some said a natural leader, so it was no surprise when he chose to be a soldier.

Soldier

With the intercession of Alexander Hamilton, a family friend, President Adams signed a commission for Macomb for the Light Dragoons. Assigned to administrative duties in the office of the adjutant general, Macomb became acquainted with the structure of the tiny army, but, of more importance, he gained the advantages garnered close to the flagpole. As a well-educated staff officer, his facility with mathematics and his manipulation of the English language were sought from those in high position who struggled to express their point of view. Soon his civil engineering talent was needed to construct fortifications along the coast and at the entrance to harbors, basic to the defensive posture of the United States. Major General James Wilkinson knew a useful assistant when he met one and sponsored the young officer. Even though the army was reduced to an unprecedented low level after the fracas with the French, by 1801 Macomb was a staff officer with Wilkinson in the Ohio Territory, where the Northwest Indian War was in its infancy. There, he met and impressed Mad Anthony Wayne and contemporaries William Henry Harrison and Solomon Van Rensselaer. By 1802, he was a first lieutenant and sent off to join the Corps of Engineers at a horseshoe bend in the Hudson River called West Point. Among the members of the first class of what would become the Military Academy, as a graduate Macomb joined the faculty, assuming the duty of judge advocate, charged with the conduct of courts-martial. Using the British army's procedure, he authored *A Treatise on Law and the Court Martial*. In an early court, he spoke for his old boss in *Wilkinson v. Butler*, a case of insubordination in which the colonel refused a direct order to cut his white hair. This was typical of Wilkinson, who also charged Winfield Scott, very early in his career, with a similar absurd incident, causing Scott to leave the service for a few years. As a reward for services rendered, Macomb was promoted to captain in 1805, a meteoric rise from cornet to captain in less than six years. The captain praised Wilkinson openly when others in and out of the army saw the general for what he was: a dangerous conspirator. Ever the sycophant, he came to the aid of Wilkinson when he was tried for involvement in the Aaron Burr treason. With the acquittal of Wilkinson, Macomb was promoted to major in 1809 and lieutenant colonel two years later in spite of his lack of field duty. No other officer of his age received such preferential treatment.

Declaration of War: June 18, 1812

On the eve of war, Lieutenant Colonel Macomb became the adjutant general of the army, similar to the director of operations in the Department of the Army in modern times; he oversaw the running of the army on a daily basis. Knowing that the future lay in the field, he was assisted in gaining command of the 3rd Artillery Regiment, an empty structure of eighteen batteries that was yet to be recruited and equipped. Now a full colonel in the fall of 1812, showing that there was more to him than a dining room dandy, he fielded the thousand-man regiment and marched it through the wilderness to Sackets Harbor in time for General Dearborn's attack on Kingston, Canada. However, it was November, far too late to begin a campaign. Wintering on the windswept, bone-chilling, snow-driven coast of Lake Ontario turned the pen pusher into a man of purpose. The regiment had to build its own quarters, cook its rations, and remain healthy through the traitorous winter. The trial matured the colonel and by spring he saw soldiering differently. Commodore Chauncey, Brigadier General Pike, and General Dearborn left Macomb's guns behind when attacking York, Canada, that spring. Shortly, the effort moved to the Niagara, but Macomb followed too late to take part in the action. In his absence, his regiment, along with others, defended Sackets Harbor from an assault by General Prevost and Commodore Yeo that was driven off by Colonel Brown's New York militia. It seems that Macomb, for once, was not in the right place at the most propitious moment. At the end of the summer, the attack to take British Fort George, where Lake Erie met the Niagara River, Colonel Macomb, acting in a staff capacity under General Dearborn, participated in the planning for the attack. There, he worked with Commodore Oliver Hazard Perry and learned how to deploy naval assets, something that would become invaluable later.

Fortune Continues to Smile

But things were looking up for the thirty-year-old officer. General Dearborn's grand plan for 1812 was a bust, and many young enthusiastic citizen soldiers suffered and died as a result of his poor execution. As the fall of 1813 turned the forests of the north to autumn colors, Major General James Wilkinson reappeared like magic into the life of Alexander Macomb. A member of Wilkinson's staff as well as a field commander of artillery, Colonel Macomb worked on the coordination for a joint attack by Major General Wade Hampton, who was to attack Montreal from Plattsburgh, New York, while Wilkinson, with 8,000 regulars and militia, was to travel four times the distance and meet Hampton for a coup de main on the capital of Canada. As fall moved toward winter, Hampton, restless, attacked across the border twice. On both occasions, a much smaller force of uniformed French Canadian voltiguers repelled Hampton's infantry. Wilkinson did not appear. In November, the Secretary of War, John Armstrong, whose brainchild the expedition had been, returned to Washington, leaving Wilkinson to return to Sackets Harbor unbloodied and Hampton to desert the army and return to civilian life. It was left to Colonel Macomb, who appeared under a flag of truce, to work out a prisoner exchange with General Prevost in Montreal before winter shut down the frontier. The death of Zebulon Pike in the spring of 1813 had created a vacancy among the handful of brigadier generals. Before the winter of 1813 set in, Alexander Macomb was promoted to brigadier general in the regular army.

In the spring, even Wilkinson could concede that Sackets Harbor was no place to launch an attack on Montreal. Consolidating his force on Lake Champlain, forty miles due south of Montreal, Wilkinson split it between New York and Vermont, where it could be provisioned for an assault once more in the spring of 1814. Wilkinson was aware of former president Jefferson's boast in the newspapers, "I have invited General Lafayette to join me for tea in Montreal this spring." Once more, Jefferson stirred the pot.

In March 1814, Canada was about to be invaded once again. Macomb was summoned to the frontier, where Wilkinson, at Rouses Point, poised at the north end of Lake Champlain, assured of success. In less than ten miles, the sodden roads, dense forest, and marshy ground slowed the attack of 5,000 uninspired soldiers. In short order, the attack was blunted when only 500 Canadian militia at Lacolle Mill confronted Wilkinson. The general offered his resignation, but a court-martial was more likely. Relieved of command, he said, according to newspapers, "Before I could draw my sword I was relieved of command."

At Last, a Competent General

Major General George Izard was appointed in his place. Izard was a professional soldier who had been trained in Europe with the likes of Wellington and other now successful and famous foreign generals. The winds of war had suddenly changed for the Americans. Napoleon was a prisoner on the Isle of Elba, and England was free to do what it wished with the idle British army drinking its way through the wine cellars of southern France. It chose to end the War of 1812 in Great Britain's favor. Izard knew what he was up against as the hundreds of troop ships unloaded at Fort Chambly twenty miles north of La Colle Mill. That summer, he and Macomb, who had consolidated his troops with Izard at Plattsburgh, trained a new crop of recruits sent north to the border. All along the coast that summer of 1814, the Royal Navy not only blockaded the ports, holding the American Navy captive at their own docks, but also sent raiding parties and hired privateers to break into coastal cities to burn and pillage.

North of the border, Lieutenant General Sir George Prevost had spent the spring of 1814 the same way he had spent every spring for the last two years: repelling invasions. He was becoming a master of defense, never really having the troops do anything else. Through the expert use of terrain and troops of various kinds, he and his field commanders had been able to maintain the borders intact. His spies told him that things were changing south of the border and that the old politically appointed generals were gone and new, young, and competent officers of all grades had taken over. Regular American formations were experienced now, and supply lines were improving. The conduct of war was changing character within the American ranks, and the British commander feared what had happened to his father's army at Yorktown might be repeated again during his watch. Prevost had lost some of his best commanders, and England was not hearing his repeated pleas for assistance.

THE BRITISH ARE COMING

In Washington, overtures were heard for a renewal of peace talks that had been sponsored by the Czar of Russia and that broke down the previous year. Lord Bathurst, colonial and war minister, was talking peace and writing war:

> From
> Earl Bathurst
> 3rd June 1814
> To Sir George Pervost, Governor-General of Canada
> > Reinforcements
> > allotted for North America
> > and the operations contemplated
> > for the employment of
> > them.
> SECRET
> Downing Street
> 3rd June 1814
> Sir,
> I have already communicated to you in my dispatch of the 14th of
> April the intention of His Majesty's government to avail themselves of
> the favorable state of affairs in Europe, in order to reinforce the Army

under your Command. I have now to acquaint you with the arrangements which have been made in consequence, and to point out to you the views with which His Majesty's Government have made is considerable an augmentation of the Army in Canada.

The 2nd Battalion of the Royal Scots of the strength stated in the margin—768—sailed from Spithead on the 9th alto. direct for Quebec, and was joined at Cork by the 97th Regiment destined to relieve the Nova Scotia Fencibles at Newfoundland; which latter will immediate proceed to Quebec.

The 6th & 8th 2nd Regiments of the strength as per margin—980 8 /2. 8 37—sailed from Bordeaux on the 15th alto. direct for Quebec. Orders have also been given for embarking at the same port twelve of the most effective Regiments of the Army under the Duke of Wellington together with the three companies of Artillery on the same service. This Force, which/when joined by the detachments about to proceed from this country will not fall far short of ten thousand Infantry, will proceed in three divisions to Quebec. The first of these divisions will embark immediately, the second a week after the first and the third as soon as the means of transport are collected. The last division however will arrive in Quebec long before the close of the year.

Six other Regiments have also been detached from the Gironde and the Mediterranean four of which are destined to be employed in a direct operation against the Enemy's Coast, and the other two are intended as a reinforcement to Nova Scotia and New Brunswick, available / if circumstances appear to you to render it necessary / for the defense of Canada, or for the offensive operations on the Frontier to which your attention will be particularly directed. It is also in contemplation at a later period of the year to make a more serious attack on some part of the Coast of the United States, and with this view a considerable force will be collected at Cork without delay. These operations will not fail to effect a powerful diversion in your favor.

The result of this arrangement as far as you are immediately concerned will be to place at your disposal the Royals, The Nova Scotia Fencibles, the 6th and the 82nd Regiments amounting to three thousand one hundred and twenty seven men; and to afford you in the course of the year a further reinforcement of ten thousand British troops—10,000—

When this force shall have been placed under your command His Majesty's Government conceive that the Canada's will not only be protected for the time against any attack which the Enemy may have the means of making, but it will enable you to commence offensive operations on the Enemy's Frontier before the close of this campaign. At the same time it is by no means the intention of His Majesty's Government to encourage such forward movements into the Interior of the American territory as might commit the safety of the force placed under your Command. The object to your operations will be, first, to give immediate protection. Secondly, to obtain if possible ultimate security to His Majesty's possessions in America. The entire destruction of Sackets Harbor and the Naval Establishment on Lake Erie and Lake Champlain come under the first description. The maintenance of Fort Niagara and so much of the adjacent Territory as may be deemed necessary, and the occupation of Detroit and the Michigan Country came under the second. Your successes shall enable us to terminate the war by the retention of the Fort of Niagara, and the restoration of Detroit and the whole of the Michigan Country to the Indians. The British frontier will be materially improved. Should there be any advance position on that part of our frontier which extends towards Lake Champlain, the occupation of which would materially tend to the security of the province, you will if you deem it expedient expel the Enemy from it, and occupy it by detachments of the Troops under your Command, Always however, taking care not expose His Majesty's Forces to being cut off by too extended a line of advance.

If you should not consider it necessary to call to your assistance the two Regiments which are to proceed in the first instance to Halifax, Sir J. Sherbroke will receive instruction to occupy as much of the District of Maine as will secure an uninterrupted intercourse between Halifax and Quebec.

In contemplation of the increased force which by this arrangement you will be under the necessity of maintaining in the Province directions have been given for shipping immediately for Quebec provisions for 10,000 men for 6 months.

The Frigate which conveys this letter has also on board one hundred thousand pounds in specie for the use of the Army under your Command. An equal sum will also be embarked on board the Ship of War which may be appointed to convoy to Quebec the fleet which is expected to sail from this country on the 10th or at latest on the 15th instant.

I have the honor to be

Sir

Your most obedient

Humble Servant

(signed)

BATHURST[2]

Prevost had replaced a popular governor, Sir James Craig, at the start of hostilities in the spring of 1812. While 80 percent of the population in Upper Canada was French, Craig, an Anglophile, had filled his government with Englishmen, many of whom had migrated north after the Revolutionary War. The London government, like Jefferson, expected the French citizens of Canada to choose the United States if American troops crossed the border. Sir George, a French speaker whose family originated in Switzerland, brought many French Canadians into power and raised the salary of the Catholic bishop. Sir George had the confidence of the government and the Crown, who paid no attention to the venomous campaign in the London newspapers conducted by the Anglophiles of Canada. To the many citizens of Canada, he had earned the title of "Savior of Canada" because of his defense of the territory from the invasions conducted over the past two years. Prevost showed great personal courage at the battle of Sackets Harbor, though some questioned his actions. But the press never gave him credit. At age forty-six, the governor general possessed considerable energy and strength of will and was known for his graciousness and personal charm. He was described as a suave diplomat but was in declining health, a result of his years of military service in the tropics. A judge in Canada said of him that "he was a tiny light gossamer man, cheerfulness of demeanor, with his simple unassuming manner and consideration of people of every rank."

The British Take the Offensive

Now Sir George not only had the means to defend; more importantly, he could attack. The master plan was most comprehensive. A diversionary force of considerable size was to be formed from London to deceive the American government and military into thinking that an English invasion of the Eastern Seaboard was eminent. President Madison knew that the great victory in France, over Napoleon, would allow England's mighty and experienced armed forces to be let loose on America. With it, they could easily avenge losses of the past two years. The American armed forces were still small and spread very thinly, no match for the veterans of the Napoleonic Wars, which had been going on unending since the turn of the century. If squadrons of Royal Navy, embarked with masses of troops, appeared in New England and along the undefended shoreline of Delaware and Virginia, there would be little to contain them.

Prevost knew that such a diversion would keep reinforcements from appearing on the northern frontier. He need only contend with the enemy he had known. In the far west of Detroit and beyond, there was militia, no real threat. At Niagara, there was little more, with the exception of some regular army units under Brigadier General Winfield Scott. At Sackets Harbor, the key support base for the American western forces, again, only 2,000 army and naval forces were in attendance. The major force was at Plattsburgh, refitting and training after the abortive attack of March on the border of Canada. Its new commander, Major General George Izard, was a formidable officer who had 6,000 regulars, as well as a burgeoning naval flotilla under Commodore Macdonough. In the summer of 1814, as the redcoated regulars arrived, Sir George felt confident that the forces under his command could fulfill the full extent of the instructions contained in the secret order.

His first inclination (and probably that of his boss in London) was to continue the campaign in the Great Lakes. He could overwhelm Sackets Harbor and move against Detroit. But his experience told him that it was hard going on the shore of the Great Lakes and that resupplying a large army would be very difficult, to say nothing of the transport problems. Captain Sir James Yeo could support a portion of the attack, but he was not so sure that 10,000 reinforcements added to the burden of the 3,000 already on the ground would not grind to a logistical halt in that wilderness before winter. He could never sustain them when the lakes and rivers froze. It could be true that the freeze might provide passable tracts if the ice was smooth and the snow was not too deep. But winter along the great length of the St. Lawrence and the shoreline of Lake Ontario could be brutal. He might well repeat the folly of Napoleon in Russia. As a professional soldier, he had studied the New York campaign of Burgoyne in 1777. If he had used Lake Champlain, Lake George, and the headwaters of the Hudson River prudently, it could have been successful. That was a neat little campaign because of the directness of the route, which stabbed like a dagger straight at New York City, the gatekeeper for New England. The opportunity that it now offered seemed irresistible. The London order plainly called for the disarming of Lake Champlain, which was only a few miles due south of Montreal and would satisfy the government's intentions. It could be more easily supplied because his army had always been fed by the farmers of Vermont and New York who used the lake to smuggle goods north since 1807. There was no real threat to his rear from the American troops in the west, which he had contained for the past two years with his formations that were still in place.

He could add a bit of deception to his own plan by sending a small portion of the reinforcement west, making the American commanders believe that he was indeed going to attack Sackets Harbor, thus fixing them in place. They would expect that. By launching a combined army and naval attack straight south, he could break the American army at Plattsburgh instead, while his navy could destroy Macdonough's small fleet and secure the entire lake. There were no regular American forces between Plattsburgh, New

York, and Washington, D.C. The state militias, modeled on the minutemen of Massachusetts from the American Revolutionary War, were not the same force in 1814. He had dealt with them on numerous occasions and found them skittish, ill-equipped, and led by amateurs. After eliminating the front lines at Plattsburgh, he could winter on the edges of Lake Champlain a hundred miles south of the Canadian border and in spring continue down Burgoyne's old route toward New York City. He also believed that his predecessor's, Governor Craig's, assessment may have been correct and that northern New Englanders, faced with the occupation of British soldiers, might give allegiance back to England. His military field position, with the treaty talks now under way again, this time in Ghent, Belgium, would result in the establishment of a new border for Canada at the point where his lines rested. It was a bold plan and an old plan and one that he believed would be well received by Bathurst. After all, had this not been the road to war in North America for nearly a hundred years?

By Land and Lake

The ball was now in Prevost's court for the first time since 1812; he could do what he liked. While the British army gathered at Chambly twenty miles south of Montreal and twenty miles north of the American border, he turned his attention to the Royal Navy. Wellington had said that the key to the control on the frontier was the waterways. This may be the only war in which the front or battle lines and the lines of communications (logistical lines) were the same. Captain Daniel Pring requested to build a frigate on Lake Champlain that was considerably larger and more powerful than the whole of Macdonough's American fleet put together. It was the answer to waterborne warfare. The frigate could easily sweep the lake of the sloops, brigs, and rowed gunboats that were built and armed only to stop smuggling. While Sir George was in command of both the civil government and the military establishment in Upper and Lower Canada, Sir James Yeo, under the Admiralty in London, directly controlled the Royal Navy in North America. This meant that Sir James was tasked in cooperating with but was not commanded by Governor General Prevost, clouding the lines of responsibility.

Disunity of Command

The two men did not get along and maintained separate headquarters. But Sir James agreed that the building of a lake frigate was an excellent idea. He also supported Prevost's plan of attack, which hinged on cooperation between navel and land forces in the upcoming offensive.

In July, Sir James selected Captain Peter Fisher from his staff for the task; to go to the Isle aux Noix, where he began to build the largest ship ever afloat on Lake Champlain. The new ship would be 160 feet overall and mount the new Congreve seven-foot six-inch 24-pound cannons in addition to several carronades mounted in the bow and stern. A third larger than any American vessel in size, it was armed with long-range cannons that could terrorize both ship and shore. This new gun could fire a 24-pound solid iron cannonball over a mile and a half with great accuracy. She would be built using material provided by smugglers from New York and Vermont.

Guns and Rockets

In addition to the infantry, there was a considerable body of artillery. Five companies of field artillery were added to the Canadian army. The initial group, 536 men and forty guns, were shipped from France. Others were to come from the arsenal at Woolwich, only a few miles from London, the home of the Board of Ordnance.[3] At this time, the artillery was not part of the army and like the navy was a separate defense entity. The guns and crews were sent to the army in the field by the Master Gunner of Ordnances, who was equal to the Commander of the Army at Horse Guards, in London. Royal Artillery units, once in the field, were then placed in direct support of the infantry and cavalry. Once under the army commander's eye, they obeyed orders like any other unit. Their firepower on the battlefield was often decisive. In Canada, they were equipped with siege artillery that was soon to be invested in the attack at the defenses of Plattsburgh.

The leaders added one special unit to the expedition by the Ordnance establishment. A troop of Congreve rockets was sent.[4] The 172 rocketeers, all mounted, were the most mobile of the artillery elements. It was as surprising to us today as it was to opponents of the British army that there were operational rockets on the battlefield at Plattsburgh. Employed by the Board of Ordnance for both the Royal Navy and the British Army, they were more than just a curiosity.[5] So extraordinary in 1814, they come down to us today in the very words of our national anthem, "the rockets red glare, the bombs bursting in air."

The Plight of the American Defenders

American Major General George Izard was getting reports of increased military activity in Canada from Peter Sailly, the Customs Collector, for the north country. Sailly was a true patriot and a zealous spymaster. Ezra Thurber, a customs officer at Champlain, reported to Sailly that one of his spies on the

Isle aux Noix told him that the British were building a frigate, bigger than anything seen on the lake. Other spies confirmed that there were so many troop transports in Quebec Harbor that the estuary looked like a pine forest. General Izard, headquartered in Plattsburgh, hurried his training program. Secretary of War Armstrong had ordered the new commander in the north to establish camps of instruction and to school the regular soldiers and officers in drill and hygiene. While they trained, new uniforms, supplies, and weapons arrived. This was in response to Izard's complaint that his forces consisted of inexperienced officers and green troops with too little time left in their enlistment to teach them essential skills. First at Albany and then at Plattsburgh and Burlington, Vermont, he and his second in command, Brigadier General Alexander Macomb, spent the spring and summer making ready to defend against an invasion. For the past two years, these officers had been on the offensive. Now the roles were reversed. It was plain that Redcoats on the waterways of Quebec and Montreal were soon to be found on Lake Champlain, headed south into the heartland of New England.

Reinforced by Army Headquarters, Izard's complement numbered 6,000 in round numbers by midsummer. Those numbers flatten out when the sick, well over 1,000 were added to the hospital list and the military prisoners in the stockade of more than a hundred were subtracted from the active ranks.

It was said that the best of Izard's soldiers were equal to the worst of Prevost's. True or not, the Americans certainly looked like underdogs. The U.S. infantryman wore a dark blue long-tailed coat that buttoned down the chest, doing away with the need for a waistcoat. The blue color was inherited from the uniform of a father or grandfather who fought for liberty from England. It contrasted with the red of the British soldier. There was no grand guardsman or king's special troops to adorn the American ranks. As the cost of uniforms drained the federal war chest, the colored facings were removed. The number stamped on their buttons could separate one regiment from another. The musicians in each regiment wore the only colorful uniforms. The drums, fifes, and bugles were the communications systems of the army and were found in each company.

The American infantry was divided into regulars, federal troops under the authority of the central government, and the militia, those who belonged to the state governor. There were two grades of militia, those that were formally organized and supported from federal funds and the backup militia who were interested farmers who treated it more like a social obligation. When invited to attend, as militia troops were when the call went out, some came and some didn't. It depended on the time of year, crop conditions, and the danger involved. Generally speaking the troops in the militia were as good as the men who led. In the case of the regulars, the men were better than the officers, political appointees who sought commissions and later regretted the boon when faced with the conduct of a war, for which they were untrained

The standard weapon issued was the "model 1775" musket. For its day, it was superior to the British Brown Bess. It was lighter and more accurate, and it fired a slightly smaller ball. Loaded with "buck and ball," it could be more effective against dense formations. The idea had come from fighting the Indians in the wooded frontier. The Indians moved quickly through the brush, and a clear shot was rare. At one point, the muskets were loaded with nothing but buckshot. The paper-wrapped cartridge contained black powder, a small amount of which was poured into the flash pan of the lock. The remaining powder was poured down the front of the barrel. The torn paper and metal ball were then rammed down the barrel to form a tight fit. The American ammunition differed from the British in that, in addition to the musket ball, there were three pieces of rather formidable buckshot included for that extra spray of lethal fragmentation. The British army considered this to be a minor atrocity of war, along with the American habit of sniping.

Izard first had to teach his troops how to shoot the musket. Today, we think of all early Americans as sharpshooters honed from clearing the wilderness of Indians and hunting for the family table. But the reality was that most recruits were from the towns. Farm boys were busy on farms. Many had never held a firearm and had to be taught from the very beginning. The musket was capable of being loaded and fired three times in one minute. The British soldier was famous for doing just that, in the teeth of a French charge. To attain that rate of fire, the recruit must follow a twenty-step procedure religiously. Skill came only with a great deal of practice. Repetition and supervision were the answer. No soldier of any time wants to spend days on the shooting range, but General Macomb knew that it was the only way to ensure survival. Once skilled, it was required that the officers instill the confidence that the musket and formation could withstand a ground assault. This was going to be a battle fought from cover if the Americans had their way. A protected static soldier in the defense could hold against superior numbers. The new commander knew that he could not risk his force to the open field. Drill, or command and control of the forces on the battlefield, was essential. In a day without radio, only packing men into formations that moved as a block could accomplish this. To maintain that integrity of fifty or more, the officer trained his men in simple voice and hand signals that directed them on the field in conjunction with other blocks of the same regiment. Maintaining shoulder-to-shoulder lines that were twenty-one inches behind the line to their front had the effect of encouraging valor, or steadying up the skittish. It also made them a great target for artillery and cavalry. Musket fire was highly inaccurate at anything over a football field's length away. Therefore, it is easy to see that colored uniforms in the open were not that dangerous, since few weapons could reach out and kill them, especially if they were moving. In fact, the reason the British wore red was to scare the enemy. The color, combined with the very tall hats, was designed to make the wearer look much larger and more fierce than he really might be. Such training was provided by the drill regulation of General Von Steuben's Blue Book of 1779 and upgraded by the French drill manual of 1791. But the northern army of America did not have time to match the offensive skill of the British regular, who wanted to get this over with in a hurry and go home. Izard expected the red columns to come smashing down from the north with only one thing in mind: the destruction of the Yankee army in the field.

Before long, all the American troops would be digging for their lives. But the presence of the black soldiers caused ill will and was used as an excuse that increased the numbers of deserters.

Guns

There were five full companies of artillery gathered that summer at Plattsburgh. They were a mix of cannon size. The primary weapon for the Americans seems to be the French 8-pounder, which was actually 8.8 pounds, therefore about the same size as the British standard 9-pounder. There were several pairs of 12-pounders that were of French design. Although the Americans had no siege guns as such, they did have naval 24-pounders mounted on fortification slides of both French and English design run on ten-inch bulky wooden wheels.

America on the Defense

George Izard knew that he could not meet the English on the open field: his troops were not steady, and being outnumbered, he used the convolutions in the land to multiply his force. The terrain north of Plattsburgh was a wilderness of virgin forest and small farms. There was only one road, to the north, that the enemy must take. He knew that they could not be embarked on the Royal Navy's lake fleet since there were no transports. Six miles north of town, the road split. At Beekmantown, the main road continued straight south, and a western spur reached the lakeshore and continued south again along Cumberland Bay and into Plattsburgh. It was an easy and natural envelopment for the English; one that Izard could not hope to defend. The Saranac River, a swift-flowing torrent, that emptied the melted snow from the Adirondack Mountains twenty miles south, cut a gorge on the south side of town. It formed a peninsula. The river on the west and north and Cumberland Bay on the east made it a natural fortress. The lake was both a curse and a blessing. He would bring the U.S. Navy's small fleet into the bay not only to protect the army from the Royal Navy, but also to add their guns to his army artillery. Using the land and the water, his force could be nearly equal to the British if he dug in on the river's edge and built redoubts with thick dirt berms to protect his static guns. It was certain that Sir George Prevost would occupy the town and attack Izard's front while the English navy attempted to attack the American right flank, which rested on Cumberland Bay. The only certain outcome was that the town of Plattsburgh, with its seventy-eight houses, mills, stores, warehouses, churches, and courthouse, would not survive this battle intact. The citizens began to slip away as the forts and blockhouses went up.

THE AMERICAN NAVY'S LAKE
FLEET UNDER MACDONOUGH

American naval Lieutenant Thomas Macdonough was brought in from his duties defending ports along the Maine coast and put in command in the summer of 1812. As master commandant, the senior naval officer on the scene, he assumed the position as commodore of the fleet of small boats. Though only twenty-eight years old when he arrived, he was nationally known as a professional sailor with deep-sea experience, having fought the Barbary pirates off the coast of Tripoli. Born in New Castle County, Delaware, his father was a physician and a major in the Continental Army during the Revolution. Thomas Macdonough entered navy service in 1798 with Decatur in the Mediterranean, where he behaved with great gallantry. Later, he gained notoriety from an incident in the harbor of Gibraltar while a lieutenant on the USS *Syren*, which was moored near an American merchant brig. A boat from a British man-of-war went along side the brig and seized a sailor who was claimed as a British subject. Macdonough, whose captain was absent, saw the incident. He armed, manned his gig, and gave chase. He overtook the boat under the guns of a British frigate, freed the sailor, and took him to the American man-of-war. The British captain, in a great rage, appeared on the *Syren* and inquired of Macdonough how he dared take a man from his boat. The following conversation took place as reported in newspapers in the United States: "What are you up to, sir?" shouted the British commander. Macdonough stood fast. "That seaman was under the protection of my country's flag, and it was my duty." Angered by the young officer's statement, the British captain's reply was strong: "You are a blaggard and pirate like all your countrymen, sir. I shall lay my frigate along side and sink your ship." Macdonough's next words went into American naval history: "While she swims you shall not have the man!" The British captain blustered, "You'll repent of your rashness, young man. Suppose I had been in that boat, would you have dared to commit such an act?" Macdonough responded, "I should have made the attempt, sir!" Continuing, Macdonough's adversary countered, "What! Would you interfere if I were to impress men from that brig?" Coolly, the young American lieutenant faced his enemy and replied, "You have only to try it, sir." The British officer wheeled about and left but did not accept the challenge.

Commodore Macdonough had previously alarmed the Secretary of the Navy with reports of both the raid by British Captain Pring, which nearly bottled up his entire complement for the duration of the war, and the news that Yeo was building a lake frigate. Frigates of that class had appeared on Lake Ontario and were feared. On a lake like little Champlain, she would rule. Jones sent his shipbuilder, Noah Brown, from the navy yard in Brooklyn, New York. He arrived at Vergennes, Vermont, with 200 carpenters. At the Otter Creek yard, they built the twenty-six-gun sloop of war *Saratoga* in forty days from native pine. Macdonough wrote in later life,

> Various reports reached me of their preparations—that the keel of a large vessel had been laid and a number of large gunboats or galleys were also constructing. On our side, as I had directions at all hazards to maintain our ascendency, we were not idle. The keel of a ship was laid at Vergennes to mount 26 guns, also the keels of 6 large galleys, the latter to be 75 feet long and 15 feet wide. Went down to Albany and New York to arrange and forward the articles and supplies for this force. In the meantime rendezvous were opened along on the seaboard at the different large places and all the necessary artificers sent to the lake from New York, from whence the guns and heavy articles were sent, though we had transported from Boston the sheet anchor of the Saratoga which weighed 3,000 pounds. Everything on both sides went on with all the dispatch which it was possible to apply.[6]

He also converted a steamboat hull into the seventeen-gun *Ticonderoga* and rehabilitated ten gunboats. The gunboats carried a 24-pounder cannon in the prow and an 18-pound cullumbiad, which was a cross between a carronade and a gun and fired explosive shells. The cullumbiad is a heavy-shell gun, combining the qualities of a gun, a howitzer, and a mortar. It required the loader to light a fuse that was cut to a length so that it would explode over or just as it struck the target. Once lit, it was stuffed down the barrel and sent down range by the main charge in the bottom of the barrel. It was possible for the lit fuse to set off the main charge prematurely, catching the crew exposed. The crew thought it so dangerous that they refused to fire the cullumbiad when fused.

When the American spy network passed on the full horror of the capability of the *Confiance*, Brown built the brig *Eagle*, a twenty-gun vessel, in nineteen days, complete with rigging and guns, ready for combat.

To crew the American vessels, few lake men wanted to serve because the presence of lake fever made the work unhealthy. Only 250 seamen, most not able bodied, could be found in New York Harbor to crew the new vessels. Macomb added another 250 soldiers. As the summer wore on, both sides trained, built, and provisioned for the invasion.

In early August, Izard agreed with his boss, Secretary of War Armstrong, that his preparation of the defenses at Plattsburgh might not be necessary. Prevost was preparing to send troops west according to the American informants in Montreal. Unknown to Izard and Sailly, Armstrong had a spy of his own who visited Canada, a lawyer who insisted that Prevost's entire force was starting to move west up the St. Lawrence. Caleb Nichols made numerous reports that may be found in the National Archives in Washington, D.C. In light of subsequent events, some of his information has proven to have been erroneous. It appears that Armstrong received military advice as well as raw intelligence from Nichols. He enjoyed the confidence of the secretary that Izard did not. Why Armstrong put such great stock in Nichols's advice is unknown since the untrained spy had no military background. Peter Sailly would have disagreed if he had known of Nichols's existence. His spies reported a coordinated attack from the north aimed at Plattsburgh. Sailly predicted that the new frigate would lead and destroy the American fleet on the lake before investing Cumberland Bay and bombarding the town while the British army attacked from the land. By mid-August, Izard received orders to take the majority of his army, 4,500, and go west to reinforce "The Niagara" between Lake Ontario and Lake Erie. George Izard had second thoughts; his training at the military school in Europe nagged at him, and he pored over the situation with his deputy commander, Alexander Macomb. He wrote to Armstrong in the strongest terms that the British would pour their whole strength down on Lake Champlain, he was sure of it. Word came back ordering him west to Sackets Harbor immediately. The War Department was relying on Armstrong's personal spy in Canada, who kept feeding bad information. It must be remembered that at that moment in Washington, the War Department had been burned out, and the cabinet was on horseback in northwestern Maryland because of the August attack on the nation's capital. Sir George's clever diversion, sending only one brigade west, had done the trick. It was plain that the London government put the diversionary portion of their strategic plan into action, churning up the Chesapeake Bay.

Izard convinced Commodore Macdonough that the army needed the navy to guard the right watery flank. It was not a hard sell. Izard and Macdonough had always cooperated, and the commodore knew he owed the victory at the mouth of Otter Creek to the cannons and troops sent by the army. The army had manned his boats for the past two years and would do so again for the upcoming battle in spite of the orders to the contrary sent him by Secretary Jones. Macdonough also knew that his flotilla had little chance on the open water of the lake against the new Royal Navy frigate armed with long-range cannons. He accepted the mission to bring his vessels into the bay and bombard the Royal Navy from one side of his ships while providing gunfire support from the other directed against British army land targets. Unaware that the federal government and therefore the War Department were no longer functioning, George Izard waited for his change of orders in vain. On August 26, he began to move south to Schenectady, New York, in stages. Once there, he waited another two days, hoping that Armstrong would rescind his orders. Nothing came. Major General George Izard's last communiqué before he fades from history was, "I must not be held responsible for the consequences of abandoning my present strong position."[7] He wasn't. His correspondence was not a priority in the War Department, wherever it was after the loss of Washington. Brigadier General Macomb was left to command the troops remaining at Plattsburgh.

Left Behind

They were a motley lot. There were seventy-seven strays from a variety of regiments, fifty from Captain Lenards artillery company, 100 from Captain Mc-Glassin's company of the 15th Regiment, and 200 of Captain Sproll's company of the 13th. Remnants from the 6th, 29th, 30th, 31st, 33rd, and 34th Regiments of regular infantry brought the total up to 1,500. No dragoons were left behind, and the rifle regiment marched off with General Izard. In addition, there were the sick and military prisoners who were more of a burden than anything else. The force was what George Izard could spare. The coming battle had now dramatically changed character. Sir George Prevost's ruse, sending General Kempt's brigade of under 1,000 to reinforce his lines in the west, had drawn off the bulk of the Yankee regular infantry. The odds on land were now 12,000 Redcoats against 1,500 regulars, plus whatever the junior American Brigadier General Macomb could muster from the militia. Major General Benjamin Mooers of the New York State militia was asked to mobilize his units in the northern counties. Mooers, a local man from Plattsburgh, was competent, but his troops were not. He called for 2,500 militia to come to Plattsburgh in the last week of August. A meager 700 showed up. Governor Martin Chittenden, of Vermont, a thorn in the side of the Army of the North, continued to hinder the use of his militia outside the border of the Green Mountain State. Leaving the decision to his commander, Major General Sam Strong mustered his militia, 2,500 of the Green Mountain Boys, on the eastern edge of Lake Champlain. Macdonough was prevailed upon to transport them across the lake on the lake sloop the *President* (and anything else that floated), all arriving the day before the main English fleet. While things looked very dark for the defense of the town of Plattsburgh, the odds on the lake between the two navies were not any better.

CHRONOLOGIES

Alexander Macomb

1782, April 3	Born at Fort Detroit, Michigan Territory
1798	Joined the New York state militia
1799	Commissioned a cornet regular army and promoted to second lieutenant the same year and discharged
1801	Second lieutenant, Dragoon Regiment, and joined General Wilkinson's staff in Pittsburgh
1802	Commissioned a first lieutenant, Corps of Engineers, at West Point academy
1802	Judge advocate
1805	Promoted to captain
1807	Inspector of coastal fortifications
1808	Promoted to major
1811	Lieutenant Colonel Macomb defended General Wilkinson in his court-martial on charges resulting in the Burr conspiracy
1812, April	Named adjutant general of the army
1812, July	Promoted colonel of the 3rd Artillery Regiment
1813	Staff officer in the Niagara campaign and later in the Montreal campaign
1814, March	With Wilkinson on the aborted Montreal campaign
1814, January	Promoted to brigadier general
1814, September 11	Brigadier General Macomb commanded at the Battle of Plattsburgh

Thomas Macdonough

1783	Born in New Castle County, Delaware
1800, May 27	Midshipman on the corvette, USS *Ganges*

1801, October 20	USS *Constellation* bound for the Mediterranean Sea
1803	USS *Philadelphia* against the Barbary Pirates
1803, October	USS *Enterprise* under Decatur
1804, February 6	With Decatur in the USS *Philadelphia* raid
1804	Promoted to lieutenant and assigned to the USS *Syren*
1806	Built gunboats at Middletown, Connecticut
1807–1808	Commanded the USS *Wasp*
1809	First lieutenant of the USS *Essex*
1810–1812	On leave
1812, Summer	Commander of a gunboat squadron at Portland, Maine
1812, October	Commander of the Lake Champlain Squadron
1813, July 24	Promoted to Master Commandant
1814, September 11	Battle of Lake Champlain

NOTES

1. Allen S. Everest, *The Military Career of Alexander Macomb* (Plattsburgh, NY: Clinton County Historical Society, 1989), 1.

2. The secret order was found among the private family papers of Sir Christopher Prevost, sixth Baronet, at his home in Portugal. The order remained "secret" into the next century. The famous naval writer American Admiral Alfred T. Mahon knew of the order and the gist of the content but had never seen it in 1905, when he wrote about the battle. It was discovered at the English Public Records Office in 1922 but lost again soon after. This order, Sir George's copy, was unearthed with the help of Sir Christopher. It does not appear in the record of court-martial held by the Royal Navy on board HMS *Gladiator* in 1815.

3. Taken from an article on famous Canadians in the *London Gazette*, found among the private papers of the Prevost family.

4. William Congreve, son of Captain William Congreve, was a scientist and inventor with the Board of Ordnance and invented the Congreve Rocket System. He was at one time the superintendent of the Royal Laboratory at the Royal Arsenal, which is where ammunition was developed.

5. William Congreve, *Details of the Rocket System* (London: Woolwich Arsenal, 1814), made available through the courtesy of the Royal Artillery Institute Library, Woolwich, England, Brigadier K. Timbers, curator.

6. William S. Dudley, ed., *The Naval War of 1812: A Documentary History*, vol. 1 (Washington, DC: Naval History Center, Department of the Navy, 1985), 371.

7. John R. Elting, *Amateurs to Arms: A Military History of the War of 1812* (New York: Da Capo Press, 1995), 220.

British Invasion, September 11, 1814; John Wool; and Benjamin Mooers

The English never draw a line without blurring it.

—Winston Churchill

URING THE last week of August, Sir George Prevost received very good and very bad news. First, the good news: General Izard had pulled out with the majority of his command, taking the bait, and had gone west. Within a few days, the northern army of the United States would be so committed to the rutted forest tracks of northwestern New York that they could not turn back and influence the battle planned for Plattsburgh. In addition to their treachery, the smugglers provided the last of the deck planks to complete *Confiance*. The very bad news was as unexpected as a thunderbolt. At the last possible minute, Commodore Sir James Yeo relieved his personal appointee, Captain Peter Fisher, the commander of the Royal Navy on Lake Champlain and builder of the new frigate, whom he had appointed to the job only a few months before. Yeo, never a supporter of the governor-general, confiding to a friend, said, "One hot head [referring to Prevost] was quite enough for the battle." The eighteen-year-old daughter of Sir George Prevost, Anne, records the event in her diary:

August 1814, Montreal, Canada.
During the summer, my Father was employed in frequently visiting the out posts, and he appeared to be greatly interested in the fitting out of a small Squadron in Lake Champlain. Captain Fisher was the Senior officer and he and my Father always appeared to be on the most cordial terms— he was several times at Montreal; but just as the Fleet was nearly ready, Sir James Yeo thought proper to supersede Captain Fisher, whose local knowledge must have been of value, and to appoint Captain Downie to

the command. About 9,000 men were concentrated in the Champlain frontier and it was generally understood that as soon as the equipment of the Squadron was completed, an expedition would be effected into the Enemy's territory.[1]

Sir George, who agreed to the replacement of Captain Pring only because Sir James insisted that he could not handle the flotilla destined for the battle, was amazed when Fisher fell from grace and was also replaced. Captain Downie reported to Montreal and was briefed by his governor-general on the importance of the naval action within the overall strategy outlined from London. He understood the urgency of the situation and left immediately for the shipyard where his new flagship was to be launched within days:

This brave hero, Captain George Downie, was the son of a respectable clergyman in the county of Ross, Ireland. At an early period in his youth he entered the navy as a midshipman, and served on board the Circe frigate in the memorable battle of Camperdown. He acted in the same capacity for sometime, in the Melampus, and afterwards in the Appollo frigate, in the West Indies for several years. In this station his uniform good conduct and strict attention to his duty received the most flattering approbation of his superiors and recommended him to the particular notice of Admiral Montague, the commander of the Jamaica station, who promoted him to the rank of Lieutenant. On his return to England for the recovery of his health, which had been much impaired, his promotion was confirmed by the admiralty and in 1804, he was appointed by Earl St. Vincent to the Sea Horse frigate, 36 guns, then commanded by the Honorable Captain Boyle. After seeing a good deal of service, he was promoted to the rank of commodore and placed in command of the fleet on Lake Champlain in 1814.[2]

Captain Downie was now the commodore of the Champlain flotilla and arrived on a dead run. He was tasked to take over a new command of four ships, one of which, *Confiance*, was launched on his arrival at the dockyards. His new boss called his portion of the invasion critical to the success of the plans set in motion by his betters at the highest level of His Majesty's government in London. George Downie was the center of attention. It was plain to him that if he failed, in spite of the fact that his force numbered only a fraction of the total troops committed by England, that he would indeed have let his nation down. At Isle aux Noix, master shipbuilder Simons took him around his flagship, whose bottom was wet for the first time on that day, August 25. She was like the other frigates that he had sailed on the Great Lakes for the past two years, but there was simply no time to get to know her.

CONFIANCE, THE KEY TO VICTORY

Everything aboard the *Confiance* was a third larger than her adversary, *Saratoga*. Longer, wider, and faster, she carried one-third more sail on her three contraband masts. Not only did *Confiance* have more guns, but they could shoot farther and were more accurate. There were four determining factors in the days of sail that rated ships: the weight of gun projectiles on target, the speed of the ship under sail, the competence of the crew to exploit both, and the ability of the captain to fight the ship. The first two went hands down to the English. The crews on either side were equally inept. Each suffered from a lack of trained sailors and gunners. The British had a leg up, though, because the Royal Marines were embarked on all the ships. They were trained gunners and drilled the 39th Foot Regiment at every possible opportunity. The masters of the fleets, Downie and Macdonough, destined to meet in combat, were a toss-up. Each was professionally trained during years before the mast, in waters around the world. Each had been specially chosen by higher authority for this very battle, taking the place of men thought to be "not up to the task." A frigate, *Confiance* looked different to the casual observer. She was slightly longer than *Saratoga* at 147 feet but sported an additional upper decking fore and aft. This quarterdeck and forecastle provided extra gun space and elevated her high above her opponent. This great warrior, however, was not ready. Out on the lake, she handled well, but on deck, the carpenters were as numerous as the crew. Raw lumber lay in stacks near workbenches, deep in shavings. There was no magazine below, and the gunpowder was tugged along behind in a series of small boats dragged like a string of sausages. The gun crews would have two days, that first week of September, to practice shooting the huge Congreve long guns. Mounted on wooden slides, supported by small, thick wooden wheels, the guns jumped back a dozen feet when fired. The decks were so rough from the green lumber that the wheels became stuck between the ridges. The ship's master, Mr. Brydon, declared, "The guns in general worked very heavy, owing to the decks being rough-scraped and a quantity of pitch on them; there were temporary locks fitted from carronade locks."[3] Guns had to be lifted and pry-barred into place, rather than run up in the customary procedure. At 2,500 pounds, the crews tired quickly. Downie was told that the American fleet carried carronades, the maximum effective range of which was no more than 500 yards. In addition to the cannons, Downie's vessel carried six carronades in the stern and bow. While *Confiance* came about and test fired once again, her companions, *Linnet*, *Finch*, and *Chub*, were only a few miles away within the Canadian waters of the northern end of Lake Champlain.

American Commodore Thomas Macdonough never considered facing more than small, agile gun-mounted sloops or cutters, escorts for smuggler's barges. But then, who could envision that England would defeat Napoleon and turn her wrath on this little landlocked lake? The young commander of the American navy knew the power of a frigate, having served on board several. He knew that he could not match her on the open waters of the lake, which was known for strong southerly winds in September. General Macomb requested that the navy defend the army's right flank, well within the confines of Cumberland Bay, which appeared open, three miles across and nearly circular, with docks along the far shore, giving the appearance of fair sailing. Hidden by the blue water were shoals and sandbars that crept out like long, thin fingers, just under the surface, that would snag a keel and hold her fast. Additionally, the winds in the bay were undependable. While the lake blew well, the bay suffered from swirling breaths of air, hardly able to sustain a ship's way. Macomb's mandate to come into the bay for the sake of the army could offer the best chance against the marauding English flotilla.

A PLAN WITHOUT A CREW IS NO PLAN

While Macdonough conjured up his battle plan, the American ships were made ready for battle. The commodore lacked the help of trained marines, but was given nearly two months to turn his soldiers into naval gunners. Still short of men, he appealed to General Macomb for more men to crew his gunboats and the brig *Eagle*. But the general had no more to offer. While Izard was still in residence, he had given 250 soldiers to the navy. In desperation, Thomas Macdonough asked for the prisoners in the stockade, men confined for drinking, disrespect, disruption, and desertion. Macdonough promised the general that they would not cause mayhem on a seventy-foot boat, powered by their own oars. Indeed, like galley slaves, there would be little energy left after rowing across the bay. When Macomb's regimental band members heard of the appeal, seven of the thirty volunteered, along with one wife. A Negro sailor, who had come up from Boston, stepped forward to join the musicians.

DOWNIE'S PLIGHT

Captain Downie had never sailed or ever seen Lake Champlain, which put him at a considerable disadvantage. Downie looked to the destruction of the enemy fleet but was unaware of the water hazards on the long, thin lake. While the Redcoats headed for Plattsburgh and the destruction of the American army, he would seek out the American navy, which he believed was on the southern end of the lake. Anne Prevost, who frequently witnessed military talk at the supper table where Downie dined, provides perspective in her solitary writing:

> August 1814, Montreal, Canada.
> The Principal object of the expedition, as I afterwards understood, was the destruction of the American Dock Yard at Vincennes on the opposite side of the Lake—and the capture of Plattsburg would be merely the first service affected by the Expedition on its way to an ulterior object. Of course it was first of all most necessary that the American Squadron should be defeated, and our command of the Lake quite established.

While the British commodore did his war gaming with the officers of his flotilla, the Army was on the move. Sir George could wait no longer for the navy, and he would have to coerce Downie into battle if necessary, because there were other things to consider than a ship that was not up to snuff. If he waited until Downie was comfortable, this thing would never be run. September was the last month in the year that he could count on good campaign weather. It would not be too long before the Americans realized that both his and Admiral Cochrane's deceptions were discovered and their true intentions revealed. Then the Americans could adjust their forces accordingly, and all advantage would be lost. Sir George Prevost was no military adventurer: unlike "Gentleman" Johnny Burgoyne, he took his profession seriously and coveted his soldiers. He was not a waster of men. To quote Colonel John Elting, "Prevost was not a death or glory boy." Sir George had tigers by the tail with those three young strident major generals Brisbane, Powers, and Robinson. They wanted to get it over and return to England in triumph. They had good friends in high places who could influence matters, if their carping letters home had time to ferment. Sir George was a soldier who appreciated the importance of lines of communication and supply. He called on his quartermaster general frequently and listened to a litany of logistical impediments. William Henry Robinson, who is not to be confused with Major General Frederick Robinson, commander of the 1st Brigade, advised, "The roads are worse than you can imagine and many of our wagons are broken down—The road through the woods at Beatville [Beekmantown] is impassable therefore our only dependence is upon water communication."[4]

THE FINAL INVASION

Sir George gave the order to cross the border and invade the United States on September 1. He directed the deputy commander, Major General Francis De

Rottenburg, to get the army moving and convene a conference of his field commanders at Rouses Point, New York. There, the first order of business was to issue the rules of engagement to his field commanders. "No civilians were to be harmed and no property was to be destroyed that was not directly connected with combat conditions. There would be no looting and all items requisitioned for the purpose of campaigning were to be paid for on the spot." Prevost reminded his officers that any ground taken may well become a part of Canada and that the people were to be treated not as prisoners but as subjects of His Majesty, King George III. A proclamation to the citizens of New York was distributed as the army moved south. Posted on buildings, nailed to trees, and passed out by hand, it read,

> The peaceable and unoffending inhabitants can expect kind usage and generous treatment. It is against the government of the United States by whom this unjust and unprovoked war has been declared, and against those who support it, either openly or secretly, that the arms of His Majesty are directed.
>
> (signed)
> Lieutenant General Sir George Prevost
> Governor General of Canada.[5]

Sir George still believed that there was considerable sympathy for English rule and that, once established, the British army could be favored by the surrounding communities as they moved ever south, if the army behaved itself and paid their way.

In her diary, Anne Prevost, a young patriotic English woman, sets the scene very well:

> On the 30th of August I made breakfast for my Father and his suite at half past six, previous to their departure on the ill fated Expedition. I was most sanguine that something very brilliant would be achieved. I had often thought with regret that my Father had never yet been engaged in any bright affair—he had considered it necessary to conduct the defense of the Canadas with much caution—defense, not conquest was necessarily his object. But now I thought the time had arrived when all murmurs would be silenced—I was delighted to think my Father was commanding some thousands of Wellington's Soldiers! I remember well my dear Mother saying to me one day, "I do not think your Father ought to go out of the Province—in his high situation he should remain on the frontier." No doubt her fears for his personal safety suggested this idea, but I could not agree with her. Precious as was my Father's life, still I was so true a Soldier's daughter, I valued his renown even more. "But dearest Mama" I said in reply, "you must remember that every step he takes he turns Yankee Ground into our territory—its our King's at least, for the time being,

whatever may become of it afterwards." O how high the pulse of Hope beat at that moment. I do not recollect that I had any sort of fear as to the result of the Expedition. I looked forward to certain Victory.

On the 3rd September we heard from my Father that he should be within the Enemy's territory the next day. This day too, we heard of the capture of Washington—I was delighted, and thought still better news would soon come.

The feeling of loss of the nation's capital to their former ruler arrived in Plattsburgh and Burlington as well. The reports were sketchy and a great shock. How could the nation be in the hands of the English once again? The local citizens, many of whom had never taken the war seriously, began to rally to the cause.

The British army's left flank took a toehold at Rouses Point, New York. The next few days would belong to the long columns of Redcoats marching route step, four abreast, with the southern sun in their eyes. There were no American formations at the border, not even a manned customs hut. Englishmen just walked in and made themselves at home. Initially in the lead was the brigade of Major General Frederick Robinson, who was the son of Colonel Beverly Robinson, a loyalist New Yorker during the Revolutionary War who was forced to return to England when the British lost on the field at Yorktown. He told his hostess, Mrs. Hubbell, that his father had told him that all Americans were small people. Ever the well-mannered lady, she agreed and sent for Philip Hensinger to fetch the next course. The growing lad of six feet, seven inches and 260 pounds delivered the roast joint for the general to carve. In great good humor, before his officers, the general remarked, "If the Yankees are all like him, the Lord deliver us from fighting them." The next morning, to dispel any thought that the family had been converted by the visit to the side of the king, she bid the complement of guests good-bye. Although they were quite splendid in both manner and uniforms, she said, "Good-bye, Sirs, for a very little while, but I know you'll soon be back and hanging your heads as you come." Annoyed that she had not resigned herself to British rule, the general said, "If a man had said that, I would call him out, but since it is a fair lady that has been our charming hostess, I reply that when your prophecy comes true, every officer here shall throw his purse on your door step as he passes." During the retreat, they stopped once again and gave up their money.[6]

REDCOATS ON THE MARCH

The countryside was so rough that not even the Indians had lived on the land, but their hunting parties made paths for untold generations. Their track was now the road from Canada to New York, which was little improved. Lined with tall green pines, red oaks, black cherries, and golden-leafed aspens, the fall color took the hardship off the minds of the plodding and hauling soldiers. Oxen were hired for the duration from the few farmers and loggers along the way to increase the size of the teams struggling with the siege artillery and wagons filled with powder and cannonballs. This army was used to foraging nearby communities to add to their rations of biscuit and salt beef. But these towns, Rouses Point, Champlain, and Chazy, which were separated by wilderness, contained only clusters of houses where trails met, and could barely sustain themselves, much less an army. Movement was so slow that officers of the navy and army convened at Chazy and chipped in on an elegant dinner served on casks covered with boards and fine tablecloths. For the enlisted men, one in every ten wives, sometimes with accompanying children, walked along with the baggage, a mile or two behind the brigade. In England the night before departure, lots had chosen the followers. If the husband died on campaign, the wife often married another man from the regiment. Their duties were to keep house for the ten fellow soldiers in the same unit. This entailed cooking, sewing, fetching water, and setting up and striking camp. Since the medical corps was in its infancy, they also tended to the sick and wounded and helped infirm soldiers keep up with the column. A thousand followers had passage on the ships from Europe and England. The Royal Navy also had women on board for the same reasons.

THE NEW YORK STATE MILITIA

There were great numbers of militiamen who could be called on in the first week of September to defend the land from all the king's men. Major General Benjamin Mooers, the commander of the New York State Militia of the northern counties, called for 2,500 to meet him at Plattsburgh. Many took their time and thought it over, some arriving after the battle. Sadly, only 700 showed up and brought with them nothing more than ragged clothes, native dirt, and large appetites.[7] The red tide was swallowing up the land and with it the courage of the people who watched them pass. Disappointed by the thin ranks, Mooers addressed them at the camp established near his home in Plattsburgh.

> Attention and good order are expected by the Major General and he would feel mortified to hear of any depredations on the inhabitants or ill usage to any one, as the object in calling militia out is for the purpose

of repelling the enemy and protecting the citizens in their persons and property.

Delivered in the third person as was often the custom of the day, particularly in public matters, it got right to the heart of the matter. The militia was not a disciplined body of men, and some joined for other than honorable reasons.

The first action on the part of the militia was a bold one. Reconnoitering alone behind enemy lines, Lieutenants Matthew Standish and Roswell Wait of the New York State Dragoons pretended to be officers returning to their unit from a hunting expedition. The two young American lieutenants, whose New York militia unit still wore red tunics and sausage roll hats from before the Revolution, were nearly identical to the dress of British cavalry. Their wandering among British formations was a clever ruse. Since the force was so large, not all officers were known at road control points. Not only did they provide "order-of-battle" information, but they also identified the capability and positions of the British advance guard.[8]

FIRST CONTACT

On the evening of September 5, near Beekmantown, Standish and Wait, leading two companies of their dragoons, struck the first blow since the enemy had crossed the border five days before. They attacked the British picket line with a force of New York State Dragoons and sent it fleeing to the rear. It triggered the 3rd Foot Regiment to arms. The Americans were no longer illusive, but would they stand and fight?

A side road at Sampson's corners, eight miles north of Plattsburgh, offered Provost an attractive opportunity. His men and supplies were strung out nearly nine miles. By splitting his force into two lines of march, he could relieve the traffic jam, and since the new spur road led to the edge of the lake and then to Plattsburgh, he could envelop the town from two sides while gaining gun support from his naval flotilla that should be on its way. He was not afraid that splitting his force would weaken it. He held in his hands an overwhelming land force, and he knew it. His intelligence agents informed him that there was nothing of consequence to his front. He sent Major General Brisbane to the left with his brigade and the light brigade, which consisted of a dozen Canadian fencible battalions, the voltigeurs, chasseurs, militia, and De Meuron's Swiss regiment. An attached company of Indians was split, half to each column, to act as scouts now that they were getting close to the American lines.

On September 4, Macomb sent Mooers's 700-man militia farther north to intercept the British army. He was not expected to engage but to harass and delay the oncoming enemy, abbatis the roads, and burn the bridges.[9] They were also expected to gather intelligence to send back to Macomb outlining the intentions of the invading army. A letter was written by Macomb on September 5 to General Mooers that had a sketch of the signaling rockets he was forwarding (modern sky or distress rockets seen today for celebration or used at sea on boats):

> I send you six rockets for signals—as it may not be understood in which manner they are set off the following is the way of using them
>   A—is the rocket tied to the stick B
>   C is the quick match is to be touched by the fire which will set it off
>   D fire brand applied
>   The rocket is held perpendicular or set up against a fence.
>   Two or more of these Rockets set off we shall consider a signal for the certain approach of the Enemy. Tomorrow before day light I shall advance a Battalion of regular Light troops under Major Wool on the Beekman town road, also six pieces of Light artillery under Capt. Leonard, which pieces will also be supported by regular and your troops must lend their aid. The positions on the road are admirable & every way calculated for troops of the Discription you command—In Heaven's sake do not let the militia retire without fighting—the more they fight the better they will become & will soon get over the alarm of a few muskets.
>   Rockets will be fired at Dead Creek in like manner[10]

However, the militia was unreliable, and at the first whiff of British gunpowder, most deserted, compelling Mooers to send a dispatch to the Governor, their commander-in-chief in Albany that evening. He spoke not of his own shortcomings that had caused the incident but rather of the men. It reads:

> A portion of the militia have entailed an eternal disgrace on themselves, many of whom have left the ranks and gone home. The General regrets that there are some who are lost to patriotism and gone home. After coming forward in obedience to his call, fled at the first approach of the enemy, and afterwards basely disbanded themselves and returned home; thereby disgracing themselves and their fellow-soldiers an example of all that brave men detest and abhor.[11]

His outrage is understandable, but during the summer, as Macomb and Izard resupplied, trained, and prepared for the attack, there is no evidence that Major General Mooers did the same. The militia members were reluctant to undergo training, but, of course, that is the responsibility of those who seek officership. The failure appears to be that of leadership and not the courage of the individual soldiers. Benjamin Mooers was a fine man, a real patriot, but the battlefield is not the place to prepare. The numbers who answered the call to arms reflect other evidence of his shortcomings as a military leader.

General Macomb agreed with the assessment by Mooers but does not mention their commander. "The Militia, except for a few brave men, fell back most precipitously in great disorder." But in the same correspondence, he concludes that "the militia behaved with great spirit after the first day, and the volunteers from Vermont were exceedingly serviceable."[12]

HELP FOR THE MILITIA

On September 5 Macomb had added a follow-up force to Mooers's mission once he found out that the British column had split and early reports came in that the militia was having difficulty. He sent Captain Robert Sproul and 200 of the 13th Regular Infantry with two 6-pound artillery pieces up the lakeside road to abbatis and destroy bridges. They were to set up a defensive position at the Dead Creek Bridge, which is less than a mile northeast of the town where the creek enters the bay.

Lieutenant Colonel Daniel Appling, dressed in the field green of the rifle regiment, took his 110 riflemen and a troop of New York Dragoons, led by Captain Safford and Lieutenant Standish, and tracked up the lakeside road due north of town directly into the path of the 5,000-man redcoated column led by Major General Brisbane. There were conflicting reports as to how much the militia had done to delay the enemy on the Beekmantown road. It is certain, however, that the first attempt to stop the British movement was made by the men under regular army Major John E. Wool of the 29th Infantry Regiment. Here it is best to use Major Wool's own words, which not only describe the action but also give an account of the day. Historians have disagreed for years over the actions of the New York militia. Since history is usually written by the victor, there is no account that has been found written by the English. It is very difficult to find anything on the battle in official British army history other than a paragraph or two. Here, Wool is responding to an inquiry about the disputed conduct of the New York militia nearly forty years later as a major general in the Union Army during the Civil War:

Troy, New York,
May 10, 1860.
My dear Lossing,
In his account of the battle of Plattsburgh Mr. Dawson says, in page 379 and 380, that "the enemy on the 5th, continued his march, in the course of which he met serious obstructions from the trees which had been felled in the roads and from the removal of the bridges on his route—a duty which had been efficiently performed by General Mooers, of the New York Militia, seven hundred strong." General Mooers, on the 4th, as it appears from Macomb's report, "collected about 700 Militia and advanced seven miles on the Beekmantown Road to watch the motions of the enemy, and to skirmish with him as he advanced—also to obstruct the roads with fallen trees and to break up the bridges." It is due to truth to say that the General, nor his Militia felled trees in the roads, removed bridges or skirmished with the enemy previous to, or on the morning of, the 6th when the enemy took possession of the village of Plattsburgh.

On the 5th, General Mooers with his Militia was encamped on the Beekmantown road, four or five miles from Plattsburgh. Majors Appling and Sproul were ordered on the direct road to Chazy with directions to obstruct the enemy's advance on this road. This service was performed by them on that, and on no other road was a similar duty performed. Up to the 5th not a shot had been fired at the enemy. It was this circumstance which induced me to call on General Macomb, when I remarked I thought we ought not to permit the enemy to reach Plattsburgh without some evidence of a determination to resist him and to defend our position; and requested permission to go out on the evening of the 5th with the troops under my command, the 29th regiment, only then 200 strong, when I would reach the enemy's camp before morning, beat up his quarters and perhaps take from him some prisoners from whom the General might learn the state of their forces. This he objected to saying I might be captured and he had no men to lose. In the course of the day I again called on the General and made the same application but with no better success. About sun down however he called at my quarters and directed me to go out the next morning at sunrise with two hundred and fifty infantry, and at the same time said Captain Leonard with his Artillery will go with you—the Captain was present and heard what the General said. Afterwards I induced the General to change the order from sunrise to 3 o'clock. Captain Leonard refused to march with me, because, as he said, he had not received orders to do so. The remarks of the General that he would go with me he did not consider an order. I halted at the camp of General Mooers when I learned the enemy was encamped at the junction of the two roads leading to Chazy, about four or five miles from the General's camp and nine miles from Plattsburgh. I recommenced my march and at daylight I met the advance of the enemy at Howes, seven or eight miles from Plattsburgh, and from this point I disputed every inch of ground . . . I received no aid or assistance from General Mooers' Militia save about thirty men who volunteered to join my command and remained with it until my arrival at Plattsburgh. It is however due to General Mooers to say that he endeavored to bring his troops into action but did not succeed. They fled without firing a gun, and did not stop until they crossed at or near Pike's Cantonment, except a small party, which defended the upper bridge. These I am under the impression, were the twenty-five young men of the village, who formed themselves into an independent Volunteer corps for the occasion.[13]

An excerpt from an earlier letter from Major General John Wool written to Mr. Philip B. Roberts of Beekmantown, New York, challenges some of the folk myths that abound in Plattsburgh even today. The language is archaic and in the third person:

Troy January 6h, 1859
Sir,
Your communication of the 1st instant, relating to the "Battle of Beekmantown," which occurred on the morning of the 6th of September 1814, was received on the 3rd.

In reply to your request I would remark that on the evening of the 5th of September, 1814, Major John E. Wool, having volunteered his services, was ordered by Major General A. Macomb with 250 regular infantry and Captain Leonard with two pieces of Artillery, to march early next morning, the 6th of September, on the Beekmantown road "to support the Militia and set them an example of firmness" by resisting the advance on Plattsburgh of the British column on that road commonly reported to be 4,000 strong. The United States Militia under Major General Mooers, 700 strong, were encamped on that road about four or five miles from Plattsburgh.

Agreeably to the orders of Major General Macomb, Major Wool with 250 regular infantry afterwards joined by 30 Volunteer Militia, left Plattsburgh about twelve o'clock at night—Captain Leonard refused to accompany him, not having been as he said ordered to do so by General Macomb—and marched about seven miles when he met the advance of the British column under the command of Lieut. Colonel Wellington of the 3rd Buffs. From this point the command of Major Wool disputed every foot of ground until it arrived on the right bank of the Saranac in the village of Plattsburgh. On his reaching Culiver's Hill the Major made a stand and compelled the British troops to fall back—when Lieut. Colonel Wellington and a Lieutenant of the 3rd Buffs were killed—but the troops soon rallied and compelled the Major to retreat. On his arrival at the brook, some half a mile or more from Culivers Hill, he made a short stand and tore up the bridge erected over the brook. From this position disputing every inch of ground, he again made a stand at Halseys Corner, a half of a mile or more from Plattsburgh, where he was joined by Captain Leonard with two pieces of Artillery, which were well served and did great execution. Being driven from his position he again made a stand in front of Judge Bayly's House, and again at Gallows Hill in the village of Plattsburgh. From this position he crossed and formed his troops on the right bank of the Saranac. the Major ordered Captain Rochester with his company to tear up the bridge, which he promptly executed under a severe fire from the enemy. The British troops took possession of the stores and houses on the opposite bank [north] from which they were driven by Major Wool's Infantry and the well directed fire of four pieces of Artillery under Captain Leonard, and from the fire of two block-houses near by. The enemy retired in the rear of the village, where the whole British force, 11,000 strong, concentrated, and where they remained until the 11th September, 1814.[14]

AMERICANS BRUSHED ASIDE

The leading British infantry unit was the East Kent Regiment, the Third Foot, or "Buffs." The name comes from the color on the facings, collar, and cuffs of their uniforms. The regiment was one of the first formed in the British model army of the 1600s and was distinguished on the field by the light brown color that edged their coats. When they encountered Major Wool's little force, they dropped their packs and charged with fixed bayonets. Lieutenant Colonel James Willington (no relation to the Duke of Wellington as many thought because of a misspelling of his name) led the charge. The Duke's family name was Arthur Wellesey. On his arrival in Canada, Brevet Major Willington was again brevet promoted to lieutenant colonel several days before he was shot dead by Private Samuel Terry of Peru, New

York.[15] In addition, Lieutenant West and Ensign Chapman were also killed, along with twelve other British soldiers. Their comrades buried them near Ira Howe's house in Beekmantown. Two Americans were wounded and captured: privates Goodspeed and Jay. When the two artillery pieces joined the running fight, many more Redcoats fell. Lieutenant Kingsbury, also of the 3rd, was wounded and later died and was buried at Isaac Platt's farmhouse. Captain Waite, commander of the Plattsburgh garrison and veteran of the battle, moved the bodies of all the slain British who had not been claimed by relatives to the cemetery at Plattsburgh on September 11, 1843.[16] It was done with considerable pomp and ceremony, as had the first hasty interment just after the battle. Dignitaries from the United States, Canada, and England were present. Full military honors were accorded. Today, each year on September 11, a joint commemorative ceremony is held at the graves of Americans and British who lie side by side.

Wool's attempt to delay the British was futile. The formation never left its column, nor did it deploy skirmishers. They just kept coming. The speed of the British army was determined by its long tail, which slowed it down, rather than the attempt of a few hundred Americans who risked their lives to blunt the juggernaut. On the lakeside road, Lieutenant Colonel Appling called on the American fleet that had moved into the bay on September 2. Along with the four men-of-war were twelve gunboats, each with two heavy naval guns and crewed by thirty men, most of whom were soldiers. At 10 a.m. on September 6, Major General Brisbane's brigade of nearly 5,000 marched in an unbroken column along the road that hugged the northern edge of the bay. The town of Plattsburgh was well within sight, as was the American flotilla. The lead British regimental band played "The Girl I Left Behind Me," while over on the Beekmantown Road, the 88th (Connaught Rangers) played their regimental march on bagpipes. The noise of the drums and the "skirl" of the pipes reached across the water like a mailed fist and announced the arrival of the most successful army in the world. The English red rim drawn along the shore was out of the range of the carronades that lined the decks of his ships. Macdonough, therefore, ordered the gunboats to take on the mission of supporting Appling's defense of the bridge and attacked the British column. The naval cannon flanking fire scattered the attackers and caused them to find cover while they called for the Royal Field Artillery to come up the crowded road to their rescue. The gunboats had dropped their sail, and half the crew rowed in order to point the gun since it was fixed in the prow. The rate of fire was slow. These seventy-foot-long whaleboats were meant to attack smuggler's rafts. The gun was to be fired once or twice as they closed in for boarding. Now they were called on to act like men-of-war and take on a land target of moving men. At the pointy end of the boat, it was difficult to clean out and reload the muzzle of a gun that weighed over a ton. But they did the work as the current drove them closer to shore. They came close enough to receive rifle fire, and some of the crew were wounded. But they accomplished something that Major Wool had been unable to do. They stopped the forward movement of the left arm of the British army and deprived Prevost of the simultaneous envelopment of the town. He and the remainder of his army were just then arriving in Plattsburgh, chasing Wool's men across the Saranac River back into the arms of General Macomb.

THE REDCOATS FIRED ON
BY THE AMERICAN NAVY

The tricky winds shifted against the gunboats as the British field artillery's 6-pounders took up the battle and found their range. Macdonough, from his quarterdeck, saw that the flotilla near the shore would be destroyed and sent Midshipman Silas Duncan from the *Saratoga* in a gig with orders to retrieve the gunboats and place them behind the American fleet. Duncan was severely wounded as he ventured too close to shore in an attempt to gain control of the boats and lead them to safety. In spite of his wounds, he accomplished the mission and was taken to Crab Island, where a hospital had been established.[17]

    C. S. Forester remarks that Macdonough, a student of military history, had in his possession a copy of Nelson's battles in which it is recorded how he attacked fleets that were anchored, at both the Battle of the Nile and the Battle of Copenhagen, destroying the enemy totally. It also noted that at the Battle of Algciras, the Royal Navy lost when the French rotated their vessels in place. Therefore, he believed that the Royal Navy commander, who may have even been at those battles or most certainly knew of the tactics, would refight those engagements. Macdonough therefore fought from anchor and lured the Royal Navy into the seemingly safe waters of the bay. First, the bay, which he had maneuvered in during the previous summer, had perfidious waters. Second, he had been required by Macomb to provide fire support against the British land forces to increase the artillery fire of the army's cannons. A stationary position would suit both requirements. This battle was shaping up to be a duel of cannons. He anchored in a line nearly north and south and prepared to fight. He also deployed kedge anchors. These auxiliary anchors were placed both ahead of and behind his flagship. They were tied with hawsers that were wrapped along and around the ship. Called "springs," they were commonly used to rotate a stationary vessel in place. Often used in port, they were known by every sailor for ease in moving a heavy vessel a short distance without having to put up the sail. With the free end of the spring attached to the capstone, it could be wound around 180 degrees exposing the other side of the ship. Macdonough knew that whatever he did to prepare, it would be a hot day and one he was very likely to lose. The worry came from the overwhelming power of the British fleet. Their ships were equipped with cannons that could outrange his by more than double. If the British stood off, they could engage the Americans, who would be unable to return fire. After retrieving his gunboats, the commodore prepared to act with Macomb and fire on the British army when they came into range on the streets of Plattsburgh.

THE LAND BATTLE AT PLATTSBURGH

Macomb shared the same fear of the sheer mass of his terrestrial opponent. The British army had him nine to one. The militia that he had hoped for, ever since Izard left with the bulk of the regulars, had not materialized. The New York militia had left the field, and there was still no word on the Vermont militia. But Alexander Macomb had not been idle. With the help of Major Joseph G. Totten and Lieutenant R. E. Darusie, military engineers, the entire command had labored all summer to construct field fortifications. Earthworks, easy to construct in sandy soil, were dug, taking advantage of the lay of the land on the southern side of town. The "fastness" was contained on a natural peninsula formed by the Saranac River and the bay. Across the center of the peninsula were positioned three large redoubts to house the artillery, which could range any potential target in the town of Plattsburgh. Two blockhouses were built near the water's edge, covering the two bridges. Trenches and laterals were dug the length and breadth of the line to protect the infantry. It looked very much like Yorktown or the more contemporary battlefield of Flanders. Large stockpiles of food, water, and ammunition were put into the dugouts for the troops so that they did not have to leave and expose themselves to enemy fire. Macomb was urged by members of his staff and townsfolk to abandon the position after Izard left. It was suggested that he go farther south, perhaps as far as Albany. "If the British wanted to take another licking at Saratoga then we will do it again," one local businessman remarked. But he may have been motivated more by declaring Plattsburgh an open city and therefore saving his shop. Macomb knew that his men, though regulars, were apprehensive, especially now that the New York militia was gone. Morale was his concern. He told his troops that they "must defend to the last extremity." A general order was issued on September 5, the day before the Redcoats arrived in town:

The eyes of America are on us, fortune always follows the brave. The works being now capable of resisting a powerful attack, the manner of defending them the General thinks is his duty to detail, that every man may know and do his duty. The troops will line the parapets in two ranks, leaving intervals for the artillery. A reserve of one-fifth of the whole force in infantry will be detailed and paraded fronting the several angles, which it will be their particular duty to sustain. To each bastion are assigned, by the several commanders of forts, a sufficient number of infantry to line all faces (in single ranks) of each tier. Should the enemy gain the ditch, the front rank of the part assailed will mount the parapet and repel them with its fire and bayonet. If the men of this rank are determined, no human force can dispossess them of the position.

He was correct. A good defensive position, hugging the raging Saranac River, spanned with only two bridges that had their flooring removed, could be held against a frontal attack of infantry for a considerable time.

Fort Brown, commanded by Lieutenant Colonel Huckens Storrs, put the 13th and 31st Infantries in the trenches in front to ensure the safety of the guns. This was the most important of the three earthen forts because it sat on a high ridge that commanded the majority of the river below. Fort Moreau, the largest of the works, was 200 square feet. It was armed with heavy artillery: 18 and 24 pounders mounted on naval gun carriages with the exception of six of the 18 pounders, which were on field carriages. The fort was named by Izard for a French general exiled by Napoleon and was commanded by Lieutenant Colonel Melancton Smith and defended by the 6th and the remnants of the 29th that had been out on the road with Major Wool. Fort Scott, on the lakeshore, was named for Macomb's old comrade, Winfield Scott. Major Thomas Vinson was put in charge of the remnants of the 33rd and 34th Infantries. The blockhouses at the mouth of the river were manned by Lieutenant Fowler's artillery, while the sick and some of the 1st Rifle Regiment under Captain John Smith garrisoned the second. Those too sick to fire or load were sent to Crab Island in Cumberland Bay to a hospital run by Doctor Mann. By the start of the battle, he had nearly 1,000 men in tents and lying on the open ground. With the help of the few who were ambulatory, he constructed wooden tent floors. Macomb sent two 16-pounder guns to place on the point of the island to prevent the Royal Navy from landing. Invalids serviced the guns. Earlier, the diseased had been evacuated to Burlington, Vermont. But now, with the battle near, all extra boats were busy moving supplies. The weather reports vary according to who is read, but it seems to have been rather wet the first two weeks of September, but there was some talk of bright, beautiful days. There is no indication that the threat of bad weather, which was high on Prevost's agenda, ever materialized. But it was ominous. To this point, the casualty lists vary widely as they will throughout the battle. Each side will exaggerate the others' losses. It appears that the British lost a total of about 200 killed and wounded before September 6 and that the Americans lost about fifty. The desertion rate was higher for the Americans, nearly 700 for the New York militia and a hundred or so from the English. Posters were put up in all the border towns to the effect that if a British soldier presented himself to local authorities with the desire to become an American citizen, he would be welcomed and given cash and 100 acres of land on the western frontier. The British thought this was no way to fight a war that that it was most unsporting.

THE BRITISH ARMY WAITS FOR THEIR NAVY

On the morning of September 6, Lieutenant General Sir George Prevost established his headquarters at the Allen farmhouse on the northeastern side of the town, barely out of range of the American cannon. While he waited for Brisbane to break through over Dead Creek Bridge, he ordered the town cleared of enemy soldiers and reiterated his order not to destroy private property or harm the citizens. Being driven before the three enemy brigades, Lieutenant Colonel Appling and Major Wool continued to fight as they crossed the bridges, pulling up the planking as they went. Wool put his two guns into immediate action on the south side of Bridge Street Bridge. At Inland Bridge, nearer to the Pike's Cantonment, Appling managed to escape the soldiers of De Meuron's Swiss regiment who boasted at the end of the battle that they had routed all the Americans from the town by dark.

By the morning of September 7 the battle lines were drawn on the banks of the Saranac River. The casualties of September 6 were repeated as another day of carnage took place among the houses of the village. The killing was not as high as one might expect, because it was infantry against infantry. The British artillery was not in place, and the American guns could not fire because so many of the skirmishers in Plattsburgh were intermingled in a hit-and-run melee. Captain Noadie, of the King's 8th Regiment, took a scouting party of a hundred men west along the Saranac River looking for a crossing point. The New York militia, that stayed, was allotted to the defense of the ford at Pike's old cantonment, three miles west, up the twisting riverbed. The woods on both sides of the river at this point were a convoluted wilderness of underbrush and maple trees. The red, gold, and rust color of the fall foliage helped to hide the Redcoats. As they tramped noisily through the undergrowth. Militia Captain Vaughan lined the south side of the stream with his riflemen. Some perched in the giant trees that nearly reached across the stream. Here, at a quiet point, where the water slipped by in thin sheets over the solid rock bed, the militia was tested once more. The ford was of tactical importance; it was the chink in Macomb's armor. If it was not held, the British could roll up the Yankee left flank at will.

Eleven-year-old Benjah Phelps tells the story with the excitement of a boy on a great adventure, nearly unaware of the gravity of the situation:

> My father was a Sergeant in the mill and protecting the ford at Pike's Cantonment on the Saranac River. His company guarded the ford all day. The British did not know they was there, but they did pooty quick when they tried to cross. The woods was thick and the big trees and bushes came right down to the water on the other side, they shot them right down. Some of them dropped in the stream and was carried away by the current. Captain Dixon, he was cap'n of the company, was hit right on the brass plate on his sword belt where it crossed his heart. It made a big dent. I seen it myself.[18]

Two militiamen were killed in addition to several invaders, while others were wounded. Back in the town, a company of Canadian Chasseurs, under Captain Mattley cleared the last Americans from the north side of the river.

Major Wool's letter to Lossing stated, "In page 383 Mr. Dawson gives credit to Captain Leonard of driving the enemy out of the houses in the village with hot shot. This service was performed by Captain Brooks of the foot Artillery. Captain Leonard was with my command at the bridge." To the great dismay of the citizens of the town who stayed behind, General Macomb ordered the American artillery to fire hot cannonballs into the structures of the town and set them on fire. The British were using the houses, barns, and outbuildings for concealment and protection. They kept up a constant rifle fusillade, pinging away from niches on roofs and upstairs windows, at anything that was exposed. Cannonballs were heated on the cook fires behind the forts and brought into the battery at Fort Brown. The river, though swift and unfordable, was only thirty yards wide. The American trenches were hung on the very edge of the precipitous south side, so that the infantry could fire down at the other side, which was flat for miles. It was nearly foolhardy to shove a red-hot cannonball down the barrel that was primed with a bag of black gunpowder. Even the damp wadding, placed between ball and charge, began to smolder immediately. The gunner with the ram was afraid that the charge would explode prematurely and the hot shot, the ram, and hapless gunner would go down range together. An eyewitness describes the mood of the townspeople:

Plattsburgh Sept. 20 th, 1814

Dear Brother

I was in the village the morning the British came in and was every day in the cantonment during their stay. The first engagement commenced in Beekmentown, five miles from the Village. Our troops were driven in every direction, nor could they make a stand until they crossed the river. How the enemy stopped and it appears made no trial to cross over that day, although a continual fire was kept up between the two armies on the banks of the river. Many of our men were either killed or wounded by the enemy's musketry from the houses where they had taken shelter. And in consequence of this our General ordered hot shot to be thrown into the buildings and burn them down. My house has shared the fate of many others. The whole block of buildings where it stood has been swept away by a single clash. Mr. Griffin's house and store and outhouses, Mr. Wait's house and store and Mr. Barker's house, also on that street, were burnt by our shot. The number of buildings burnt are about 30, with the courthouse. Such has been the conflagration and destruction of private property in this place caused by fortifications erected for the purpose of defending our frontier.[19]

The British slowly filled the little town to overflowing that once boasted seventy-eight fine homes. Prevost had two concerns: the establishment of the heavy artillery to bombard the American infantry out of their strong defenses and the location of his navy. To his surprise and delight, the entire American navy was in the bay. Captain Downie would have to look no farther than Cumberland Bay. First, the Royal Navy could destroy Macdonough's ships, which was the primary objective of Sir George's plan, and then turn their considerable guns on the American forts. He relayed the good news to Downie on September 7 and categorizes each ship in the American fleet and its capability. Then he goes on:

> If you feel the vessels under your command are equal to a combat with these I have described, you will find the present moment offers many advantages which may not again occur. As my ulterior movements depend on your decision, you will have the goodness to favor me with it, with all possible promptitude.[20]

Anne Prevost, writing in her diary, relays her father's thoughts: "The 8th of September, we heard that my Father had established his Head Quarters within sight of Plattsburg—they directed red hot shot at the house he occupied. The Army were waiting for the Fleet, as the attack on the Squadron and the Fort was to be simultaneous." There had been no word from the Royal Navy flotilla commander, Downie, in days. The last contact had been the visit paid by a staff officer who met with Captain Pring at Rouses Point whose vessel, *Linnet*, was in for provisions. Pring relayed that Downie was in and out of the lake as he struggled with the new vessel and trained the crew. Sir George dispatched a message to his naval commander informing him of the progress of the army and expanded Downie's instructions, which were passed to him by Daniel Pring:

> 8th of September, 1814
> Captain Downie, RN
> Commodore of the Lake Champlain Flotilla.
> I only wait your arrival to proceed against General Macomb's last position on the South Bank of the Saranac. Your share in the operation in the first instance, will be to destroy or capture the Enemy's Squadron if it should wait for a contest, and afterwards cooperate with this Division of the Army, but if it should run away and get out of your reach, we must meet here to consult on ulterior movements.
>
> (signed,) Prevost

WILL THE ROYAL NAVY EVER COME?

Downie's reply is not what Sir George was expecting. The captain had been working with his new ship and crew for the past week, and things were not coming together. He promptly replied, the same day,

> Lieutenant General Sir George Prevost, Bt.   8th September, 1814
> I stated to you that the ship was not ready—she is not ready now, and until she is ready, it is my duty not to hazard the squadron before an Enemy who will even then be considerably superior in force.
> (signed,)   Your Obedient Servant
>   Downie

Why Downie remarks that the enemy is "superior" is a total mystery. The following quote was found among the papers held by the family of Sir George Prevost:

> The strongest confidence prevailed in the superiority of the British vessels, their weight of metal, and in the capacity and experience of their

officer and crews; and as the commander of the forces was informed by an officer of the staff, who had been dispatched to Capt. Downie, that Capt. Downie credited himself with his own vessel alone a match for the whole American Squadron.

Naval statistics of the day show that the Americans could come somewhat close to the throwing weight of the British because carronade had heavier projectiles. But the British flotilla had the long-range guns that overwhelmingly outstripped the Americans.[21] Here, Mahon compares cannons to carronades.

Prevost mentions again on September 9 that he has postponed his attack on the American army, but, "I need not dwell with you on the evils resulting to both Services from delay." Sir George can see in front of him a golden opportunity to destroy both the American army and navy in one stroke and does not want to let Macdonough's fleet, his primary concern, get away. But Downie has been plagued with problems that all new ships go through. Nothing works properly on the series of little shake-down cruises, confined to the safety of the northern waters of the lake. His crew of converted soldiers is not responding to the nautical life. He has kept the shipyard carpenters on board since she was launched, fixing leaks and reinforcing gun platforms.

Finally, on September 10, he mentions to Prevost that "I would have sailed on the 10th but the winds prevented it." Sir George replied,

> I received at twelve last night your letter acquainting me with your determination to get under weigh about that time in the expectation of rounding Cumberland Head at dawn of day; in consequence, the troops have been held in readiness since six o'clock this morning to storm the enemy's works at nearly the same moment as the naval action should commence in the Bay. I ascribe the disappointment I have experienced to the unfortunate change of wind and shall rejoice to learn that my reasonable expectations have been frustrated by no other means.

Downie added that he would be in Plattsburgh as soon as the winds allowed. Prevost instructed him to scale his guns when he intended to begin the attack and that he would set the army in motion against the land fortification.[22] While the messages flew back and forth between the army and navy bosses, the army was assembling all 11,000 in and around the village. The artillery, which was critical to the siege, was going into battery.

THE GUNS MAKE ALL THE DIFFERENCE

Eight gun positions began to be dug on the northern rim of the Saranac River and bay side. The burning of the houses plagued the American gunners. The smoke, from the smoldering town obscured the Royal Artillery activity as they threw up dirt berms to protect the guns that would soon be registered. The Royal Artillery set up its headquarters at the Delord house at the northern end of the line of six batteries near the mouth of the bay extending to the south following the path of the river's northwestern bank.[23] The house was abandoned, and the officers laid their kit on the floors and put together additional boards for beds. The house was large, more than a dozen rooms with considerable outbuildings. It was next to Sailly's home, which was also an artillery billet. The officers were careful not to destroy any of the furnishings that had been left behind. Some of the valuables had been buried in the backyard garden:

> The guns had started late due to the bad roads and weren't available to go into position until the 9th of September. Captain King, RA was separated from his company and sent to the two 8 inch siege mortars. Captains Maxwell, Wallace and Sinclair of the 4th battalion, were joined in the construction of the earthen batteries by J Addams the commander of a company from the 10th battalion, who worked day and night to prepare for the battle.[24]

From these locations, the heavier siege guns not only could hit the American forts but could also menace Macdonough's anchored fleet, which looked like decoy ducks on a pond. The American commodore was forced to weigh anchors and reposition his entire fleet farther to the southeast. Macomb watched with dread. He had just lost the ability to bombard the British army with naval artillery. Macdonough was also out of range of the friendly guns at Fort Scott. The simple move of establishing the Royal Artillery had split the American defensive plan without having to fire a shot. It was now going to be two separate battles. Neither navy could be struck by, nor could they strike the army. Even though the civilian spectators, who lined the northern shore of the bay and spread blankets to picnic, could see good portions of the combined battle, they did not realize that land and water conflict were no longer connected.

To most civilians, though, the threat to their homes and property was more than they could stand. Dr. Beaumont described the scene in the village,

> The people are all frightened nearly out—out, did I say? rather into their wits—if they have any—moving everything off—under the expectation that all will be burnt or destroyed—poor souls. many of them love & uphold the British—censure & condemn our own Government—complaining they have no protection—neither will they take up arms to defend themselves—Indeed I pity their depravedty—but don't care much for their losses—if they should maintain, any.

VERMONT MILITIA COME THROUGH

Major General Sam Strong, Commanding General of the Vermont Militia, strolled into Macomb's headquarters. He told Alexander Macomb that he would have 2,500 of his "Green Mountain Boys" near Pike's Cantonment by morning. Macomb was overcome with emotion. He plucked a sprig of pine from a nearby tree and placed it in Strong's hat as a mark of zeal shown by his men who volunteered to serve outside their home state, against the desire of Governor Chittenden. Strong told Macomb several tales of his journey:

> At Horatio Seymour's law office in Middlebury Vermont, men and boys worked all night making cartridges. Afraid of using candles, they worked in the dark and the next morning the floor was blackened with powder, leading one to exclaim: We Certainly Have Been In More Danger Here To Night Than Any Of Our Volunteers Will Be In Plattsburgh.

He also told about a Vermonter from one of his lakeside hamlets:

> He started for the lake shore, his zeal pushing him ahead of his companions, "Come on boys, lets kill some red coats," he shouted. Apparently, he was scared by his own cry. Soon he began to hear heavy firing in the direction of Plattsburgh, across the water of the lake. Those whom he had outstripped met him in rapid retreat toward home. He explained breathlessly that "I have on my best Sunday shoes and my wife would feel dreadfully if I spoilt them." He went back to change: "I will catch you up."[25]

In spite of his claim, he was not seen again in the ranks of the courageous Vermont Militia.

By early the next morning the Green Mountain Boys, descendants of Ethan Allen's heroes, were on the ramparts of the peninsula. Benjah Phelps takes up the story:

> The British tried to get across in Plattsburgh, but they couldn't. Why, you see, all the Vermont milishy was there, I remember Uncle Colonel Tim Allen set in the grist-mill winder. He had a long rifle. The barrel was five feet long. The river was about 80 rods wide there. There he set in the winder and killed every soldier that come down for water. That was the morning when they was gittin breakfast. Colonel Tim stayed right there until he killed nine or ten of em before they stopped comin down.[26]

The morning of September 11 would prove to be more than expected.

NOTES

1. Provided to the author at Albufeira (this is the correct spelling), Portugal, with permission of Sir Christopher Prevost, Bt.

2. Henry J. Morgan, *Sketches of Celebrated Canadians and Persons Connected with Canada* (London: Hunter, Rose and Co., 1952), 222.

3. Morgan, *Sketches of Celebrated Canadians and Persons Connected with Canada*, 222.

4. Testimony from the court-martial aboard HMS *Gladiator* at anchor in Portsmouth Harbor, August 1815.

5. Public Archives of Canada, 24 I 21 MG, W. H. Robinson to Mr. Clarkson, September 10, 1814.

6. North Country Notes, Clinton County Historical Association, November 1965.

7. John R. Elting, *Amateurs to Arms: A Military History of the War of 181* (New York: Da Capo Press, 1995).

8. "Order of battle" is a listing of the units, attachments, and affiliations of a military force.

9. "Abbatis" is a military term meaning to fell trees on either side of a road so that they fall, often in a herringbone pattern facing the oncoming enemy column, thereby creating an obstacle to movement. If there was time, the ends pointing at the oncoming enemy were sharpened. They are very difficult and time consuming to breach even today with modern engineering tools.

10. North Country Notes, Clinton County Historical Association, No. 103, May 1974. Extract taken from the Bailey Collection, Burnt Hills, New York.

11. North Country Notes, Clinton County Historical Association, No. 104, May 1974. Extract taken from the Bailey Collection, Burnt Hills, New York.

12. Dawson's writings and Benson Lossing in his book, *The Pictorial Field Book of the War of 1812*, give the militia more credit for interrupting the British movement (New York: Harper & Co., 1898).

13. Taken from a letter to B. J. Lossing from Major General John E. Wool (1784–1869). Wool became the Inspector General of the Army and served in the Mexican War and the Civil War until his retirement in 1862.

14. Clinton County Historical Society, Courtesy of Mrs. Addie Shields, custodian.

15. Historical Records of the Buffs (East Kent Regiment), 3rd Foot, 1814–1914. C. R. B. Knight text made from original letters. Made available at the East Kent Regimental museum, Canterbury, England.

16. Note the graves of all the combatants are at the Riverside Cemetery in Plattsburgh.

17. Silas Duncan's heroic actions were recognized in 1826 by the U.S. Congress, which passed a resolution of thanks for his gallantry. There were no medals issued at that time in American history, and Congress had to act on each event.

18. Published in *Outlook* (1901), Memories of Benjah Phelps. Plattsburgh Historical Society pamphlet published for the centennial of the battle.

19. Letter from George Freligh to his brother, Dr. Michael Freligh, in Watervliet, New York. Courtesy of the Feinberg Library, State University of New York, Albany.

20. Court-martial proceedings of the Royal Navy, August 1815, on board HMS *Gladiator*, Portsmouth, England. Whenever there was a military disaster, a court would be called to inquire into the circumstances and fix blame. If a commander, officer, or sergeant were deemed derelict or culpable, they would at least be removed from a position of trust to protect the troops under their scrutiny.

21. John K. Mahon, *War of 1812* (Gainesville: University of Florida Press, 1972).

22. To "scale the guns" meant to fire without a cannonball in place. The guns are here used as a signaling device. It was a common practice even on land, and Napoleon would fire them in a certain rhythm to provide a variety of commands, like drumbeats.

23. Sketch of the Battle of Plattsburgh prepared by Major DeRussy, USA, accompanying General Alexander Macomb's official report dated September 18, 1814.

24. Francis Duncan, *History of the Royal Regiment of Artillery* (London: John Murray, 1874), 188–89. Provided by the Secretary of the Old Royal Military Academy Library, Woolwich, England.

25. From the archives of the Antiquities Collection of the University Library of the University of Vermont, courtesy of Ms. Campbell, librarian.

26. Transcript of a conversation record in the archives of the office of the Clinton County Historical Association.

8

BATTLE OF PLATTSBURGH
AND LAKE CHAMPLAIN

The most decisive battle of the War of 1812.

—Winston Churchill, *History of the English Speaking People*

LATE ON September 9, 1814, Downie was determined to cooperate as best he could and sent Prevost a battle plan that could be disrupted only by the weather:

> It is my intention to weigh and proceed from this anchorage about midnight in the expectation of rounding into the bay of Plattsburgh about dawn of day and commencing an immediate attack on the enemy, if they shall be found anchored in a position that will offer any chance of success. I rely on any assistance you can afford the squadron.

It was, however, not until late evening of September 10 before the wind swung around from the north and the anchors were pulled out of the mud off Rouses Point. Inky darkness greeted George Downie, the thirty-three-year-old captain of the Royal Navy frigate when he gave in to Prevost's incessant urging and set his flotilla into motion up Lake Champlain toward Cumberland Bay. As Yankee water passed under the black keel, the British commodore felt confident. The clouds blocked the stars and moon, leaving only a bobbing daisy chain of flickering yellow lamplight as the Royal Navy fleet plowed south into history.

Standing on the quarterdeck, a red glowing sky greeted Commodore James Macdonough, the thirty-year-old commander of the little American fleet, early on the morning of September 11. He heard Downie's juggernaut scale her guns before he could see her. That morning there was no need for his heavy brass-fitted telescope to find the British: they were all too close. Two miles north by east, around the point of land called Cumberland Head, the rising sun silhouetted the black tops of their mastheads, yards spread and hung with puffy blankets of canvas, there above the treetops. Ominous, the long narrow white pendant with the red cross flying from the masthead informed him that *Confiance* was all too real. He had read many reports about her launch, and from the height of her contraband main mast he could tell she was a giant.

Rousing the British army at the sound of the naval guns, Sir George directed the two brigades, that of Robinson and Powers, to prepare to move and left Brisbane's to finish breakfast. The apparent inactivity of the British army brigade directly in front of the American position was expected to calm the alarm set off by the Royal Naval guns on the lake.

At first there was just *Confiance*, but within minutes other skeletons joined the horizon. As early as seven o'clock there was a mass of naked pines scratching the damp dawn sky, beyond the finger of land that separated the combatants. Downie had started the passage with the fleet all in a bunch. The winds had separated the sailing vessel from the gunboats. All six principal ships—*Confiance*, *Linnet*, *Chub*, *Finch*, and sloops, *Icicle* and *Canada* (the last two support vessels)—dropped anchor above the point in the channel between Grand Island, Vermont, and the New York shore. They were waiting for the eleven row galleys to catch up. The galleys intended to punch great holes to let in the shimmering lake water. Then, cutlass in hand, the crew would board like pirates and subdue the crew.

DOWNIE TAKES A PEEK

Going forward in a small boat, Downie noted the number and anchored position of the Americans. Taking advantage of his long-range cannons, Downie would not anchor at first but rather would lead his ships in a racetrack pattern, before the Yankees, around the top of the bay, firing the guns from one side and then the other as they reversed field. It would rest the crews and the guns, giving the gun captains time to restore any battle damage on the return trip. Destroying his opponent at long range, he would turn his attention to the American army, snug in their dirt forts, and reduce them to dust. It was all within his reach. The boast that he could defeat the entire American fleet with just his flagship alone was certainly true. It would make entertaining reading in the London newspapers.

THE WINDS ARE EVERYTHING

The Naval tactics of the day were complex because of the wind. It was true that fleets often could see each other but be unable to engage in battle because of unfavorable winds. As his boat crew pulled him back around the point, he had a chance to see his own force gathered together at anchor. He noticed that the gun captains had run out the cannons, whose blunt noses formed a solid line of black, dotting the white band that ran from stem to stern on her black shiny hull. The barrels were bronze but painted with a mixture of coal tar and salt water to protect them from the corrosion of salt water and foul weather. His other ships looked grand clustered together and arrayed in all black, a ploy devised by the Royal Navy to make the vessels appear small and attackable.[1] The last of the gunboats were now moored together ahead of the line, at the tip of the point, nearly within sight of the enemy.

Puffed up with confidence after viewing both combatant fleets, the youthful Downie sat down in his cabin with his captains. Daniel Pring, his second-in-command, captain of *Linnet*, was not afraid of the Americans and had nearly put an end to their fleet the summer before. The primary mission was the destruction of the American fleet.

> I am happy to inform you that I find from deserters who have come over from the enemy that the American fleet is inefficiently manned, and that a few days ago after the arrival of the new brig [*Eagle*] they sent on shore for the prisoners of all descriptions in charge of the provos to make up a crew for the vessel.[2]

This message shows the level of intelligence at General Prevost's fingertips. It buoyed the spirits of the English captains, which were running a little low, as all of them had observed the poor state of the flagship and her army crew. The formidability of the *Confiance* had faded: to a trained eye, "she was not up to snuff." Earlier, Downie had described the plan of attack from the intelligence gained on September 9. In the communiqué to Sir George, he laid it all out, never having seen Cumberland Bay:

> Should the enemy be attacked at anchor, it is the intention of the senior officers to confine the attack to their large ship, and the smaller vessels that may be moored on the windward side of her—*Linnet*, *Chub* and *Finch*—to go down in line abreast with the *Confiance*: the first division of gun boats on the opposite beam of the *Confiance*, and the second on the beam of the *Finch*, and go down the line abreast with the others.

ROYAL NAVY'S BATTLE PLAN

Now the instructions were finalized. The visit to view the enemy had enhanced the intelligence reports and served to confirm Prevost's earlier plan with the exception of the *Finch*. *Confiance*, *Chub*, and *Linnet* would enter the bay abreast of the flagship and attack the head of the line, *Eagle*, and broadside *Saratoga* as they passed by out of American range. The three would make a turn about to starboard, exposing their starboard guns, and start back up the line. *Chub* and *Linnet* would concentrate on the destruction of the American brig, *Eagle*, while *Confiance* would continue across the upper bay, parallel to the American *Saratoga*, and finish her off. *Finch* would be at the tail end, splitting off on the run in and attack the American *Preble* at the south end of the line assisted by the British gunboats. Lieutenant Hicks would proceed with the gunboats and board *Ticonderoga*. Downie was confident that the first and second pass would do enough damage to allow the flotilla to anchor close in so that his first three ships could complete the job of killing first the *Eagle* and then the *Saratoga* from a standing position. From there, all the British naval guns could then reach *Ticonderoga* if she had not already been taken by the *Finch*.[3]

While the skippers returned to their commands, Commodore Downie inspected the progress of the oven. It was against naval regulations to have a furnace on deck to broil cannonballs in the Royal Navy since fire was a prime danger on a wooden ship. French frigates were known to carry shot furnaces in spite of the obvious danger. The prime result of cannonballs was to dismount guns; kill, wound, or terrify the crew; and impair the running gear. If the sails, masts, spars, or rudder could be shot away, the ship must surrender. The Royal Navy considered it too dangerous and attributed the defeat of the French at the Battle of the Nile to its use. The hot shot, just as it did on land, could add another horror to war. A sizzling cannonball wedged in the structure could turn the vessel into a blazing inferno. The crew would have to abandon the guns and repeatedly douse the area with buckets of water or attempt to pry it loose and roll it overboard. If the fire took hold, the ship would soon be uninhabitable.[4]

THE BATTLE OF LAKE CHAMPLAIN, SEPTEMBER 11, 1814

At nearly 8 a.m., Downie brought the Royal Navy into harm's way, around the point, while *Icicle* and *Canada* were left behind. In their holds were supplies for the fleet, timbers to repair battle damage, and medicine to treat the wounded. *Confiance* hugged the northern shoreline and turned the corner with sails puffed out, driving the big ship at top speed. She needed to keep up with *Chub* and *Linnet*, quicker craft, which were abreast on her port side. Downie didn't want to get too far behind after the turn but planned to pass parallel to the Americans, in ships-a-trail formation, following *Chub* and *Linnet*, who were just off his bow and racing at full speed. The northern wind kicked up the waves to whitecaps and the crews were sprayed as the bow bit in and tossed the water over the gun deck. Each would deliver a broadside first into *Saratoga* and then into *Eagle*, before turning 180 degrees for the return bout. Careful to stay outside the range of the American carronades, each healed over on the starboard as they plowed in a straight line nearly north by northeast. The British *Finch* lay behind. On either side was a horde of gunboats, or "bateaux," since they were crewed mainly by French Canadians. *Finch* detached from the Royal Navy flotilla and headed straight for *Preble*, engaging her before the others hit their marks. Faster, she outreached the oarsmen, who were fatiguing. The long oars, or "sweeps," were fifteen feet in length and weighed fifty pounds. Even the drummer who beat out the pace was beginning to flag after half a mile.

Turning to the words of a young Teddy Roosevelt,

As the English squadron stood bravely in, young Macdonough, who feared his foes not at all, but his God a great deal, knelt for a moment, with his officers on the quarter deck; "[Stir up Thy strength O Lord, for Thou givest not always the battle to the strong, but can save by many or by few." Then ensued a few minutes of perfect quiet, the men waiting with grim expectancy for the opening of the fight.

A Coordinated Attack, the English Army Moves

Lieutenant General Sir George Prevost stood outside the Delord house beside his guns and watched the first naval cannonade, as did the civilian spectators all along the northern shore of the bay. The regimental bands on both sides began to play the men into battle but were nearly drowned out by the roar of the field artillery. All six batteries opened up on the American lines at once, only adding to the cacophony of the naval guns across the water. The rocket battery was in full glory. There 6- and 10-pound rockets lit the sky with contrails that took the breath away of the American infantry that were about to receive them. Fired in salvo, the "whoosh" could be heard above the guns. Twenty at once passed over the river, and several impacted against the walls of the bridge blockhouse, "first go." The house was set on fire, and the invalids inside were killed. With the guns came the white smoke that consumed both the land and the lake within minutes. The smoke foretold an ominous tale that the English commodore was the first to notice. It hung in the air, swirled a bit, but did not dissipate. It certainly obscured targets on both land and water, but, more than that, it denied the British both speed and control of all their ships. No one on either side of the land battle paid it any mind except the gunners at Fort Brown, who had the same problem created by the fires in the town, namely, smoke, which again plagued their target acquisition. The Redcoats' advance couldn't be seen, but they were sure that they were there and they continued to match the Royal Artillery round for round. Major General Brisbane was a little slow to get his men from breakfast, thinking that perhaps this would be like the previous four days, waiting for the Navy who would not show up. But his troops were not critical to the plan at that moment. Their job was to put up a front and pretend to be the entire land force. They began to harass the American lines with musket fire while bagpipes rent the air and men marched about in block formations pretending to prepare for another frontal assault. Major Generals Robinson and Powers had combined into one column again and were about to strike out for the ford at Pike's Cantonment, three miles upstream. With the naval battle going on loudly in the bay, the artillery keeping the Americans' heads down in their trenches, and Brisbane parading, Macomb would be too busy to look for the other brigades. The battle was becoming a slugfest of land and sea artillery. The noise of cannons was also of great tactical effect. One of the main criticisms leveled against light guns was that their noise failed to terrify the enemy, whereas the 8-pounder and particularly the 12-pounder made a very frightening blast. This materially enhanced their effect in battle, so it should not be assumed that the importance of firepower in Napoleonic battles could be measured entirely in terms of the number of physical casualties produced. Gunfire also spread confusion and hesitation in the ranks by its intrusion on morale, especially in the case of howitzer fire.

The renowned military historian and mentor, Prussian General Carl Von Clausewitz, wrote of his experience fighting Napoleon that "no plan ever survives the presence of the enemy."[5] At Plattsburgh, the enemy was found to be in the "direction of the wind." Just when it was needed most, by the English aggressor to maintain separation between the two fleets, it failed them, baffled, and fell away. With only swirls to flutter his canvas, which flapped like wash on a laundry line, Downie's plan fell to nothing. Unable to steer without the push of the wind, his three leading men-of-war drifted toward the motionless American naval line. Everything changed when the Royal Navy had to stop the progress of their attack and anchor 300 yards in front of Macdonough's floating gun platforms.

Commodore Macdonough fired the first American naval cannon. Nearly on his knees, chin just above the breach of the short fat black iron tube, he waited until he had the prow of the oncoming *Confiance* resting above the front blade sight. His gun crew stood by breathless: the master gunner holding the smoldering matches above his head. Macdonough cried "fire" and sidestepped. The fuse sputtered in the goose quill filled with powder, stuck in the touch hole, and set off the main charge, and the 42-pound cannonball emerged from the fiery blast of the muzzle, bursting out of a white cloud of smoke, and went down range. According to English reports, the ball struck the bow of the flagship and careened along the deck, killing and wounding several British sailors and destroying the wheel. Not only did the remainder of the guns follow the captain's lead, but the entire American fleet opened up with a fusillade on the now precarious Royal Navy formation. Captain Pring was quick to return the fire for his comrades, as *Linnet* drifted by, destined, she hoped, for her assigned station opposite *Eagle*. While cannonballs were indeed destructive, on the lake they were more so. At sea, where the guns were designed to take on ships made of oak, which quickly seasoned in the salt air and turned to near iron, all the vessels in this battle may look like ships of the line, but they were not. On Lake Champlain, they were constructed mostly of unseasoned soft pine plank seven inches thick that was easy to saw and warp into shape. The effect of cannons was therefore much more devastating. Pring's shot splintered everything in its path and kept going right out the other side. Before dropping anchor, he poured a full broadside into *Eagle*. The crew became bewildered by the noise and shocked by the sheer power of the strike. All the British ships had loaded with double shot as their first round. It meant two cannonballs for the price of one, with the blast from her port side guns. That would have been twenty, counting the carronades in the prow and stern, that raked the eighty-five-foot-long hull and gun deck. The American captain, Lieutenant Henley, was wounded along with much of the crew.

Plodding before the thin wind, *Confiance* had stopped and anchored. It was her turn to return fire from her array of ordinance, the most powerful afloat in the bay. *Saratoga* had allowed *Confiance* to close in without inhibiting her after Macdonough's first salvo. The uninjured members of the crew were taking the wounded below and busy clearing the deck of battle debris from the attack of the passing *Linnet*. Even though the advantage of long-range gunfire was lost, the sheer power of the Congreve cannon, combined with the four carronades on *Confiance*'s main, was formidable. Downie had held his fire even after the severe racking he had taken, ensuring that his ship was secure before fighting. He dropped the anchors and had them tied on with springs (hawsers) that were laid out by men in rowboats in spite of the fire all around. George Downie stood behind his favorite gun and prepared a broadside for *Saratoga*.

Battering Close Range

The effect of the double-shotted guns was terrible. The *Saratoga* trembled to her very keel, pushing the ship sideways against her anchors. Nearly forty of her crew's 250 were disabled, including her first lieutenant, Peter Gamble, who was killed outright as he sighted a bow gun. He was kneeling down, checking the sights on the rear of the massive barrel, when a shot entered the open gun port, split the wooden quoin (pronounced "coin") elevating wedge, and drove a portion of it against his side, nearly cutting him in half. Gamble was dead. It is said that the survivors, caught up in the maelstrom on the open deck, carried on the fight with undiminished energy. Macdonough himself, worked like a common sailor, in pointing and running a gun up into firing position. When fired, the "equal and opposite effect" sent the cannonball flying, and the 2,000-pound bronze and wood mass jumped backward. There was no recoil mechanism at that time to absorb the shock, and the gun came careening out of position. It was arrested finally by restraining ropes attached to blocks in the deck, near the rail.

On board the *Saratoga*, the full weight was caught a dozen feet from the bulkhead by the restraining ropes. The bore was swabbed out with water to extinguish any remaining fragments of powder that might still be burning. A powder monkey, a lightweight sailor or boy who had run to the magazine below, brought the powder bag, which was rammed in first. The cannonball, taken from a stack in the center of the gun deck, was carried to the muzzle and pushed in with a rammer. In the meantime, the gunner would have replaced the goose quill primer. It took the crew of ten to get the gun back into position, which rested solemnly on stout little wheels. With the gun fully forward, the muzzle stuck out through the bulkhead, clearing the side of the ship. When fired, the muzzle blast, filled with flame, could ignite nearby wood. A fully fit and trained crew could fire the massive gun, which weighed more than a ton, three times in two minutes if not distracted or reduced in number. That morning, in the heat of battle, one round in two minutes was the standard. Commands from above ceased now that both fleets were at anchor, and gun captains fired to their front at their own pace. Coordinated firing at "one go," a true broadside, was not recommended since the shock could break the spine of the ship.

A British cannonball from the first broadside of the *Confiance* split in two a spanker boom high up in the rigging of the *Saratoga* that fell across Macdonough's shoulders and struck him senseless for several minutes. While Macdonough was lying on the deck, the crew rushed to his aid. They picked him up and began to carry him to the safety of the medical station in the hold. Coming back to his senses, he had them put him down near to where he fell. He pushed them aside and stood unsupported and sent them back into the fight. He returned to his gun, which had been neglected during his brief absence. Gathering his reduced gun crew, they began the weary work again amidst the fire, smoke, and noise. Everyone on both sides was becoming deaf, and only shouts could gain the attention of the man next to Macdonough. There was no longer a plan on either side; it was gun-to-gun, ship-to-ship. Well within the danger zone, he witnessed his ship being shot to pieces by the guns of the British frigate. Farther along the gun deck, was Midshipmen Bellamey, a young officer who had shown Macdonough much promise. Captain Macdonough was looking at Bellamey's gun crew in action when a cannonball entered the ship, ricocheted off the metal gun barrel, and severed young Bellamey's head. The skull flew along the deck and hit Macdonough full in the face with such force that it knocked him to the opposing rail of his ship. Stunned again, a cannonball that came careening along the deck missed him, taking down a whole row of sailors.

Leaderless

The Americans were giving nearly as good as they got. "The firing was terrific, fairly shaking the ground along the shore, and so rapid that it seemed to be one continuous roar, intermingled with spiteful flashing from the mouths of the guns, and dense clouds of smoke soon hung over the two fleets."[6] Within fifteen minutes of the opening engagement, Captain George Downie found it necessary to assume the aiming of one of his big Congreve guns. A cannonball from *Saratoga* sought revenge. It struck the muzzle of Downie's gun, and the force of the blow ripped the gun barrel, which weighed 2,500 pounds, out of the wooden carriage. Flipping the tube up on end, like a coin in the air, Downie caught it with his arms and pulled it to his chest. The two went to the deck together, crushing the life out of the unlucky naval officer and commander of the Royal Navy fleet fifteen minutes after the onslaught had begun. Taken below by his gun crew to the makeshift infirmary, it was found that the skin was not broken but that a black and blue mark the size of a dinner plate was over his heart. His waistcoat pocket watch, one with a second hand, was found to have stopped at the precise moment of his death. The British flotilla was now leaderless.[7] Lieutenant Robertson took command of the flagship but not the flag. He was unable to send word to Captain Daniel Pring of the death of the commodore. Not only had the captain's gig been shot away from the davits during the action, but also, in the confusion of battle, the signal book had been lost. Most of the casualties were from splinters of all sizes. While missiles smashed men and ships, most casualties were the result of shrapnel, not of metal but of wood.

Flawed Gun

The Congreve cannons were unbalanced and climbed in elevation if the quoin was not tended to. That would explain why the entire rigging and masts of the American flagship were shot away while the hull and main deck received no further damage. The crew was saved from further direct fire; however, that did not reduce the casualties since falling sail and split masts continued to maim. The red-hot cannonballs appeared among the succeeding waves of fire from *Confiance*. Twice, the crew of Macdonough's ship had to break away from their artillery duties and concentrate on putting out the fires. The smoldering missiles set the port bulkhead ablaze after they had passed through the starboard planking just above the waterline.

As the contest went on, the gunfire gradually decreased in severity. The guns were becoming disabled, one by one. On the *Confiance*, the confusion was even worse: after the death of her commander, some of the crew refused to resume their posts. Lieutenant Robertson, the new skipper, was able to re-store order. A frightened British gun crew loaded a cannon with double shot but forgot to precede it with powder, wrecking the gun. One gun had been rammed with wadding first, thus preventing the firing of the main charge. On other English combatants, haste caused a crew to recharge a gun that had not been swabbed out with water. The heat and embers fired the gun before the ball was seated, killing the loader. It was said that not a man escaped without injury from the morning's work.

At the head of the line, *Eagle* encountered both *Linnet* and *Chub*. But the *Eagle* had some advantage since she was moored and her fire was not sub-ject to movement. While attempting to maneuver, the *Chub* caught a broad-side from ten carronades, the smashers, ripping her gun deck asunder. Here are the words of her captain, Lieutenant James McGhie:

> When getting near enough for the carronades to the *Eagle*, the vessel I had orders to engage in support of the *Linnet* under your command, be-fore I could choose a good situation for anchoring, my peak and throat halyards with the fore stay were shot away. This obliged me to let go an anchor in the way of the ship and brig's fire. We suffered so much from galling fire of the latter that it obliged me to strike for humanity's sake alone.[8]

In addition to McGhie's description, there is evidence that *Chub* had absorbed such damage that she became uncontrollable. Her jib boom had been shot away, the head of the bowsprit shattered, forestay gone, fore sail rove (half overboard and dragging), and the main boom damaged right over the hatch-way. She still spread some sail, but the throat and peak halyards were gone.

As she drifted between the *Confiance* and the *Saratoga*, the mainsail crashed. She provided a lull in the battle as she blocked the fire of the two flagships, slowly drifting into the American line between *Saratoga* and *Ticonderoga*. Captured, Midshipman Charles Platt boarded *Chub* and had her towed to shore by a gunboat. Of her crew of forty-one, six were dead and sixteen wounded so badly that they could not serve; not a man was untouched. There were only six men left on deck when she was taken.[9]

American Eagle *Driven Off*

The American *Eagle* was suffering as well. The prisoners who had been released to crew the ship were prominent among the dead and wounded. A wife found her husband, one of the three bandsmen killed, as she brought gunpowder up from the magazine. Both remaining British ships at the head of the line forced *Eagle* to pull up her anchor and slide behind *Saratoga*. Only two guns were functioning, and her crew was wounded and dying. She had intended to leave altogether, but when *Eagle* was released from the grip of battle, the captain and crew rallied, and she took up a position between her two sisters, the *Saratoga* and the *Ticonderoga*. There with the port side guns exposed, she fought the battle once again.

The British *Finch* accomplished half of her mission. Taking on the American *Preble* at the start, she had swept her aside without the assistance of the gunboats that had lagged behind. Coming about, she changed course and charged *Ticonderoga*. Some galleys pursued and veered close enough to *Preble* to fire grapeshot. The little American, with only four of her seven 9-pounders operational, could barely range *Finch* as she lay off and fired both cannon and carronades. *Preble* turned away, out of line.

Here are the words of Lieutenant Charles A. Budd, captain of *Preble:*

> U.S. Sloop Preble off Plattsburg
> 13th Septr. 1814
> Sir; I have the honor to express to you the satisfaction which the officers and men of the U.S. Sloop Preble under my command afforded me in the late action of the 11th inst. When the enemy's fleet were standing in for the purpose of laying their larger vessels alongside of those of our, the sloop Finch of 11 guns with several galleys outside of her made for may sloop with her peak down and tack triced up. When within shot the fire was opened on her from the Preble with coolness and deliberation, the galleys having taken in their sails and lying at long gun shot. The Finch continued edging down on my starboard quarter with an intention of getting a raking position which I prevented with my spring, which proving too short in consequence of the wind having shifted 2 or 3 points to

the Easwd, was obliged to let it go entirely and keep her broadside to bear with 2 sweeps out of her stern ports. About this time my boatswain Joseph Rose was killed on the forecastle. I could now perceive confusion on board the Finch, when wishing to avoid the incessant and well directed fire of the Preble she endeavored to go about but failed, which gave me a chance, and I did not miss it, of raking her. At this instant 4 galleys were coming down on my weather bow within grape distance with a visible intention of boading me and which the officers commanding those galleys have since assured me when I was down to the lines with the flag of truce was actually their intention and that "in five minutes they would have been along side of me," which is the fact, to prevent which, as each galley had more men than my whole crew, I thought it best, with the concurrence of all my officers, to get under way, more especially as my having been obliged to slip on of my cables when the Saratoga drifted on board of me in consequence of the sudden shift of the wind from south to north the preceding evening which occasioned me to be so far to leeward that no assistance could be afforded me from any of the rest of the squadron. I accordingly cut my cable and wore round under my jib toward the Finch, who at the same time wore from me and stood out of the bay. In the act of wearing I manned my larboard broadside and gave the galleys its contents of grape, which, from their short distance from me, must have had good effect. At this time Sailing Master Rogers Carter was severely wounded with a grape shot from one of them, of which he has since died. I then got my mainsail on her and brought her by the wind, the galleys persuing me closely and firing immense quantities of grape, which fortunately being directed too high did no other damage than cut my sails very much. I made one stretch in shore, then stood off.

Closing in on *Ticonderoga*, *Finch* cornered hard starboard to bring her guns to bear. The same wind that defeated the other three Royal Navy vessels stopped her in her tracks as she attempted to sail to the northeast. When *Finch* drifted within carronade range of her target, she got a face full of shot and shell. Nearly locked together, *Finch*, along with her escort of gunboats, attempted to board *Ticonderoga*. The American changed from solid shot to canister and leather bags filled with rifle bullets, turning the carronades into giant shotguns. When the fighting was at its hottest, the enemy attempted to board once again. Light swivel guns on the rail that were meant more for signaling were pressed into action at the intruders. Elevating the breach to its highest setting, the carronade discharge went down into the gunboats near the hull, killing the crew and blowing holes in the bottom of the boat. Many of the new flintlock-firing devices installed on *Ticonderoga*'s recently manufactured carronades were defective. Midshipman Hiram Paulding, an American lad of only sixteen years, fired the four guns of his division by the flash of his pistol for two hours.[10] When the enemy boarded, he fired at them with the same pistol. Captain Cassion put out fires on the deck that were started by the hot shot that they received from the carronades on the bow of *Confiance*. One of the American gunboats under Midshipman Conover attempted to support Cassion's vessel and attacked the British gunboat crew that was attempting to board. Three of his crew were killed.

Wrecks

In the middle of the engagement, Royal Navy Lieutenant Hicks's vessel, *Finch*, received five wounds below the waterline and attempted to maneuver away, but was grounded on a sandbar near Crab Island. They came under immediate fire from the invalid soldiers manning the two–gun shore battery. Finch fired grapeshot at the guns in an attempt to silence the position. Hicks attempted to free the ship, stuck in the sand, by throwing overboard four 6–pounders and all her ballast. He sent a boat crew out with a line from her stern to pull her free. But it was too late: she had two feet of water in her hull, and Lieutenant William Hicks struck his colors. American Naval Lieu-tenant Charles Budd, captain of the *Preble*, described the action of the *Finch* at the close of his after–action report:

> In the meantime the galleys had left me to assist the Finch, who I after-wards understood was aground. Whether she was got there accidentally or purposely I will not pretend to assert. After the ship Confiance had struck and the galleys left the vicinity of the Finch, who had her colours still flying, I prepared for lying alongside of her and bore up for that purpose, which she, perceiving, struck her flag. I still stood down for her and discov-ered she was ashore. She has 4 nine-pound shot below the surface of the water, which impressed me very forcibly with the opinion that she was in a sinking condition when she grounded. The Preble I have the pleasure to state is not materially injured. She has got 2 eighteen pound shot through her hull about a foot from the water; her larboard wales considerably started; 1 eighteen-pound shot lodged in her stern, having carried away the head knees and shattered the stern; one 24 lb. shot through her quar-ter bulkwards & the dents of two 18 lb shot from the Finch's columbiads.

The other combatants had fought to a standstill. The absence of *Eagle* at the head of the line exposed the American flagship to the cannonades of both the *Linnet* and the *Confiance* shooting away the remaining rigging that fell to *Saratoga*'s gun deck, crushing, maiming, and killing in furious proportions. A cannonball from *Linnet* struck the one remaining gun on the starboard side of Macdonough's ship and sent it careening down the main hatch into the deck below, taking the crew with her. The decisive moment had arrived. Neither the *Confiance* nor the *Saratoga* was capable of defending themselves. The *Linnet*, though heavily damaged, was still operational, and she continued to pour hellfire onto the defenseless decks of the *Saratoga*. Of the 250 members of the crew, fewer than 100 were still fighting.

The Master Stroke

It was then that Commodore Macdonough played his cards, which had been held close to his chest. During the preparation for battle, he secured his vessel by the bow and stern. Additionally, he positioned kedge anchors that had been rowed out to either end and dropped. Now, with all his guns gone on one side, he was able to cut some anchor lines and pull in others and thus rotate the stricken ship in place and expose the port side, which bristled with a fresh battery that had yet to be fired. While the maneuver took place, he sheltered most of his crew from the fire of the *Linnet* below deck. Mister Brum, the sailing master of the *Saratoga*, had his clothes torn off by splinters while he supervised the turning of the capstan, which wound the ship around. The Royal Navy lieutenant commanding *Confiance* tried to duplicate the maneuver but was unable because of tangled lines and succeeded in moving forward only a few yards. It was as if a new ship had suddenly taken the place of the shattered combatant *Saratoga*. Now a dozen fresh guns were trained on both the remaining British men-of-war. When Macdonough spun the *Saratoga* around and fired, the *Confiance* lost over half her crew. There, on the rude deck that was strewn with the wreckage of war, 140 lay dead or wounded. Most of the British guns on the engaged side were dismounted, and her stout masts had been splintered, looking like bundles of matches strung together with knotted string. Her sails, which had been torn to rags, hung limp in strips above the heads of the exhausted sailors:

> 14th September 1814
> Dear Mother
> The havoc on both sides is dreadful. I don't think there are more than five of our men, out of three hundred, but what are killed or wounded. Never was a shower of hail so thick as the shot whistling about our ears. Were you to see my jacket, waistcoat, and trousers, you would be astonished how I escaped as I did, for they are literally torn all to rags with shot and splinters; the upper part of my hat was also shot away. There is one of our marines who was in the Trafalgar action with Lord Nelson, who says it was a mere Flea-Bite in comparison with this
> > Midshipman R. Lea,
> > Royal Navy, aboard H.M.S. *Confiance*.

In fact, Lea was counted among the wounded but failed to tell his mother. The carnage aboard the defenseless British flagship under the renewed cannonade was terrible. It was no longer a battle: it was a shipwreck and slaughter. Blood poured from her scuppers as would water after shipping a heavy sea.

It was nearing 10:30 when Robertson further informed Commodore Pring that he could no longer sustain the action and intended to strike his colors. *Linnet* was in no better shape. Her masts were shattered, and her spars and sails lay on the deck, mere debris of battle. There was no hope for her to escape unless the gunboats could tow her from harm's way.

The spectators, British and Canadian men and women, watching from a private vessel that lay out in the lake, could see little of the fleet through the smoke, but it was apparent that the ships had become nothing but hulks.[11] None of the eight ships were capable of moving under sail. *Confiance* had 105 holes punched in her side when she lowered her white ensign crossed with red, which had the Union Jack in the upper corner. At that moment, with the *Finch* and *Chub* prisoner, the *Linnet* stuck her colors.

The exhausted Americans gathered all remaining ships, British and American, together, and everyone gave a hand with the salvage work. Wounded on both sides were put into the gunboats and taken to Crab Island for treatment. The surviving commanders from the Royal Navy were conducted, when all was secured, to Commodore Macdonough, who received them on what remained of the beleaguered quarterdeck of *Saratoga*. Captain Daniel Pring, his old adversary for the past two years of hit-and-run warfare, presented his commanders, Lieutenants McGhie, Hicks, and Robertson. The British officers drew their swords and presented them, in the presence of the victorious American crew, to Thomas Macdonough. The young American commodore graciously declined to accept their arms, the symbol of command and authority, and said, "Gentlemen, your gallant conduct makes you worthy to wear your weapons; return them to their scabbards."

Meanwhile, on Land

Sir George Prevost had dispatched the two brigades off to flank Macomb shortly after Downie entered the bay. The force of 7,000 marched in a column four abreast to the southwest, heading for the river ford where the Vermont militia of 2,500 waited. Both sides of the river were choked by tangled forest and underbrush. The only cleared area was the old cantonment that Zebulon Pike had clear-cut in 1813. The militia formed up for battle in straight lines, some dressed in fragments of uniforms. All were armed with issued muskets but had no artillery to back their play. The redcoated column was accompanied by field artillery in addition to the overwhelming strength of veteran regiments. It was going to be a short fight there in the open field, and General Sam Strong decided, after taking a look at the lines of amateur soldiers, to break them up and withdraw most of them into the edge of the forest on the southeastern side of the clearing. The others he put in reserve block formations that he could shift as needed. The British force was led by a staff officer from the quartermaster general, who had been at the ford two days before. If Macdonough had been blessed by the winds, Macomb was about to be saved by the "fog of war." The misguided five-mile-long line of anxious British soldiers tramped west for an hour without finding the river and its vital ford. During that valuable time, between 8:30 and 9:30, the naval battle could be heard in the distance. Lost, the column reversed itself to the starting point and struck out once more. Later, back in England, Robinson said, "A full hour of precious time had been irretrievably lost by the unfortunate mistake." Not until nearly 10:00 was Major General Robinson able to send his first line across at Pike's Cantonment. They were all from Major General Manley Powers's brigade and supported by Royal Artillery 6-pound field pieces. Powers waded into the militia and immediately dislodged them. He pursued them through the thickets for four miles, taking so few casualties that there is no record of losses. The retreating Vermonters headed south for the Salmon River, where perhaps they could make a stand. This gap left Macomb's left flank wide open. Robinson, trailing Powers, crossed the Saranac, and turned ninety degrees to the left with his brigade of 3,400 led by the 27th Infantry Regiment, the Inniskillings, in red with pale yellow facings and white cross belts. The Irish were most aggressive, crashing through growth on the southern side (the American side) of the Saranac. It was less than a three-mile trek, as the crow flies. Topping a wooded ridge, they gained the road, closing Macomb's main supply and escape route. Robinson could see the backs of the regular American infantry defending the upper bridge less than a mile away. The British were behind American lines in great force, primed for the final and fatal assault.

Dishonor Rather Than Death?

But time had been wasted that could not be reclaimed. Following the path beaten down by the marauding redcoats, an aide from General Prevost, Adjutant Baynes, caught up with General Robinson and delivered a message. Breaking the wax seal, stamped with Lieutenant General Prevost's coat of arms, he was shocked to read,

> I am directed to inform you that Confiance and the Brig having struck their colors in consequence of the Frigate having ground, it will no longer be prudent to persevere in Service committed to your charge, and it is therefore the Orders of the Commander of the Forces that you immediately return with the troops under your command.

In a letter home, Major General Frederick Robinson's feelings are revealed:

> Never was anything like the disappointment expressed in every countenance. The advance was within shot, and full view of the Redoubt, and in one hour they must have been ours. We retired under two 6 pounders posted on our side the Ford in as much silent discontent as was ever exhibited.

In the letter to Lossing, at Troy, New York, dated May 10, 1860, Major General John E. Wool, who was a major during the battle, fills in the details:

> On the 11th on the approach of the British Fleet to attack McDonough, the troops on land opened their batteries upon the works of General Macomb, but without much effect. Their fire was briskly and efficiently returned from Forts Moreau, Brown and the block-houses. The enemy formed in two columns preparatory to an assault intended as soon as the anticipated victory obtained over the fleet of McDonough. One column moved near the bridge in the center of the village to be in readiness to cross, and the other crossed the ford at Pike's Cantonment without resistance from the Militia, who retired as the column advanced, the head of which halted within a short distance of the rear of our works and remained there until the engagement of the two fleets was decided. This being in the favor of the Americans, Prevost recalled his columns of assault and immediately commenced preparations for retreating to Canada. The column in rear of the American works recrossed the Saranac without interruption, excepting the company in advance which not receiving the order to fall back and after waiting some time for the main column, went back to learn the cause of the delay, when they come in contact with General Strong's Vermont Militia, who killed and took prisoners the greater part of the company. Thus ended the battle of Plattsburgh, excepting on the retreat of the enemy some of the Militia followed and picked up as prisoners 250 or 300 deserters.

The British nearly echo the words for Clausewitz: "It may be considered as one of those misfortunes incidental to warfare which human prudence can neither foresee nor prevent."

NOTES

1. Philip J. Haythornthwaite, *Wellington's Military Machine* (Tunbridge Wells, UK: Spellmount Limited, 1951), 154.

2. Oscar Bredenberg, *The Battle of Plattsburgh Bay: The British Navy's View* (Plattsburgh, NY: Clinton County Historical Association, 1978).

3. The following comes from court-martial testimony in 1815 and appears very convenient, if not contrived, to support the charge made by Sir James Yeo that Prevost was at fault in the battle, not the Royal Navy. Downie said to his crew, "There are the enemy's ships; at the same moment we attack the ships, our Army are to storm the enemy's works at the moment we engage, and mind, don't let us be behind."

4. Interview with Captain Adrian Caruana, Royal Artillery, noted gun expert, regimental historian, and author, conducted at The Old Royal Military Academy, Woolwich, England, January 1994: Patrick Griffith PhD. *French Artillery: Nations in Arms, 1800–1815* (New Malden, UK: Almark Publishing Co., 1995), 11.

5. Carl Von Clausewitz, *On War*, edited and translated by Michael Howard and Peter Paret (Princeton, NJ: Princeton University Press, 1976).

6. Julius Hubbell's account seen from the road on Cumberland head, courtesy of the Clinton County Historical Association records.

7. Note: The gun that killed Captain George Downie is mounted in front of Macdonough Hall at the U.S. Naval Academy, Annapolis, Maryland. The muzzle is clearly marked where the American shot struck.

8. Personal letter from Lieutenant James McGhie, Royal Navy, to Captain Daniel Pring, Royal Navy, written while in American custody the day after the battle, court-martial record, Public Records Office, Kew Gardens, London.

9. Bredenberg, *The Battle of Plattsburgh Bay*.

10. Bredenberg, *The Battle of Plattsburgh Bay*.

11. Bredenberg, *The Battle of Plattsburgh Bay*.

CHARLES STEWART AND
THE BARBARY PIRATES

There is nothing more enticing, disenchanting and enslaving than the life at sea.

—Joseph Conrad

CHARLES STEWART

THE TREATY OF GHENT was signed by the delegates in Ghent, Belgium, ending the War of 1812 on Christmas Eve 1814. Major General Andrew Jackson defeated the British at New Orleans in January 1815. The Senate ratified the treaty before the president signed it on February 16, 1815. Unaware of those events, Commodore Charles Stewart on board the USS *Constitution* fought the last major battle of the War of 1812 when attacked on February 20, 1815.

Charles Stewart Sr. was a sea captain out of Philadelphia and partner in the East India Trading Company. His wife Sarah shared two things with the sea captain: a British Isles heritage and eight children. Their youngest was a boy, Charles Junior, indicating that their firstborn son more than likely died in infancy. Within eighteen months, baby Charles's father died in the fall of 1780. Sarah, left with four children in a time of high child mortality, married Captain Britton, who appears to have been with the Pennsylvania militia in the waning days of the Revolutionary War. A man of some importance, when Charles was just twelve, he introduced the boy to George Washington. A member of the Episcopal Church, Charles's education was grounded in useful subjects that prepared him for business and refined culture. In that small, insular world, Charles's best friend was Stephen Decatur, whose father was a fellow sea captain in the same firm as Charles's father. At thirteen, like many of his age, Charles was sent to sea as a cabin boy on a merchantman bound for the Caribbean. Ashore in Haiti, he witnessed the other side of slavery. At home, house slaves were common, as were slaves on the docks, but in the tropics, slavery took on the brutality of the sugarcane plantations, where black men toiled, starved, and were sold like sacks of grain or dumb farm animals. On his return to shore at seventeen, he became one of Princeton's class of thirty-three who would graduate in 1797. Charles's world was centered on sea trade and the good life among the upper classes. The new Americans were traders, buyers, sellers, brokers, agents, and merchants who were bringing, selling, or making the best of everything for the expanding opulent and plantation class who were filled with the exuberance they earned defeating the king.

At just the right moment, April 30, 1798, Congress was forced to put a new navy to sea. England saw no reason to continue to defend American merchant shipping now that the colonies had turned their back on the mother country. The French and Barbary pirates of the Mediterranean were feeding on the American merchant fleet. The Continental Navy, which had been sold off in 1786, had an impressive record but was an expense that the new nation could not afford. In those times, a ship was the most costly movable item in the world. It called for the best of everything, including timber, ironwork, cording, canvas, and highly skilled labor. Once in the water, the crew had to be fed, trained, and paid. Sea captains and their complement of officers were the heroes of their day, in high demand, and scarce on the ground. The risk of long sea voyages was extremely high, maintenance was incessant, and the longevity of the vessel was from twenty to thirty years, depending on the quality of wood and usage. Commissioned a lieutenant at age nineteen, the month before the inauguration of the Navy Department, meant that he was one of the founders of tradition. Charles Stewart was a lucky man. His first assignment was under Captain John Barry, an Irishman of renowned sea adventures who became known as the father of the U.S. Navy. As the fourth lieutenant on the new forty-four-gun frigate the USS *United States*, he was privileged to be on the best ship in the navy fleet. She was faster than the other frigates, according to those who sailed on or with the *Constitution* and *President*. On board were three officers who would become legendary seafarers: Lieutenant James Barron, Midshipmen Stephen Decatur, and Richard Somers.

Revolutionary France looked on the United States as allied with the Royal House of Bourbon and so seized American merchantmen in the Caribbean as well as off the coasts of Europe. A year's apprenticeship with Commodore Barry earned him command of the USS *Experiment*, a twelve-gun, three-masted, single-decked schooner that had been bloodied the previous year in a fight against Caribbean pirates.[1] Stewart's lieutenant was David Porter, who would command a famous ship during the War of 1812. At the end of July 1800, Stewart sailed for St. Kitts to join Captain Stephen Decatur Sr.'s command. Operating independently, he chased down the *Deux Amis*, a privateer, and captured her, sending her off as a prize under Lieutenant Porter.

Replenishing at port at Prince Rupert's Bay, it came to his attention that an American seaman had been impressed into service on an adjoining British man-of-war. When a plea in writing failed, Stewart confronted the captain on board the fighting ship. The British claimed that any man born in Great Britain was a citizen at risk of serving during wartime in the Royal Navy. Naturalized citizenship was not recognized. Amos Seeley was not born in England but was native born. Seeley pleaded his case, backed by the American captain, in such convincing terms that Seeley was released to Stewart. Stewart was not only a seafaring captain, but also a diplomat, something that surprised those who read about his exploits in the Philadelphia newspapers. It was a valuable skill needed far from home when the appearance of his ship meant that the captain represented his country.

Ranging off St. Bartholomew, he encountered two armed vessels: a brig and schooner flying British colors. Stewart was about to fall in with them when they switched colors to the tricolor of revolutionary France. Stewart, gaining the weather gauge, attacked. The ships drew up close while *Diana* began to pound with her guns, some loaded with metal fragments. Stewart sustained a minor wound to his shoulder that was not serious enough to send him below, but he was treated by the surgeon on the pitching deck. There, remaining at his station, he relentlessly directed fire into the enemy craft until she surrendered. Lieutenant David Porter later chronicled the event:

> The "Experiment" now opened fire with all her guns, [half of fourteen] and began to close with the stranger, intending to carry the latter by boarding.
>
> It was blowing quite fresh at the time, and the Experiment being very light, owing to a short supply of provisions in the hold, laid over so much on her side as to be unable to depress her guns sufficiently to strike the supposed enemy's hull; and all her shot was expended among the rigging. But this difficulty was soon remedied, and the resources of the trained seamen made manifest; planks were cut and placed under the trucks, which expedient made it possible to depress the Experiment's guns sufficiently, and the fire told with so much effect that in a few minutes the stranger struck her colors.
>
> This action showed the superiority of the Experiment's fire; and it will be observed that in all the fights in which this vessel was engaged the battle was finished in a short time. The vessels captured by the schooner

were not, it is true, ships of war, except in the case of the "Diane," which was a superior vessel to the "*Experiment*" in guns and men, if we include the thirty soldiers on board and when we consider the rapid manner in which that contest was brought to a close, we cannot but admire the precision of the "*Experiment's*" fire. Up to this time, The "Experiment" had given an excellent account of herself, and the reputation of her commander and first lieutenant stood high a compliment not to be despised when so many gallant fellows were vying in a noble zeal for their country's service.[2]

DRAWDOWN

The Quasi War ended quietly. It was more of a misunderstanding than a war. The navy benefited from the conflict even if the nation didn't. In 1801, with the arrival of President Jefferson, who earlier as a diplomat to France had cried out for the creation of the navy, called for the reduction of the men-of-war to thirteen, seven of which were put in reserve. The officer corps numbered just enough to sail the active ships while crews were recruited off the docks at the start of each voyage. It was a sorry state of affairs for the Navy Department, which understood the importance of establishing a regular force rather than one ginned up at a moment's notice. Since the states didn't contribute to the federal treasury, Congress could not produce a stream of funds to keep a navy on station. A cruising navy required naval agents in distant foreign ports to pay in local currency for provisions collected and repairs completed. The U.S. Treasury had to guarantee payment. Some in Congress looked at the navy with the same eyes as the unpopular standing army. They couldn't see an outside threat to the nation that would justify the expenditure.

Only one of thirty-six lieutenants retained on active service, Stewart had the good fortune to join the company on board the thirty-eight-gun USS *Chesapeake*. Not in office six months, Jefferson, for the second time in his life, was confronted by the Bashaw of Tripoli, who not only preyed on undefended American merchant ships but was the first state to declare war on the United States. When Ambassador to France in 1784, Jefferson had protested paying a tribute to Tripoli for allowing American trading vessels to operate in the Mediterranean. Jefferson had advised the new American government to sign a mutual trade treaty or else go to war with the pirates. It doesn't sound like Jefferson, so quick to offer a military option, but he was embarrassed that his country allowed a foreign tin-pot power to steal ships, murder seamen, and enslave Christian passengers on board their rowed xebecs. One witness to the affront had told Jefferson of seeing miserable starved white men chained to oars at a port in Morocco. When the Bashaw was questioned about the declaration, a standard reply that went back to the Crusades was given:

the Laws of the Prophet, as written in the Holy Koran, reads that all nations who should not have acknowledged the authority of Islam were
sinners, that it was the right and duty to make holy war upon them
wherever they could be found, and to make slaves of all they could take
as prisoners.

Such a response to a "man of the enlightenment," as Jefferson saw himself, was
nonsense and was used as a veiled justification for stealing, which, he reminded
the potentate, was condemned in the Koran. John Adams of Massachusetts supported the tribute. The merchants of New England saw it as a practical matter since the country could not afford to send a significant naval force. George
Washington had opposed the tribute. As a show of force, Jefferson sent three
frigates to the Mediterranean in May. By the end of the year, the fleet required
replacement. By January, a replacement flotilla was mounted, but the chosen
ships needed to recruit able seamen, ordinary seamen, and ships' company.
The established American merchant fleet paid higher wages, leaving the navy
to scrape the bottom of the barrel and floors of the taverns for crews. Slowly,
the thirty-eight-gun frigates *Constellation*, *Chesapeake*, and *John Adams*, plus the
thirty-six-gun frigate *New York*, were brought into service that spring. That
year Stewart had been transferred to the *Constellation* under her new skipper,
Alexander Murray, whose long experience as merchant captain qualified him
for the transit of the North Atlantic to Gibraltar and the confining waters of the
Mediterranean. The big frigates, USS *Philadelphia* and *Essex*, were on station
waiting in May 1802, when the fleet congregated outside Tripoli. America was
not alone; Great Britain and Sweden collaborated, plying the same waters to
form a blockade of North African ports.

Blockade duty wasn't rewarding. Maintaining station off the mouth of
the harbor was difficult, requiring constant attention to minor alterations in
sail and yards. The enemy corsairs, xebecs, and row galleys could oppose the
wind and range inshore where the waster was shallow. Frustrated, the captain
of *Constellation* gave chase to a flotilla of eighteen such craft and managed to
split them in half. Those caught were racked with heavy cannon fire and prevented from entering the harbor.

REPLACEMENTS

In Washington the following year, naval officers complained that they were
not equipped to maintain an effective blockade since the waters were shallow and the American frigates' draft ruled out dangerous pursuit into shal-
lows. The Navy Department constructed four vessels, and, in May 1803, the
secretary gave one, the *Argus*, to Stephen Decatur and another, a sixteen-gun

ninety-four-foot-long, two-masted, shallow-draft brig, *Syren*, to Charles Stewart for deployment with the blockade of North African ports.[3] Stewart and Decatur took a keen interest in their respective vessels under construction in the Philadelphia shipyard that summer. On the last day of August, Stewart drove *Syren* out into the Atlantic on a passage to Gibraltar to join Commodore Edward James Preble and *Constitution* on station off Morocco.

While finalizing an agreement with the king of Morocco, Preble split his fleet and sent Captain William Bainbridge, captain of the frigate *Philadelphia*, ahead with an escort to resume the blockade of Tripoli. Many had warned that it was bound to happen. The shoals would get the better of the blockade. The *Philadelphia*'s draft was too deep for the sandbars that protected the mouth of the harbor. While in chase, suddenly her prow violently rose up, and she shivered to her keel before grounding. Her escort *Vixen* came up and tried to pull her off. The pirates, expert at boarding and subduing the crew, took them and their captain prisoners. The frigate and all on board were in the hands of the enemy and likely to remain so. Within two days, the pirates were able to unstick her and bring her in, tacked into the inner harbor. They could claim her as a prize of war and sell her off or convert the frigate to their flag, a common practice.

HUMILIATION

The winter of 1803 humbled Commodore Preble, who promised Jefferson that the Bashaw would never sail his new frigate, for he had drastic plans to prevent the eventuality. While Preble planned, he left the operation of the blockade in the hands of his first lieutenant, Charles Stewart, who, in spite of appalling weather conditions, maintained a constant parade off the harbor entrance with the *Argus, Nautilus, Enterprise*, and *Vixen*.

Preble's plan called for a sneak attack by a single vessel at night to board *Philadelphia*, subdue the prize crew of pirates holding her at anchor, and fire the magazines. Stephen Decatur jumped at the chance and volunteered his crew of the *Enterprise* to board the *Intrepid* (a captured ketch) and sail her under false colors to the side of the *Philadelphia* and set her on fire. Stewart was to follow *Intrepid* into the harbor and provide cover if necessary and transport back to the fleet waiting anxiously outside the harbor of Tripoli in the freezing water of a February night.

Stewart's crew on *Syren* were at last going into action after months of sailing in circles chasing and not catching the pirates who took their frigate and imprisoned their fellow sailors. Two days were needed to prepare *Syren* to look like a pirate ship in silhouette returning to port. As the two raiders approached the entrance to the harbor, a freak squall erupted, tossing the little vessel around like a cork. Both captains could not hold to their stations and independently strove back to sea. *Syren's* anchor was stuck in the mud, and the pressure exerted by the storm on the line prevented pickup. Stewart and his crew were flung from the capstone when it spun out of control, splattering the men with the sweeps' bars. There was nothing to do, but to cut the anchor loose and escape to the open sea. The two distressed vessels stayed together even though the storm increased, driving them away from Tripoli and their own fleet. For a week, they bailed, replaced torn sails, lashed together cracked spars, and ate nothing but ship biscuits and drank bad-tasting water. The storm turned and drove them back toward shore to within sight of the rocks, and Stewart feared that both vessels would be broken up on the African shore.

On February 16, Tripoli was once again within reach. The two captains realigned their crews and spoke for the last time before beginning the run after dark. Stewart anchored in forty feet of water off the entrance and watched the dim yellow lantern light on *Interpol's* masthead bob into the quiet harbor. The first indication of the attack was the sound of musket and pistol fire. Through his glass, Stewart could see the lights of the city reflected in the water and considerable movement. Soon, bright orange flames began to rise in the vicinity of the *Philadelphia*. Now he scanned the darkness on that nearly moonless night for evidence of *Intrepid*. The fire on the frigate grew quickly and eliminated *Interpol's* attempt to escape to *Syren*. Caught in a pool of reflected light, they took fire from all sides, but remained unhit as the tiny craft slipped slowly out to sea propelled by the enthusiastic rowing of the exhilarated crew. Safely back on board *Syren*, only one man was injured, while a count confirmed that all hands were accounted for.

One result was a request to promote Decatur to captain, the youngest of the rank to this day. That summer, in an effort to put pressure on the Bashaw to release the crew of the *Philadelphia*, Stewart and Decatur came up with a plan to attack the harbor fortress defenses and rake the harbor. Stewart silenced the fort, and Decatur bombarded the harbor, to no avail. Stewart landed at the head of a small amphibious assault group made up of sailors and marines mixing it up on the shore east of the fortress, but again they could not sustain the attack.

PREBLE, EXASPERATED, ATTACKS TRIPOLI

Determined to rescue Bainbridge and crew, Preble turned from diplomacy to a more direct approach. He mounted a three-tier attack. *Constitution* and bomb ketches would lay off with heavy gunfire support. His flagship could put cannonballs on several of the Bashaw's fortresses. Stewart would take the flotilla of brigs and schooners as close as the depth of water would allow and rake, suppressing fire on the pirate craft that lined up across the entrance of the harbor. Decatur and Lieutenant Richard Somers, another boyhood friend of Stewart, would each command a group of three gunboats and break into the inner harbor. On August 3, as the attack was moving into position, the pirates countered with a morass of armed craft of all kinds. Decatur plunged into the line along with Somers and managed to capture three enemy craft. In the middle of the fray, Master Commandant Isaac Chauncey blundered in, booming away on the twenty-six guns of the *John Adams*. The multiplicity of Tripolian gun platforms, combined with the formidable defenses surrounding the harbor confines, expelled the American fleet from the harbor in disarray once again.

Before he was relieved, Preble took one more shot. He sent *Intrepid* into the harbor loaded with gunpowder, skippered by Lieutenant Somers. Somers was expected to sail into the inner harbor and mingle with the pirate fleet before setting fire to her and escaping by boat. The complicated currents passing through the narrow entrance to the harbor denied Somers completion of his trajectory, and his incendiary vessel, though catching fire and exploding, did no harm other than killing Somers and the crew.

CHANGE OF COMMAND

It was the end for Preble, who had fought all odds in a very faraway place with a strange-sounding name. Chauncey was just the vanguard of the relief sent by the president. The new commodore was on the way. Samuel Barron would try to finish off the Barbary pirates and free Bainbridge's crew, who, stuffed in the Bashaw's prison, were much worse for the wear. Chauncey brought the long-expected promotion list confirming Stewart's promotion to master commandant, a grade below captain. The years 1804 and 1805 saw the quick departure of Commodore Barron because of illness, and he was replaced by Commodore John Rodgers; back in America, Commodore Preble died of tuberculosis.

Stewart, age twenty-seven, was given an exclusive mission and a flotilla with sufficient power to enact change to the status quo when he sailed en masse into the harbor of Tunis under the gaze of the Dey of Tunis. The American Council, at his wit's end dealing with a determined head of state, could not convince the Dey that it was ultimately in Tunis's interest to stop seizing American merchant ships and sign a trade agreement. In desperation, he looked to Stewart to bombard the port and bring about the destruction of the city. Stewart showed more than naval gun tactics:

> Stewart sailed with the squadron for the purpose of checking in that regency of Tunis a rising disposition to commence depravations on our commerce. The feeling there became so hostile that Mr. George Davis, our consul, deemed it prudent to seek refuge on board the fleet. In this critical state of affairs our consul-general, Colonel Lear, advised that the Commodore ask the advise of his principal officers. A council was convened on board the flagship, the situation of affairs was explained, and the opinion of the officers demanded whether hostilities ought not to be immediately commenced. Captain Stewart gave it as his opinion, that there was no power under the *Constitution* which authorized hostilities and wars on others, but that which was lodged exclusively with Congress; that the President could not exercise this power without the action and authority of Congress, much less the Commander of an American squadron; that due respect for the laws of the nations forbade aggression, and only justified property and commerce, but where hostile attempts, were made on either, he would be justified in seizing all persons engaged in them, but no further would his country sanction his acts. This sound reasoning and discretion prevailed, and the Dey of Tunis sent a special minister to the United States. When President Jefferson received from our consul-general a copy of that opinion as delivered in the council, he expressed to his cabinet the high satisfaction he felt at having an officer in the squadron who comprehended the international law, the constitution of his country and the policy of his government.[4]

Such insight, perhaps rare today for one so young, was to be expected in a man of his responsibility, education, experience, and background. With the submission of the Barbary governments, the Mediterranean fleet was called home, leaving behind only a token to serve the nation's needs. Within the next year, Stewart was recognized for his service and promoted to captain in April 1806, serving in the effort to design and construct a fleet of gunboats to protect the harbors of the Eastern Seaboard, a pet project of President Jefferson.[5] The western expansionist did not favor building expensive oceangoing men-of-war when there was no clear enemy to oppose American merchant shipping. They wanted the effort to go toward new states and territories creeping toward the Mississippi. The navy and her supporters favored big powerful warships, which were most impressive, or small poky harbor craft to protect the 2,000-mile coastline of the nation. Stewart sought a balance of some of each. He witnessed the wisdom in being able to block the harbor entrance with small agile craft as deployed by the Tripolian pirates who stymied Preble's efforts for two years. He also recognized the need for juggernauts to dominate future commitments on the high seas. He realized the instability of the continental conflicts and expected the United States to be drawn into its web regardless of intentions to remain aloof. Like most naval officers, he was not an isolationist. However, there wasn't money for a balanced fleet and perhaps not enough for harbor craft either. The federal government would have to find funds somewhere other than those collected by revenue cutters and customs offices.

ON THE SHELF

Within a year, Stewart was called back to supervise the boatyard of New York City with the design and launching of a fleet. On June 22, 1807, everything changed when the fifty-five-gun HMS *Leopard*, in an attempt to stop and board the thirty-two-gun frigate *Chesapeake*, raked her decks, killing and wounding American sailors as she sailed out of the harbor unprepared for attack and within sight of horrified citizens of Norfolk, Virginia. The nation and the president were incensed by the cowardly and unprovoked act of war. Jefferson imposed an embargo of all American trade with Great Britain that would turn out to be highly ill-conceived. The navy court-martial board included Decatur and Stewart, who convicted Commodore James Barron for not preparing his ship for action, which was a lesser charge and suspended him from service for five years. Free from naval service by 1808, he joined the merchant marine trade and accumulated a considerable fortune over the next four years. When Congress declared war in the summer of 1812, Stewart was placed in command of an old friend, USS *Argus*, but before the year was out, his seniority, the watchword in the navy, gave him command of the USS *Constellation*. Stewart knew that, with a weapon like her, he could not prowl the seas seeking British trade vessels and hurt the empire like no other element. His intent was to assemble a small flotilla of men-of-war and disrupt the enemy's commercial shipping, the only way the British Isles, which depended on links to her colonies, could be disrupted by a small newborn nation like the United States. A hit-and-run tactic would disrupt the Royal Navy, which preferred static targets for their dreadnaughts to shatter or the wooden walls of an enemy warship that could be turned to splinters. The Royal Navy officer corps excelled at blockade and bombardment and hated slow, methodical escort duty. As raiders of commerce, the American navy could break up British maritime formations and fight single-ship battles, which Stewart assured Secretary Hamilton they could win. While waiting on shore for the *Constellation* to complete repairs, which flowed like molasses that fall of 1812, her captain marched the halls of

Congress and the parlor of the White House lobbying for an offensive naval posture. He engaged with the seldom-sober secretary on many occasions over nautical trivia—how many guns on one side equal how many guns on the other. It was not until late December that his ship was afloat in the Chesapeake Bay. February found him waiting orders at Annapolis for sailing orders from the new Secretary of the Navy, William Jones. Released at last, he sailed down the Bay but found his passage to the Atlantic obstructed by the arrival of Admiral Warren's Royal Navy flotilla across the mouth of the Bay. *Constellation* was forced to skirt the western shore and slip behind the defenses of Norfolk, Virginia. Month by month, Stewart contrived and constructed elaborate land and water defenses to protect his valuable frigate from attack by the Royal Navy. He was bottled up for sure, and as long as the blockade ships weaved across the opening to the broad Atlantic, *Constellation* settled in the backwater awaiting her chance to fly. By May, the long spring waning, Stewart sat moored in shame and steamed over his inability to get to sea. He became a victim of his own warnings put to the president at the start of the conflict. "If the navy did not get out to sea quickly, it would remain bottled-up, beached."

CIRCUMSTANCES AND LUCK

The seniority system came to his rescue. In June 1813, William Bainbridge was relieved of command of the USS *Constitution* and was succeeded by Charles Stewart, who took the rest of the year to prepare Old Ironsides for service once again. The most valuable ship of her day, Stewart took from fall right up to Christmas to prepare her to meet the Royal Navy. The repairs took a considerable time. It seemed that everything was rotted through, particularly the masts and yards. Some deck beams had to be replaced and the ship completely provisioned. In spite of the great victories she had achieved, it was difficult to maintain the crew once in port. The U.S. Navy was not yet a standing regular service. Soon the crew was paid off. The ship would remain idle from February to December 1813 while refitting as the war raged around her. Once it was determined that she was to voyage once again, a call was put out for able and ordinary seamen. Some of the warrants remained during refitting. It was most difficult to recruit after the defeat of *Chesapeake*, which took place just outside Boston harbor. The British blockage was intended to deny, divert, disrupt, disorient, destroy, and demoralize the United States, her commerce, and her navy. It was having a devastating effect.

It was not until the first day of January 1814 that *Constitution* was completely clear of the blockading Royal Navy fleet that crisscrossed the trading lane leading to the Atlantic. Nearly an entire year had gone by since she had acquired her title "Ironsides."

Over the past year, victories and more recently disasters had befallen the American navy as the war dragged on toward another year. Stewart had been shipmates with the heroes and carried the coffin of the losers. Captain Stewart's situation was not very different in Boston than it had been for the past ten months in the Chesapeake Bay. Just outside Boston harbor waited the haughty Royal Navy captains who ran newspaper blurbs baiting Stewart to try his luck running the blockade. Others, like *Chesapeake* Captain Lawrence, had taken the challenge and paid the price with his ship and his life. The opponents, now three years later, were more wary and girded for single combat against the American navy, which had earned its good reputation since the start of the conflict. British commanders sought fame and fortune in the defeat of American frigates, especially the *Constitution*, victor over two vanquished British frigates, the pride of the King's navy. By the end of 1813, the formidable blockade had completely shut down trade all along the Eastern Seaboard and the Gulf Coast. The American navy was captured, sunk, or marooned in port.

FREEDOM AT LAST

On December 31, a dark and stormy evening, word came from Halfway Rock that the weather had forced the blockading ships off station. With his ship ready, Stewart moored out in the channel. When the heavy weather closed in, he called all hands to set the fore, main, and mizzen gallants and courses. The mighty vessel pulled confidently into the storm and out of sight. The bow came up, forcing the captain to stand on the rail amidships to see forward, straining in the gloom for the dreaded enemy. She slipped unnoticed into the Southern Atlantic as easily as you please.

ON PATROL IN 1814

Constitution's winter and early spring patrol into the Caribbean was not a notable success. Stewart chased a number of ships that turned out not to be British. The hard, pounding Caribbean weathered the crew and damaged the wooden ship. Captain Stewart realized that his mainmast was severely cracked and decided to go home to Boston for the repair. A passing ship told him that the *President* was blockaded in New York Harbor. As *Constitution* came up on Marblehead from the south, he was not surprised to find two Royal Navy frigates in chase. HMS *Junon* and *Tenedos* were nearly in range and closing fast. With a mast that could snap at any time, he was not prepared to fight, nor was he about to make Ironsides a prisoner. Turning for the shelter of the American harbor, he was nearly becalmed. Thoughts of kedging his way to safety crossed his mind as he lightened ship. The two enemy frigates gained on him, and he jettisoned water and spars while adding "stun sails," reaching for both a slight breeze and the estuary at the same time. His skill, coupled with *Constitution*'s ability to sail, brought him past Halfway Rock, where the pursuers dared not risk their keels. Not a glorious victory, but Charles Stewart had saved his crippled ship, the one mandate that all captains shared.

TRAPPED

After six months in port, Charles Stewart's vigil was realized when a temporary letup in the blockade was seized on December 18, 1814. Painted with a yellow ocher gun hatch stripe rather than the black-and-white checkerboard, she looked the part of an Englishman and not a runner. The USS *Constitution* was free. The only warship to break the blockade in six months, she went hunting across the Atlantic.

Sailing south and then east across against the trade winds, progress was slow and tiring. Supplies were consumed at a high rate. By Christmas, everything was in short supply, yet they were well out at sea. Providence smiled on this lucky ship. A Royal Navy supply ship, *Lord Nelson*, was delivered into their outstretched hands on the new year. Acting Chaplain, Asherton Humphreys, who was also the ship's clerk, wrote,

> There were lots of corn beef in rounds, smoked salmon, dried beef and codfish, tongues and rounds, fine apple cheeses & barrels of loaf sugar of the most superior kinds, pipes of best brandy, gin and port wine, chests of imperial and gunpowder tea, barrels of flour, hams inferior not even to Smithfield Virginia, etc.[6]

As she neared the West African coast and began to mingle with the commercial vessels, contacts came frequently. They were mostly neutral and not fair game for the crew, who wanted prize money. Sailing in January, the worst month of the year in the faraway waters of the Bay of Bisque, the winds were blowing with great strength, providing speed but not comfort. The crew dreaded going into the tops where their hands froze to the lines and their hair and eyelashes became crusted in ice.

Asherton Humphreys's diary tells a touching tale of a terrier dog named Guerriere that belonged to Second Lieutenant Beekman Hoffman:

> Beloved by the deck hands, he joined in on the end of lines, lending his pulling ability, which was always welcome. By February, the wind blew fiercely in the face of the lookouts at the tops. On deck Chaplain Humphreys and First Lieutenant Henry E. Ballard paced the quarterdeck on late afternoon. Guerriere kept the step, the watchdog so to speak. Guerriere who was playing about the heels of Mister Ballard appeared uncommonly frisky and was rather troublesome at length. Becoming a nuisance he attracted the particular attention of the Lieutenant when he jumped up on the hammock clothes tied on the top of the rail and stretching his head to windward and commenced barking most vehemently. Upon looking to discover what attracted his notice lo! & behold! There was a large frigate standing down before the wind under a press of sail, which the gentlemen at the mast head had not yet discovered.[7]

The dog was rewarded with food, and the lookouts had twelve strokes of the whip laid on by the boatswain's mate. The ship was the *Amazona*, a Portuguese frigate going into Lisbon. Such a dereliction could have cost the sailors and the ship their lives.

THE LAST MAJOR BATTLE
OF THE WAR OF 1812

The lesson learned by the Royal Navy during the war was, "When confronted by one of the large American frigates, do not attack." The unprecedented loss of the *Guerriere, Macedonia,* and *Java* in one-sided battles was not to be replayed ever again in London newspapers. Ships that had been at sea for the past several months were unaware that a final solution to the war had been reached at the peace table. In January, *Constitution* had contact with a passing vessel that reported the rumor of a treaty, but Stewart had heard such claims for nearly a year, all of which turned out to be misleading.

On February 20, 1815, over the horizon, the lookouts, who were much more keen than before the alert terrier's bark, shouted and pointed to the horizon, where two ships were approaching. Soon it became plain from the Union Jacks flying from their mizzens that they were men-of-war. The Royal Navy ships weren't running. Their officers knew from her unique cut which was the American frigate, but the warning to lay off had been for single ships. The British sailors were game—what a prize it would be to bag Ironsides. Traveling west, the wind was on their beam, giving them the high hand. The twenty-gun *Levant*, in lead of the twenty-four-gun *Cyane*, closed on *Constitution*'s starboard side. *Levant* was a single-decked corvette ship rigged with all nine yards. Her courses were drawn up in fighting position—some called

A political hack, Jacob Brown lead the militia of the northwest corner of New York state to splendid victories. A true transformer, he became a premier self-taught regular army commander. A practical innovator and natural leader, he consolidated the losses of the Niagara and turned them to victories. Engraved by Thomas Gimbrede, one print from stipple engraving, © 1816, courtesy of the Library of Congress, LC-USZ62-48105.

Winfield Scott began his early rocky career prior to the War of 1812. First in command at Queenston, Canada, he lead a "forlorn hope" that resulted in the capture of his command. A self-schooled warrior, he built the army of the north and lead it under a most oppressive superior. In the end, free to express his abilities, he triumphed. Engraved by T. B. Welch, one print from engraving with etching, courtesy of the Library of Congress, LC-USZ62-46717.

Alexander Macomb was the son of an influential New Yorker. Quickly promoted through sycophantic efforts, he defended the machinations of his commander in court. Once on his own, late in the war, he changed his demeanor and became one of the most effective field commanders of the war. His unassisted victory at the most decisive battle of the war saved the nation from invasion. U.S. Army Military History Institute.

Commodore Thomas Macdonough's defense of Lake Champlain while supporting the army at Plattsburgh is a thing of legends. Building his own fleet, training soldiers to be sailors, staring unflinching into the eye of the tiger, places the thirty-year-old officer in a class of his own. U.S. Army Military History Institute.

Lieutenant Colonel Winfield Scott and Major John E. Wool fought together heroically in the War of 1812 (Queenston and Plattsburgh), the Mexican War, and the Civil War. It was a rare partnership blended together by wounds on the fields of battle, which did not end until each had served more than fifty years in uniform. By Auguste Edouart, lithograph, pencil and cut paper on paper, © 1843, image/sheet: 28 cm x 19.2 cm (11" x 7⁹⁄₁₆"), National Portrait Gallery, Smithsonian Institution; gift of Robert L. McNeil, Jr.

Little is known of militia Major General Benjamin Mooers except that he was a military man in name only. Appointed by the political machine, he failed to train his troops or inspire them to stand and fight. He faded from history as quickly as he arrived. Yet if he had taken advantage of that which was offered, things would have been different. U.S. Army Military History Institute.

Commodore Charles Stewart a founding rock of the U.S. Navy. His many commands at sea and adventures with pirates are legendary. A mentor to the officer corps, political advisor, and diplomat put him in a class of his own. He commanded the USS *Constriction* in the last battle of the War of 1812 off the coast of Africa, which occurred in late February 1815 after the president signed the Treaty of Ghent. Wood artist; Goodman engraver, print from stipple engraving, courtesy of the Navy Art Collection, Naval History and Heritage Command.

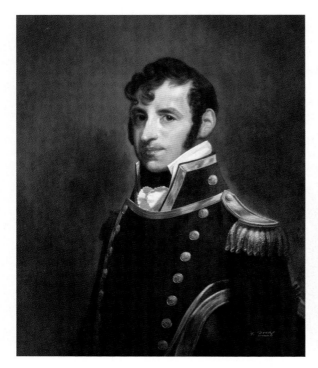

Commodore Stephen Decatur Jr. was the darling of the navy. Smart, fearless, dedicated, and a leader of men, he affected everyone and everything he touched. His storming of the *Philadelphia* and taking of the *Macedonia* are classic swashbucklers. His sense of honor was his downfall. By V. Zveg, oil painting on canvas, © 1976, Navy Art Collection, Naval History and Heritage Command.

Accepting the challenge to fight his ship USS *Chesapeake* against HMS *Shannon*, Captain James Lawrence uttered his last heroic words, "Don't give up the ship" before dying of his wounds. Commander Perry emblazoned those words on a flag flown on the USS *Lawrence* at his victory over the Royal Navy on Lake Erie in 1813. Print from engraving, courtesy of the Navy Art Collection, Naval History and Heritage Command.

Commodore John Rodgers was first mate at seventeen. Once at sea, in 1812 he established the merchant raider tactic followed by the navy throughout the war. By Gilbert Stuart, oil painting on canvas, courtesy of the Navy Art Collection, Naval History and Heritage Command.

Captain James Lawrence touched a chord with every officer in the navy for his sailing skill, professionalism, and leadership. Given at the end to pride, he risked it all, which cost him his ship and his life. Gilbert Stuart, artist; Edwin, engraver, print from stipple engraving, © 1813, courtesy of the Navy Art Collection, Naval History and Heritage Command.

Major General James Wilkinson, who called himself the "scientific soldier," was the most successful sycophant of the time. As commanding general of the American army, he earned the scorn of the nation for being a paid agent of the Spanish government. "He never won a battle or lost a court martial." Oil on canvas, © 1820, Stretcher: 74.9 cm x 62.2 cm (29½" x 24½"), National Portrait Gallery, Smithsonian Institution.

her a sloop of eighteen carronades and two 9-pound cannons. However, the American count adds one 12-pound cannon that was shifted about as a chaser. Robert Gardner, in *War Ships of the Napoleonic Period*, wrote, "A sloop can refer to a single-masted rig or a ship so rigged or a small warship, in the royal navy. It was also used as a rating—in effect any vessel in charge of an officer with the rank of master and commander by the 1790s, the type name was not related to rig."

In spite of the conspicuous yellow ocher gun stripe used earlier to conceal *Constitution*'s identity, there was never any doubt that their enemy was at hand. *Cyane* followed *Levant* close behind. The light was fading, but there was quite enough to identify the stars and stripes that topped the mizzenmast.

Night Battle

It was a classic engagement, as all three ships opened up with broadsides at nearly the same moment. The *Cyane*'s shot screamed through the rigging's snapping lines and punching holes in the yellowed flaxen topgallants. Wooden spars, the size of telephone poles, came crashing down. They were momentarily slowed by the crisscross of cables strung above the quarterdeck protecting Major Archibald Henderson's marines, who stood ready to repel boarders. Fortunately for the Americans, the shorter-range 32-pound carronades on *Levant* were at their range limit, while *Constitution*'s long 24-pounders sizzled straight through the Englishmen's rails and hull. Both royal Navy vessels turned toward the path of the *Constitution* to close the gap and improve the effectiveness of their short-range carronades. Captain George Douglas, Royal Navy, commander of HMS *Levant* and the senior officer described the instructions he passed by speaking horn to Captain Gordon Thomas Falcon, skipper of HMS *Cyane*. Captain Douglas wrote later in third person,

> Cyane arrived and Douglas hailed and indicated to Falcon to attack *Constitution*. They were attempting to protect two convoys from Gibraltar in their company. Superior sailing ability of *Constitution* prevented maneuver. Captain Falcon returned fire but his shot fell short while the enemy's long 24's were producing their full effect.[8]

Levant attempted to cross in front of *Constitution* and rake her as he went. Douglas's two 9-pound cannons did little damage to the great ship but played around the heads on the forecastle. The American captain saw it coming and slowed. "In 15 minutes the *Constitution* ranged ahead and became engaged in the same manner with the *Levant*. The *Cyane* now luffed up for the larboard

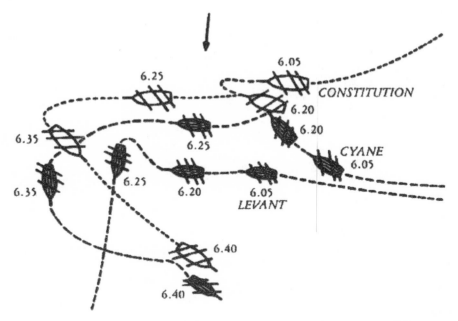

HMS *Cyane* and HMS *Levant* attack the USS *Constitution* in February 1815 off the coast of Africa.

quarter of the *Constitution* where upon the latter, backing astern, was enabled to pour into *Cyane* her whole broadside."[9]

The *Cyane* didn't injure Ironsides, but *Constitution*'s 24-pound solid shot crashed through the hull and became embedded in the opposite side. Soon, water gushed in, breaking loose barrels of food and water that became buoyant. Floating debris prevented the powder monkeys from ready access to the magazine. Water lapped around the ankles of the surgeon and his mate treating the first of a flood of bleeding and broken shipmates. The keelson was covered with water, which was rising at an alarming rate. The carpenter was commandeering men to help plug the holes in the hull. The noise of the American cannonballs thudding on the bulwarks sounded like the muffled drums of death in the dark, belowdeck. The moon was bright, but the smoke hung in the air and obscured the American captain:

> Meanwhile the Levant had bore up, to wear round and assist her consort. The *Constitution* thereupon filled, shot ahead, and gave Levant two stern rakes. Seeing this, Cyane, although without a brace or bowline except the larboard fore brace, wore, and gallantly stood between the *Levant* and *Constitution*. The latter then promptly wore, and raked the *Cyane*

astern. The *Cyane* immediately luffed up as well as she could, and fired her larboard broadside at the starboard bow of the *Constitution.* The latter soon afterwards ranged up on the larboard quarter of the *Cyane*, within hail, and was about to pour in her starboard broadside, when at 6h 50m p.m. having had most of her standing and running rigging cut to pieces, her main and mizzen masts left in a tottering state and other principal spars wounded, several shot in the hull, nine or ten between wind and water, five carronades disabled, chiefly by the drawing of the bolts and starting of the shocks, and the *Levant* being two miles to lee-ward still bearing away to repair her heavy damage, the *Cyane* fired a lee gun and hoisted a light as a signal of submission.[10]

While the larger of the two Royal Navy ships, *Cyane*, had capitulated, HMS *Levant* had slipped away into the darkness. Captain Stewart's blood was up. His own decks were smashed and shattered, while piles of debris brought down from above littered the quarterdeck. Below, the gun deck had little damage, and the men serving the cannons were looking past the muzzles of their run-out 24-pounder peering into the darkness for sight of *Levant*.

The captain, the Honorable George Douglas, the son of Lord Doug-las of Lancaster, though outgunned, had cleared away the busted yards and tangled lines and was coming on. He made a large sweeping turn to the wind and came back at Ironsides once again with blood in his eyes. Bearing straight at *Constitution*, they came together head-on and passed at twenty-five yards on their larboard sides.

More than two hours had passed since the engagement began. The sail-ors on all the ships would not have noticed. They were overwhelmed with their individual tasks. "Shift the wounded, stack the dead, clear the rails, and run up the guns." The tangled sheered-off spars were cobbled together by shredded lines that were hung from broken blocks. The decks were slick with men's blood pumped out by the last thumps of their stout hearts. The disci-pline of silence was maintained in those who were unharmed. Others could not keep their tongues quiet, wrapped in pain as they slipped into shock at the sight of their ghastly wounds, dark red and black:

At 8h 15m which was as soon as the *Levant* had rove new braces, the gallant little ship again hauled her wind, as well to ascertain the fate of her companion, as to renew the desperate contest. On ap-proaching the *Constitution* and *Cyane* the *Levant*, with a boldness bordering on rashness, ranged close alongside the *Constitution* to leeward, being unable to weather her, and at 8h 30m these two ships while passing on opposite tacks, exchanged broadsides. The *Consti-tution* immediately wore under the *Levant's* stern and raked her with a second broadside. At 9h 30m finding that the *Cyane* had undoubtedly surrendered, Captain Douglas again put before the wind, but in the act of doing so, the Levant received several raking broadsides, had her wheel shot away and her lower mast badly wounded. . . . Seeing the *Constitution* ranging up on her larboard quarter, the *Levant,* at 10h 30m p.m. struck her colours.[11]

The casualties among the Royal Navy, according to their own count of 300 on both ships, suffered nineteen killed and forty-four severely wounded. The American navy had six killed and six wounded. In a way, this is exactly how a naval battle should come to pass. The actions were not designed to either sink the ships or wipe out the crew. It was to cause one to surrender, not to kill sailors. The wooden ships were susceptible to heavy iron projectiles that struck with terrific force. Their masts, yards, and ropes would disintegrate in spectacular displays, blown to smithereens and scattered like glass in all directions. Once the running gear was destroyed, the ship was immobilized, and defeat was a matter of course left in the hands of boarding parties. The mental and physical exhaustion must have been all-consuming. It was only then that the iron men of wooden ships succumbed.

While the British account does not mention that it was two vessels against one, Captain Charles Stewart does in his after-action report:

Considering the advantages derived by the enemy, from a divided and mere active force, as also their superiority in the weight and number of guns, I deem the speedy and decisive results of this action the strongest assurance which can be given the government that all under my command did their duty and gallantly supported the reputation of American seaman.

The battle became moot since it occurred after the war was concluded and is of interest only to the respective navies, which still argue over its implication. To my surprise, the newspapers in London were absolutely silent. It quickly passed into history, and, as we all know, "history is an unending argument."

CHRONOLOGY

Charles Stewart

1798, March	Lieutenant Charles Stewart entered the Navy at age nineteen as the fourth lieutenant on the USS *United States*
1799, April	Appointed captain of the schooner USS *Experiment*

1800, May	Captured *Deux Amis* (a French privateer) off St. Kitts: Stewart wounded in the capture of *Diana*
1801, June	Lieutenant on board USS *Chesapeake*
1802, June	First lieutenant on board USS *Constellation* in the Mediterranean
1803, May	Lieutenant Stewart captain of the new brig USS *Syren*
1804, January	Lieutenant Stewart second in command to Commodore Preble's Mediterranean fleet
1804, February	Supports Decatur in the burning of the *Philadelphia*
1805, September	Stewart commands the thirty-two-gun frigate *Essex*
1806, April	Promoted to captain
1807, June	Napoleon establishes the Continental Economic system, excluding Great Britain from participation: England blockades Europe and restricts trade by neutral nations
1807, June	HMS *Leopard* attacks USS *Chesapeake*
1812, June	Captain of the USS *Argus*, followed shortly by command of the *Constellation*
1812, November	HMS *Macedonia* captured by Decatur on *United States*
1812, December	*Constellation* under way in Chesapeake Bay
1813, June	Captain of the USS *Constitution*
1813, December	*Constitution* escapes the Boston blockade
1814, December 24	The Treaty of Ghent is signed by delegates
1814, December	*Constitution* escapes the Boston blockade once again
1815, January	Battle of New Orleans
1815, February 16	The Senate ratifies the Treaty of Ghent
1815, February 20	*Constitution* captures HMS *Cyane* and *Levant*

NOTES

1. Most historical accounts describe her having three masts, but Paul Silverston's *The Sailing Navy, 1775–1854* (Annapolis, MD: Naval Institute Press, 2011), 50, shows a drawing of her with two masts.

2. Claude Berube and John Rodgaard, *A Call to the Sea: Captain Charles Stewart of the USS Constitution* (Washington, DC: Potomac Books, 2005), 20.

3. Silverstone, *The Sailing Navy*, 6.

4. Berube and Rodgaard, *A Call to the Sea*, 54.

5. A commander wore one epaulet on the left, a captain one on the right shoulder, and a post captain one on each shoulder.

6. Tyrone G. Martin, ed., *The USS Constitution's Finest Fight, 1815: The Journal of Acting Chaplain Asherton Humphreys, US Navy* (Mount Pleasant, SC: The Nautical and Aviation Publishing Company of America, 2001), 20.

7. Martin, *The USS Constitution's Finest Fight, 1815*, 20.

8. Admiralty Library, Whitehall, London, *Marshal's Naval Chronicle*, page 161 Cyane, Gordon Thomas Falcon, Esq., description written 28 April 1815.

9. William James, *The Naval History of Great Britain*, vol. 6 (London: Conway Maritime Press, 2002), 372.

10. James, *The Naval History of Great Britain*, 373.

11. James, *The Naval History of Great Britain*, 373.

10

STEPHEN DECATUR, JAMES BARRON, AND JOHN RODGERS

If our officers cannot be inspired with the true kind of zeal and spirit which will enable us to make up for the want of great force by great activiy, we had better burn our ships and commence a navy at some future time when our citizens have more spirit.

—Secretary of the Navy Benjamin Stoddert

STEPHEN DECATUR

"OUR COUNTRY! In her intercourse with foreign nations, may she always be in the right; but our country, right or wrong."

In 1779, the middle of the Revolutionary War, Stephen Decatur was born in a tiny Maryland town adjacent to the Atlantic Ocean. The family had resided in Philadelphia, but had been chased out by the British. Priscilla (Ann) French, wife of Sailing Master Etienne Decatur, nurtured their two children while her husband fought the British from a privateer under letters of marque issued by the Continental Congress. Offspring of a mixing bowl of ancestors, Dutch, French, Irish, and Scots—two generations before the name was spelled De Kater—allowed the growing boy to associate with anyone without discrimination when the family moved back to Philadelphia at war's end. His father, quite wealthy from exploits during the war, was a sea captain in the shipping firm of Gurney & Smith, which also employed Captain Charles Stewart Sr. In spite of the father's travels, every few months to Europe, two brothers were added to the family. Because of the close business affiliation between the fathers, Charles Stewart Jr. and Stephen Decatur Jr. became childhood friends. Stephen contracted whooping cough when eight years old, a serious complaint, but since no treatment existed, a long sea voyage was recommended. Many a child and adult experienced the curative power of the sea in those days of rampant infectious diseases that ran through the congested cities. Common sailors often found that their health improved at sea, especially if they had their ears pierced with gold rings. The clean, clear salt air was not only refreshing, but also efficacious. The sick son was added to the passenger list on board his father's ship, *Ariel*, for a turnaround voyage to Europe. While convalescing, the boy fell in love with the life of a sailor. Schooled at home by a widow of a friend, his mother, a devout Episcopalian, didn't want to lose him to the sea and hoped that he would take the cloth. But his poor mother hadn't a chance once Stephen had witnessed his father in command of a ship. The son found the nautical life most interesting, demanding, and worthwhile. At fifteen, his father secured a job in the boatyard, where in 1794, with money provided by the Naval Act, the yard began construction of one of the large frigates designed by Joshua Humphreys. President Washington, a vital supporter of a navy and personal admirer of Humphreys, was a frequent visitor to the yard.

THE NAVY

In 1798, with the commissioning of the great frigate USS *United States*, Stephen Decatur Jr. assumed the title "midshipman" in the U.S. Navy alongside Lieutenant Charles Stewart, his friend from youth. Handsome with a long French nose, thick dark wavy hair, and athletic build of nearly six feet, Decatur looked splendid in his dark blue uniform, according to his mother. She felt some comfort in sending her son to sea on a warship since his schoolmate Richard Somers shared his accommodations.

JAMES BARRON

While Stewart was the fourth lieutenant, James Barron was the third lieutenant charged with the starboard watch, which included Decatur. Also the son of a sea captain, Barron had served as a cabin boy in the Virginia State Navy during the Revolution. James Barron was thirty-three years old, an experienced sailor who would teach Decatur the ropes, the names of which were a puzzle to the young midshipman, who was not as bright as the others. Decatur was fortunate to serve under the giant of a man who had a genuinely friendly manner confident in that he was more than qualified for the job. In letters home to his doting mother, Decatur often praised Barron for his help with the indecipherable world of archaic nautical terminology that the lad had difficulty remembering. Barron was battle hardened, having fought skirmishes in the Mediterranean against pirates. He was well known to the naval officer corps and admired by the secretary of the navy. Decatur was doubly fortunate to serve under Captain John Barry, a prominent warrior in the Continental Navy with many prizes to his name.

THE USS *UNITED STATES* AT SEA

The frigate was originally designed to fight the Barbary States, but that dispute was put on temporary hold. In the meantime, the long, slow process of funds, design, and construction, which was interrupted for lack of congressional interest, was completed. The odd Quasi War took center stage that year when the revolutionary French government was put out over America's improved relationship with its old adversary England, which was taken as a snub to Napoleon's France. At sea, French privateers captured hundreds of American merchant vessels, particularly in the Caribbean. The New England merchants traded heavily with the islands for sugar, spice, and medical herbs that were sold not only in American ports but in Canadian ones as well. Boston newspapers were screaming, "Why did we build the navy if not to protect us from more than a few Arab pirates?" The navy had been thrown together on provocation since there was no more expensive department than the navy. Turning it on for the pirates and then off only to be turned on once again for the Quasi War was no method for ensuring protection for a world trading nation. The warships had to be built for a purpose. Navy ships had to be twice as strong and therefore took twice the live oak, pine masts, and spares from the forests of the east and the south. The cost of gunmetal to make cannons was immense, but the real cost, in addition to a corps of sailors, was ship maintenance in government and civil shipyards abroad. Ships rotted, rusted, snapped, and withered just sitting at anchor. It was becoming obvious that America must launch a navy no matter the expense.

OCEAN GOING

The *United States* was a hunter seeking Frenchmen returning home with ships full of sugar and tobacco. The secretary of the navy's instructions paid particular attention to the retaking of pirated American vessels for return to their owners. In addition to pay, the captain and crew were excited at the prospect of prize money that was shared by every member of the crew (albeit in unequal shares). Once an enemy ship was taken, it would have a skeleton crew put aboard, sailed to a nearby port, and sold. A major portion of the sale was rendered to the victorious crew. In mid-July 1798, the *United States* passed out of the Delaware River and into the open sea, turning south off the southeastern banks of the Carolinas. Ship handling came first followed by gun drill.

The shakedown cruise of six weeks was a show of force that woke up the French to the new threat from the heavily armed frigate that scattered the pirates who scuttled away to hide in island coves. Back on station after recaulking, the ship leaked profusely: she was caught by an October gale that took hold of the ship and shook her to the keel. Hurricane winds battered the *United States* so fiercely that she had to give up her course and run before the storm. The sailmaker prepared a cone from light sailcloth with a bridal at the mouth attached to a line that was thrown off the stern and fastened above the rudder. The drogue slowed the forward progress of the ship driven by the fierce trailing winds and kept the bow up. Her sails were clued up, with the exception of the fore sail and main topsail, which strained the masts. With her bow plunging and lurching, a monster wave split her bowsprit, allowing the standing rigging to slacken and give up vital support to the fore- and mainmasts. The loosening allowed the giant three-tiered masts to move independently and distort even the hemp ratlines. Masts, the mainstay of the propulsion system, creaked alarmingly, indicating that they were no longer resting securely on the step above the keel. With each passing minute, the standing rigging, so vital to the composition of the ship, slipped one after the other. It was obvious to Captain Barry that the integrity of the vessel was in jeopardy. Lieutenant Barron asked permission to take his starboard watch forward and secure the masts by rigging purchases from the solid deck to the standing rigging, recovering the stability that had been rent by the menacing wind and waves. It was the only way to save the *United States*. Barron took his watch, led by Decatur and other midshipmen, who cobbled together blocks, and with multiple sheaves and rove lines through creating tackle that was anchored to the deck; they spliced each one to the loose rigging. It took tremendous and heroic service in the face of the raging waves that broke across the decks, deluging the sailors and taking their feet out from under them. Once completed, the waste of the frigate was a tangle of blocks and sodden ropes crisscrossed in a spider's web. For young Decatur, it was a demonstration of what was expected of a leader, a lesson he would emulate in voyages to come. The captain and crew told the remarkable story of Barron's watch back in Norfolk. Barry recommended to the secretary that Barron be given command of the *United States* since John Barry was elevated to commodore. Benjamin Stoddert agreed.

THE TWENTY-SIX COMMANDMENTS

The handbook of instruction for Naval midshipmen, their "Bible," contained a passage on the *Code Duello* taken from the Irish rules of 1777. The honor code contained twenty-six hard rules on insults, challenges, apology, weapons, attire, location, etiquette, seconds, and aftermath. The stilted language is chilling. It appears that an accidental affront could lead inexorably to death.

Two of the rules are as follows:

> Rule 1. The first offense requires the first apology, though the retort may have been more offensive than the insult. Example: A tells B he is impertinent, etc. B retorts that he lies; yet A must make the first apology because he gave the first offense, and then (after one fire) B may explain away the retort by a subsequent apology.

> Rule 13. No dumb shooting or firing in the air is admissible in any case. The challenger ought not to have challenged without receiving offense; and the challenged ought, if he gave offense, to have made an apology before he came on the ground; therefore, children's play must be dishonorable on one side or the other, and is accordingly prohibited.

Somers and Decatur, great friends from youth, were engaging in harmless banter, criticizing each other in their quarters below deck when overheard by other midshipmen. Their fellows demanded that the two buddies fight a duel, but Somers refused and was treated as a coward for not defending his honor. Somers then challenged the accusers to duels with pistols for treating him as a coward without cause. With Decatur as his second, the duels were fought one after the other, and Somers and the others were wounded in their legs. It was common to wound in the leg rather than shoot for the trunk or head to satisfy the breach of honor.

However, it was not long after that, Lieutenant Decatur, while leading a recruiting party ashore in Philadelphia, went on board the *Indianman* merchant ship to retrieve recruits whom he had paid to join the *United States*. The recruits had been induced to join the other ship by the first mate. A verbal conflict erupted, resulting in Decatur's losing out and walking away. Decatur's father, an old sea dog and supporter in the *Code Duello*, insisted that his son find and fight a duel to defend the family honor. A few days later in a provisioning port, the two men met, and Decatur challenged according to the rules. With Somers as his second, Decatur, a renowned shot, wounded the first mate in the leg, while he remained untouched.

The Quasi War droned on in the Caribbean until the Treaty of Mortefontaine was negotiated in 1801. However, the lack of a constant source of funds required a severe reduction in the number of active officers and sailors along with their ships, which were put in reserve. Decatur was retained along with a third of the hundred fellow lieutenants.

THE BARBARY PIRATE WAR

In June of the same year, President Jefferson, who in the past was always watchful of the size of the defense establishment in the country, believing that standing forces were a European bad habit, sent six ships to Tripoli to quiet Yusuf Karamanli, the Dey, with whom he had crossed swords when ambassador to France. Decatur, serving on the thirty-two-gun *Essex*, a small, 145-foot-long frigate with a complement of 300, was under Captain William Bainbridge, a former commercial skipper. Jefferson, ever cautious, limited the mission to convoy escort duty along the North African coast. In the fall of 1802, the *New York* under Captain James Barron was sent to Tripoli with a tribute of $30,000 in gold. On arrival, at the request of Barron, Decatur was transferred to the thirty-six-gun frigate as first lieutenant, a step up once again. The presence of the naval squadron and the payment of the tribute to a state that had declared war on the United States didn't make sense to other nations much less to the officers of the navy, who wondered just what were they expected to do. While protecting American interests, they could be attacked by Tripolian pirates funded by America.

While on Malta, Midshipman William Bainbridge, Captain Bainbridge's brother, became involved in a dispute with Royal Navy officers and was called out by a sporting Englishman who had a reputation for provoking duels and killing his opponent. The dueling Mr. Cochran was secretary to the governor of Malta. Decatur, as second, chose pistols at four paces rather than ten. When adding the length of an outstretched arm, the muzzles would be seven feet apart. Cochran's second said that was murder, knowing that both men could certainly be killed. Decatur replied, "No Sir, that looks like death. Your friend is a professional duelist while mine is wholly inexperienced. I am no duelist but I am acquainted with the use of pistols, if you insisted on ten paces, I will fight your friend at that distance."[1] No modification was agreeable, and the duel was scheduled. The Englishman showed signs of stress when he fired and missed, while Bainbridge's pistol ball penetrated Cochran's hat. Cochran stated that he had not received satisfaction, and Decatur once again lined up the men, telling the midshipman to shoot lower. Bainbridge put the next ball through his opponent's eye and walked away unhurt. Decatur and Midshipman Bainbridge were chased from Malta on the USS *Chesapeake*, which was on rotation to America, under James Barron.

Six months later, in September 1803, with all forgiven, Decatur was back in the Mediterranean to take command of the twelve-gun sloop *Enterprise*, assigned to Commodore Edward Preble's fleet blocking Tripoli harbor.

LOSS OF THE USS *PHILADELPHIA*

On October 25 at Algiers, Preble was astonished by word from a passing British ship that the American navy frigate *Philadelphia* had been captured in Tripoli harbor. Captain William Bainbridge was chasing a Tripolian xebec and ran aground on a shoal just outside the fortified harbor. The attitude of the ship caused her to list. Defenseless, since her guns could not be brought to bear, Bainbridge instructed his carpenters to scuttle the ship by breaking through the hull and allowing the seawater to flood, but a dozen Barbary pirate gunboats were at her almost immediately, preventing any serious vandalism by her own crew. The *Philadelphia* surrendered, and the crew was taken to prison. Two days later, a storm surge lifted the stricken frigate off the shoal, and her new owners patched the hull. She was taken into the broad harbor, a highly valuable gift for Bey Yusuf.

Commodore Preble could not permit the enemy to sail *Philadelphia* under the flag of the Barbary pirates, a mammoth disgrace to the fledgling American navy. To deal with the crisis, in December he had moved his supply base from Gibraltar, after a dispute with the Royal Navy, to Syracuse on Sicily closer to the action to come with Tripoli. The week before Christmas 1803, Preble pressed outside the enemy harbor to get a look at the status of his former frigate. Decatur's *Enterprise* was sent after the Tripolian ketch *Mastico* as it attempted to slip past the Americans. Decatur closed on the ketch and took her without destroying her integrity and was found to be carrying bits and pieces of *Philadelphia* to be offered for sail. Bad weather drove the fleet apart that week. The Mediterranean sailing season was closing.

At Malta, Preble convened a strategy conference. Unlike his two predecessors, Preble was a fighter and vowed to avenge the loss of the frigate and release the captain and crew from Bey's dungeon. Decatur's prize vessel was renamed *Intrepid* under U.S. colors with Lieutenant Decatur in command. Specially equipped for return to the enemy harbor, the commodore led the American fleet back to the entrance to Tripoli and waited in deep water with *Intrepid* and her crew of volunteers, one of which was Midshipman Thomas Macdonough. In darkness, they slipped in under her old colors, her familiar silhouette well known by the defenders to be friendly, while Lieutenant Charles Stewart lay off waiting to rescue any of the surviving *Intrepid* adventurers. It was impossible for Decatur's sailors to seize the *Philadelphia* and sail her out of the protected harbor at night. The plan called for Decatur to set *Philadelphia* on fire and prevent the pirates from exploiting their good fortunes. "The *Philadelphia* was moored in the inner harbor . . . and within easy range . . . of the batteries of the harbor. She mounted 40 guns . . . a full complement of men was on board to serve them."[2] Lieutenant Decatur's report to Commodore Preble reads,

> Stealthily *Intrepid* slunk along in the gloom with all but a few of her crew concealed. . . . Unchallenged by guard boat or sentry she crept by the forts and had drawn quite close to the Philadelphia when the [enemy's] frigate hailed her . . . the Intrepid's pilot replied that the ship was a trader from Malta, that she had lost her anchors in the recent storm and that they desired permission to make fast to the frigate during the night. It was then about half past nine o'clock. Mean while a boat's crew from the Intrepid attached a line to the *Philadelphia's* fore chain. . . . Hauling on these lines the crew, still concealed, had brought their vessels almost alongside when the Turks were aroused; the cry "Americanos" rang through the ship.

Decatur led the boarding party on to the dark decks of the unfortunate *Philadelphia* and was immediately engaged in hand-to-hand combat with the pirates. At a critical moment, Boatswain Mate Ruben James stepped between a sword-swinging pirate and his leader, taking the blow and saving Decatur's life. James recovered and spent the next thirty-two years in naval service.[3] Thomas Macdonough led ten crewmen below and set fire to the berth deck and forward storeroom. In less than half an hour, Decatur had accomplished his mission to destroy the American frigate and had escaped with only one casualty. Decatur's action caught the eye of the great English naval hero, Lord Nelson, who said that it was "the most bold and daring act of the age."[4]

In 1820, Charles Stewart commented on Decatur's exploit:

> The recollection of the difficulties and dangers he had to encounter in this expedition, of which I was an eye witness, excites more and more my admiration for his gallantry and enterprise, and although the results shed a luster throughout Europe, over the American character, and excite an unparalleled emulation in the squadron, in our country alone it has never been duly estimated or properly understood.

Sad was the fate of the *Philadelphia*'s captive crew, whose only bright spot was the "prison school," conducted by David Porter, which figures high in American naval history.[5]

AUGUST 1804: ANOTHER TRY

In August, Preble recognized from Decatur's raid on the *Philadelphia* that it was possible to put a large raiding party ashore and destroy the accumulation of vessels and stores while his fleet blocked anyone who tried to escape. Such a bold act could persuade the Dey to release the imprisoned crew of the *Philadelphia*. Preble's intention was "to beat the Bashaw into a better humor."[6]

Two clusters of three-armed flat-bottomed gunboats, seventy feet long, were trailed by a bomb vessel, all of which had to be rowed through the narrow passage that led to the inner harbor. In addition to the long 24-pound cannons in the prow of each boat, a bomb ketch carried mortars with exploding shells that were to be lobbed into the fortress and city. With just under 300 sailors and marines, Somers, who was slightly senior to Decatur, was placed in command, but the two would act independently once inside the harbor. Charles Stewart's brig *Syren* shepherded the tiny flotilla toward the harbor entrance at midday but laid-off because of the shallow water. The pirates were not surprised and put up a wall of armed craft stuffed with screaming brigands armed with swords and pistols. The Americans plunged into the fray in a spectacular display of bravado—but to no avail. The American expedition was outnumbered four to one in the churning green water that was squeezed between the wheeling boats as they clashed amid white smoke from the bomb ketch, harbor defenses, and seaside fleet. Decatur's brother James, a midshipman commanding one of Somers's boats, was the only one in that division capable of lending Somers, who was heavily engaged, a hand. His other boat had grounded on the rocks, and the crew had been captured.

Fighting through the enemy line, the Decatur brothers and Somers reached the inner harbor dock and cleaned the pirates off with blasts from their bow cannons, which were loaded with musket balls. Separated, James's crew stormed aboard an enemy craft, but the midshipman was shot through the body and fell into the water gap between the boats. He was fished out, and his crew went looking for his older brother, who was engaged nearby. When Lieutenant Decatur saw his brother's bleeding body, he turned into a mad avenger and took on the pirates on a third vessel followed by his own crew. The enemy captain, a massive Turk, attacked Decatur with a boat pike. Decatur parried with his sword, which broke off at the guard, leaving him defenseless. Grabbing the shaft, he pulled the man to the deck, and they wrestled, rolling over and over until Decatur ended up on the bottom. The Turk pulled a curved knife from his sash, but Decatur blocked it with one hand, while the other drew a pistol from his sword belt and fired it into the back of the assailant. Fortunately, it killed the attacker, and the bullet was absorbed into his body, or it could have gone through and killed Decatur. Decatur, wounded in the scuffle, rose to find that Preble had raised the signal to pull out. Captain of a captured boat, Lieutenant Decatur brought his severely wounded brother out to the fleet. Sadly, James died later that evening. He was the only one killed, while nearly all the men had some wounds from the day's adventure. Soon, though, another would die. Somers sailed *Intrepid* into the harbor filled with a huge charge of powder and was killed when the vessel blew up. Considerable damage was done in the attacks, but it did not change the Dey's mind, and nothing was altered.

NATIONAL HERO

At home, the young naval captain took the nation by storm. Drawings of his handsome face and classic uniform were in every newspaper in the country along with grotesque drawings of mustachioed pirates dying at the hand of the naval officer. In the west, where towns were springing up from the Canadian border to the Gulf of Mexico, the people of America thanked the young hero by naming schools, villages, and counties after the noble sailor. After George Washington, *Decatur* was on everyone's lips. The country was proud, but Congress balked at awarding prize money to him and his crew; they gave him a decorative sword and the crew two months' pay, which they refused.

USS *CHESAPEAKE* VERSUS HMS *LEOPARD*

Captain Decatur, on the beach at Norfolk, Virginia, building boats, was not directly involved in the eradication of the Royal Navy's impressment of American seamen. However, in March 1807, he received a demand to return three men who had deserted an English frigate moored in the port of Norfolk. He didn't have any knowledge of the men and said so, then let the matter pass.

On June 22, 1807, the USS *Chesapeake*, a thirty-six-gun frigate, was under way, leaving Norfolk. Just after dropping her pilot, HMS *Leopard*, a fifty-gun frigate, hailed her to stop, claiming to have a dispatch for Captain James Barron. American naval regulations called for the crew to come to battle stations when approached by a warship of another nation as a precaution since the switching of flags was an old trick used by navies since the beginning of time. Both ships were well within American waters. There was no message, but instead a letter from the Royal Navy fleet commander was handed over, demanding a search for British seamen believed to be stowed away below. Barron refused to allow the search and sent the boarding party away. Barron could see that the *Leopard*'s gun hatches were open and that her guns had run out. At that moment, he ordered some precautions to be taken, but it was too late. His crew had not yet stowed the baggage and other loose boxes that were to be put away once at sea. The gun hatches were still closed, and powder had not been drawn from the magazines below. When the party returned to the *Leopard* empty-handed, *Chesapeake* was attacked at a range under 200 feet. A twenty-gun broadside was fired, reloaded, fired, reloaded, and fired once again, splintering the *Chesapeake*. The American ship was totally unprepared to defend herself so close to port, and even though efforts were made during the fusillade, only one gun was fired in reply. Captain Barron had failed to have the cannons loaded and other precautions taken that were expected of a warship at sea. However, there was no state of war either. Both ships had been in the same port under peaceful conditions, and no overtures were made to Captain Barron prior to leaving. Three American sailors were killed and nearly twenty wounded. The British captain ordered her to stop, and a boarding party was sent to search for the British sailors. The following letter reveals the British version of the incident:

Letter to Vice Adm. Berkely, Chief of Halifax station 15 Aug 1807
from the Right Honorable Lord James Towshend,[7]
Sir.—I beg leave to represent to you, that the fine man named in
the margin belonging to HM Sloop Halifax, under my command,
who sent a petty officer in a jolly boat, in Hampton roads, on the 7th
of March last, to weigh a kedge anchor, which had previously been
dropped for the purpose of swinging the ship by, taking advantage
of the dusk of the evening, mutinied upon the petty officer, some of
them threatening to murder him; but the rest interfering they desisted.
However, taking the boat under their own command, they succeeded
in deserting, by landing at Sewoll's Point. The whole of the above
mentioned deserters I have since been informed entered on board the
US frigate Chesapeake and were seen by me and several of my officers
parading the streets of Norfolk in triumph, under the American flag.
A few days after their desertion, I accosted one of these men, Henry
Sounders, asking the reason of his desertion, and received for answer,
that he did not intend anything of the kind, but was compelled by the
rest to assert, and would embrace the first opportunity of returning. At
that moment Jenkins Radford, one of the said deserters, coming up,
took the arm of the said Henry Sounders, declaring with an oath, that

neither he, nor any of the rest of the deserters, should return to this ship, and with a contemptuous gesture told me that he was in the land of liberty, and instantly dragged the said Henry Sounders away.

Finding that my expostulating any longer would not only be useless in obtaining the deserters, but in all, ultimately have collected a mob of Americans, who no doubt would have proceeded to steps of violance, I instantly repaired to the house of Colonel Hamilton, the British Counsil there, and related everything circumstance which occurred, and applied to him, as also to Lieut. Sinclair, of the rendezvous of the US service, went to recover the said deserters, but without effect.

Being since informed that Jenkin Radford has been recovered in action on board the US frigate Chesapeake with *HBM* ship Leopard, and is now a prisoner on board *HMS* Bellona, I have to request that you will be pleased to direct a court martial may be assembled for the purpose of trying the said Jenkin Radford, for the within—mentioned charges of mutiny, desertion and contempt.

I Have the Honor to be
Signed
Captain James Towshend, RN

Jenkin Radford was found hiding in the coalhole of *Chesapeake* by the purser of *Leopard* and was recognized as the deserter from *Halifax*. He said that he was hiding to prevent the Americans from forcing him to fight against his own country. He claimed that Lieutenant Sinclair of the U.S. Navy had persuaded him to join the U.S. Navy. He was hanged on August 31, 1807, by the yardarm of the HMS *Halifax*.

James Radford and Henry Sounders were two of the four men taken from the USS *Chesapeake*. American accounts differ, reporting that three of the four were Americans: the British disagree, believing that all were long-standing members of the crew of HMS *Halifax*. However, Vice Admiral Berkely was transferred along with an apology by the British government. What made the incident so noteworthy was the proximity to Hampton Roads, clearly inside the borders of the United States. There were other similar occurrences in which the Royal Navy boarded American merchant ships, but they were out of sight and received much less publicity. There were hidey-holes in between the decks on merchant ships used by the best sailors as they came into British ports so that the Royal Navy could not take them off.

Jefferson and the nation considered this an act of war. Jefferson's call for retaliation was in the form of an embargo against all trade with Great Britain. Seen as a punishment, it backfired and created the smuggling industry, which would plague the war on the northern frontier, New England's manufacturing, and the South's sale of tobacco and cotton.

CHANGE OF COMMAND

On July 1, Commodore James Barron was relieved of command of the *Chesapeake*, and Stephen Decatur was put in his place. Within days, Decatur reported thirteen holes to her gunwalls and a great deal of destruction to her spars, sails, masts, and lines. With the excellent facilities at the Norfolk yard, it would be only three weeks before she was fit for sea duty.

Three senior naval officers conducted a preliminary hearing in October. Testimony was heard from the officers and crew, who spoke openly about the conduct of the captain. While some soft pedaled the words out of respect and friendship of a thoroughly honorable man, the truth damned him. The result was that a court-martial would be convened in the New Year. Secretary of the Navy Robert Smith named Decatur to the court. Decatur had formed a prejudicial opinion of Barron over the years since he had been his midshipman on the *United States* at the start of his naval career. In a letter, he explains,

> When the unfortunate affair of the 22nd of June occurred, I formed an opinion that Commodore James Barron had not done his duty: during the Court of Inquiry, I was present when the evidence of officers was given in, I have since seen the opinion of the Court, which opinion I think lenient. It is probable that I am prejudice against Commo. Barron, and view his conduct in this case with more severity than it deserves; previous to her sailing, my opinion of him as a soldier was not favorable. Although, Sir, I hope and trust I should most conscientiously decide on Commodore Barron's case, still, Sir, there is no circumstance that would occasion me so much regret as to be compelled to serve on a court-marshal that tries him. I have therefore to solicit that I may be excused from this duty.

The secretary's problem was that no senior officer wanted to serve on the court that had to be convened, and he assigned William Bainbridge, Hugh G. Campbell, Stephen Decatur Jr., John Shaw, John Smith, David Porter, Jacob Jones, James Lawrence, Charles Ludlow, and Joseph Tarbell, with Charles Stewart as president. Barron saw a copy of Decatur's letter to recluse and never forgot the words "as a soldier was not favorable." For the battle hero of the nation to write those words, which would not remain private, only one path was clear to Barron, and Decatur must have known what it would invoke. It was a clear breach of the *Code Duello* and must be answered.

Barron was suspended from duty without pay for five years.

HIS BROAD PENNANT

When Decatur assumed Barron's command, he hoisted his broad pennant as commodore of the Atlantic Squadron responsible for the East Coast from Maine to Virginia. In the spring of 1809, he relinquished command to supervise the refurbishment of the forty-four-gun frigate *United States*, the ship he joined as a young midshipman on her first voyage. It must have been a joy to tread her weathered decks that he had known as new and review the years she had plied the waves defending the country of the same name. Before Christmas in 1811, Decatur rested in Norfolk: during the winter, the *United States*'s bottom was coppered. In spring, with the ship still undergoing extensive restoration, Congress declared war on Great Britain, and preparations for sea were hurriedly concluded. In the summer, Decatur joined Commodore John Rodgers's squadron a hundred miles off New York City, where Rodgers had become involved with chasing HMS *Belvidera*.

October found the *United States* split off from the rest of the fleet, a lone hunter, sailing the faraway sea-lanes north of the Canary Islands off the west coast of Africa. Decatur was searching for an East Indianman or merchant ship laden with expensive cargo bound for Liverpool. A sail was spotted on the horizon to windward, but it would be an hour or two before she could be made out. At sea, from the tops on a clear day, a lookout with a glass could see nearly fifty miles. By mid-morning, it was clear that she was a Royal Navy man-of-war. Decatur took the time to maneuver to the weather gauge—most important, for, if she was too big, he could run off. If she was a typical frigate of thirty-eight guns or less, he could press and defeat her. At the same time, the British captain must have been measuring his chances. Her large silhouette easily identified as the *United States*. As it became clear who was who, both captains savored the battle that they knew would make them rich. The Royal Navy captain's prize money would be large enough to buy an estate and comfortable retirement. Decatur would be the most famous man in the country, respected in all quarters at only thirty-three years of age. He too would be rich if he could capture her intact.

Decatur's frigate, a sister of *Constitution*, was most powerful. Hull's encounter had taught him just how deadly his cannons and carronades would be when taking on an enemy frigate. He didn't intend to repeat Captain Hull's mistake and sink his opponent and thus lose out on the prize money for himself and his crew. He therefore, in consultation with his officers, devised a plan of attack *that* would defeat, but not destroy, the lucrative target.

If possible, he could take her and sail her into port under an American flag, a feat never seen before in Royal Navy history. Also at play in the mind of the officers was to avenge the attack of *Leopard* on *Chesapeake:*

Captain John S. Carden, R.N., to
Secretary of the Admiralty John W. Croker
American Ship United States
At Sea 28th October 1812
Sir,
It is with deepest regret I have to acquaint you for the information of my Lords Commissioners of the Admiralty that His Majesty's late Ship Macedonian was Captured on the 25th Instant by the United States Ship, United States, Commodore Decatur Commander. The detail is as follows.

    A short time after daylight steering NW b W with the Wind from the Southward in Latitude 29° N and Longitude 29° 30 W in the execution of their Lordships orders, a sail seen on the lee Beam, which I immediately stood for, and made her out to an large Frigate under American Colours, at 9 OClock, I closed with her and she commenced the Action, which we returned, but the Enemy keeping two points off the Wind I was not enabled to get as close to her as I could have wished; after and hours Action Enemy back'd and came to the wind, and I was then enabled to bring her to close Battle, in this situation I soon found the Enemy's force too superior to expected success, unless some vary fortunate chance occur'd in our favor and with this hope I continued the Battle to two hours and ten minutes when having the mizzen mast shot away by the board, Topmast shot away the caps, then Main Yard shot in pieces, lower Mast badly wounded lower Rigging all cut to pieces, a small proportion only of the Foresail left to the Fore Yard, all Guns on the Quarter Deck and Forecastle disabled but two, and filled with wreck, two also on the Main Deck disabled, and several shots between wind and water a vary great proportion the Crew Killed and wounded, and the Enemy comparatively in good order, who had now shot a head, and was about to place himself in a raking position without our being enabled to return the fire, being a perfect wreck, and unmanagable Log.

    I deemed it prudent th'o painful extremity to surrender. . . .

    On being taken on board the Enemys' Ship I ceased to wonder at the result Battle; the United States is built with the scantline of

a seventy four gun Ship, mounting thirty long twenty four pounders [English Ship Guns] on her Main Deck, and twenty two fourty
two pounders, Carronades, with two long twenty four pounders on
her Quarter Deck and Forecastle. Howitzer Guns in her Tops and a
travelling Carronade on her upper Deck with a Complement of four
Hundred seventy eight pick'd Men. . . .

    And have the honour to be [&c.]

                                                         Jno S. Carden

Decatur notified his headquarters two days later. The message could have
been carried by USS *Argus*, which had been sailing with Decatur just before
the incident:

Commodore Stephen Decatur to Secretary of the Navy Hamilton
USS United States at sea
October 30 1812

Sir,
I have the honour to inform you that on the 25th Inst. Being in the
Lat. 29. N. Long. 29.° 30. W., We fell in with, & after an action of an
hour & an half, captured his Britannic Majesty's Ship Macedonia commanded by Captain John Carden, and mounting 49. Carriage guns
[the odd gun shifting]—She is a frigate of the largest class—two years
old—four months out of dock, and reputed one of the best sailers in
the British service. The enemy being to windward had the advantage
of engaging us at his own distance, which was so great, that for the
first half hour we did not use our carronades, & at no moment was
he within the completed effected of our musketry or grape—to this
circumstance & a heavy swell which was on at the time. I ascribe the
unusual length of the action. The enthusiasm of every officer Seaman
& marine on board this ship on discovering the enemy, their steady
conduct in battle & the precision of their fire could not be surpassed—
where all have met my fullest expectations it would be unjust in me
to discriminate. Permit me however to recommend to your particular
notice my first Lieutenant Wm H. Allen, who has served with me
upwards of five years & to his unremitted exertions in disciplining the
crew is to be imputed the obvious superiority of our gunnery exhibited in the result of this contest.
    Subjoined is list of Killed & wounded on both ships our loss com-
pared with that of the enemy will appear small. Amongst our wounded

you will observe the name of [acting] lieutenant Funk, who died a few hours after the action he was an officer of great gallantry & promise and the service has sustained a severe loss in his death. The Macedonian lost her mizzenmast, fore & maintopmasts and mainyard & was much cut up in her hull. The damage Sustained by this Ship was not such as to render her return into port necessary, and had I not deemed it important that we should See our prize [in?] should have continued our cruise. With the highest consideration and respect I am [&c.]

Stephen Decatur[8]

Decatur's first order of battle, as his first Lieutenant Allan understood, was to capture, not sink, the *Macedonian*. The lieutenant directed his gunner to dismast the enemy and let the spars, sails, and rigging fall into the waste to make the deck untenable. The shot splintering the mast showered the crew with splinters and covered them with debris. Those sent into the rigging to service the sails and the marines posted aloft to snipe at the officers on the American ship came crashing down as well. The crews on the gun deck were treated to huge careening carronade shot breaking through the gun walls, scattering wounded men and boys and grinding blood mixed with sand and black powder into the planks. Allan did his best to keep from breaking *Macedonian*'s hull. With the lowering of the enemy flag, the salvage of crew and ship began.

Initial reports to Decatur were all the same: "Fragments of the dead were distrusted in every directions, the decks were covered with blood, one continued agonizing yell of the unhappy wounded, a scene so horrible of my fellow creatures, I assure you, deprived very much of the pleasure of victory."[9] Lieutenant Allen was appointed prize captain and given the duty of making *Macedonian* seaworthy for the slow journey home to America. Allen used both American and Royal Navy sailors to repair nearly a hundred breaches in her hull while rigging the two forward masts to accommodate sails. Decatur gambled that he would not meet any other Royal Navy warships on the month-long voyage. In company, the two warships encountered merchantmen on the way home treating them to a sight that they could report across Europe and the New World.

Arriving in Connecticut, Decatur sent the British battle flag with Lieutenant Hamilton, son of the secretary of the navy, to Washington and handed it to Dolly Madison in the midst of a White House ball. Decatur was a master at not only warfare but also publicity, and *Macedonian* was positioned in New York Harbor for all to inspect prior to the prize evaluation. He was intent on more than a decorative sword this time.

USS *PRESIDENT*

By the spring of 1814, the Royal Navy blockade of the major eastern ports was as tight as a drum. Madison offered command of the big frigate *President*, languishing in New York Harbor, to Decatur, who jumped at the opportunity. "The well known rapidity of the *President*'s sailing places her in my estimation above all others. . . . Having been so long blockaded, I dread being placed in such an unpleasant situation." He knew the challenge that an overly rested crew faced when stressing the masts, lines, spars, and timbers of the great ship out of service so long.

While he waited that long summer and fall of 1814, the land war swirled around him. Plattsburgh was invaded, and his colleague from the raid on the *Philadelphia*, Thomas Macdonough, stood on the hero's dais beside him. Washington was burned and Baltimore attacked. John Rodgers left to assist in the land battles. Decatur made plans to follow the lead of David Porter and sail to the Pacific to disrupt England's East India Company.

News arrived of Jackson's victory at New Orleans, and the city of New York celebrated as a howling westerly snowstorm struck on the evening of January 14, 1815. Seventeen days before, the British monarch had signed the peace Treaty of Ghent ending hostilities between the two nations. That night, the storm drove the four British blockade ships off their station and out into the Atlantic. Waiting at Sandy Hook, New Jersey, for the pilot, the *President* sat heavy in the water filled with supplies to take her around the horn of South America. Decatur weighed anchor as the tide rose and moved toward the channel. Within minutes, she grounded fast—stuck. While she sat, supplies were jettisoned, and everything except her guns were thrown into the teeth of the gale-force winds, which wrecked the main mast, tore the sails, and twisted the keel. She was suffering, and nothing could be done except to wait for the flood tide that lifted off. Decatur hoped to return to port for repairs, but the westerlies would not allow it. Driven against her will to the east in the dark, *President*, crippled, reluctantly went to sea.

With light came the return of the blockading British fleet, first one, and within hours, all four hunters were on *President*'s wake. HMS *Majestic*, a *raizer*—a French alteration copied by the British that cut away the upper gun decks, leaving a strong keel and gunwales while increasing speed—of fifty-four guns, was the first to fire, but her cannonballs fell short. Of the three smaller frigates, only the forty-gun *Endymion* began to close the distance. The stiff winds blew spray on the sails, yards, and ratlines, which began to cake with ice, adding weight and slowing *President* even more. The fastest sailer in the American fleet, crippled to her core and hogged fore and aft, was not the spry young lady of 1799: the years and wear had slowed her to within reach of her ardent pursuer. The chase slowed into a slugfest between two warriors of nearly equal throwing weight. Decatur began to lose leaders to the cannonade, and then suddenly he was slugged by a huge splinter in the chest that knocked him to the quarterdeck unconscious. The British gun crews recovered quicker, increasing the tempo of the blasts. Darkness comes early in January, and the dim glow of the lanterns on the gun deck only hindered those still able to fight after four hours of noise, carnage, freezing cold, and hopeless battle. *Endymion* was the first to wear away smashed and broken, but she did not strike her flag.

President slipped northeast in the darkness to lick her wounds, but within a few hours, before midnight, the British blockade fleet of four ships came up strongly and contended. When they reached cannon range, Decatur struck his colors.

REAP OF THE WHIRLWIND

> Hampton Virginia, June 12, 1819
> Sir, I have been informed in Norfolk that you have said that you could insult me with impunity, or words to that effect, If you have said so, no doubt you will avow it, and I shall expect to hear from you.
> I am, sir, your obedient servant
> James Barron[10]

Decatur felt strongly, in the years after the war in which he held an unassailable position among the naval community, that Barron should not serve in an active capacity among naval ranks. Such feelings, repeated by those who had some stake in the dispute, were repeated and exaggerated to a great extent. A long exchange of notes began, quoting the rules of *Code Duello* and charges of assault on a gentleman's honor. The letters containing charges and counter charges continued until the following March. Decatur accepted a valid challenge to a duel and appointed Commodore Bainbridge as his second. The place was Bladensburg, Maryland; the weapons were pistols; the time was 9:00 a.m. on March 22, 1820; and the distance was eight paces. As a rule, thirty-six feet was standard, but since Barron's eyesight was poor, it was agreed that twenty-four feet would be the distance between shooters. That was a deadly choice.

In the cold morning calm, next to a small branch of the Anacostia River, on the wet grass, the seconds and their minions walked off the course and conferred in hushed voices while Decatur's doctor hid in the woods not far off. It was a well-known ritual of the gentry and one proudly coveted.

Often both men would fire into the ground or deliberately point the barrel of their gun well off target to indicate that he had no intention of hitting the other. It was a mad forum. Decatur, in spite of his jawing about Barron, had no real animosity and indicated to Bainbridge that he would wound Barron in the leg.

Bainbridge: "Present, One—Two." There was no "Three." Both pulled the trigger on "Two." Both men were hit with a small pistol ball. Barron whirled around, hit in the hip, and went to the ground—wounded. Decatur grabbed himself, "Oh, lord, I am a dead man."

JOHN RODGERS

The son of Scottish parents, John Rodgers was born in 1772 in Havre de Grace, Maryland, seven years before Stephen Decatur, close to the water of the Chesapeake Bay to a father of the same name who would become a colonel during the Revolutionary War. Educated locally, young John was fascinated with the sailing vessels that floated peacefully by along the shoreline. At age fifteen, his father apprenticed his son for five years to a shipbuilder in Baltimore with whom he had served during the war. Trusting that his boy was well looked after, he agreed that he should go to sea. At seventeen, young Rodgers was a first mate on a merchantman, and at the end of his commitment, he was named captain of the *Jane* out of Baltimore. On revolving voyages to and from Europe, the teenage skipper learned his trade so that, by 1795, he was considered a master mariner. A "man's man," during a voyage to the North Sea, a storm drove them off course and into the grip of severe winter weather—three crewmen froze to death. When the crew refused to go aloft to chip ice from the yards that threatened to capsize the ship, Rodgers cursed them. He removed his coat and shirt and bid them watch as he climbed into the tops with a hand ax. They soon followed his example.[11]

With the kindling of the Quasi War with France in 1798, John Rodgers was appointed a second lieutenant on board the U.S. Navy frigate USS *Constellation* under Captain Truxtun. The next year, the crew of the *Constellation* captured the French frigate *Insurgent*, and Rodgers, along with Midshipman David Porter, was charged to take the prize ship, with the crew of 100 still on board, to St. Kitts to be sold. The enemy crew got loose. Rodgers with his crew of eleven confined the prisoners within a narrow passage and held sway with blunderbusses for three days and two nights. The USS *Insurgent* was refitted and flagged and was skippered by newly promoted Captain Rodgers when it joined the fleet in the spring of 1799. A favorite of Secretary of the Navy Stoddert, Rodgers was sent to Baltimore to supervise the construction of the USS *Maryland*, a twenty-gun sloop-of-war, taking command in the spring of 1801.

BARBARY PIRATES

During the past 200 years, all along the southern Mediterranean coast, Barbary pirates from the Levant to Morocco captured ships and enslaved crews regardless of flag. A constant scourge, the pirates alarmed and terrified even the hardiest of sailors.

In 1802, Rodgers took command of the twenty-eight-gun frigate *John Adams* and sailed for Tripoli, joining the *Constitution* and *President* on patrol. The frigates, the light cavalry of the sea, were quick and well gunned. In the hands of a skilled captain who could use the wind direction to his advantage, the pirates on board their unorthodox xebecs feared them. Within two weeks, the *John Adams* captured the twenty-gun corsair *Meshouda* trying to run the American blockade of Tripoli harbor. Singled out for his brilliant performance, Rodgers was appointed commodore of the Mediterranean Squadron in 1805. By July, the squadron had grown to a dozen fighting ships that dominated the waters to such an extent that the Dey of Tripoli, though not defeated, signed a peace treaty. The crew of the *Philadelphia*, held since 1804, were released.

TROUBLE WITH GREAT BRITAIN

By 1805, the landscape switched from alliance with the British against the Barbary pirates to open hostilities. After the Barbary pirates were subdued, Rodgers was sent to New York City to build a fleet of gunboats to defend the inner harbor from the British, selecting Oliver Hazard Perry to oversee operations. In 1807, with the unprovoked attack on the USS *Chesapeake* by HMS *Leopard* off Norfolk, Rodgers was appointed commodore of operations along the Atlantic coast for protection of cargoes, ships, and crew. With the coming of war in June, Rodgers was the first to point out the vulnerability of the American navy.

1811: ARROGANCE OF THE ROYAL NAVY

In spite of all the missions, diplomatic communiqués, best of intentions, and years of restrictions imposed and reimposed, it all fell apart on May 1, 1811.

Americans were to learn the name of the HMS *Guerriere*, one of His Majesty's frigates for the first time—but not the last. In those times, ships and their distinctive names were known by every newspaper reader in the country. The only source of mass media, in 1811, newspapers were read religiously in every corner of the new republic. The *Guerriere* had kicked in the golden door at the mouth of New York Harbor. While just off of Sandy Hook, New Jersey, a stone's throw from where the Verrazano's Bridge stands today, she attacked and boarded the American brig *Spitfire*, taking off American citizen John Deguyo. Within days, she also impressed Gideon Caprian and Joshua Leeds, both Americans from a second ship. It was widely reported in the newspapers as yet another flagrant assault on American sovereignty. Deguyo and Caprian would be repatriated, but Leeds was not. Secretary of War James Monroe ordered American warships to sea to "protect the coast and commerce of the United States."[12] Captain John Rodgers was in command of the frigate USS *President*, the best sailing frigate of the fleet. Eleven days later, she put to sea from Annapolis, Maryland, in a hunt for HMS *Guerriere*.

The captain of a passing vessel in open water outside the entrance to Chesapeake Bay told Rodgers that he had seen the quarry to the north. The captain prepared the ship for combat and plowed toward New Jersey. Soon the Royal Navy ship-rigged sloop *Little Belt* was sighted heading south. She was carrying dispatches for *Guerriere*'s captain from Bermuda Station. Mistakenly thinking that the frigate on the horizon at midday could be the *Guerriere*, she approached the *President* and hoisted the encrypted signal of the day, a three-digit number. *President* was flying her American colors, but Royal Navy Captain Arthur Bingham was not put off because ships often disguised themselves with false flags. When *President* did not respond to the code, *Little Belt* turned away and continued on her course. She did not expect to be attacked since the two countries were not at war.

The American closed in and signaled that the captain wanted to speak. By early evening, before dark, Captain Bingham slowed his progress and allowed *President* to approach. The Royal Navy vessel readied her guns just in case. Seeing the crew at their guns in furious activity, *President* passed by and soon found herself in a raking position. This dance continued as each vessel maneuvered close in; shouts from both went unheard and therefore were unacknowledged by either. A gun was fired accidentally. It is not known by whom. A general melee ensued. Within half an hour, it was over when the British ship was incapable of defending herself. The British account in James said:

> The greater part of her standing rigging and the whole of her running rigging were cut to pieces, not a brace or a bowline was left. Her masts and yards were all badly wounded, and her gaff were shot away. Her upper

works were completely riddled, and her hull in general were much struck: several shots were sticking in her side, and some had entered between wind and water.[33]

Eleven were killed and twenty-one wounded on board the Royal Navy sloop. *President*'s damage was slight, mostly to the sails and rigging. The ships separated for the night for repair. By morning, *Little Belt*'s suffering was very apparent to Captain Rodgers, and he drew up and sent a lieutenant across with his apologies when he realized how inferior his opponent had been. The *Little Belt* limped to Halifax Station, and *President* continued to search for *Guerriere*, but it was *Little Belt*, a courier intended for *Guerriere*, that reaped the aftermath of the attack on *Spitfire*. England expressed its regret over the incident, and America continued to rage over *Guerriere*'s behavior.

MORE PROVOCATIONS

In the spring of 1812, England published Orders of Council in the *London Times* newspaper. They instructed all Royal Navy ship commanders to bring into port all ships belonging to the United States of America. At the same time, the government recognized the need to protect its merchant fleet from attacks by marauding American navy and privateers. It reinstated the Convoy Act, which required her merchantmen involved in the Caribbean and North American trade to travel within the confines of protected convoys.

Soon, President Madison's plea to Congress for war, which described "intolerable grievances," brought action and a declaration of war. In short, they were as follows:

1. Impressment of Americans into the Royal Navy.
2. The violation by the Royal Navy of the sovereignty of the United States at sea. Highlighted by the *Chesapeake* and *Leopard* as well as *Guerrier*'s attack on *Spitfire*.
3. The intermittent naval blockading of American ports.
4. Orders of Council, which restricted neutral ships from trading with European countries, and favored British traders over American.

WAR OF 1812

Now lads, we have got something to do that will shave the rust from our jackets. War is declared. We shall have another dash at our old enemies. It is the very thing you have long wanted. The rascals have been bullying over us these ten years, and I am glad the time has come when we can have satisfaction.

Captain John Rodgers

June 18th, 1812
Sir:
The day war has been declared between the "United Empire of Great Britain & Ireland" and their dependencies and the United States of America and their territories and you are with the force under your command entitled to every belligerent right to attack and capture and to defend—You will use the utmost dispatch to reach New York after you have made up your complement of men & c at Annapolis. In your way from thence, you will not fail to notice the British flag, should it present itself—I am informed that the Belvidera is on our coast, but you are not to understand me as impelling you to battle, previously to your having confidence in your crew unless attacked, or with a reasonable prospect of success, of which you are to be at your discretion to Judge. You are to reply to this and inform me of your progress.

    Respectfully yrs.

Paul Hamilton[14]

The next day, one day following the beginning of the hostilities, Commodore Rodgers sent the secretary of war his assessment of the enemy situation (not yet aware that war had been declared):

U.S. Frigate President
New York 19th June 1812
British naval force at present on this side the Atlantic consists of one sixty four—seven frigates—seven sloops of war—seven Brigs, & two or three schooners—Hallifax & Bermuda are their ports of rendezvous; & permit me to observe, Sir, that should war be declared, & our vessels get to sea, in squadron, before the British are apprised of it, I think it not impossible that we may be ale to cripple & reduce their force in detail; to such an extent as to place our own upon a footing until their loss could be supplied by a reinforcement from England.

    The President & Hornet are ready for sea & the Essex will I hope be ready in ten days from this date.

    It is this moment reported that the frigates UStates & Congress are off the Bar. The British frigate Belvidera & sloop of War Tartarus were seen off Sandy Hook yesterday morning—The schooner

Macherel with Mr. Ruff (English messenger) sailed last evening for
Hallifax,

    With the greatest respect

Jn Rodgers.[15]

THE U.S. MARINE CORPS

As might be expected, fighting infantry was a primary concern to Secretary of
War Eustis. The rapid expansion of the army was not going well. An incen-
tive of $16, part paid on sign up and the rest when the new soldier mustered,
was augmented by the promise of a severance pay of three months' salary and
160 acres. The land was in the west (Ohio, Indiana, and Illinois), part of a
plan to move the frontier west. A death benefit was also to be included if the
soldier did not survive. The recruitment for seagoing marines, in a sense a naval infantry, could not compete without some stimulus. None was forthcom-
ing from Congress:

    The secretary of the navy took it upon himself to assist the recruiters.

To: Lieutenant Colonel Commandant Franklin Wharton,
19 June, 1812
Sir,
After having performed your business in N York you will proceed to
Hudson.

    Congress having offered extraordinary inducements to Soldiers
to enter the army, it becomes proper that some additional inducement
should be offered to persons to enter the Marine Corps. You will
therefore consider yourself at liberty to allow to each man who shall
enter the Corps—Twenty dollars bounty—of which 10$ are to be paid
at the time of signing the articles—& 10$ on their being first mustered
    I am Sir etc
    Paul Hamilton,
    Secretary of the Navy.[16]

    In September 1776, the uniform coat of green with white facings and
a leather stock was prescribed for the Continental Marines—green because
it was all that was available. Their recruiting drum sported a coiled American rattlesnake and the words "Don't tread on me." The four-inch leather
detached collar was to protect the neck from saber cuts but in reality was, as
in the British army, meant to keep the head up on parade and improve the
stature of the Marine. Of course, like the British "Tommy," the men hated

them and seemed to loosen them at every opportunity. However, the name "leatherneck" stuck.

On Christmas 1776, as a part of Washington's crossing of the Delaware River, Marines took part in the action against the British garrison at Trenton, New Jersey. Later, aboard *Ranger* with John Paul Jones, they raided the English coast in 1778. Maintained on active service in a very small number, the Marines were stationed aboard a revenue cutter, a most important and vital source of money for the Federal government. Samuel Sewall's bill to formalized the Marine Corps for service rather than placing a quota on newly commissioned ships for a marine contingent authorized the creation of a Corps of Marines. With central authority, the corps would recruit, equip, and train while managing on behalf of the U.S. Navy. The old blue coats with red facings, left in storage by Anthony Wayne's Continental Legion at West Point, were issued to the Marine Corps in place of the green. Round, black, broad-brim hats, edged in yellow with the left side pinned up, was the most impractical for wear on the windy seas. The hats were not unlike the Royal Marine hat with the turned-up brim piped in white.

TO SEA

The secretary had his hands full during preparations to send the American fleet out against the Royal Navy. Initially, he deployed two squadrons. Commodore Rodgers took *President* and *United States* (both with forty-four guns), *Congress* (thirty-six guns), *Hornet* (eighteen guns), and *Argus* (sixteen guns), and assumed a station east of New York Harbor. They extended far out to intercept English Caribbean prizes. Commodore Decatur's squadron, which consisted of the frigates, *United States* and *Congress*, took the southern approaches and waited outside Norfolk for the British convoys from the Caribbean. *Constitution* under Isaac Hull struggled out of Chesapeake Bay after hosting a visit by Secretary Hamilton at Annapolis and sailed north to join Rodgers. Soon, Hamilton had second thoughts and sent orders that restricted Rodgers's operation closer to the Atlantic coast so that he could accomplish two things at once. Not only could he pick up British vessels that Decatur missed, but he could also protect American shipping near New England ports. He feared the Halifax Royal Navy squadron to the north. But his afterthought was too late; Rodgers was moving east, now out of reach, that summer of 1812. Hull also missed his rendezvous and was left alone off Massachusetts.

CONTACT

Rodgers, secure in the center of his clustered squadron, was called to the quarterdeck when the lookout in the tops spotted the sail of a square-rigged ship that could not be American. It was a gift. The frigate, the thirty-two-gun HMS *Belvidera*, which Rodgers had reported to be off New York Harbor, was making tracks north:

> Belvidera's Captain Richard Byron kept away as soon as he noticed the five ships of war were approaching. He was under the impression that the ships were sent out to chase away British ships of war that were in territorial waters and had no desire that his ship should figure in another *Little Belt* affair when he was opposed to odds of some ten to one.[17]

Almost immediately, his big forty-four-gun frigate *President* outpaced the squadron in pursuit of the smaller English frigate. Winds were light, and the sea was nearly calm a hundred miles off the New York coast. The studding sails (pronounced "stun sails") were hauled up and spread like billowing white wings. Water was sprayed and dumped on them to improve performance. The British Lion was tracked by the Yankee, but little to no gain was achieved hour after hour. The USS *President* was about to fire the first shot of the War of 1812. Rodgers's account is telling:

> I gave orders to commence a fire with the bow chase guns, at his spars and rigging, in the hope of crippling one or the other, so far as to enable us to get alongside: the fire from our bow chase guns he instantly returned with those from his Stern, which was now kept up by both Ships without intermission until 50 minutes past four when on of the Presidents chase guns burst and killed and wounded sixteen persons among the latter myself. This was not however the most serious injury, as by the bursting of the Gun, and the explosion of the passing box, from which it was served with powder, both the Main and Forecastle decks (near the gun) was so much shattered as to prevent the use the Chase Gun, on that side, for some time: Our main deck guns being single shotted I now gave orders to put our helm to Starboard and fire the starboard broadside, in the expectation of disabling some of his Spars, but did not succeed, altho I could discover that his rigging had sustained considerable damage, and that he had received some injury in the Stern.

This maneuver was repeated several times, yawing the *President* one side or the other to fire a broadside rather than the single bow chaser that was left in action. Each time he did so, the *President* lost what little of the closure he had worked so hard to gain.

The British ship was unaware that the American government had declared war. The report of Richard Byron, the *Belvidera*'s captain, confirms the American account, but does not seem to realize the amount of destruction caused by the Royal Navy's fire and is unaware of the burst gun. Byron reported:

> At 4:20 he opened his fire from his foremost Guns I had given the most positive orders to my Lieutenants to prick the Cartridges but not to prime the Guns. Although ignorant of the War, we were of course prepared, and about five Minutes afterwards opened ours with two Carronades 32 Pounders and two long Eighteens from the Stern. In light Winds the President sail'd better than the Belvidera, and as his second, a very heavy Frigate, sail'd as well. I acknowledge I was much surprised at the nearest Ship, yawing repeatedly and giving starboard and larbard Broadsides, when it was fully in his power to have run up alongside the Belvidera. I thought it may duty to make a firm retreat from three Frigates of the largest Class accompanied by a small Frigate or sloop and a brig of War two of which bore broad Pendants.

Belvidera also deployed studding sails to increase her speed. The first three shots from *President*'s bow chasers struck *Belvidera*'s stern, ripping through the captain's cabin just below the stern carronades, killing and wounding a dozen "tars." What he fails to mention is that he jettisoned a considerable amount of weight in the end to outdistance the American pursuit. The use of the carronades by the British ship indicated that they were indeed close—not more than 500 yards apart at times.

RODGERS'S LAST CHAPTER

Through 1814, the Royal Navy, once in an eastern port for repair and replenishment, blocked Rodgers's squadron, like all other primary warships of the American navy. When the Battle of Bladensburg and the burning of Washington occurred in August, Rodgers, knowing that the sailors under his command in Philadelphia could not reach south by water, mounted a force to march south. Within the month, a second attack, this time farther north at Baltimore and the surrounding area, threatened his home at Havre de Grace. A shore party of tars set fire to his family home, but when his wife asked for the assistance of the Royal Navy, they returned and put it out. Rodgers's sailors and marines went on to Arlington, Virginia, and assisted in the defense of that city. Rodgers finished his wartime service as a soldier.

CHRONOLOGIES

Steven Decatur

1779, January 5	Born in Sinepuxent, Maryland
1798	Midshipmen, U.S. Navy, on *United States*
1798	Quasi War
1801	Fought Barbary pirates
1802	Promoted to lieutenant and commanded *Argus* and then *Enterprise*
1803, October	Captures ketch *Mastico* and converts to *Intrepid*
1804, February	Sets fire to USS *Philadelphia*
1807	Captain of the USS *Chesapeake*
1808	Commodore, northern coast of the United States
1809	Captain of the USS *United States*
1812	HMS *Macedonia* captured intact by Decatur
1814	Commander of the *President*
1815	*President* captured by the Royal Navy
1820	Decatur killed in a duel by James Barron

James Barron

1768, September 15	Born in Hampton, Virginia
1776	Cabin boy in Virginia State Navy
1798	Lieutenant in U.S. Navy
1800	Commander of the sloop-of-war USS *Warren*
1807	Commodore of the USS *Chesapeake* attacked by HMS *Leopard*
1807	Relieved and court-martialed for surrendering the USS *Chesapeake*
1820	Killed Stephen Decatur in a duel

John Rodgers

1772, July 11	Born in Havre de Grace, Maryland
1789	First mate on merchant ship *Harmony*
1793	Master of the merchant ship *Jane*
1798	Second lieutenant of USS *Constellation*
1799	Capture of the French brig *Insurgent*
1801	Captain of the sloop USS *Maryland*
1801	Captain of the frigate *John Adams*
1805	Commodore of the Mediterranean squadron

1805	Treaty ending the Barbary War
1806	Commander of New York Harbor
1807	Embargo Act: Commanded operations on Atlantic coast
1811	Appointed commodore of the Eastern Seaboard
1811	Commander of USS *President* attacks HMS *Little Belt*
1812	Commodore Rodgers chased HMS *Belvidera*
1814	Commander of USS *Guerriere*
1814	Aids in the land defense of Alexandria, Virginia

NOTES

1. James Tertuis de Kay, *A Rage for Glory: The Life of Commodore Stephen Decatur* (New York: Free Press, 2004), 44.

2. Virginia Mason Burdick, *Captain Thomas Macdonough: Delaware Born Hero of the Battle of Lake Champlain* (Dover: Delaware Heritage Commission, 1991), 20.

3. Peter Lamborn Wilson, *Pirate Utopias, Moorish Corsairs and European Renagadoes* (London: McCord, 1984), 129.

4. Robert Gardiner, ed., *The Naval War of 1812* (London: Catham Publishing, 1998), 46.

5. C. S. Forester, *The War of 1812* (London: Michael Joseph, 1957), 21.

6. de Kay, *A Rage for Glory*, 61.

7. James Towshend was the youngest son of George, 1st Marquis Towshend, born September, 11, 1785, with the rank of post captain on June 2, 1809.

8. William S. Dudley, *The Naval War of 1812: A Documentary History*, vol. 1. (Washington, DC: Naval History Center, 1982), 549–53.

9. de Kay, *A Rage for Glory*, 120.

10. de Kay, *A Rage for Glory*, 182.

11. C. O. Paulon, *The Life of Commodore John Rodgers* (1910), New York: Biblio Bazaar, 2009 (reprint), 27.

12. William M. James, *The Naval History of Great Britain, 1808–1811: During the French Revolutionary and Napoleonic Wars* (Mechanicsburg, PA: Stackpole Books, 2003), 7.

13. James, *The Naval History of Great Britain, 1808–1811*, 11.

14. Dudley, *The Naval War of 1812*, 136.

15. Dudley, *The Naval War of 1812*, 138.

16. Dudley, *The Naval War of 1812*, 139.

17. C. S. Forester, *The Age of Fighting Sail* (Sandwich, MD: Chapman Billies, 1956), 29.

11

WILLIAM BAINBRIDGE, DAVID PORTER, AND JAMES LAWRENCE

A gunner having a lite match in his hand behind a gun, had his arm taken off by an enemy shot. The match fell to the deck clenched in the severed hand. He looked down at his severed arm, seized the match with his other hand and touched off the gun, then went off to the cockpit for care.

—Memoirs of John Nicol

WILLIAM BAINBRIDGE

ORN JUST two years before the Declaration of Independence, his family remained loyal to the Crown. His father Absalorn Bainbridge and wife Mary served the British army in the field hospital while on campaign. Returning home to Princeton, New Jersey, at the close of the war, Absalorn was tried for high treason by the state; however, the American Loyalist Claims Commission mitigated the finding on humanitarian grounds and restored the family's property. William's father abandoned the family for life in England, leaving the three children to be raised by a delicate mother and her father. A born sailor, William became a seaman at age fourteen on a commercial trading vessel that made the rounds of the Caribbean shifting contraband between restricted ports. He became the captain of a merchant ship at age twenty-four in 1798, when he converted over to the U.S. Navy as a lieutenant. Not a handsome man, he was husky and gruff with thick, unruly, dark brown hair. His experience rated him command of the USS *Retaliation*. A French privateer schooner of fourteen-guns, she was captured by the USS *Constitution* in July 1798 during the Quasi War. Cruising the waters surrounding the French possessions in the Caribbean that November, seeking recapture of American merchant vessels, he was accosted by two French frigates off Guadeloupe. *La Voluntairer* and *L'Insurgente*, carrying more than twice the through weight of his little schooner. Bainbridge surrendered in the face of arms, something that was considered not a disgrace but the proper action to save the lives of his crew.

Tribute

Bainbridge was promoted to master commandant of the eighteen-gun brig USS *Norfolk*. Thoroughly reliable, Bainbridge was put in command of the twenty-four-gun USS *George Washington*, built in Providence, Rhode Island, in 1793. He had the onerous duty of delivering the pirate tribute to the Dey of Algiers and was forced under diplomatic obligation to take on board the gifts of livestock and slaves to the sultan of Turkey in Constantinople.

THE USS *PHILADELPHIA* CAPTURED

As the senior officer on station, Captain Bainbridge was given command of the USS *Philadelphia*, which was leading the blockade of the harbor of Tripoli. On the last day of October 1803, the thirty-six-gun frigate, while in hot pursuit of a Berber xebec, ran aground on a riff at the entrance to the inner harbor of Tripoli. Naturally, the crew turned to lightening the ship, but the enemy swarmed around in minutes in small boats heaped with screaming pirates. The decks teemed with armed men slashing with long, narrow, curved swords that cut like razors and soon subdued the 300 American sailor and officers, who were taken to the dungeon of a fortress prison. Captain Bainbridge and the officers, led by Lieutenant David Porter, settled into two years of miserable treatment. The only thing keeping them from being sold as Christian slaves for the benches of the row galleys favored by the North Africans was the hope of a large ransom payment expected from the United States. Bainbridge explained to the Dey that if they were harmed, the United States and her allies (whoever they were in 1803) would invade his country. The Barbary pirates were a loose group of despotic states that hovered along the coast from the Levant of Turkey to the tip of Morocco. They acted independently and didn't process land armies and war machines outside their coastal forts. While Commodore Preble and others came up with scheme after scheme to crack open the Tripolian harbor defense, Lieutenant David Porter ran a school for his crew to keep them occupied over their long wait. One of the plans, the burning of the *Philadelphia*, was a blow to the pride of the Dey, who planned to reflag the ship and flaunt it around the

Mediterranean. Bainbridge and his crew were not released from captivity for two years and eight months. He faced a Naval Court of Inquiry for misconduct. Porter and the others stood up for Bainbridge's actions, stating that he did the best that could be expected of any man under the circumstance and credited him with prolonging their lives under the most adverse conditions. Bainbridge was released from service with no prejudice. Bainbridge returned to commercial command of merchant ships. Experienced ship captains were in very high demand in the days of sail. They were the most technically competent experts of their day, much more so than doctors. The world, as today, ran on sea trade, and there was nothing more complex, valuable, and risky than a sailing vessel on the high seas.

Change of Command

After the attack of the *Leopard* on the *Chesapeake* in 1807, Jefferson sent the American navy back to sea. In the summer of 1809, Bainbridge was called back to command the forty-four-gun frigate USS *President* patrolling the Eastern Seaboard protecting American merchant vessels from attack by Royal Navy's hunters looking to impress seamen into servitude on their men-of-war. A year later, he was sent to supervise the Boston navy yard. With his country at war, Bainbridge was given a new command, the forty-five-gun USS *Constitution*, shortly after she had sunk the HMS *Guerriere*. A solid, quiet man who was not caught up in the hoopla surrounding the amazing victory, he, along with Captain Hull, went about the task of repairing the ship's battle damage and training a crew for whatever was to come. An old sea dog with both good and bad experience behind him, he had great respect for the Royal Navy and was acquainted with serving officers on her noble ships. Repeating Isaac Hull's accomplishment never entered his mind. He was duty driven and planned the next phase of *Constitution*'s fighting life.

COMBAT COMMAND

Not surprisingly, the loyalty of the crew was with the departing captain. Like all new commanders, he would have to earn their respect. Bainbridge was not a warm human being, and the crew knew it from the first moment he was piped on board. He was not only captain but also commodore; his second vessel, *Hornet*, joined him off Castle Island on October 16, 1812, looking for favorable winds to carry them out into the Atlantic. His orders were vague. He was to protect American commerce in any way and anywhere he saw fit. The navy secretary perhaps had learned that it did no good to pass out detailed instructions since none of his captains seemed to follow them. By the end of the month, he was edging his way down the Eastern Seaboard looking for trouble in the sea-lanes that carried British commercial prizes. He expected to find a convoy escorted by a Royal Navy frigate that might net a victory comparable to his predecessor. It was important that Bainbridge clear his name. The farther south he went, the less he found. Perhaps it was getting too late in the year. The sailing season would soon be deteriorating into hurricanes and winter storms.

BLACK SKY AND WHITE WATER

The weather was certainly more challenging than any enemy. It came at him from the south, a bad omen. The most prominent danger in storm conditions was the fear of being run up on the rocks near shore as the storm surged. But *Constitution* was several hundred miles off Norfolk, Virginia, and free of the outer banks—fingers of land that would reach out and run his ship aground once again. As the sea came up, the ship was prepared for storm running. The hours were going to be long and wet. Just when they needed a hot meal the most, it would not be available. The fire was put out in the caboose. Glowing coals were shoveled into heating buckets to hang from the overhead, where at least their warming heat could provide some comfort. Soup was heated by the red-hot cast-iron range, providing a last hot meal before it slowly cooled.

While sails were shortened, the rudder came in for serious alterations. In a storm, four helmsmen manned the double steering wheel. Tacking into the face of the southerly gale demanded brute force to maintain course. A square-rigged ship cannot steer into the wind. Its forward motion is best served from winds on the beam or the aft. In fact, thirty-three degrees on the compass either to port or starboard of the direction of the wind can't provide forward motion. In other terms, that is six points on either side of a wind in the face of the ship (a point is just a shade over eleven degrees).[1] Tacking back and forth across the wind, Bainbridge was able to maintain a heading. It called on the crew to be standing by to brace the yards around, which swung the bow sharply in front of the wind, installing a distinct zigzag into forward progress.

As the force of the southerly wind rose and the sea swelled, further modification to the rudder was begun. On the orlop deck, the manual tiller was reinforced with added lines and blocks. A lit compass was set up below in case the wheel and binnacle were damaged and steering had to be transferred below. Exterior rudder tackle was rigged from the rails over the side to the rudder in case it broke free. If allowed to flop or slam against the buttock, the heavy panel would damage the hull, where it beat itself to death.

Guns were an enormous danger. Weighing over two tons on their wheeled carriages, they couldn't be allowed to career around the deck like mad bumper cars, crashing into the masts and rail or running down the crew. The most effective method was to lash the muzzle tightly to the rail in a nose-up condition while the carriage was trussed to eye and ring bolts in the deck. The bower anchor was next to be secured. A painter, or additional small rope, was applied to the cat lines that held it to the outside of the rail. It was wrapped around both flukes and shank ringed when at sea.

Signals at Sea

With embargoes in effect and wars underway, nearly every vessel sighted had to be "spoke," meaning that the warship would come up for identification. Hailed by voice shouted through a speaking trumpet, the merchant captain would announce the ship's names, port of origin, and destination along with the mix of cargo. Since nearly everybody flew false flags, a suspicious engagement meant that an armed boarding party rowed over in heavy seas. Intimidated by a line of loaded cannon at "pistol shot range" (twenty-five yards), few refused to brace around their sails in opposite directions, nearly bringing a halt to their progress. The warship could have been on station for several months and was always interested in the news or perhaps put a sick sailor or prisoner aboard to be delivered on land.

Code Books

Warship encounters were quite different. Many combatant ships were recognized by their silhouette. The news that a particular enemy ship was in the area was most valuable. True national colors were unfurled until the last moment. A series of signals could save time. A coded signal book was issued by the nation's naval headquarters and distributed to outgoing vessels. Small, long, and narrow, they would fit in the tailcoat pocket of the officer's uniform.

On stiff paper, they consisted of about fifty pages. It contained the names of Royal Navy ships with a number assigned to each. It assigned letters and numbers to colored, configured, small square pennants. There was also a section on commonly used phrases, such as "will depart," "acknowledge," "you shall," "I am intending," and so on. The names of ports of call and nations were assigned numbers as well as prominent personages and offices. One of the lesser lieutenants was assigned the duty of reading and making up strings of signal flags as directed. When a message was confirmed, it was stung up on a running rigging line from the mast.

Most prominent was the identification or "private signal." An annex to the common book, it was issued by a command and changed more often. Looking like a matrix, the challenge would be taken from one column, which, when read across the field of random numbers, would evoke the proper response. The signal would be spelled out in a series of flags that were hoisted on encountering a ship of war. That signal should have prompted a counter response. At that point, the enemy could raise his true national colors instead and fire on the inquirer or, perhaps, if he were the lee, run away as fast as possible. The last page told the user to notify the originator if lost so that a new set of codes could be issued as soon as possible to prevent the captured one from compromising the operation.

Any ship flew common messages. The most important proclaimed the health of the crew. Ships liable to quarantine were supposed to fly a large yellow flag of six breadths of bunting from the maintop masthead if free of disease, but a similar yellow flag with a black circular mark or ball equal to two breadths of bunting in the middle if there were illness on board.[2] Outside of ports, there was a quarantine station or buoy where incoming vessels would lie for fifteen days before being allowed to discharge cargo. When visibility was poor or nonexistent in fog, which was common along the northeastern coast of North America, sound signals were employed. Particularly in convoy, it was important to prevent collisions or to change the course of the entire body. Course change was done by drums or cannon signals. There was a set of instructions contained in the signal books for that process. Two guns, followed a minute later by one more, would turn everyone to starboard. A different series would instruct them to slow down by changing sails. If heard, there was a response as well as the obligation to pass the signal along to vessels farther out. It was not always effective but was a little better than nothing. If nothing else, it signaled the proximity of another ship. To see a man-of-war loom up and out of the blue-gray sea fog, prow up and with bowsprit poised like a battering ram, must have been frightening.

Gale

Now the wind and water were the culprits that must be fought. It whipped up the water into swells. The little flotilla of *Constitution* and *Hornet* kept a respectable distance for fear of being driven into one another. The storm rose higher, forcing them to alter course and scud before the wind. Scudding, or running with the wind, meant abandoning the southerly course for the duration of the blow. Sails were brought down and courses furled, leaving near bare polls. The jib and two stays were allowed up to help with the steering. Scudding with the wind could be very dangerous since the ship could be pooped. Pooping occurs when a heavy sea breaks over the stern. It usually comes about when the speed of the ship is approximately the same as the speed of the sea so that the rudder has little or no grip on the sea. In such cases, a sea that poops a ship is apt to swing her off course until she is broadside on the sea, with the danger of rolling over.[3] Even if a prize was sighted, there was no chance that either vessel could fight under those sea conditions.

To prevent water from gushing down the open waist of the frigate, canvas was stretched and blocked in place, cutting out the light to the decks below. Lifelines crisscrossed the open quarter and forecastle. The helmsmen were secured in position with rope. Tarpaulin weather cloths were taken to the fighting top to protect the lookouts that crouched behind them and waited out the storm. A sea anchor was made up of metal rods in a circle with sailcloth attached in the form of a parachute. It was hooked to a length of line and tossed off the stern. The drogue filled with water and acted as a drag, providing more control for the helmsmen. Naturally, all hatches were battened down, and the waisters were sent to the pumps. The roar of the sea deafened the sailors. Commands could not be heard, especially in the tops. Runners were sent with messages of command at critical moments to ensure the safety of ship operations. If the helmsman could keep the ship turned slightly to the lee, it could reduce the rolling.[4] Ships floundered far more than being taken by pirates or men-of-war. The skill of the captain and crew, based largely on experience, both good and bad, coupled with the physical condition of the ship, was pitted against nature. In the case of *Constitution*, all became well as they resumed their sail south through the Caribbean and to the trading lanes favored by the British merchantmen.

Java versus Constitution

Commodore Bainbridge was unaware of Decatur's victory over *Macedonia* but was "spoke" by a passing ship of the momentous event. Waiting on station for the wayward Captain David Porter and the frigate *Essex* to join him on patrol off the coast of Brazil, Bainbridge reviewed the tactics employed by Hull.

Christmas passed in the sunny waters of the South Atlantic, while *Constitution* and *Hornet* maintained their station. Captain James Lawrence took *Hornet* into San Salvador to acquire supplies for both vessels. There, he was told by the American naval agent that His Britannic Majesty's frigate *Bonne Citoyenne*, loaded with gold for England, was about to depart. Lawrence challenged the commander, by letter, to meet him at sea and fight it out. The

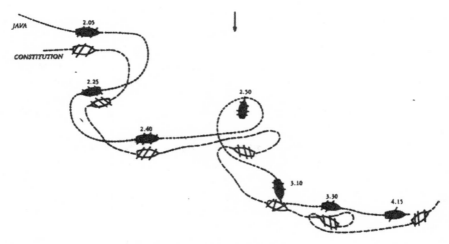

HMS *Java* attacks the USS *Constitution* in December 1812 off the coast of Brazil.

commander declined and rightly so, as his mission didn't include endangering the English Treasury. Bainbridge ordered Lawrence to remain near the port and engage the prize ship when she attempted to go to sea.

Leaving Lawrence in place, the *Constitution*, now resupplied, continued to patrol the coastline. On December 29, Commodore Bainbridge came face-to-face with his destiny. HMS *Java*, heavily embarked with a hundred extra men and a high-ranking diplomatic party destined for India, fell into his hands. English built along the pattern of the famous French frigate *Renommee*, she was transiting to St. Helena with dispatches.[5] *Java* was a thirty-eight-gunner that carried forty-nine cannon and carronade. James disagrees writing that "she carried forty-six." A little smaller in tonnage, she was nontheless capable of defending herself. She had taken as a prize an American merchant ship, the *William*, which she sent off at the sight of the big American. Her captain was H. Lambert, whose career had been as spotted as Bainbridge's. He had lost a ship and been a captive. If the captain had any trepidation when confronted by the *Constitution*, he didn't show it and went straight into the attack.

Royal Navy Account

Letters of which the following are copies of an extract, have been transmitted to this office, by rear admiral Dixon, addressed to John Wilson Croker, Esq. By Lieu Chads, late first Lieut. of his majesty's ship Java;

United States Frigate Constitution, off San. Salvador, December 31 1814

Sir:

It is with deep regret that I write you, for the information of the Lords Commissioners of the Admiralty, that his Majasty's ship Java is no more, after sustaining an action on the 29 instant for several hours with the American Frigate *Constitution*, which resulted in the capture and ultimate destruction of his Majesty's ship. Captain Lambert, being dangerously wounded in the height of the action, the melancholy task of writing the detail devolves on me. . . . We soon found we had the advantage of her in sailing, and came up with her fast, . . . Both ships now maneuvered to obtain advantageous, our opponent evidently avoiding close action, and firing high to disable our masts, in which he succeeded too well. Having shot away the head of our bow sprit with the jib-boom, and our running rigging so much cut as too prevent our preserving the weather gage.

At five minutes past three, finding the enemy's racking fire extremely heavy, Captain Lambert order the ship to be laid on board—the intention was to board the *USS Constitution* at that instant—in which we should have succeeded, had not our fore-mast been shot away at this moment, the remains of our bow-sprit, passing over his taffrail, (the railing at the stern of the quarterdeck) shortly after this the main top-mast went, leaving the ship totally unmanageable, with most of our starboard guns rendered useless from the wreck lying over them.

At half passed three our gallant Captain received a dangerous wound in the breast and was carried below; from this time we could not fire more than two or three guns until a quarter past four when our mizzen mast was shot away; the ship then fell off a little, and brought many of our starboard guns to bear; the enemy's rigging was so much cut that he could not now avoid shooting ahead which brought us barely broadside and broadside. Our main-yard now went in the slings both ships engaged in this manor till 35 minutes past four, we frequently on fire in consequence of the wreck lying on the side engaged. Our opponent now made sail ahead out of gun shot where he remained and hour repairing his damages, leaving us unmanageable wreck, with only the main-mast left, and that tottering. Every exertion was made by us during this interval to place the ship in a state to renew the action. We succeeded in clearing the wreck of our masts from our guns, as sail was set on the stump of the fore-mast and bow sprit, the weather half of main-yard remaining aloft, the main-tack was got forward in the hope of getting the ship before the wind, our helm still being perfect; the effort unfortunately proved ineffectual from the main-mast falling over the side, from heavy rolling of the ship, which covered the whole of our starboard guns. We still waited the attack of the enemy, he now standing towards for that purpose. On his coming nearly within bail of us, and from his maneuver perceiving he intended a position ahead, where he could rack us without a possibility of us returning a shot, I then consulted the officers, who agreed with myself that our having a great part of our crew killed and wounded, our bow-sprit and three masts gone, several guns useless we should not be justified in wasting the lives of more of those remaining, who I hope their Lordships and the country will think have bravely defended his Majesty's ship.[6]

The news of the loss of another Royal Navy vessel in single combat reached England by the end of January. The capture of *Guerriere*, *Macedonia*, and now *Java* was a terrific blow that could not be covered with thin alibis. It was the last straw as far as the British people were concerned. They demanded to know what had happened to their great navy. The news that Napoleon lost mightily in the Russian winter campaign was of far more importance in the war with France, which they had been fighting for twenty years. However, the newspapers were consumed with England's own naval losses against a former colony. The following account taken from American Commodore Bainbridge's journal was published in the *London Times* nearly four months later as if it had happened yesterday.

Tuesday, Dec. 29, (1812) at nine am, discovered two strange sail on the weather-bow. At 10, discovered the strange sail to be ships. One of them stood in for the land, and other stood off shore, in a direction forwards us. At 10:45 AM we took ship to the northward and westward, and stood for the sail standing towards us. At 11am tacked to the southward and eastward, hauled up the mail-sail and tack in the royals. At 11:30 made the private signal for the day, which was not answered; and then set the main sail and royals, to draw the strange sail off from the neutral coast, and separate her from the sail in company.

Wednesday Dec 30 (nautical time). In latitude 13.6 longitude 33.W. ten leagues from the coast of Brazil, commences with clear weather and moderate breezes from East, N.E. hoisted our ensign and pendant. At 15 minutes past meridian, the ship hoisted her colors, and English Ensign having a signal flying at her main.

At 1:26 PM being sufficiently from the land and finding the ship to be an English frigate, took in the mail sail and royals, tacked ship, and stood for the enemy. At 1:50 the enemy bore down with an intention of racking us, which we avoided by wearing.

At 2 PM the enemy being within half a mile of us, and to windward, and having hauled down his colors, except the Union Jack at the mizen-mast head, induced me to give orders to the officer of the Sd division to fire a gun ahead of the enemy, to make him show his colors, which being done brought on a fire from us of the hole broadside. On which the enemy hoisted his colors, and immediately returned our fire. A general action with round and grape then commenced, the enemy keeping at a much greater distance then I wished; but could not bring him to a closer action, without exposing ourselves to several racks. Considerable maneuvers were made by both vessels, to rack and avoid being racked. The following minutes were taken during the action;

At 2:10 PM commenced the action at good grape and canister distance, the enemy to windwind, (but much farther than I wished).

2:30, our wheel was shot entirely away, at 2:40, determined to close with the enemy, not withstanding his racking; set the fore and main sail, and luffed up close to him. (intention of the American was to board the Englishman) The captain of Java had the same plan at that time. Cannonade fire was directed into the helpless Java whose nose was hung up, three quarters of the way down the hull of the Constitution. The 32 pound solid shot, fired from the forecastle and quarter deck shatter the rails and chop down masts on Java, A hail of splinters, striped from oak planks, saturate the air. Boarding parties were formed of marines and sailors armed with bayoneted rifles, pikes and cutlesses on both vessels. Firearms were of little use after the first shot. Long rifles could not be reloaded in the middle of a melee. The parties huddled in two groups, while marines on both ships fired their rifles down into the cluttered decks below. Smoke rose in acrid clouds and obsured the accuracy of the men in the tops. The captain of Java was fatally wounded by an American marine in the tops.)

At 2:50, the enemy's jib-boom got foul of our mizzen-rigging. at 3pm the head of the enemy's bowsprit and jib-boom shot away by us.

At 3:05 shot away the enemy's fore-mast by the board.

At3:15, shot away his maim-top mast just above the cap.

At 3:40 shot away the gaff and spanker boom.

At3:55, shot away his mizzen-mast nearly by the board.

At 4:05, having silenced the fire of the enemy completely and his colors in main rigging down, supposed he had struck, and then hauled down the course to shot ahead to repair our rigging, which was extremely cut, leaving the enemy a complete wreck; soon after discovered that the enemy's flag was still flying, hove-to to repair some of our damage.

At 20 minutes past 4, the enemy's main mast went nearly by the board. At 50 minutes past four, woreship, and stood for the enemy. At 25 minutes past five, got very close to the enemy, in a very effectual racking position, athwart his bows, and was a the very instant of racking him, when he most prudently struck his flag; for had he suffered the broadside to have racked him, his additional loss must have been extremely great, as he lay an unmanageable wreck upon the water.

After the enemy had struck, woreship and reefed the top sails, then hoisted out one of two only remaining boats we had left out of eight, and sent Lieut. Parker, first of the Constitution, to take possession of the enemy, which proved to be his Britannic Majesty's Frigate Java, 38 but carried 49 guns, and manned with upward of 400 men, commanded by Captain Lambert, a very distinguished officer, who was mortally wounded.

The action continued from commencement to the end of the fire, one hour and 55 minutes. The Constitution had 9 killed, and 25 wounded. The enemy had 60, killed and 101 certainly wounded: but by a letter written on board the Constitution, by one of the officers of the Java, an accidentally found, it is evident the enemy's wounded have been considerably greater that stated above, and who must have died of their wounds previously to being removed. The letter states 60 killed, and 170 wounded. the Java had her own complement of men complete and upwards of 100 supernumeraries, going to join the British ships of war in the East Indies, also several officer passengers going out on promotion.

. . . . the force of the enemy in the number of men, at the commencement of the action, was no doubt was considerably greater than we have been able to ascertain, which is upward of 400 men.

The officers were extremely cautious in discovering the number. By her quarter bill, she had one more man stationed to each gun than we had. the Constitution was very much cut in her sail, rigging, and many of her spars injured.

At seven PM the boat returned with Lieut. Chads the first Lieutenant of the enemy's frigate, and Lieut. General Hislop, (appointed Governor of Bombay), Major Walker, and Captain Wood. Bruce, no matter what I do I can't make the red go away?

Captain Lambert was to dangerously wounded to be removed immediately. The cutter returned onboard the prize for the prisoners, and brought Captain Marshall, master and commander in the British Navy, who was passenger on board, also several other naval officers.

. . . . the Java was and important ship fitted out in the completest manor, to carry Lieut. General Hislop and staff to Bombay.[7]

Lieutenant Henry Ducie Chads, the son of a naval captain, at his court martial in May of 1813 at Spithead said that, "the crew was exceptionally bad, a large portion had never been to sea and drafted from prison. Crew drill was neglected since the ship was overcrowded. By June Chads was promoted to captain and serving as commander of the sloop Columbia.[8]

Postmortem of Captain Lambert

All the wounded were transferred at sea by boat along with the officer's baggage to the *Constitution*. The account of the captain's treatment on the sinking ship by the *Java*'s surgeon, Thomas Cooke Jones, is most descriptive:

> Captain Lambert was wounded about the middle of the action with a musket ball fired from the tops of Constitution. I saw him almost immediately afterword and found that the ball had entered the left side under the clavicle fracturing the first rib, splintering of which had severely lasorated the lungs. I put my finger in the wound, detected and extracted several pieces of bone, the hemorrhage was particularly trifling, his pulse became very quick and weak, the respiratory organs did not appear much affected, he said he felt no agony from the wound in his breast, but complained of pain extending the whole length of the spine. In a short time, he became very restless, his pulse hardly perceptive and his countenance assumed a most piteous appearance of anxious solicitude; from this state of irritability he became exhausted and generally fell into a partial one of asphyxia from which I hardly expected him to recover.[9]

Before *Java* was abandoned, members of the American crew were reported to have gone on board and removed her double steering wheel and installed it in the place of the original on *Constitution*, which had been splintered to smithereens by an English cannonball. Captain Lambert was the last to leave the sinking frigate. Carefully secured in a boat, he was taken to the *Constitution* and cared for in the captain's cabin. An American lieutenant took a party to the wreck, which was rapidly filling with water. They fired the ship to ensure that it would not float just below the surface and become a hazard to navigation. The wounded captain lived for two more days on the American ship. On the morning of January 2, 1813, he, along with the crew, was landed at San Salvador, Brazil. Surgeon Cooke Jones continues: "there he talked incoherently during the greater part of the day. At 10 o'clock his pulse grew faint and he died."

Royal Navy Captain Lambert could not defend himself. The *London Times* could. On March 23, 1813, the *Times* printed the following:

> We find it stated in an American paper, that when the Java fell in with the *Constitution* she mistook her for the Essex, which is a frigate of less force, carrying carronades (42-32pounders and 4 long guns), and, therefore kept at a long range of shot, (farther than he supposed the carronades would carry): and that it was til the Java top-mast were shot away and she was otherwise disabled; that the mistake was discovered. Captain Lambert had heard a few days before, that the Essex had been into Porto Braya, which lead him to believe that the frigate he was chasing as he had not heard of any other being upon the coast, was her: It was the

Constitution, when commanded by Commodore Hull, which captured the Guerrier.

Three days before, they had exposed the public to Commodore Bainbridge's personal account. (*London Times*, Saturday, March 20, 1813):

> The public will learn with sentiments, which we shall not presume to anticipate, that a third British frigate has struck to an American. On 29th of December, his Majesty's frigate *JAVA* captain H. Lambert, was captured by the United States Frigate *Constitution,* Commodore Bainbridge, after a desperate action, of an hour and fifty five minutes, in which the *Java* lost 60 killed, and 101 [other accounts say 1,700 wounded]. Among the latter, we lament to say, was the gallant commander of the Java, and it is added, mortally.
>
> This is an occurrence that calls for serious reflection—this, and the fact stated in our paper yesterday, that Lloyd's contains notices of upward of five hundred British vessels captured, in seven months, by the Americans. Five hundred merchantmen, and three frigates! Can these statements be true; and can the English people hear them unmoved? Anyone, who had predicted such a result of an American war, this time last year, would have been treated as a mad man, or traitor.[10]

Today, it is hard for us to understand the impact the taking of the Royal Navy frigates had on the public. Their "wooden walls against invasion" had kept the island kingdom safe for hundreds of years. The Royal Navy was not only revered also but depended on to keep the nation safe. It had done so against the Spanish Armada and the scourge of Napoleon's combined navy in 1805. The frigate contest in no way indicated that the twenty-one Americans that began the war could ravage the Royal Navy's 600 ships. It was a matter of pride. There was no finer profession than that of a Royal Navy captain: now three were captured in six months by a former colony. The newspapers drove the Naval Board to alter its strategy and clutter the Eastern Seaboard of the United States with warships, while others took up convoy duty. The Royal Navy hated what they saw as a misuse of navy ships, but the people would not stand for another defeat. The instructions were clear. It wasn't until January 1815 that the USS *Constitution* was able to slip out of New York Harbor under the cover of a storm. Bainbridge enjoyed life on the beach after the war and died at age fifty-nine.

DAVID PORTER

A Bostonian, David Porter was born in 1780 into a family of ten children. His father, captain of *Eliza*, took sixteen-year-old David with him to the West

Indies. In Haiti, British privateer Captain Reynolds, who was impressing men into service on his vessel, approached. Although unarmed, the crew refused and drove Reynolds from their deck. He retuned with an armed press crew and was engaged by the crew of the *Eliza* once more. Beaten off with clubs, Reynolds returned a third time, but the entire crew had abandoned the *Eliza*, so Reynolds vandalized the *Eliza*. It was a memory carried by Porter the rest of his life.[11] Later, when Porter's father became ill with tuberculosis, George Farragut and his wife took him in and nursed him until his death in 1808. When Mrs. Farragut died, Captain Porter agreed to take eight-year-old James Glasgow Farragut to sea with him. In 1809, living with the Porter family in Washington, he changed his name to David Glasgow Farragut when he became a midshipman in the navy and sailed with Captain Porter. (His fame would come in another era.) Porter's father, a merchant captain during the Revolutionary War, had lost a ship to the Royal Navy. Porter held a grudge against the British for the treatment doled out to his father and his crew. Porter, like so many of his contemporaries, worked the decks of merchant ships prior to applying for a billet when the Navy formed to fight the French in the Quasi War. He was a midshipman on the USS *Constellation* when she was deployed.

Lieutenant Charles Stewart took command of the USS *Experiment* in 1799 and asked that Lieutenant David Porter sign on as his second in command. *Experiment* was small: only eighty feet long and twenty-five feet wide and drawing only nine feet of water: with twelve guns, she could go inshore to chase privateers. The Baltimore-built, three-masted, single-decked schooner had been in a fight with a French privateer earlier and won. Operating off St. Kitts, *Experiment* captured the French privateer *Deux Amis*, and Porter was put in command to take her to the nearest prize court. Back on board *Experiment*, she chased down *Diana*, which carried more guns that *Experiment*. But the skill of the crew put *Diana* in a poor position, and she was forced to surrender. Within the year, Stewart moved on to captain the *Syren*.

Lieutenant William Maley was appointed captain of the *Experiment*, while Porter remained first lieutenant, escorting American merchant convoys north. The twenty-gun schooner was attacked by ten pirate craft intent on taking the entire convoy once *Experiment* was disposed of. The captain ordered his colors struck before firing a shot in defense. Porter seized command, rallied the crew, and beat back the pirates, sinking three of them in the fight. The captain didn't make an issue of the mutiny.[12] It is just one example of the impetuous disregard for rules and regulations as a whole, something that would be the hallmark of Porter's career. However, his audacious behavior fit a captain of a vessel at sea who was charged with a mission. He also was aware of the importance of training his crew and maintaining the standards of the service, which he recorded every day he was in command.

Recognition

On December, 20, 1801, President Monroe authorized Porter to establish a fleet of shallow-draft craft that could pursue pirates into their lair and exterminate them. He established a naval base on Key West and gathered craft of all sizes. He armed a merchant ship as a decoy and sent it into hostile waters backed by half a dozen gunboats, schooners, transports, and sloops-of-war. The notorious pirate Diabolito was captured by the West Indies Squadron under Lieutenant Porter and, together with many other encounters in the Caribbean, paid the half million dollars spent on the venture. The success of the Mosquito Fleet against light craft that previously hid in bays and shallow water, spawned five more similar units over wars to come. David Porter was the founder of the naval concept.

USS Philadelphia

Back in the Mediterranean in 1802, Porter changed ships several times, landing on the frigate USS *Philadelphia* captained off Tripoli. Imprisoned for nineteen months, Lieutenant Porter made himself schoolmaster and busied the starving crew. Asking the Danish council for assistance, he taught naval history and tactics, French, and art. On release, he was given acting command of the USS *Constitution* and later command of *Enterprise*. Porter made numerous trips across the Atlantic as convoy master.

Tar and Feathers

In June 1812, the *Essex* was laid up in the Brooklyn Navy Yard for extensive repairs. Her hull was damaged, and her masts were being replaced. In addition, her long-barrel 12-pounders were being replaced with short-range 32-pound carronades that her new captain, David Porter, objected to in the strongest fashion. Left with only a few 12-pounders, he knew he could not engage or indeed defend *Essex* from an attack beyond 500 yards. However, if he could get in close, the carronades were devastating. A long discussion ensured with Secretary Hamilton over the cost of cannon versus carronade and the range disparity between weapons relative to the weight of the shot delivered on target. In the end, the secretary compromised and exchanged several 12-pounders for 18-pound cannons to give Porter the reach he needed to fight a British frigate. Porter was not happy, nor should he have been. *Essex* was too small and needed more cannons than carronades, as were found on larger frigates.

     While the *Essex* was undergoing repair, Porter administered an oath of allegiance to the crew. One man, born in England, refused to take the oath.

Sailmaker John Erving's lack of patriotism angered his messmates, and they asked the captain for permission to tar and feather Erving. Porter agreed. Erving was stripped, hot tar was poured over his entire body, and then chicken feathers were supplied by the cook, blown onto the hot tar. Of course, it was a ludicrous and highly painful sight when Erving was pushed into the street and arrested by the police. In custody and for his own protection from the local citizens, he was turned over to the British Council.

The secretary of the navy was concerned with the publicity brought by the newspapers and asked Porter for an explanation. Porter took an aggressive attitude in his reply and admitted that the incident got out of hand, but the sending of Erving to a British ship to be transported to Halifax meant that the man was a spy and could obtain valuable information about the *Essex* and our intentions and that someone should look into other spies like Erving on board all U.S. ships. There was no reply, and the incident was dropped.[13]

Challenged

On July 3, 1812, *Essex* sailed, but her repairs had lingered on, and she missed Commodore William Bainbridge's fleet. Alone, within eight days she intercepted a British convoy and cut out two prizes. Porter challenged the *Minerva* to single-ship combat, but she sailed on, escorting the remainder of the convoy. Highly successful and taking everything in sight through the month of August, *Essex* was becoming a thorn in the side of the British merchant fleet. Not satisfied with the commercial ship, Porter disguised *Essex* as a merchantman, laying a trap for the Royal Navy. HMS *Alert*, armed with only carronades, fired first, even though they suspected that *Essex* was a warship. Porter made her a prize in just ten minutes. Porter's behavior was obscene, according to Sir James Yeo, who sat on his frigate off the coast of Halifax and who then issued a challenge. Like a knight of old, he sought single combat. Issued through a newspaper, the story was carried far and wide:

> Captain Sir James Yeo . . . would be glad to have a tete-a-tete anywhere between the capes of Delaware and Havana, where he would have the pleasure to break his own sword over Captain Porter's head, and put him down forward in Irons.

Countering, Porter responded,

> Captain David Porter accepts with pleasure his [Yeo's] polite invitation. If agreeable to Sir James, Captain Porter would prefer meeting near the Delaware, where Captain Porter pledges his honor to Sir James, no other American vessel will interrupt their tete-a-tete. The Essex may be

known by her flag bearing the motto, "Free Trade and Sailors' Rights," and when it is struck Captain Porter will deserve the treatment promised by Sir James.[14]

The ship duel never took place since the *Essex* was ordered to conjoin with *Hornet*, which was under command of Lieutenant James Lawrence off Africa. In October 1812, adventurer Porter played his strongest card. News came of Decatur's victory in single-ship combat, and this must have had an effect on Porter. Bainbridge missed the first scheduled meeting, and Porter pressed on to the coast of Brazil but found no joy there either. Both *Constitution* and *Hornet* were separated chasing different quarries. Rather than waiting, Porter, all alone and without orders, took on provisions for the Pacific and left for a voyage around Cape Horn to take on the Pacific Royal Navy. Weathering the horrific sea conditions and uncharted hazardous passage, the *Essex* rounded the southern tip of South America and took up station on the trade route. Porter sailed on with the money he had taken from a British mail-packet boat caught on a return trip to England. The $50,000, found in species, would pay for his patrol of the Pacific. He never explained why he went to the Pacific, and no one at the Navy Department ever asked.

Capture of the Essex

Sailing off the coast of Chile, Porter was looking for a Royal Navy man-of-war that had been taking New England whalers. One didn't have to see a whaler, but he could smell it if he were downwind. He could justify protecting commerce since that was his broad mission, but he could also take British whalers, which brought the greatest prize. In the days of open flames, only the best-quality whale oil was used in the finest places. It was pure and odorless. He called at ports to make himself known, calculating that it would disperse the Royal Navy even farther. It was a bold and brave mission that he had cut out for his crew, but they were happy with the quest for prize money. He called at Valparaiso for provisions and to let the crew go ashore to make as much noise as possible so that the world would know that an American warship was on patrol. He learned that Chile was friendly, but Peru was still under Spanish rule. It gave him another quarry on the way north. Near the Galapagos Islands, he captured a dozen hapless British whalers who were inclined to defend themselves against a mighty warship.

Porter was a remarkable commander. *Essex* was hove down at Nuku-hiva in the Marquesas Islands in true buccaneering fashion, her bottom was cleaned, and her lines were reset. Porter maintained his ship at sea as a fighting unit from October 1812 to March 1814. For seventeen months, his crew was in good health and well disciplined, without once calling at a home port. However, he was reckless in the matter of sending his prizes home. Nearly all were recaptured along with the American crews.[15]

Porter knew that the Royal Navy's frigate *Phoebe*, captained by Captain James Hilyar, had long 24-pounders and could outrange Porter's formidible cannons. In close, it was a different story. There, the American had the advantage with her massive carronades. They passed outside the neutral port, and while Porter had the opportunity to fire a raking broadside, he didn't. The two gentlemen sailors met in the town and agreed to respect the neutrality of Valparaiso. The *Phoebe* left but maintained a blocking position outside the harbor in conjunction with the eighteen-gun *Cherub*, a Royal Navy sloop waiting for *Essex* to appear. *Cherub* fired a weather gun that was interpreted as a challenge to Porter. (Ship captains, in their role as knights of the sea, called out an opponent to give up the sanctuary of the harbor to a fair fight.) Porter stood out in the bay, itching for a fight. The onshore winds drove *Essex* out into the bay. There was a sudden shift in the opposite direction, and a storm began to beat down. Porter ran with the storm in an attempt to slide between *Phoebe* and the shore for open water. The gale-force wind damaged the tops, preventing any attempt to return to the protected harbor. Backtracking was out of the question for the square-rigged *Essex*. Porter anchored to prevent being driven against the rocks. The British had him in their grasp and closed in, preventing Porter from putting out boats with anchors and springs to revolve or move the ship. *Essex* took a pounding from both enemy warships. Porter was taking on water, and many of his crew were down.

Phoebe jumped at the chance to rake her stern while *Essex* moved three guns forward into position to ward off the attack. Porter decided to attack; he cut his anchors and rushed at *Phoebe*. Hilyar backed off, planning to move off beyond Porter's cannon range. *Phoebe* was able to maintain a station ahead and continued to rake *Essex* with 18-pound long guns that Porter could not match.[16]

Porter's journal tells the story:

I now sent for the officers of the divisions to consult them; but what was my surprise to find only Acting Lieutenant Stephen Decatur M'Knight remaining, who confirmed the report respecting the condition of the guns on the gun-deck—those on the spar deck were not in a better state. Lieutenant Wilmer, after fighting most gallantly throughout the action, had been knocked overboard by a splinter while getting the sheet anchor from the bows, and was drowned. Acting Lieutenant John G. Cowell had lost a leg; Mister Edward Barnwall, acting sailing master, had been carried below, after receiving two wounds, one in the breast and one in the face; and acting Lieutenant William H.

Odenheimer, had been knocked overboard from the quarter instants before, and did not regain the ship until after the surrender. I was informed that the cockpit, the steerage, the ward-room and the birth-deck could contain no more wounded; that the wounded were killed while the surgeons were dressing them, and that, unless something was speedily done to prevent it, the ship would sink from the number of holes in her bottom. And, on sending for the carpenter, he informed me that all his crew had been killed or wounded, and that he had been once over the side to stop the leeks, when his slings had been shot away, and it was with difficulty he was saved from drowning.

The enemy . . . was now able to take aim at us as at a target; his shot never missed our hull, and our ship was cut up in a manner which was, perhaps, never before witnessed—in fine, and I saw no hopes of saving her, and at twenty after six, gave the painful order to strike the colors.[17]

The British Captain sent his sailors on board to save the American ship and render medical aid to the wounded. Hilyar, who had known Porter for many years, offered the courtesy of parole. Porter was sent back to the United States a free man with the promise not to engage in warfare with the British for the duration of the war.

JAMES LAWRENCE

James Lawrence's mother, Martha, died giving birth to her son in June 1781. His father, a Loyalist, fled to Canada at the conclusion of the Revolution, leaving the baby boy in the care of his sister. She raised and educated him in Woodbury, New Jersey. With the crisis of the XYZ Affair in 1798, he abandoned the study of law to join the navy.

Lawrence seemed to be everywhere there was action during the war with the Barbary pirates. On a daring raid to destroy the captured USS *Philadelphia*, he was second in command to Oliver Hazard Perry. (Perry would name his flagship on Lake Erie the *Lawrence* after his friend.) Whenever a good, dependable man was needed, they turned to Lawrence for leadership.

In the fall of 1812, Lawrence took command of USS *Hornet*, part of Bainbridge's squadron waiting for David Porter to arrive on *Essex*. Lawrence discovered that the *Bonne Citoyenne*, with eighteen 32-pound, and two long 9-pound carronades, crewed by 150 men, was loading gold coin aboard bound for England under the command of Captain Pit Barnaby Green. Lawrence sent a challenge to Captain Green inviting him out and pledging that the *Constitution* would not intervene. Green refused and honored his mission to get the cargo to England. Bainbridge left Lawrence to blockade Green inside San Salvador harbor and left because word had arrived that a Royal Navy frigate was passing through the area. Lawrence remained on station until January 24, when the seventy-four-gun *Montagu* arrived. *Hornet*, out-gunned, sailed away and within a month stumbled on HMS *Peacock*, a brig armed with 24-pound carronades, north of San Salvador under the command of Captain William Peake. Lawrence lost no time and came up strongly, pass-ing starboard. Peacock suffered immensely from the American broadside. Peake was killed along with a high number of his crew. The ships wore and came at each other once again, like two boxers, now only twenty-five yards apart. The pass on the lee finished off *Peacock*, and Lawrence luffed up and sent a boarding party aboard. The battle took fourteen minutes. It is a dra-matic lesson because *Hornet*'s carronades were not 25-pounder but 32 pound-ers. *Hornet* took damage in the tops, while three American crewmen were killed and several wounded. It should have been a lesson to Lawrence that good gunnery from the start would prevail.[18]

USS Chesapeake

Although captured by HMS *Leopard* in 1807, once the British completed their search, they left James Barron in command of his smashed ship, dead in the water within sight of Norfolk, Virginia. Stephen Decatur took command from Barron and supervised her repair in his Norfolk yard before taking her to sea once again. In early May 1813, Captain James Lawrence took com-mand of the famous frigate *Chesapeake*. Deceptively known as a thirty-eight-gun frigate, she actually carried fifty guns, twenty-six to a broadside. The mix of twenty-eight long 18-pound cannons, two long 12-pound cannons, eigh-teen 32-pound carronades, and two 12-pound carronades made her a lethal customer (gun counts vary widely according to the source and date of the survey). While the ship was a match for any Royal Navy frigate, the crew was not established on board when Lawrence accepted command at the dockyard. In those early navy days, seamen signed on for the voyage at dockside or when recruiting parties traveled about the area. Since the Royal Navy block-ade had shut ports on the Eastern Seaboard, navy ships didn't come and go at will. There was a glut of idle, able seamen. Some signed on from the nearby *Constitution*. Other American sailors who had not been happy on other men-of-war thought that they would give Captain Lawrence a try. Dozens were British who felt safer on a warship than a commercial vessel that might be captured. Just prior to sailing, all were welcome when it came to filling the last 150 billets of the complement of 379. His first lieutenant was Augustus Ludlow, a competent officer. Lawrence had served with only a few of the crew on other ships and at other times. He was well aware of *Shannon*'s presence just outside the harbor, and those he left behind on the beach thought that the captain was planning on a few weeks at sea to train before challenging the audacious blockader. Lawrence should have been thinking of his mission, which was to operate in the Gulf of St. Lawrence to disrupt the flow of men and supplies into Canada in aid of the army plan of invasion that year. Slipping along the coast, he anchored for the night and the next morning was told that there was only one block ship in area: HMS *Shannon*.

HMS Shannon

Shannon was a very different situation. It is true that the two vessels were nearly identical with the advantage going to the American in its throw weight of guns. Royal Navy Captain Philip Bowes Vere Broke had been in command of his frigate for seven years. Broke didn't fit the mold of the staid, sedentary mariner who rarely rehearsed gun crews and who preferred to drill the crew on ship handling. It is unfair to criticize, though, since in the days of sail, putting the vessel in just the right place at the correct moment while being driven by an unhelpful wind does take a great deal of experience. But Broke managed to do both. He fired his guns at least once a week; he used targets and timed on-target drills, giving prizes of a pound of tobacco to the best crew. At any moment, he would throw a cask into the water and call for a crewman by name to hit it. The officers conducted musket, sword, and pike practice in competitive boarding groups. His ship was the standard British frigate of her day, rated at thirty-eight guns when commissioned but with a complement of armament just under that of the *Chesapeake*.[19]

Dual at Sea

Captain Broke, commander of one of the blockade ships, had missed *President*'s departure and was not going to let another slip out. The *Shannon*'s captain kept an eye on *Chesapeake*'s progress, and when his spies told him she was ready to go to sea, he sent a challenge letter ashore on June 1 to her captain. The letter called Lawrence out, but he was already exiting the confines of Boston harbor and missed the missive.

Lawrence didn't need a letter from Broke to bring him out. He had been watching *Shannon* flaunt herself just off the coast for the past two weeks. Lawrence knew that if he could take the British blockader within sight of land and then bring her in as a prize, it would make his career. The capture of the *Peacock* had given him national fame: now *Shannon* too was within his grasp.

Broke picked the ground, twelve miles off shore, and each was armed with similar weapons, setting the stage for the drama—only one would survive. Both ships took the wind, which was light, into consideration, bringing out all sails, to include the royals. They were flying now at top speed and beginning to wheel like great birds looking for an opening—a faux pas. At 5:00 p.m. on the weather gauge, Lawrence clewed up his courses, readied the decks, organized his boarding parties fore and aft, and streaked directly for *Shannon*. Lawrence was not planning to stand off and trade broadsides all day. His crew couldn't sustain that kind of engagement. He didn't plan to destroy or sink her. He was prepared to take her by force with his boarding parties once one or two broadsides knocked *Shannon* off balance. Just before 6:00 in the evening, *Chesapeake* fired a broadside that sent screaming cannonballs thudding into her sides and wrecking the exposed deck, causing terrific damage to ship and crew. The first shots from *Shannon* were sent high to shatter her running rigging, sending it crashing to the main deck along with her marines firing from the tops. Lawrence couldn't maintain station and slid ahead, removing the sight picture from his gunners below on the crowded gun deck. The loss of position allowed Broke to continue to sweep fire to *Chesapeake*'s aft section. The merciless black iron cannonballs stitched the hull and scattered the crew. Lawrence lost his first lieutenant, Ludlow, and other key officers in the chaos of flying splinters and crashing spars. The light winds allowed the puffs of acrid smoke to linger around the two vessels like a shroud. *Chesapeake*'s four helmsmen were killed, the wheel was fractured, and the ship was sent out of control, her bow turned away. With a wind shift, Broke slid the starboard side of his ship tight against the Americans' port rear quarter. The British boarding parties scrambled aboard and were met by swinging cutlasses:

> The frigates were kept in this position by the fluke of the Shannon's anchor catching in the Chesapeake's quarter port. . . . Broke ordered the two ships lashed together and the great guns to cease firing. . . . Lawrence himself, while standing on the quarter-deck, fatally conspicuous by his full dress uniform and commanding stature, was shot down . . . by Lieutenant Law of the British Marines. He fell dying and was carried below, exclaiming—Don't give up the ship![20]

Wounded Captain Broke boarded with the first party and cut his way past the defenders with his straight sword. He later wrote, "The enemy fought desperately, but in disorder." *Chesapeake* was captured.

Epilogue

The tragic death of Lawrence and the quarterdeck of the *Chesapeake*, many believed to be a jinxed ship, crackled through the ranks of the naval community.

Oliver Hazard Perry, a shipmate of Lawrence, kept the captain alive when he emblazoned "Don't give up the ship" on his battle flag on Lake Erie, leading the men and ships to the destruction of the Royal Navy, an enormous contribution to the war in the west. It is one of few items remembered from that long-ago war.

CHRONOLOGIES

William Bainbridge

1774, May 7	Born in Princeton, New Jersey, to a Loyalist doctor
1798	Commissioned a lieutenant in the Navy in command of the schooner USS *Retaliation*
1799	Captain of the brig USS *Norfolk* and promoted to master commandant
1800	Captain of the USS *George Washington*
1802	Captain of the USS *Philadelphia*; run aground and captured
1806	Released from prison in Tripoli
1809	Commodore of the USS *President*
1812	Commodore of the USS *Constitution*; captured HMS *Java*
1820	Decatur's duel with Barron

David Porter

1780	Born in Boston
1789	Midshipman on *Constellation*
1799	Capture of *L'Insurgente:* taken as prize to port
1799	First lieutenant on *Experiment*
1801	First lieutenant on *Enterprise*
1801	Captain of *Amphitheatre* in the Barbary Wars
1802	First lieutenant on *Chesapeake* and *New York*
1802	First lieutenant on *Philadelphia*; taken prisoner by pirates
1805	Released from prison
1805	Acting captain of *Constitution*
1806	Captain of the *Enterprise*
1808	Commander of naval forces at New Orleans
1811	Promoted to master commandant
1812	Captain of *Essex*
1814	Captured by HMS *Phoebe* and *Cherub*

James Lawrence

1798	Midshipman on the *Ganges*
1800	Midshipman on the USS *Adams*
1802	Lieutenant on the USS *Enterprise*
1804	Second in command on the *Philadelphia* raid
1804	Commanded the *Enterprise*
1805	First lieutenant on the USS *Adams*
1806	Commanded the USS *Vixen*
1807	Commanded the USS *Wasp*
1809	Commanded the USS *Argus*
1810	Master commandant of the USS *Hornet*
1813	Captain of the USS *Chesapeake*

NOTES

1. Captain Kenneth Johnson, USN, retired Naval Historical Center, Navy Yard, Washington, D.C.

2. Dudley Pope, *Life in Nelson's Navy* (Annapolis, MD: Naval Institute Press, 1981), 207.

3. Peter Kemp, ed., *Oxford Companion Ships and the Sea* (London: Oxford University Press, 1976), 669.

4. John Harland, *Seamanship in the Age of Sail: An Account of the Ship Handling of the Sailing Man-of-War 1600–1860* (London: Conway Maritime Press, 1984), 215.

5. William James, *The Naval History of Great Britain*, vol. 6 (London: Conway Maritime Press, 2002), 188.

6. Record of Court-Martial, HMS *Java*, Lieutenant Henry Chads, May 15, 1813, Admiralty Library, Scotland Yard, Whitehall, London.

7. *Times*, April 15, 1812, British Library, Newspaper Annex, Colondale, England.

8. Brown-Chaldner, ed., *Dictionary of National Biography since 1900*, vol. 3 (London: Oxford University Press, 1968).

9. Ira Hollis, *The Frigate Constitution: The Central Figure of the Navy under Sail* (New York: Houghton Mifflin, 1901), 258.

10. Andrew Lambert, *Trincomalee: The Last of Nelson's Frigates* (London: Chatham Publishing, 2002), 13.

11. Frances Diane Robotti and James Vescovi, *The USS Essex and the Birth of the American Navy* (Holbrook, MA: Adams Media Corp., 1999), 141.

12. Robotti and Vescovi, *The USS Essex and the Birth of the American Navy*, 142.

13. William S. Dudley, *The Naval War of 1812: A Documentary History*, vol. 1 (Washington, DC: Naval History Center, 1982), 173.

14. Dudley, *The Naval War of 1812*, Vol. 1, 137.

15. C. S. Forester, *The Age of Fighting Sail* (Sandwich, MD: Chapman Billies Inc., 1956), 206.

16. Theodore Roosevelt, *The Naval War of 1812* (New York: Putnam, 1882), 271.

17. Robotti and Vescovi, *The USS Essex and the Birth of the American Navy*, 234.

18. Roosevelt, *The Naval War of 1812*, 168.

19. Roosevelt, *The Naval War of 1812*, 178.

20. Roosevelt, *The Naval War of 1812*, 182.

12

WILLIAM WINDER AND
JAMES WILKINSON

*Strike now. . . . Chastise the savages for such they are. Make them pay.
Our demands may be couched in a single word—Submission!*

—*London Times*, August 5, 1814

WILLIAM WINDER

BORN IN Somerset County, Maryland, to a prominent family in 1775, William was brought up in the law profession, graduating from the University of Pennsylvania in 1798. The nephew of Governor Levin Winder (a considerable advantage), William Winder sought a colonel's commission in the regular army as war loomed. He had no military education or experience, but that was not a stumbling block in the heyday of sycophants. Assigned as the deputy commander to Brigadier Alexander Smyth, who commanded the rifle regiment ensconced near Buffalo, Winder was promoted to brigadier when Smyth abandoned his post and returned to Washington to resume his law practice. In May 1813, after burning York, Ontario, Canada, it took more than a month for General Dearborn to consolidate his army at Fort Niagara near the northern mouth of the Niagara River, across the water from the British stronghold of Fort George. One of his four brigades was given to Winder, who would join the amphibious assault on Fort George, which had been reinforced against an American attack. Winder's brigade held back during the primary assault, which was successful, driving the British commander Brigadier General John Vincent's force west and south. The following day, Winder's brigade was sent in pursuit. Fearing that he hadn't sufficient strength to engage Vincent, he halted until Chandler's brigade was sent, doubling his own. Unable to catch the retreating British, the two American brigades, 1,500 strong, camped for the night at Stoney Creek, Ontario, Canada. A true amateur soldier, Winder failed to put out scouts or adequate trip wire outposts to protect his sleeping brigade. British officers backtracked to reconnoiter and found the camp settling in for the night ill-prepared to defend itself. Just after midnight, 700 British regulars attacked the tightly formed encampment. In the confused fracas, both Winder and Chandler, along with a number of their men, were captured.

Winder's most valuable contribution to the nation came in the arrangements made of his own parole and those made for many other soldiers captured by the British along the northern frontier. As a lawyer, he traveled between the two capitals during 1813 arranging prisoner exchanges. Endearing himself to the Washington community by the summer of 1814, his negotiating at an end, he was placed in command of the palace guard, 10th Military District, defending Washington. When the threat of a British invasion from the Chesapeake materialized, Madison knew that he needed the Maryland state militia because of the scarcity of regular troops in the area. The president rightly believed that with William Winder in command, nephew of the federalist governor, Madison could prevail on Levin Winder to contribute more troops to the defense of the capital.

AUGUST 1814

On August 1, British harassment turned into seizure. Vice Admiral Sir Alexander Cochrane turned loose his hired turncoat Captain Richard Coote on the trusting folks of New London, Connecticut. Flying false colors, he brought the *Comet*, into port on the evening tide. On board, hidden below deck, was a company of Royal Marines. After landing, they rampaged through the town, turning their drunken attention to the waterfront and setting alight twenty-seven moored craft before leaving the citizens traumatized. The Royal Navy, not two days later, at Buzzards Bay, Wareham, Massachusetts, put armed sailors ashore, in the dead of night, to burn, rape, and pillage. To their surprise, the militia confronted the pack and trapped them. To save themselves, American hostages were taken as shields during the British escape. At Fort Phoenix, New Bedford, Massachusetts, American artillery got the best of the Royal Navy frigate HMS *Nimrod* when it attacked the USS *Fairhaven*, which sat helpless at anchor.

BRITISH MILITARY PLAN

Some communities were already lost. Royal Navy Admiral Cochrane seized the defenseless island of Nantucket. He issued an ultimatum to the undefended population to surrender and swear allegiance to King George. Devoid of protection by the federal forces, they had no alternative except death and so signed away their precious freedom—won by their forefathers. Behind the sudden aggression was the military plan to end the war in England's favor.

The plan, "The Re-enforcements allotted to North America and the Operation Contemplated for the Employment for them," was issued from London in June. It was dispatched to the navy commander in Bermuda who was in support of the army commander, Sir George Prevost, in Montreal. Prevost was to conduct the main attack. At the conclusion of the third paragraph, it offers Prevost the assistance of the Royal Navy with 7,000 troops:

> It is also contemplated at a later period of the year to make a more serious attack on some part of the coast of the United States, and with this in view a considerable force will be collected at Cork without delay. Those operations will not fail to effect a powerful diversion in your favor.

THE DIVERSION OF AUGUST 1814

Within a week of Coote's attack on New London, the president called a meeting of the cabinet at the executive mansion. Professor Donald Hickey reminds us in his landmark book *Don't Give Up the Ship* that it was known as the "White House" as early as 1810.[1] Of the notables present were Secretary of War John Armstrong and Secretary of State James Monroe, who was not a supporter of Armstrong's view of the increased activity of British forces. Armstrong had a message from Commodore Barney, who led a small gunboat flotilla in the Chesapeake Bay. A sailor brought word that the Royal Navy fleet in the Chesapeake under Admiral Sir George Cockburn had doubled in size. Barney's feeble fleet of gunboats had been sniping at British ships in the Chesapeake for the past year. Barney's alarming communiqué also warned that his flotilla was boxed in and that Cockburn intended to land a large force on the Patuxent peninsula. Commodore Barney's meager force was the last American navy element in opposition to the rapacious Royal Navy. The message recommended beaching the fleet and converting to infantry.

Seated at his table, one of a dozen in the great room, the secretary of war declared that the Royal Navy was sure to attack Baltimore, not Washington, which had no military value. James Monroe took exception. He saw the political value of taking the capital of a nation—believing that Armstrong was wrong—and he was urging preparations for the defense of Washington.

Armstrong believed that the avaricious Royal Navy was interested in Baltimore, home port of the fleet of privateers that had taken so very many British merchantmen and sullied their reputation over the past two years. He believed that their motive was a combination of vengeance coupled with the pursuit of prize money and not political. When questioned about his action resulting from Barney's message, he replied that he had directed the governors of Maryland, Virginia, and Delaware to call out the militia at federal expense. In addition, Armstrong instructed the commissary general of ordnance to open the arsenals and armories to supply the troops on the march. When Monroe asked what had been done to prepare for the defense of the city, Armstrong repeated that there was no danger. Armstrong was not cooperating with Winder, whom he had opposed as the 10th district commander.

Some in the room took the secretary of war's statement at face value. Armstrong was the most trusted military man in the capital, having written *Hints to Young Officers by an Old Soldier.* He had seen war both in the Revolution and in Europe. Surprisingly, the cabinet believed that the defense of the nation should not be in doubt. The memory of the Revolutionary War was very much alive among the cabinet members, most of whom had served under arms in their youth. To a man, they believed that another land war in America favored Americans and not the British. This time, England was at even more of a disadvantage than in 1776. Then, they had a standing army in the country with depots and fortifications. The main British army was 4,000 miles away, with the exception of troops in Canada, who were decisively engaged on the northern border. The local militia, which had not been committed in recent years, could take the field in great numbers if necessary as they did before. Of course, they were untrained, untried, badly equipped, and poorly led. It was agreed before they adjourned that Commodore Barney should give up the boats and convert to infantry.

WINDER'S DEFENSE OF THE CAPITAL

Monroe's assessment of the situation was correct. Even though Winder had been in command since June, he hadn't begun to assemble a plan for defense of Washington until the start of August. British Admiral Cockburn had spent the summer raiding Chesapeake Bay communities from Havre de Grace to Hampton, 200 miles of interior coastline, but Winder did not budge. It never occurred to him that Cockburn was learning the tributaries for an approach to the capital. The American lion, Commodore Joshua Barney, had opposed the British fleet with a handful of undergunned gallywampus (low flat-bottomed crude often rowed, fit to operate in shallow coastal swampy water) craft.

Brigadier General Winder had retained 380 regular infantry, 125 light dragoons, 120 marines, and a military band under his direct control. It was nothing more than a palace guard. When he finally pulled together a staff, it turned out to be a gathering of party cronies. The militia in the capital region was comprised of bands of friends who trained on weekends to get away from their wives. Their drill sessions were short and succeeding parties long. Uniforms were in short supply, as were blankets, tents, shovels, axes, field kitchens, and transport. There was no system to resupply flints, which were good for only forty shots. Even if there were supplies, no one was under contract to move the army. The men were told to bring personal items to maintain themselves in the field. Some had joined up to drink and loot.

Like Congress, Winder bet on the strength of the state militias to meet him on the battlefield. The brigadier general's inaugural order came on August 4. Unaware that Congress had summoned the militia to action the previous month, Winder activated 4,000 militia for the defense of the 10th Military District. Just 250 citizen soldiers answered the call.

COCHRANE'S DIVERSION

Vice Admiral Sir Alexander Cochrane briefed his principal commanders at Government House, Bermuda, on August 8, 1814. He had repositioned his headquarters to Halifax to be a little closer to the action. He had been faithful to his admiralty orders that spring and summer. The trade, so vital to New England merchants, was choked off. Royal Marine raiding parities had burned out numerous coastal communities. The American navy was shut down. He and his officers had become rich from the prize money paid for captured American ships and cargoes.

LAND RAIDER

Among the military men that day was army Major General Robert Ross, who was appointed land commander of the expedition. Newly promoted, he had commanded an infantry brigade for Wellington at San Sebastian, Spain, in the closing campaign of the war with France. General Ross had embarked at St. Malo, Brittany, on June 2 with four battalions. The veteran 4th Foot, Royal Lancaster (two battalions of the 44th East Essex regiment and the 85th

Shropshire Light Infantry) had been resting in the wine cellars of France since the capitulation of Napoleon in April. At Bermuda on July 25 a battalion of the 21st Royal Scots Fusiliers from Genoa and a company of field artillery embarked at Gibraltar. The welcome addition brought the complement to nearly 4,000 fighting men. There was no transport or cavalry escort assigned to his expedition. The troops, once ashore, enjoyed the relief from the storm-driven passage.

THE KING'S MEN

Robert Ross, age forty-eight, was the son of Major David Ross of Rostrevor, County Down. His mother was the half-sister of the Earl of Charlesmont, his patron for many years. The earl provided for his education at Trinity College, Dublin. A brilliant combat leader, Ross rose from ensign to regimental commander of the 20th Foot in fourteen years. A drillmaster and strict disciplinarian, he talked tough but took care of his men as if they were kin, sharing their hardships. Leading from the front, Ross was popular. His three wounds, two of which were serious, attested to his courage. He came to Wellington's attention at the Battle of Vitoria in 1812. A highly decorated personal aide to the king, the duke picked him from dozens of good commanders to promote to major general. A tall, trim, dark-haired warrior who had begun to gray, his fitted short military coat bore four gold campaign medals, while at his side hung a engraved sword of honor.

Sir Alexander Cochrane articulated the mission to General Ross and the naval officers who were in support. The council of war could see Cochrane's blood rise as he began the briefing. He was a man of passion bent on settling this war, which tied down half his fleet with a boring and wasteful blockade. The admiral was confident of victory.

Major General Robert Ross was not a passionate man, but he was a calculating provider of the military art. He had no ax to grind with Americans. On August 16 the ships bearing British soldiers slipped into the Chesapeake Bay through the narrow opening between the tip of the Delmarva Peninsula and the long, sandy shore of Norfolk, Virginia.

COCKBURN'S SHOW

George Cockburn, the master of independent action, had his orders, needing no umbilical cord to higher headquarters. On the morning of August 18, he landed Major General Robert Ross's 4,000 soldiers and sailors from the fleet anchored on the Patuxent River. They were near the fishing community of Benedict, just forty miles as the crow flies from the capital of the United States. But that crow would have to walk dusty, rutted farm roads through several towns before reaching the outskirts of the capital city. He was sure to face stiff resistance unless other diversionary elements could decoy away the American defenses. Hidden in the steamy morning river mist, they were unopposed. Unit commanders sought local avaricious farmers for horses and carts. The British always paid in gold coin. Unable to find enough draft animals, British sailors spelled each other in dragging borrowed wagons loaded with powder and ball. The inactivity of the veteran infantry on the long sea voyage had sapped their strength, turning once sinewy legs to rubber. Ross could see that progress was going to be slow and that the element of surprise would be lost. His column sent up clouds of dust that could be seen for miles over the rolling green fields. With no cavalry to screen his approach, he feared ambush. Several platoons of infantry were mounted on saddle horses purchased from locals along the way. They reported a cordial reception as they probed carefully northward. Ross paused just north of Nottingham the next day, a ten-mile march.

Cockburn, who shared the trek on foot, made note of all harbor installations, shipping, and storehouses to be destroyed on the return. The field artillery picked up at Gibraltar was left on board the fleet in favor of a troop of Royal Rocketeers. Their lightweight "A" frames and unguided rockets were more mobile, but less effective than the cannons. Yet, as Wellington was fond of saying, "they were only good for scaring horses." Ross thought that they would have the same effect on militia.

One of his subordinate commanders, Captain Sir Peter Parker, Royal Navy, had suffered the loss of numerous British merchant ships under his protection to mercenary American privateers. Now on board his frigate *Menelaus*, he ventured an additional sixty miles north with a flotilla of a dozen empty transports to confuse and confound the American defenders. The movement, made to look like an attack, was a feint at Baltimore, reinforcing Secretary of War Armstrong's prediction and tying down Governor Levin Winder's Maryland militia. Parker did not engage but laid-off outside the range of Fort McHenry. Simultaneously, Royal Navy Captain James Gordon entered the southern Potomac River where it met the Chesapeake Bay and made a great show of moving ever northward, burning settlements as he slowly closed on Fort Warburton. His impressive fleet of two frigates, three bomb vessels, and Congreve rocket ships swept naval gunfire all along the shore to terrorize local civilians. Several smaller craft, filled with troops, harassed the riverbank, challenging the militia to fight. The militia refrained. Local folks abandoned their homes at the sight of a forest of tall masts and billowing sails moving upriver past plantations and farms that hugged the muddy river. Fishing boats fled upriver ahead of the British spreading alarm to Alexandria.

> *That vast array, so formidable of aspect, lacked the moral force without which physical power, given it its most terrible form, is but an idle show.*

—British military commentator

WINDER'S WAR

William Winder, wearing his usual blinders, was unaware and therefore unaffected by enemy diversions. He was drawn to the outskirts of Washington by reports of Redcoats on Marlboro Pike. James Monroe borrowed a contingent of regular dragoons from the force husbanded by Winder and went looking for trouble. South of Upper Marlboro, he met the first American refugees fleeing before Ross. They told of Redcoats at Nottingham headed northwest at a slow pace.

Monroe, in dark civilian dress, was quite a contrast to the dragoon officer beside him, clad in a short indigo bluejacket crossed with eight rows of straight silver braid that finished in curlicues. Monroe was buoyed knowing that he was headed in the right direction. Others had told him that the enemy was far to the south. None of the refugees questioned mentioned cavalry. The absence of cavalry was most encouraging. There were no indications of where the British were headed. It could mean Baltimore or Washington, but it's sixty miles to Baltimore, so why pick a route so far south? Monroe was confirming his initial assessment that if they stayed on that road, they would go to Bladensburg, a junction with the best route to Washington. Proving Armstrong wrong seemed more important than anything else at that moment. There was nothing more important to that politician than proving his judgment superior to others.

CONFUSION AND CONTRAST

Monroe, the statesman turned intelligence officer, sent a trooper back to tell the army what he had found and that he intended to press on to see the color of their coats for himself. Monroe questioned more travelers while the troopers' horses rested. Accounts differed slightly, but nothing changed with the exception of the enemy strength. He encountered the magistrate from Nottingham (fleeing on a cart full of records), who tagged the British advance guard at 6,000. Without checking the figure, Monroe sent another dispatch. It caused a panic in the city.

It was late on August 20 when a messenger, carrying a note from Monroe, found Brigadier General Winder dithering at the bridge over the eastern branch of the Potomac River just west of Bladensburg. The assessment was sent on to Armstrong and the president. Armstrong held fast to his assessment that Baltimore was to be attacked. The president recognized the capital city for the prize that it was and began to organize the district militia to defend the mansion and Capitol.

The thought that Baltimore may not be the objective filtered into the capital city. Now concerned that he might have miscalculated, Armstrong sent his only military engineer, Decius Wadsworth, the commissary general of ordnance, to Bladensburg to organize a blocking position. Winder had left the bridge over the eastern Potomac by the time Wadsworth arrived. To the east of Bladensburg, the hills folded together into open fields. Finding a point where vision was unrestricted, Wadsworth directed that defensive dirt revetments (barricades) be constructed. A scattering of troops arrived to form a crescent-shaped line on the low ridge. The Potomac was fordable farther south of Bladensburg. The bridge was the gateway to Washington.

Several thousand American militiamen were beginning to gather in small groups on dusty roads south of the eastern branch of the Potomac. They meandered toward Upper Marlboro like water through fingers. The British marched unmolested in the same direction, foraging for transport and buying friends who thought it best to play both sides until the final battle. While Ross's men were not cheered, neither were they stoned. Local folks recognized the contrast between citizen soldiers and professionals. They were surprised to see Admiral Cockburn walking with common sailors. They knew his name and sinister reputation from the newspaper accounts. His presence was widely reported to both Baltimore and Washington. The only thing operating at capacity was the rumor mill that added confusion to the crisis.

UPPER MARLBORO IN BRITISH HANDS

Early on August 21 a platoon of redcoated infantry, with muskets slung across their bodies, mounted on barebacked horses and blew through the provincial towns and out the other side. By late in the day, the first elements of the British column were nearing Upper Marlboro. By morning, the sanded cobblestone streets would be teaming with their brothers by the thousands. Marching in order of fours, to the sound of ominous drums, they appeared irresistible.

Winder vacillated with every rumor. Camped at the Woodyard, a few miles southwest of Upper Marlboro, he sat surrounded by regular troops waiting for good news. His palace guard consisted of 750 regular infantry and cavalry, some marines, and five guns. In the last twenty-four hours, he dispersed an army of 9,000 men along the roadways that served Baltimore, Annapolis, Washington, and Fort Warbuton. He had single-handedly constructed a battle line over a hundred miles long. The majority of cannons were in Baltimore. The army transport that he had been expecting to cross the bridge at Bladensburg had been commandeered by government clerks to move files and furniture west across the Potomac and north to the Harpers Ferry arsenal. The night of August 21, the American field army was sleeping on the ground and eating whatever they could forage.

DIGGING IN TO MEET THE BRITISH

The *Nile's Weekly Register*, a Baltimore newspaper, reported that General Tobias Stansbury, commander of the 20th Maryland Infantry Brigade, commented on the heroic march he was about to undertake. They didn't march far. Five miles south of the city, they halted to set up camp and remained in place as a blocking force to protect Baltimore.

At the other end of the overextended battle line, Winder's reinforcements had arrived at Fort Warburton with new orders for Captain Dyson, the commander. He was to blow up the fort if seriously attacked by a large British force. There was no sense to the order, but it served to illustrate the hopelessness that Winder embraced.

Monroe appeared at the Woodyard on the night of August 21 in hopes of solidifying the situation. Earlier, Monroe had seen the British column from a considerable distance without a telescope, leading to his highly overestimated report of enemy strength. He did convince Winder to send Sterrett's regiment to Bladensburg.

THE BLIND LEADING THE HELPLESS

On the morning of August 22 Monroe led Winder and 2,000 American men on foot north toward Upper Marlboro. There should be an explanation for taking the long route, but there is none. They had nearly covered the five miles when, to their shock, they stumbled across the advance guard of the British army. At the sight of the distant Redcoats, Winder lost heart and ordered a retreat that turned into a rout. Monroe dispatched another message to the president stating that the British intended to attack the capital.

THE BRITISH KEEP COMING

Ross continued to consolidate at Upper Marlboro while wondering what the Americans were up to. Little did he realize that he would be unopposed until the following day, when he reached Bladensburg. He was protected in the center of the British formation by a fifty-man detachment of Royal Sappers and Miners. These men were specialists trained and equipped to blow up military fortifications. More coal miners than soldiers, they wore tight black leather caps with a protective plate that extended down the back, covering the neck. Their short red jackets were closed by a single row of white metal buttons. Dark blue stand-up collar and cuffs gave them the appearance of soldiers. Their white pants were protected under medium-blue coveralls. Unmistakable at first sight, they carried shovels and picks instead of muskets. If Monroe had been the intelligence officer he claimed to be, he would have identified the unit and concluded that the British not only intended to occupy the capital but also were determined to destroy the public buildings. In addition to the sixty 40-pound rockets of the Royal Rocket Corps, the navy dragged one 6-pounder and two 3-pounder field pieces. Ross's mounted scouts reported Bladensburg, nine miles north, to be the enemy camp and strong point. While Ross consolidated at Upper Marlboro, on August 23 he conferred with Cockburn. The admiral had brought his own cask of wine, not trusting the water in the hot climate. Ross traced his plan on a map laid at Cockburn's feet. Although a naval officer, the admiral had considerable experience with small land forays.

On the evening of August 23, General Ross listed the troops available for the attack the next morning. It was an old habit from the Peninsula War, where he had been a subordinate commander.

> Four regiments, infantry
> Battalion, royal marines
> Company, black colonial marines
> Light rocket, royal artillery
> Naval rocket, royal marine
> Naval gunners, 90
> Navy sailors, 275
> RS&M, 50
>   Total 4,300

THE BLADENSBURG RACES

A substantial wooden bridge crossed the marshy eastern branch of the Potomac. The bog that extended for miles was one of the finest mosquito breeding spots in the east. Situated on a low ridge above the crossing, the village blocked the British approach. Traditionally, it was the last rest stop before entering the confines of the District. Comprised of services for travelers, Bladensburg provided rented rooms, eateries, livery stables, and a post office. Just to the east, the American military elements began to congeal to the left and right of Wadsworth's hasty redoubt that blocked the road from Upper Marlboro. Upon arrival on the evening of August 22, Tobias Stansbury's command soaked up small elements from all directions as his hodgepodge grew to over 4,100. With little control exercised by the Baltimore general, the force ebbed and flowed all day until nothing was certain. The road network that converged at Bladensburg became knotted with disparate elements of fifty to a hundred confused units.

WHERE IS WINDER?

On the afternoon of August 22 the bewildered American commander was grasping at every crazed passing rider who jabbered that he had seen the enemy column. Unfortunately, no coherent picture emerged from such ravings. All Winder knew was that the British were in a column headed toward Bladensburg and would intersect with a considerable number of his troops perhaps that very day.

On August 23 General Winder and his followers remained in bivouac six miles south of Bladensburg at Battalion Old Fields. Winder and Monroe conferenced in the open that morning when President Madison emerged from the tree-covered road on horseback. Armstrong and the entire cabinet accompanied the president. Unprotected by a military escort, the group included grooms and civil aides who followed closely, leading remounts like a pack of itinerant polo players.

Winder, always the sycophant, left the discussions and greeted the president, bowing to the others in turn. The diminutive Monroe stood up in his stirrups to gain the lay of the land and disposition of the troops. The president felt obliged to do something faced with so many soldiers.

Madison accepted the offer, and a formation of the 800 regulars was thrown together while the militia formed a crowd at and around the edges. The president remained on horseback so that he could be both seen and heard. In the open, Madison's voice was difficult to hear.

Winder took the principal members of the party to a tent for an incoherent briefing. Surprisingly Armstrong had switched horses and now supported Monroe's estimate. Winder painted a fluid picture, sticking to Monroe's estimate of 6,000.

ACTION

A dispatch rider pulled up and tossed down a message. Winder, more to show the president that he was a man of action than anything else, issued a verbal order to Major Peter to take the regular battalion south down the Marlboro Pike and fix the British main force but not to take any risk. Then Winder dispatched a messenger for Stansbury to abandon his position on Lowndes Hill and move the entire formation south toward Upper Marlboro. To further confuse the situation, he ordered the District militia of 1,700 to stand fast. Even the president, who was supposed to be impressed by the decisive display, could not accept the fragmenting of the command so near the enemy. Armstrong urged Winder to take the entire army back to Washington and build a revetment around the Capitol and executive mansion.

Winder bid good-bye and rode off, without the president, Monroe, or Armstrong, north toward Bladensburg to intercept Stansbury while calling for more troops from the north to join them on the Marlboro Pike.

Meanwhile, an officer who reported that the British were coming straight at them only five miles away stopped Stansbury's column only a mile or two east of Bladensburg. Stansbury ignored Winder's order and returned his entire command to the Lowndes Hill (near Baltimore) defensive position. At the dinner hour, Sterrett's 5th Maryland trudged in from their forced march. They were added to the end of the line where they stood and waited for the British—who were not coming.

When darkness fell, the men sat down where they had been standing for hours, and 1,000 campfires sprang up. The cooking fires marked the American position for the British scouts who were secreted in the line of trees a mile to the east. White chicken feathers, plucked from the birds slaughtered on the spot by the troops, clearly delineated a path for Tobias Stansbury, who tripped down the cluttered line to Sterrett's bivouac. He was noticeably nervous, unable to hide his lack of combat experience any longer. Few that he met along the mosquito-infested path were true veterans, and he despaired over the preparations to meet the enemy. Stansbury needed to commiserate with a fellow sufferer of the same rank. Alone, both could be honest and freely admit their trepidation. The companionship of a close friend was the only solace available that terrifying night before the battle. Within hours, their government, family, and fellow citizens expected them to stop thousands of Wellington's "invincibles," the finest army in the world. Both were sure that their inexperience meant that they would be either dead or disgraced before noon. The battle would expose them as parade soldiers fit for the top of a chocolate box.

Monroe arrived at Bladensburg near midnight and repeated the rumor that Winder was either captured or dead. Winder disappeared at the same time that Peter's column met Ross on the open road. After midnight, a messenger handed Stansbury an amazing message from the reincarnated Winder, who had taken his wing of the army, led by Peter, back to Washington. Stansbury, feeling abandoned to face the entire British force alone, packed up the army and vacated Bladensburg. By dawn, they were on the Washington side of the bridge, retreating toward the city. When Winder heard of the move, he countermanded Stansbury's action and ordered him back to Bladensburg. In explanation, he shared the latest interrogation of a captured enemy patrol. "The British are going to attack the capitol city from Bladensburg."

At 10 a.m. on August 24 Winder ordered Peter, who had settled comfortably in Washington, to Bladensburg, where Stansbury was waiting. However, Stansbury didn't trust Winder to reinforce him prior to Ross's arrival and settled in to wait on the Washington side of the river. Trailing behind Peter's troops, Winder slumped in his saddle, clueless. The president and cabinet followed Winder to the waves of the people on the streets expecting the British to be defeated.

Stansbury could have returned to the strong defensive position along the ridge on the east side of Bladensburg but feared that if pressed, he could not get his command across the narrow Potomac bridge and become trapped with his back against the river. On the west, or Washington, side of the river, the land did not support the defense. There was no natural high ground with open fields of fire. Wadsworth had thrown up an artillery redoubt at the intersection of the Georgetown-Washington Pike. It was too large for Stansbury's small field pieces, but could be somewhat modified. The land was marshy with an orchard dominating the center. To Stansbury's great relief, Colonel William Beall arrived in a cloud of dust from Annapolis with his brigade of exhausted marchers who had been on the road for twenty hours. They were directed to form a reserve in the rear.

DON'T HELP

While Stansbury was overwhelmed by the approaching British, who streamed over Lowndes Hill, finding it empty, James Monroe decided that the troop disposition was all wrong and as the secretary of state took command and moved the formations while Stansbury's back was turned. Before the 20th Maryland field commander could do anything about Monroe's meddling, Winder arrived, agreed with Monroe, and, to show his power, moved the artillery and rifle regiment. General Smith arrived, got into an argument with Stansbury as to who was the most senior general, and took up a position across the Washington Pike with Barney's naval guns. In the end, American units of all sizes converged willy-nilly and elbowed for a place in the front.

REDCOATS ACROSS THE POTOMAC

The British quickly cleared the observation posts from the village and broke into open order to cross the bridge. The 85th Shropshire Light Regiment was held up momentarily by the American artillery, but soon separated into clouds of skirmishers, nullifying the solid shot that was so devastating to packed formations. The light companies of the other regiments were consolidated, and they rushed across the bridge without incident. The American gun positions were poorly placed and allowed the enemy to find dead spots where they could move unopposed. Suddenly, the American six-gun battery was in jeopardy and limbered up, leaving the field and losing one gun in the race. The Americans didn't try to disable the bridge. The 44th East Essex Regiment, in red coats with yellow cuffs and collars, rushed across and attacked a weak spot in the American line. The 44th began to roll up the left flank. The Royal Rocket Battery launched 40-pound unguided rockets. They burst in fireballs, showering fragments of hot metal down on the frightened soldiers of Schultz's and Regan's battalions. Part of Stansbury's untrained brigade ran in terror. The screaming cylinders, trailing prodigious amounts of white smoke, turned over the innards of the Americans, who never knew a weapon like that existed. While the rockets caused few casualties, many men sought refuge, leaving their muskets behind.

IRONIC

General Winder determined that the British light infantry was overextended and ordered the 5th Maryland to counterattack. He misread the situation, and soon the Americans were caught in crossfire from the east and the north. The American battalions stood at close order in the center of the field and engaged the British, the enemy fighting as open skirmishers from two sides. Winder rode forward in an attempt to rally his troops. Confused in the face of enemy fire, he merely interfered. He shouted for Stansbury to withdraw and moments later recanted. The 5th broke and ran, chased by Redcoats from East Essex.

Barney's naval gunner made an impression with shot and shell, stopping three charges by the British light infantry. Killing and wounding the enemy officers leading from the front, the concentrated firepower of Commodore Barney and Major Peter drove the first wave of Redcoats back across the marsh to the north. The 1,700 men of Walter Smith's District brigade were spread out across the Georgetown Road on the north flank. They were green troops without uniforms. Ross mounted a deliberate attack. At first, Smith believed that he could hold the ground, but to his surprise was ordered to withdraw to the center by Winder. Barney was just as vulnerable, but he never got the message, if there was one, to pull back. Soon exposed, his command took volleys of fire from the north and the east. The commodore was badly wounded and made prisoner. His last order was, "Run for it men!" Smith's ordered withdrawal and Barney's capture brought Winder close to panic. Twice he ordered Smith to halt and face the enemy and countermanded the order within minutes. The entire American complement got up as one and began to move off down the Washington Pike. In the face of Redcoats streaming across the Bladensburg Bridge and the enemy formation mingling with Yankee wounded and stragglers, Winder sent word by horseback to those elements still in contact to "break away" and re-form five miles down the road from the capital. The stream of moving men, some in uniforms and some not, turned into a torrent. If the British had been blessed with cavalry, they would have decimated Winder's army before they had gone two miles.

As it was, the enemy was also walking, so it became a footrace on the evening of August 24. The militiamen broke ranks and scattered in the direction of their homes, leaving what little military equipment they possessed littering their path. Winder truly panicked when his army dissolved. He directed some formations to go to Georgetown and north to Tenleytown three miles up the Potomac.

COMMANDER-IN-CHIEF

Madison, Armstrong, and the cabinet had witnessed the engagement from a slope less than a mile from the battle line. Scared, many without weapons ran past their president without giving him a glance. The road to Washington overflowed as the regular army, still in formation, plodded toward the capital. Armstrong urged the president to join the blue-coated column for protection. Madison's reaction was overheard by a reporter. The newspapers quoted the president: "I believe I should leave military matters to military men." The reporter presumed that by "military men," he meant the British. At the suggestion of the secretary of war, Madison dispersed the cabinet, directing them to convene at Kemp Hall on Market Street in Frederick, Maryland, fifty miles due north of the capital. Madison turned his horse and cut out for Virginia. By nightfall, he was in Harpers Ferry, leaving the government, his executive mansion, and Dolly to their own devices.

Ross claimed sixty-four of his men killed and three times that severely wounded. The regular American army losses were twenty-six killed in action and fifty-seven wounded. There was no accounting for the militiamen. The battle developed so rapidly that there were only brief periods of rifle action. No units clashed in hand-to-hand fighting: bayonets didn't need cleaning. The American Army Band that had come up from town behind the presidential entourage played as the troops streamed by. Most of the soldiers, sailors, and militiamen involved at Bladensburg never fired their weapons.

THE UNDEFENDED CITY

The executive mansion was occupied, and other federal buildings along Pennsylvania Avenue were torched. Some say that looters were as responsible as the British army. Monroe and Winder watched the glow in the sky to the south as they trudged north. They spent the night surrounded by a thousand regular soldiers. There was no attempt to defend the city. Their strategy was to wait for the enemy to leave.

That night and the next day, Ross and Cockburn supervised the destruction of the Navy Yard and the Washington arsenal (today, Fort McNair) at the fork in the Potomac River, a mile south of the capital. An inquisitive element discovered a dry well at the arsenal and threw a blazing torch down to see what was dumped there before the garrison was abandoned. To their surprise and regret, it was filled with gunpowder, which exploded, killing twelve and wounding thirty. It was the most horrific engagement of the battle, but only one side was present.

MONROE WASN'T FINISHED

James Monroe went to Alexandria and took charge of what military men and equipment there was to block the southern approach. He had received reports of the progress of Captain Gordon's fleet. Captain Dylon, commander of Fort Warburton, sent word that he was about to be attacked by water and land. As the enemy came closer, Dyson expanded his orders, which stated that he was to destroy the guns and fort if attacked by an overwhelming force. Prematurely, before a shot was fired, he acted and spiked the guns and ignited the powder magazine before abandoning his command.

By the last week of August, Armstrong was asked to resign his appointment as Secretary of War. James Monroe accepted the temporary duty while remaining Secretary of State.

When found, Winder was relieved of command.

JAMES WILKINSON

Never won a battle or lost a Court-Martial.

—Robert Lechie, historian

James Wilkinson referred to himself, as the "scientific soldier" but was neither. Of the twenty-five soldiers and sailors reviewed in detail in this volume, Wilkinson is the most consistent. He failed at everything. General Wilkinson eclipsed all the other hacks, sycophants, and adventurers but never approached hero. "James Wilkinson had a propensity for intrigue and a strong desire to succeed in the world by whatever means he could employ."[2] There has never been another American more involved in the nation's affairs like him. He tainted everything he touched.

James Wilkinson was born in Benedict, Maryland, of a once-high-bound family in 1757 that sold off Stoakley Manor to pay debts. James, the second son, was educated privately by funds remaining in the hands of his grandmother. She sent him for medical studies that were interrupted by the Revolutionary War. He joined Colonel Thompson's regiment of Pennsylvania rifles who marched to Boston and joined in the battle at Breed's Hill. Appointed a captain and company commander after the battle, he remained with General Philip Schuyler. After the abortive attack on Quebec, Canada, by Benedict Arnold, who was wounded and recovering, Captain Wilkinson accompanied troops sent north to reinforce Arnold, who wintered at Montreal. Wilkinson remained as an adjutant to Arnold and accompanied the general on the retreat from Canada in 1776. He served as brigade major to General St. Clair as well as courier between Gates and Washington and witnessed the winter attack at Trenton. Washington promoted him to lieutenant colonel and sent him off on recruiting duty. Soon, he joined the military gathering at Saratoga, New York, and became adjutant to Major General Horatio (Granny) Gates. Benedict Arnold defied Gates and personally led the American army to victory in the field. Gates, along with Wilkinson, remained behind the lines, safe in his headquarters, throughout the battle. Wilkinson was sent to Congress with the official report of the victory. The journey took considerably longer than expected. When questioned, Wilkinson claimed illness, which had kept him in Albany. A note to John Hancock from Gates read,

> I desire to be permitted to recommend this gallant officer in the warmest manner to Congress and in treat that he may be continued in his present office with the brevet of a brigadier general . . . from the beginning of this contest I have not met with a more promising military genius than Colonel Wilkinson, whose services have been of the last importance to this army.

Wilkinson was never on the battlefield. It was traditional in military circles to send a junior officer of note with the message of a victory who would be specially recognized for his part in the conflict. Remaining in Philadelphia, Wilkinson became a principal member of the "Conway Cabal" an attempt within Congress to replace Washington with Gates.

CONWAY CABAL

As the infighting continued, Wilkinson began to worry that Gates and his conspirators might not be able to make their case, so Wilkinson began to play both sides of the street, leaking documents to Washington's supporters. When the conspiracy blew up, Gates accused Wilkinson of treachery, and Wilkinson offered to duel Gates to defend his reputation. According to Wilkinson's own account of the encounter, the morning of the duel, "Gates apology . . . was satisfactory beyond expectations, and rendered me more than content. I was flattered and pleased, and if a third person had doubted the sincerity of the explanation I would have insulted him."[3] We only have his words, which aren't worth much. Later, as the sniping continued between Gates and Wilkinson, now firmly in Washington's camp, the duel was fought near White Plains, New York. Although they fired at each other three times, no one was injured. Accepting the position of overseeing government contracting for uniforms, he resigned two years later claiming that he would "leave the office for his ignorance of mercantile business, which will incapacitate me under the proposed regulations."[4]

LIFE IN A NEW NATION

With independence from the mother country came the new horizon of land speculation. No longer the King's to grant, federal and state governments sold land cheaply to lure Europeans to join the western expansion free of Old World restrictions and filled with the promise of freedom. Eastern specula-tors bought large tracts, only to break them up into packages for sale at bar-gain prices. Generally, purchased unseen, new owners felt swindled when the property did not meet expectations. It was a scheme made for James Wilkin-son. With the opening of the Cumberland Gap, a flood of pioneers rushed into Kentucky (which at that time was a part of Virginia), the first of the boom states where the land was virgin and fertile. Wilkinson established him-self with a few backers to include John Armstrong, later the Secretary of War, and other notables. In 1783, after exploring much of the new territory, he settled in what is Lexington on the banks of the Kentucky River and set up a store and land office. He made a dozen land entries, adding up to nearly a 100,000 acres, and notified his backers back east to sell it off at a profit. He became prosperous when the supplies, floated down a number of rivers and packed on mule back, arrived at his store on a regular basis. Locally, he was best known as a prominent defendant in a long string of lawsuits over land deals. Kentucky had been trying its wings since 1785 to break away from Vir-ginia because it was too distant to conduct any oversight.

Wilkinson branched out into tobacco export. Sent down several rivers, through Indian-controlled land, it eventually arrived at the Spanish port of New Orleans. By 1791, Spanish gold pieces came back rather than Yankee dollars, turning his head and leading him to dark places. Wilkinson's store and land enterprises became the center of commerce, tempting him to live beyond his means. He put together collection creditors made up of some of the most prominent men in America. Wilkinson courted Spanish Governor Miro, convincing the Spaniard that he was the most influential Kentuckian and a stalwart friend. To prove his loyalty, Wilkinson applied for a Spanish passport. At the same time, he accepted a federal commission as second in command of federal troops and participated in a short campaign against the Wabash Indians. President Washington offered his personal thanks for the ser-vice. That same year, Wilkinson's plan to incorporate Kentucky into Spanish Florida faltered when statehood was granted. Undeterred, Wilkinson, a paid Spanish agent, continued to clandestinely coordinate the defection of a por-tion of his state to Spain.

BACK IN UNIFORM

With his creditors breathing down his neck, Wilkinson accepted Washing-ton's commission as a lieutenant colonel and command of Fort Washington at Cincinnati, Ohio. That spring, he was promoted to brigadier general when a vacancy of a natural death occurred, opening up a slot for a new general. President Washington wrote to Secretary of War Henry Knox, "General Wilkinson has employed great zeal and ability for the public weal since he came into service. His conduct carries strong marks of attention, activity and spirit, and I wish him to know the favorable light in which it is viewed." He joined Major General Anthony Wayne and William Henry Harrison at Pittsburgh to train and plan the coming campaign against the Indians. Wilkinson was put in command of the left wing of the small army even though Wayne realized that he was essentially a staff officer and had little to no combat experience during the Revolutionary War. That fall of 1793, Wayne's army moved to Fort Greeneville, but failed to make contact with the Indians because of a great deal of disease that incapacitated Wilkinson and his troops. That winter, Wilkinson intrigued to replace Wayne, who was "not up to the job at his advanced age."

The Indians attacked an element of the army in June 1794 just as Wayne was reinforced with Kentucky volunteers. The British allies prompted the Indians to resist negotiations in favor of war. Major General Wayne marched toward northern Ohio in late August and located a major Indian force. Wilkinson discovered 1,500 Indians and Canadian militia waiting in a line awaiting the Americans' attack. Chiefs Blue Jacket and Little Turtle rested their lines behind an abatis of fallen trees blown down by a storm months before. Wilkinson, with the support of the mounted Kentuckians, drove the enemy line back a mile. The two wings of Wayne's army rested and then moved forward once again, driving the Indians to the gates of British Fort Miami, but the gates were not opened, and the braves melted away into the forest. There was a standoff for two days between the Redcoats and the Yankees. Wayne burned the crops around the British fort as he waited for the Indians to return, but there was no sign of them. Before leaving, Wayne moved off and built Fort Defiance, stocked it, and left troops inside to control the area. His Legion was dissolved on completion of its mission.

CHARGES

Even though the battle and a new Indian treaty had been negotiated, Wilkinson and his cronies insisted that an inquiry should be made into the conduct of the campaign: "I feel reluctant to hazard my professional reputation under the administration of a weak, corrupt minister, or a despotic, vainglorious, ignorant General." He was complaining of the laxity and inefficiency in contractor supplies. He was alleging irregularities since resupply was not sufficient. Of course, what he wanted was Wayne's job. Throughout the period,

Wilkinson continued to correspond with Spanish authorities—he had renounced his oath of American citizenship in order to accept Spanish funds—since he needed the salary to pay for his lavish lifestyle. Along with some of his friends, he was attempting to ally Kentucky with Louisiana, which included a large parcel of land called the "Yazoo," as a fiefdom for himself. In 1794, Wilkinson's agent picked up several barrels of sugar from New Madrid in Spanish territory and placed it on his boat for transport to Cincinnati, where he and Wilkinson broke open the casks and separated $9,640 in gold pieces before repacking and selling the sugar. The War Department announced on December 11, 1795, that Brigadier General Wilkinson would succeed Wayne.

PROMOTION?

Alexander Hamilton was the commanding general of the entire army, but felt he couldn't control the south and west, where Wilkinson was in charge, and found the arrangement impractical in 1799 in view of the problems with the French. However, there had been more than rumors of Wilkinson's involvement with the Spanish over the future of their colony along the Gulf Coast and Mississippi River. Wilkinson knew that he was in line for promotion and pulled out all the stops when he got to Philadelphia. He hurried to Braintree, Massachusetts, to solicit a letter of support from President John Adams. But Adams didn't care for the measure of the man and simply left the state of the army as it was. Wilkinson, bitterly disappointed, wrote on his way back to New Orleans from ship, "20 years as a Brigadier, a patient one too, I pant for promotion."[5] In Philadelphia, the name of Wilkinson was followed by "that fawning flatterer, superannuated coxcomb, from the bark to core a villain, and hackneyed scoundrel if I do say so myself." While many had the measure of the man, his undoubted charm was such that his many supporters defended his honor.

LOUISIANA PURCHASE

Napoleon's treaty signed with the hostage royal family of Spain stole the claim to the Louisiana Territory in exchange for a promise of land in southern Europe that was never delivered. The transfer canceled the provisions of the old Spanish Treaty of San Lorenzo and denied Americans access to the port of New Orleans. Napoleon, planning more costly campaigns, offered to sell Louisiana to the United States, which gladly purchased it on

May 2, 1803. It took six months for the transfer, which occurred on December 20, 1803. To Wilkinson's delight, he was appointed governor of the Louisiana Territory.

AARON BURR AND GENERAL WILKINSON

Aaron Burr, born in 1756, served in the Continental Army with Wilkinson at Montreal. He was a noted war hero during the many campaigns of Washington. A lawyer, he served in the state assembly of New York, was New York's attorney general, and was elected to the U.S. Senate for one term. Thomas Jefferson chose him as vice president in 1801. He gained infamy by killing Alexander Hamilton, commander of the army, in 1804 in a duel. An influential politician, he converted the Tammany Hall social club to a powerful political entity. When Jefferson rejected Burr as his running mate in 1805, after the duel, Burr ran for governor of New York but lost. Burr went west to lease land from the Spanish government in Louisiana with the help of General Wilkinson. Burr planned to seize Spanish territory along the Gulf Coast with the help of Wilkinson. Burr also enlisted the assistance of General Dearborn, a comrade from the Revolutionary War, to lend legitimacy to his cause and intercede with General Andrew Jackson for use of his troops. Burr's exact intentions remain a mystery, but it is expected that he planned to stir up the pot and see what he could get out of the resulting chaos.

At least Burr expected to separate the land west of the Mississippi from the United States and make himself the head of state. He began by playing the Spanish, English, French, and the United States against each other to see what would happen from the instability. As early as the summer of 1804, Vice President Burr met with Anthony Merry, British minister in Philadelphia. He knew that the British government was opposed to the Louisiana Purchase, regarding Napoleon's sale to be illegal. By March 1805, Burr told Merry that in order to carry out his plans, a British fleet at the mouth of the Mississippi and 100,000 pounds were required.[6] He also asked the Spanish representative in the United States for a passport to Mexico because he was no longer welcome at home after killing Hamilton. The Spanish suspected that Burr would incite anti-Spanish feelings with the Mexicans and denied the passport. In the Richmond trial of Burr for treason, a letter to General Adair was introduced dated May 1805 in which, "the letter to me I think fully proves that some secret plan of Burr's was known to Wilkinson in May. . . . In the same year Wilkinson wrote a letter to Colonel McKee: "could not he raise a corps of cavalry to follow his fortune to Mexico?"[7] Wilkinson produced a letter at the trial in which Burr's guilt was proved. Close examination of the letter showed that it was not written by Burr but rather was in Wilkinson's handwriting. Wilkinson admitted that he had lost the original and that the letter he had submitted was his account from memory. Burr was acquitted for lack of evidence, and Wilkinson returned, unchaste, to his post in New Orleans. Winfield Scott, prior to his military service, witnessed the trial and found Wilkinson's testimony wanting. Later, Lieutenant Scott would be court-martialed by Wilkinson for disrespect, to which Scott pleaded guilty.

Wilkinson could not remain out of trouble for long. In October 1807, after Great Britain had attacked the USS *Chesapeake* and feeling in the country was running high, Congress, in special session, began an inquiry into Wilkinson's involvement with the Spanish government contrary to U.S. interests. It was alleged that the general had corruptly received money from Spain.[8] After much debate, a court of inquiry convened in January 1808, but because of a lack of hard evidence, he was acquitted. Jefferson sent Wilkinson to treat with the Spanish officials in Florida over their relations with the United States that fall. By 1809, back in New Orleans as commander of a fledgling army, he began to make plans to invade Florida with the approval of Jefferson and Madison, the secretary of war. Captain David Porter, naval commander of the port, who tried to stop the smuggling, was at odds with Wilkinson, who unofficially supported the illegal trade.

WILKINSON'S WAR OF 1812

Because of the poor treatment of his troops, Wilkinson was relieved by General Wade Hampton and returned to Washington under a cloud once again. During the trial, he made reference to "this sword [which] has been the untarnished companion at my thigh for forty years." After a long trial, Wilkinson was acquitted of all charges in February 1812 for lack of evidence. In July 1812, Wilkinson was promoted to brevet[9] major general and restored to command of the Southern District, headquartered in New Orleans. While he was gone, Baton Rouge had defected from Spain, and Wilkinson thought that Mobile and Pensacola were ripe for the taking. The new secretary of war, John Armstrong, a former business partner of Wilkinson, approved the plan to invade Florida and directed Andrew Jackson to take his Tennessee soldiers to Natchez and then to Wilkinson. In the meantime, the government changed its mind and ordered Jackson, now in Natchez after an exhausting march, to turn over his equipment to Wilkinson and "go home." Wilkinson expected Jackson to abandon his troops so that they could be enlisted into the regular army in New Orleans. Old Hickory put a stop to that plot.

FROM SOUTH TO NORTH

Armstrong, Wilkinson's comrade from Gates's headquarters at Saratoga, whisked the general to Washington and then to Sackets Harbor, New York, to command the offensive of 1813 to take Montreal. Dearborn, a close friend of Wilkinson, had been relieved over the abortive attacks on Canada during 1812. The plan called for Wilkinson's 7,000 troops to join Wade Hampton's 4,000 soldiers along the way northeast, down the St. Lawrence, and seize the capital city. Hampton and Wilkinson were not speaking, and all messages had to be routed through Armstrong. Armstrong, the former minister to France and staff officer during the Revolutionary War, would accompany the campaign. Hampton, a rich planter, joined the army in 1808 as a political appointee and was interested more in his business than in fooling around in Canada. In September, with the campaign season waning in the northern latitudes, Sackets Harbor became a repository of everything military. Units flooded in until it was bursting at the seams. Brigadier Jacob Brown, the only competent senior officer present, took to looking after the army while Wilkinson went west, the wrong direction, to inspect the Niagara formations. Wilkinson dithered while Brown moved the troops by boat into the St. Lawrence, and Armstrong, for some unknown reason, left for Washington. Hampton, moving north to meet Wilkinson, ran afoul of a small French Canadian element with big ideas and routed the American column at Chateauguay. It was November, and ice began to form around the boats that moved Wilkinson farther north. At that time he was planning an attack on Montreal even though Hampton had not arrived to support him. Splitting his force, his troops were caught by the British and were defeated at Crysler's Farm. General Brown, whose brigade had been separated from the army by Wilkinson, consolidated the American army at French Mills on the south side of the St. Lawrence while Wilkinson deserted the army for comfortable quarters in Malone, New York, claiming illness. In the spring, Wilkinson took command of the 4,000 soldiers at Plattsburgh and invaded Canada, getting six miles inland before being confronted by a much inferior formation of Canadians. After a few shots were fired, Wilkinson ended his career by retreating across the border.

THE LAST COURT-MARTIAL OF WILKINSON

The newspapers described Wilkinson at various times as unscrupulousness, addicted to sycophancy, the father of underhandedness, and the repeated subject of congressional inquiries and military courts. Wilkinson was noted for his ornate phrases and pompous strutting, and this prompted author

Washington Irving (who had created for himself the fictional Dutch historian, Fiedrich Knickerbocker) to caricature Wilkinson as "von Puffenburg," lamenting that "military preferment had spoiled an admirable trumpeter."[10]

Because of the fast-moving circumstances of the war during its final nine months, the court-martial did not convene in Utica, New York, until January 1815. There were four charges: neglect of duty, un-officer-like conduct, being drunk on duty, and conduct unbecoming an officer and gentleman, countenancing and encouraging disobedience of orders. The court found, "that no censure attaches to the accused to all or any of the specifications."[11]

Due wholly to bad character, Major General James Wilkinson, a consistent scoundrel, failed his men, his officers, and his country. Never before or since has America spawned a worse seed.

Nevertheless, the hacks, sycophants, and adventurers, in the end, were unable to undo the good work of the heroes.

CHRONOLOGIES

William Winder

1775	Born in Somerset County, Maryland
1798	University of Pennsylvania law School
1812	Commissioned a colonel in the regular army
1812	Promoted to brigadier general
1813	Captured by British at Stoney Creek, Canada
1813	Negotiates prisoner exchange and parole
1814	Commander of 10th Military District, Washington, D.C.
1814	Defeated at Battle of Bladensburg; Washington, D.C., burned

James Wilkinson

1757	Born March 24 in Benedict, Maryland
1776	Served in Pennsylvania Rifles as a captain
1776	Aide-de-camp major to Nathanael Greene
1776	Benedict Arnold's staff in Montreal
1776	Promoted to lieutenant colonel by General Washington
1777	Aide-de-camp to Horatio Gates at Saratoga
1777	Promoted to brigadier general by Congress
1778	Conway Cabal member to remove Washington
1779	Clothier general of the army until 1781
1782	Pennsylvania militia brigadier general
1783	Pennsylvania state assemblyman

1784	Split Kentucky from Virginia
1787	Became a secret agent of Spain at New Orleans
1788	Sought union with Spain for Kentucky
1791	Commissioned a lieutenant colonel in Cincinnati, Ohio
1792	Appointed brigadier general of regular army
1794	Commanded the army after Battle of Fallen Timbers
1798	Commanded army in the southern states
1803	Took possession of Louisiana Purchase at New Orleans
1804	Allied with Aaron Burr conspiracy
1805	Governor of the Louisiana Territory
1811	Court-martialed
1812	Commissioned a brevet army major general
1813	Commands the army in the northern United States
1813	Relieved after loss of two battles in Canada
1814	Relieved after defeat at Lacolle Mills, Canada
1821	Died in Mexico City

NOTES

1. Donald R. Hickey, *Don't Give Up the Ship! Myths of the War of 1812* (Champaign: University of Illinois Press, 2007), 81.

2. Hay S. Werner, *The Admirable Trumpeter: A Biography of General James Wilkinson* (New York: Doubleday, Doran & Company, 1941), vii.

3. Werner, *The Admirable Trumpeter*, 40.

4. Werner, *The Admirable Trumpeter*, 51.

5. Werner, *The Admirable Trumpeter*, 184.

6. Werner, *The Admirable Trumpeter*, 240.

7. Daniel Clark, *Proofs of the Corruption of Gen. James Wilkinson, and of the Connection with Aaron Burr* (Honolulu: University Press of the Pacific, 2005), 120.

8. Werner, *The Admirable Trumpeter*, 284.

9. He assumed the duties, privileges, and rank insignia but was denied the pay grade. It is a common practice that goes on to this day in all military services.

10. Werner, *The Admirable Trumpeter*, viii.

11. Werner, *The Admirable Trumpeter*, 330.

BIBLIOGRAPHY

Adams, Henry. *The War of 1812*. New York: Cooper Square Press, 1999.

Altoff, Gerard T. *Oliver Hazard Perry and the Battle of Lake Erie*. Put-in-Bay, OH: The Perry Group, 1999.

Bellico, Russell P. *Chronicles of Lake Champlain: Journeys in War and Peace*. Fleischmanns, NY: Purple Mountain Press, 1999.

Berton, Pierre. *The Invasion of Canada 1812–1813*. Toronto: Anchor Canada, 1980.

Berube, Claudem, and John Rodgaard. *A Call to the Sea: Captain Charles Stewart of the USS Constitution*. Washington, DC: Potomac Books, 2005.

Bowditch, Nathaniel. *The American Practical Navigator: An Epitome of Navigation*. Bethesda, MD: National Imagery and Mapping Agency, 1857.

Burdick, Virginia Mason. *Captain Thomas Macdonough: Delaware Born Hero of the Battle of Lake Champlain*. Wilmington: Delaware Heritage Press, 1991.

Caruana, Adrian. *The Pocket Artillerist*. Rotherfield, UK: John Boudroit Publications, 1992.

Chapelle, Howard I. *A History of the American Sailing Navy*. New York: Norton, 1949.

Clark, Daniel. *Proofs of the Corruption of Gen. James Wilkinson, and of the Connection with Aaron Burr*. Honolulu: University Press of the Pacific, 2005.

Clieaves, Freeman. *Old Tippecanoe: William Henry Harrison and His Times*. Newtown, CT: American Political Biography Press, 1939.

De Kay, James Tertuis. *A Rage for Glory: The Life of Commodore Stephen Decatur*. New York: Free Press, 2004.

Dudley, William S. *The Naval War of 1812: A Documentary History*. 3 vols. Washington, DC: Naval History Center, 1982.

Elting, John R. *Amateurs to Arms: A Military History of the War of 1812*. Chapel Hill, NC: Algonquin Books, 1991.

Everest, Allen S. *The Military Career of Alexander Macomb*. Plattsburgh, NY: Clinton County Historical Society, 1989.

Fitz-Enz, David G., ed. *The Final Invasion: Plattsburgh, the War of 1812's Most Decisive Battle*. New York: Cooper Square Press, 2001.

———. *Old Ironsides: Eagle of the Sea*. Lanham, MD: Rowman & Littlefield, 2005.

Forester, C. S. *The Age of Fighting Sail*. Sandwich, MD: Chapman Billies, 1956.

———. *The Naval War of 1812*. London: Michael Joseph, 1957.

Frost, D. R. *The Ropery: Visitor's Guide Book*. Unpublished document, London: Chatham.

Gardiner, Robert. *The Naval War of 1812*. London: Chatham, 1998.

———. *Frigates of the Napoleonic Wars*. London: Chatham, 2000.

———. ed. *The Heyday of Sail: The Merchant Sailing Ship 1630–1830*. London: Conway Maritime Press, 1995.

Gillmer, Thomas C. *Old Ironsides: The Rise, Decline and Resurrection of the USS Constitution*. Blue Ridge Summit, PA: TAB Books, 1993.

Goldsmith, Robert. *The Battles of the Constitution: Old Ironsides and the Freedom of the Seas*. London: Macmillan, 1961.

Goodwin, Peter. *Countdown to Victory: 101 Questions and Answers about HMS Victory*, Portsmouth, UK: Manuscript Press, 2000.

Guttman, Jon. *Defiance at Sea (Stories of Dramatic Naval Warfare)*. London: Arms and Armor Press, 1995.

Harland, John. *Seamanship in the Age of Sail: An Account of the Ship Handling of the Sailing Man-of-War 1600–1960 Based on Contemporary Sources*. London: Conway Maritime Press, 1984.

Heinbach, Craig J. *Chasing Oliver Hazard Perry: Travels in the Footsteps of the Commodore Who Saved America*. Cincinnati, OH: Clerisy Press, 2010.

Heyerdahl, Thor. *Early Man and the Ocean: A Search for the Beginnings of Navigation and Seaborne Civilization*. Garden City, NY: Doubleday, 1979.

Hickey, Donald R. *The War of 1812: A Forgotten Conflict*. Champaign: University of Illinois Press, 1989.

———. *The War of 1812, A Short History*. Champaign: University of Illinois Press, 1995.

———. *The War of 1812: Still a Forgotten Conflict? Historiographical Essay, War and Society, a Journal of the History of Warfare*. Canberra: School of History, Australian Defense Force Academy, 2001.

———. *Don't Give Up the Ship! Myths of the War of 1812*. Champaign: University of Illinois Press, 2006.

Gardiner, Robert. *The Historic Dockyard Chatham, Where the Legends Were Created*. Norwich, UK: Jarrold Publishing, 1994.

Hitsman, J. Mackay. *The Incredible War of 1812*. Updated by Donald E. Graves. Toronto: Robin Bass Studio, 1965.

Humphreys, Asherton. *The USS Constitution's Finest Fight, 1815: The Journal of Asherton Humphreys, Acting Chaplain, US Navy*. Edited by Tyrone G. Martin. Mount Pleasant, SC: Nautical and Aviation Publishing Company of America, 2001.

James, W. M. *The Naval History of Great Britain, during the French Revolutionary and Napoleonic Wars*. London: Conway Maritime Press, 2000.

Kemp, Peter, ed. *The Oxford Companion to Ships and the Sea*. New York: Oxford University Press, 1976.

Lambert, Andrew. *Trincomalee: The Last of Nelsons Frigates*. London: Chatham Publishing, 2002.

Lardas, Mark. *Constitution vs. Guerriere: Frigates during the War of 1812*. London: Osprey Publishing, 2009.

Lavery, Brian. *Nelson's Navy: The Ships, Men and Organisation 1793–1815*. London: Conway Maritime Press, 1989.

———. *Building the Wooden Walls: The Design and Construction of the 74 Gun Ship Valiant*. London: Conway Maritime Press, 1991.

Lees, James. *The Masting and Rigging of English Ships of War, 1625–1860*. London: Conway Maritime Press, 1979.

Lewis, Denis. *British Naval Activity on Lake Champlain during the War of 1812*. Plattsburg, NY: Clinton County Historical Association, 1994.

Lewis, Jon E., ed. *Life before the Mast: Sailors' Eye Witness Accounts from the Age of Fighting Ships*. London: Constable and Robinson, 2001.

Mahan, Alfred T. *The Influence of Sea Power upon History, 1660–1783*. New York: Little, Brown, 2010.

Malcomson, Robert. *Warships of the Great Lakes, 1754–1834*. London: Chatham Publishing, 2001.

Maloney, Elbert S. *Dutton's Navigation and Piloting*, 13th ed. Annapolis, MD: Naval Institute Press, 1978.

Magoun, F. Alexander. *The Frigate Constitution and Other Historic Ships*. Salem, MA: Maritime Research Society, 1928.

Marshall, John. *Marshall's Royal Naval Biography*. Vol. 2, Pt. 2. London: Longman, Hurst, Rees, Orme, Brown & Green, 1825.

Martin, Tyrone G. *A Most Fortunate Ship: A Narrative History of Old Ironsides*. Annapolis, MD: Naval Institute Press, 1997.

McKinley, Silas B., and Silas Bent. *Old Rough and Ready: The Life and Times of Zachary Taylor*. New York: Vanguard Press, 1946.

Morgan, Henry J. *Sketches of Celebrated Canadians and Persons Connected with Canada*. London: Hunter, Rose, 1934.

Morris, John D. *Sword of the Border: Major General Jacob Jennings Brown, 1775–1828*. Kent, OH: Kent State University Press, 2000.

Morris, Roger. *Guide to British Naval Papers in North America*. Compiled by National Maritime Museum, Greenwich, England. London: Mansell Publishing, 1994.

Munday, John. *Naval Cannon*. Buckinghamshire: Shire Publications, 1998.

Niles, John M. *The Life of Oliver Hazard Perry*. Reprint of William S. Marsh, Hartford, 1820. Reprint from the library of the University of Michigan, published by the Haiti Trust HP. Ann Arbor, Michigan.

Peckham, Lloyd, and Howard H. Brown. *The Revolutionary War Journal of Henry Dearborn, 1775–1785*. Chicago: The Claxton Club, 1939.

Pope, Dudley. *Life in Nelson's Navy*. Annapolis, MD: Naval Institute Press, 1995.

Roberts, William H. *USS New Ironsides*. Annapolis, MD: Naval Institute Press, 1999.

Robotti, Frances Diane, and James Vescovi. *The USS Essex, and the Birth of the American Navy*. Holbrook, MA: Adams Media Corp., 1999.

Roosevelt, Theodore. *The Naval War of 1812*. New York: Putnam, 1882.

Sauer, Carl O. *Northern Mists*. Berkeley: University of California Press, 1968.

Silverstone, Paul H. *The Sailing Navy 1775–1854*. Annapolis, MD: Naval Institute Press, 2001.

Skaggs, David Curtis. *Oliver Hazard Perry*. Annapolis, MD: Naval Institute Press, 2006.

Skaggs, David Curtis, and Gary T. Altoff. *A Signal Victory*. Annapolis, MD: Naval Institute Press, 1997.

Simmons, Edwin H. *The United States Marines: A History*. Annapolis, MD: Naval Institute Press, 1974.

Snow, Elliot, and H. Allen Gosnell. *On the Decks of Old Ironsides*. London: Macmillan, 1932.

Toll, Ian W. *Six Frigates: The Epic History of the Founding of the U.S. Navy*. New York: Norton, 2006.

Upham, N. E. *Anchors*. Buckinghamshire, UK: Shire Publishing, 2001.

Victor, Orville James. *The Life, and Military and Civic Services of Lieut-Gen. Winfield Scott: Complete Up to the Present Period*. New York: Beadle & Co., 1852.

Waters, D. W. *The Planispheric Astrolabe*. Greenwich, UK: Crown Publishing, 1976.

Werner, Hay S. *The Admirable Trumpeter: A Biography of General James Wilkinson*. New York: Doubleday, Doran & Company, 1941.

Woodman, Richard. *The Victory of Seapower: Winning the Napoleonic War of 1806–1814*. London: Chatham Publishing, 1998.

INDEX

ABOUT THE AUTHOR

COLONEL DAVID FITZ-ENZ served as a regular army officer for thirty years. In Vietnam, he was a combat photography platoon leader, paratrooper, and aviator in the 173rd Airborne Infantry and signal officer in the 10th Cavalry Squadron, 4th Infantry Division. Among his decorations is the Soldier's Medal for Heroism, the army's highest award for lifesaving at extreme risk and the Bronze Star for "Valor" with four oak-leaf clusters. An Army War College graduate and brigade commander, his command operated the Moscow Hot Line for three presidents. Random House published his memoir, *Why A Soldier?*, the stories of a combat photographer.

He wrote and coproduced *The Final Invasion*, a television program for PBS. His book of the same title won the Distinguished Writing Prize from the Army Historical Foundation and the Military Order of Saint Louis from the Knights Templar for contributions to military literature. He is published in *Military Illustrated* magazine in London and authored *Old Ironsides: Eagle of the Sea* and the alternative history novel *Redcoats' Revenge*. Fitz-Enz has lectured at the National Archives; Library of Congress; National Army Museum in London; Royal Navy London Squadron; and Royal Dockyard, Chatham, England. He was a presenter on C-Span's *Book TV* on four occasions and a contributor on the Fox News Network.

He resides with his wife of fifty years, Carol, who is his researcher and editor, at Lake Placid, New York.

1 charge
2016 last circ

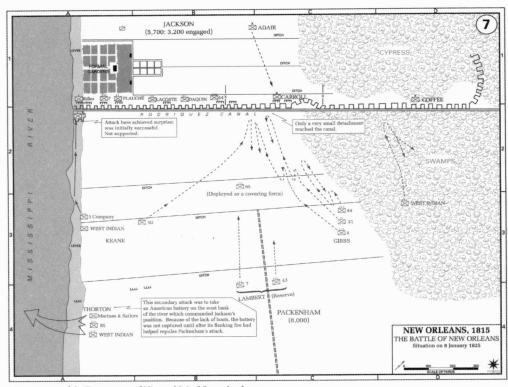

The map content includes:

JACKSON
(5,700: 3,200 engaged)

ADAIR

(7)

CYPRESS

LEVEE

FORMAL GARDENS

DITCH

DITCH

DITCH

Rifles   PLAUCHÉ   LACOSTE   DAQUIN   44   CARROLL   X   COFFEE

R O D R I Q U E Z   C A N A L

Attack here achieved surprise;
was initially successful.
Not supported.

Only a very small detachment
reached the canal.

SWAMPS

DITCH

95

(Deployed as a covering force)

WEST INDIAN

3 Company   93

WEST INDIAN

KEANE

DITCH

44

21

GIBBS   4

LEVEE

DITCH

7   43

THORTON

This secondary attack was to take
an American battery on the west bank
of the river which commanded Jackson's
position. Because of the lack of boats, the battery
was not captured until after its flanking fire had
helped repulse Packenham's attack.

LAMBERT (Reserve)

PACKENHAM
(8,000)

Marines & Sailors

85

WEST INDIAN

NEW ORLEANS, 1815
THE BATTLE OF NEW ORLEANS
Situation on 8 January 1825

M I S S I S S I P P I   R I V E R

SCALE OF YARDS
100   200   300